AF798757

Palgrave Advances in Bioeconomy: Economics and Policies

Series Editor

Justus Wesseler, Agricultural Economics and Rural Policy Group, Wageningen University, Wageningen, Gelderland, The Netherlands

More information about this series at
https://link.springer.com/bookseries/16141

Stephen K. Wegren · Frode Nilssen
Editors

Russia's Role in the Contemporary International Agri-Food Trade System

palgrave
macmillan

Editors
Stephen K. Wegren
Political Science
Southern Methodist University
Dallas, TX, USA

Frode Nilssen
Nord University Business School
Bodø, Norway

ISSN 2524-5848 ISSN 2524-5856 (electronic)
Palgrave Advances in Bioeconomy: Economics and Policies
ISBN 978-3-030-77450-9 ISBN 978-3-030-77451-6 (eBook)
https://doi.org/10.1007/978-3-030-77451-6

© The Editor(s) (if applicable) and The Author(s) 2022. This book is an open access publication.
Open Access This book is licensed under the terms of the Creative Commons Attribution 4.0 International License (http://creativecommons.org/licenses/by/4.0/), which permits use, sharing, adaptation, distribution and reproduction in any medium or format, as long as you give appropriate credit to the original author(s) and the source, provide a link to the Creative Commons license and indicate if changes were made.
The images or other third party material in this book are included in the book's Creative Commons license, unless indicated otherwise in a credit line to the material. If material is not included in the book's Creative Commons license and your intended use is not permitted by statutory regulation or exceeds the permitted use, you will need to obtain permission directly from the copyright holder.
The use of general descriptive names, registered names, trademarks, service marks, etc. in this publication does not imply, even in the absence of a specific statement, that such names are exempt from the relevant protective laws and regulations and therefore free for general use.
The publisher, the authors and the editors are safe to assume that the advice and information in this book are believed to be true and accurate at the date of publication. Neither the publisher nor the authors or the editors give a warranty, expressed or implied, with respect to the material contained herein or for any errors or omissions that may have been made. The publisher remains neutral with regard to jurisdictional claims in published maps and institutional affiliations.

This Palgrave Macmillan imprint is published by the registered company Springer Nature Switzerland AG
The registered company address is: Gewerbestrasse 11, 6330 Cham, Switzerland

Preface

Circumstances often create opportunity. This book would not have been possible without two developments. The first development has been the remarkable improvement in agricultural production that Russia has experienced since 2004. The increase in production has provided food security, allowed import substitution, and increased food self-sufficiency. A second development is the Russian government's commitment to extend food policy beyond food security and self-sufficiency and to become a seafood and food exporter. In particular, the emergence of Russia as a major grain exporter is one of the major story lines in the past decade. In 2004, not many people would have predicted that Russia would be a major player in the international agri-food system within a decade.

The purpose of this book is to assess contemporary Russia's role in the international agri-food system, which includes fish and seafood. During the Soviet period, the world was accustomed to Russia as a grain importer. During the 1990s, Russia decreased its grain imports but became the world's largest poultry importer. Despite Russia's turn toward protectionism since 2010, Russia has not withdrawn from the international food trade system, but rather has enhanced its international role, and become an active player in the system as both a food importer and exporter.

The origins of this book were rather serendipitous. Frode Nilssen, Christel Elvestad, and I have been working together since 2015 on various projects related to Russia's food policy and food trade. In May 2019, I took a quick trip to Bodø, Norway to discuss what was next for us, and during the course of an afternoon brainstorming session we came up with the outlines of a book project. During the next several weeks and months, Frode and I developed the ideas further and began to put the project together, including a proposal to Palgrave Macmillan, which subsequently was accepted.

Nord University has been especially generous in providing financial support that helped bring this book to fruition. It funded a workshop for contributors that was to be held in Brussels in March 2020 that subsequently had to be canceled due to Covid-19 and international travel restrictions. Nord University also provided funding for the index, and it funded Open Access so that more readers are able to benefit from our collective research. We are very grateful to the university for its generous support.

We acknowledge and thank two anonymous reviewers for their comments and suggestions for improvement. We thank the contributors who put aside their own work to write a chapter for this volume. Finally, we thank Ruth Jenner for supporting this project and including it in Palgrave Macmillan's book series on Economics.

Dallas, USA
Bodø, Norway
January 2021

Stephen K. Wegren
Frode Nilssen

Contents

List of Figures

Chapter 2

Chapter 4

Chapter 5

Chapter 7

Chapter 8

Chapter 9

List of Tables

Chapter 5

Chapter 6

Chapter 10

Introduction: Is Russia's Role in the International Agri-Food System Sustainable?

Stephen K. Wegren and Frode Nilssen

1 Introduction

This book examines Russia's role in the contemporary international agri-food system. For several decades Russia's role in the global food trade system was as food importer because the Soviet command economy had difficulty keeping food shelves full or providing adequate choice for urban consumers. In the contemporary period, Russia remains a significant food importer by dollar value, but its role has evolved since 2000 as Russia's food production has rebounded. If Russia as a food importer is the old story, a new development has occurred that makes this book relevant. Twenty years ago, Russia's agricultural recovery was only beginning and the country was not a significant food exporter. In recent years, Russia has returned to its historical role as a major food exporter. During

S. K. Wegren (✉)
Political Science, Southern Methodist University, Dallas, TX, USA
e-mail: swegren@smu.edu

F. Nilssen
Nord University Business School, Bodø, Norway
e-mail: frode.nilssen@nord.no

© The Author(s) 2022

S. K. Wegren and F. Nilssen (eds.), *Russia's Role in the Contemporary International Agri-Food Trade System*, Palgrave Advances in Bioeconomy: Economics and Policies,
https://doi.org/10.1007/978-3-030-77451-6_1

1909–1913, for example, Russia was Europe's largest grain exporter, and its grain exports accounted for 30 percent of the world's grain exports.[1] Since 2010, Russia has become a major wheat exporter, ranking either first or second in wheat exports by volume during 2014–2020. Grain importing countries and regions around the world have a stake in Russia role in the international food market. In calender year 2020, more than 130 countries imported Russian grain, and for the 2020/2021 agricultural year 125 nations are expected to import food from Russia.[2]

Russia's agricultural rebound has led to a qualitative and quantitative change in its role in the international agri-food trade system, and subsequent chapters explore different dimensions of that occurrence. But is Russia's rise to a prominent player as both a significant importer and exporter sustainable? The purpose of this introductory chapter is to examine this core question, with a timeframe covering the next 10–15 years. In the sections below we discuss the variables that affect Russia's trade sustainability. We adopt a macro-view and make no attempt to predict actual levels or values of food imports and exports.

2 Prospects for Sustainability as an Agri-Food Importer

A country becomes a food importer for a variety of economic and political reasons. For example, common reasons for importing include: trading opportunities via a regional free trade agreement; economic advantages of importing that allow allocation of resources to other purposes; the building or maintenance of international alliances; the constellation of political interests within a nation that favour imports; the political philosophy of an administration in power that may favour open trade; and a host of other economic and political reasons.[3] Being a food importer does not necessarily connote deficiencies in domestic production or an inability to feed its population, although in some countries those factors are certainly relevant. Importing companies may discover a new product from abroad that they think will sell domestically. Or perhaps a company detects an unfulfilled market niche. An example of a country that imports food but is not food deficient in the United States, which is the largest importer of food in the world by dollar value, but it is also one of the world's largest food producers by volume. The United States, for example, in 2017 imported more than $137 billion in food and beverages, or almost five times the dollar value as in Russia in that same year.[4] At the same time, the United States has a high per capita caloric intake, more than 3,600 calories a day, and the United States is the world's leading food exporter by dollar value. Thus, being a food importer does not have to mean that a country is food deficient.

In the post-Soviet period, four main trends characterise Russia's agri-food imports since 1992. The first three trends are well-known. First, there has been a change in the composition of Russia's imports from grain imports in the early 1990s to meat products by mid-decade and continuing into the 2000s (see Chapter 2). Meat import levels continue to decline and since about 2010 Russia's meat imports have declined from about 2.5 million tonnes per year to 600,000 tonnes in 2020. The emergence of vegetarian 'meat' should not have a major impact on the demand for real meat within Russia.[5]

Second, there was a rise in the dollar value of Russia's agri-food imports from 2000 to 2013, although the increase was not linear due to variable economic conditions. Russia's population, the largest among European nations, suggests that its food market will remain attractive for domestic and foreign business. Third, Russia's food embargo in 2014 led to a decrease in the dollar value of its agri-food imports. The dollar value of Russia's food imports has increased from its low in 2016 ($25.1 billion USD), but remains far below the peak year 2013 when imports were valued at $43.2 billion USD. During 2018–2020, for example, the dollar value of Russia's food imports was under $30 billion USD.

The fourth trend, which is less well-known, is that the share of Russia's agri-food imports as a percentage of total imports has declined significantly since 2000 even though the dollar value of food imports rose, thereby reflecting the fact that the import of non-food products was increasing faster than food imports. In short, food imports have become less important to the national economy. The decline in the share of agri-food imports as a percentage of total imports is shown in Table 1.

The table shows that the share of Russia's food imports to total imports declined during 2000–2013 even as the dollar value of food imports was increasing. This trend was due to an impressive increase in domestic food output. Since 2014, the ratio of food imports to total imports continuously fell due to import substitution policy. The decline in the share of food imports was also due to a lower-cost structure of food imports because Russia has changed its trading partners from the European Union (EU) to China and other non-Western nations where production costs are lower. The upshot of the table is that Russia over time has become more

Table 1 Russia's food imports as percentage of its total imports (billion USD)

	Dollar value of total commodity imports	*Dollar value of Russian food imports*	*Food imports as percentage of total imports (%)*
2000	$33.9 billion	$7.3 billion	21.5
2005	$98.7 billion	$17.4 billion	17.6
2010	$229.0 billion	$36.3 billion	15.8
2012	$317.2 billion	$40.6 billion	12.8
2013	$315.2 billion	$43.2 billion	13.7
2014	$297.0 billion	$39.9 billion	13.4
2015	$182.9 billion	$26.2 billion	14.3
2016	$182.2 billion	$25.1 billion	13.8
2017	$227.8 billion	$28.9 billion	12.7
2018	$238.4 billion	$29.7 billion	12.4
2019	$254.5 billion	$29.9 billion	11.8
2020	$239.7 billion	$29.4 billion	12.2

Note Percentages have been rounded
Sources Rosstat, ***Rossiiskii statisticheskii ezhegodnik***, various years; author's calculations

food self-sufficient in the production of certain basic commodities (see Chapter 4).

It is likely that Russia will remain a significant food importer simply because some of the products it imports cannot be grown in Russia. Being an importer is a natural condition for large-population nations, and with more than 146 million people Russia represents the largest single-country food market in Europe. Large-population countries import food even if they are generally food secure. Russia ranks in the top ten countries for food imports based on dollar value, trailing large-population nations such as the United States, China, Germany, Japan, and France. Thus, Russia will remain an agri-food importer, but here we note that the structure of Russia's agri-food imports has changed and will likely continue to evolve as shown in Table 2.

The table reflects the impact of food policy in terms of reducing imports for some commodities. Specifically, the dollar value of imported meat (exclusive of poultry meat) fell and its ranking based on dollar value dropped from 1st in 2005 to 3rd in 2018; the dollar value of imported poultry meat was halved and its ranking dropped from 4th to 9th; and the dollar value of imported raw sugar fell dramatically and its ranking dropped from 5th to 10th during the same period. Significant

Table 2 Top 10 commodities in Russia's agri-food imports by dollar value, 2005–2018 (USD)

	2005	*2010*	*2015*	*2018*	*Rank in 2005/rank in 2018*
Alcoholic and non-alcoholic drinks	$1.5 billion	$2.2 billion	$1.7 billion	$2.6 billion	2/1
Apples, fresh	$297 million	$669 million	$387 million	$518 million	8/6
Bananas	$451 million	$704 million	$910 million	$1.1 billion	7/5
Butter	$245 million	$504 million	$311 million	$432 million	10/8
Citrus fruits	$484 million	$1.2 billion	$1.2 billion	$1.2 billion	6/4
Fish and seafood	$926 million	$1.9 billion	$1.2 billion	$1.6 billion	3/2
Meat (exclusive of poultry)	$1.9 billion	$4.7 billion	$2.4 billion	$1.4 billion	1/3
Milk and cream	$247 million	$795 million	$598 million	$503 million	9/7
Poultry meat	$865 million	$940 million	$365 million	$364 million	4/9
Raw sugar	$744 million	$1.1 billion	$191 billion	$4.9 million	5/10

Notes
[a]2005 is used as base year for top 10 commodities
[b]commodities are listed alphabetically
[c]citrus includes fresh and frozen
[d]fish and seafood include fresh and frozen
[e]meat includes fresh and frozen
[f]milk and cream include condensed and non-condensed
Sources Rosstat, ***Rossiiskii statisticheskii ezhegodnik***, various years

increases in the value of imports and a rise in rankings occurred for fresh apples, butter, citrus fruit, fish and seafood, and milk and cream. Alcoholic and non-alcoholic drinks remained a large-value import throughout the 2005–2018 period. Given the priorities of state food policy, we expect that the value of imported meat and poultry meat to decline in the future. In the sections below, we discuss several variables that impact the sustainability of Russia's agri-food imports going forward, presented in alphabetical order.

2.1 *Food Production*

The Russian government has been explicitly concerned with food production levels since 2008 when its first food security doctrine was drafted and subsequently adopted in 2010. Since then, food security has been a core principle in Russia's food policy, although usage of the term food security by Russian policymakers has a dual meaning, referring to trade protectionism and self-sufficiency as well as the more traditional meaning of adequate caloric intake.[6]

For the past decade, in order to fulfil the goals of the 2010 Food Security Doctrine, the volume of raw food production has increased thereby creating more supply for Russian processors and exporters, and reducing the need for imports of several commodities. Domestic production of pork and poultry meat currently meets domestic demand, which means that Russia is basically self-sufficient. Domestic poultry meat production has increased from 3.4 million tonnes in 2009 (90 percent of which produced by farm enterprises) to 4.9 million tonnes in 2019 (91 percent from farm enterprises).[7] Russia has become self-sufficient in poultry meat and started to export. Through the first ten months of 2020, poultry meat exports were about 280 thousand tonnes which ranked Russia 11th in the world, and equalled a 33 percent increase over the same period in 2019.[8]

Russia's pork production rose from an average of 2.7 million tonnes during 2011–2015 to 3.7 million tonnes in 2018. In 2019, Russia became self-sufficient in pork production.[9] At its annual meeting in November 2020, the National Union of Pork Producers noted that the combination of Russia's 25 percent import tariff and rising international pork prices due to African Swine Flu curtailed Russia's pork imports by 93 percent.[10] In 2020, Russian analysts argued that for the first time in 30 years, Russia will be essentially import-free, in comparison to the mid-2000s when imports comprised 50 percent of consumption.[11] By 2025, Russia's pork production is forecast to reach 6 million tonnes, 1.5 times the level of 2019.[12] With the expected increase in pork production, the need for imports will disappear and exports should increase. Pork exports were around 143 thousand tonnes in 2019 and were projected to reach 200 thousand tonnes in 2020.

Other branches of animal products are trending positively too. There are indicators that production in the beef sector may be ending after a 25 year slump, as the rate of decline in number of cattle has slowed.[13] A tariff-rate quota on beef imports has been in place since 2003. The quota will be retained for 2021, but starting in January 2022 the tariff-rate quota on imported beef may be replaced by a flat tariff of 27.5 percent.[14] That policy change is expected to lead to a retail price increase of up to one-third, which, if occurs, will put downward pressure on demand and lower the need for beef imports. Higher retail prices should also attract investors and perhaps lead to higher domestic production.

After many years of decline, domestic milk production increased in 2017, 2018, and 2019. In 2020, raw milk production exceeded 32 million tonnes, up from its low of 29.8 million tonnes in 2016, and equal to meet 84 percent of national demand.[15] The target in the January 2020 version of Russia's Food Security Doctrine is 90 percent of demand.[16] Russian experts expect that when the food embargo ends, Russia will no longer need to import milk from the European Union (even assuming that supply chains could be reestablished, which have already been disrupted for seven years).[17] The point is that positive production trends in Russia's animal husbandry put downward pressure on the need for imports.

In addition, domestic vegetable production is supported by a rise in greenhouse vegetables, which more than doubled in volume from 2013 to 2019. In 2019, greenhouse vegetable production reached about 1.3 million tonnes and was estimated at 1.4 million tonnes in 2020. Production is on track to reach 2 million tonnes by 2024.[18] The rise in domestic vegetable production is reducing vegetable imports. In 2019, Russia imported 558 thousand tonnes of tomatoes and about 100 thousand tonnes of cucumbers. By 2025 those volumes are expected to decrease to 347 thousand tonnes and 36 thousand tonnes, respectively.[19]

2.2 Constraints on Food Production

Going forward, we identify three variables that will affect Russia's food production. First, Serova argues that the 'resource curse' affects Russia, by which she argues that 'the availability of vast land and water resources and relative biodiversity do not yet pose an urgent need for the country to preserve'.[20] Environmental degradation is widespread, evidenced by soil leached of its nutrients; wind erosion; streams, rivers, and ponds polluted with animal waste; rivers fowled with chemical runoff; and a degradation in soil biodiversity. Although Russia has a large amount of agricultural land (in 2019, Russia had 193.3 million hectares of agricultural land, of which 115.7 hectares were arable, and 79.6 million hectares were sown), it faces a range of problems related to land use: 20 percent of agricultural land has saline soils, 18 percent is subject to water erosion, 12 percent is marshland, and 8 percent is subject to wind erosion.[21] Russia's federal government adopted a land reclamation project that ran 2014–2020 with the goal to improve more than 3 million hectares by draining, irrigating, and repairing irrigation systems. By 2025, the Ministry of Agriculture hopes to bring back into production 4 million hectares of arable land that previously was abandoned or unused land, which it claims will add 1 million tonnes of grain production.[22] The problem is that formerly unused land has lower yields per hectare and is more expensive per unit of output.

Second, the country lacks a national strategy for food losses. Food loss is defined as a decrease in quantity or quality along the supply chain and this loss affects the amount of food that is available to consumers.[23] Serova notes that in some branches of Russian agriculture food losses reach 40 percent of output, which means that resources are used to produce food that is never consumed.[24] For context, throughout Europe in 2016, post-harvest food losses averaged just over 15 percent.[25] The implication for Russia is that food losses need to be remedied, but Serova argues that Russia's taxation system is an obstacle.

Third, the financial aspect is important. The rise in Russia's food production correlates with an increase in state financial assistance to agriculture, including credits, loans, subsidies, and investment. Private sector investment also increased as the agricultural sector became profitable, but state assistance has led the way. Russian state assistance has not come close to the level of state support in the United States or EU. Moreover, companies involved in production, processing, storage, and transportation expect state assistance. We cite just two examples from 2020. In December 2020 the State Duma considered a first reading of bill for a new state insurance policy for 2021. The government is interested in increasing the participation in crop and animal insurance due to the frequency of weather anomalies that can have devastating financial effects (see Sect. 3.2 below). In the proposed new system, federal subsidies for insurance premiums will double from the R2.2 billion level of funding in 2020. In addition, the state will pay 80 percent of the insurance premiums for small and medium-sized farms. For other farms, the state will pay 80 percent of the first year's insurance premium, which in subsequent years would decline to 50 percent of the premium.[26] The second example also comes from December 2020 when the Ministry of Agriculture suggested to compensate grain millers for their grain purchases, up to 50 percent of the difference between current domestic market prices and the average price for the previous three years during a comparable time period, adjusted for inflation.[27] Put in perspective, financial trends in agriculture could be worrisome in that expectations may exceed capability. Depressed oil prices and the economic effects of the pandemic led the Russian government to lower its budget allocation to agriculture in 2021 to R256 billion, down from R308 billion in 2020.[28]

2.3 *Knowledge-Based Innovation*

Knowledge-based innovation in the agricultural sector affects food production and food imports. Although there are indicators of a nascent technology boom in Russia's agriculture through the introduction of automation and robotics on farms, pilotless driver equipment, and other 'smart' technology, Russia remains far behind agri-firms in the West. A big reason for Russia's disadvantage is a severe generation gap in its agricultural sciences, exacerbated by the fact that during the 1990s the influx of a new generation of scholars into science declined dramatically. In addition to a deficit in human and intellectual capital in the agricultural sciences, state funding for agricultural sciences is only a fraction received by other branches in the economy. Serova notes that the planning horizon for Russia's agribusiness companies is four to five years whereas the research and development cycle of new technology can span 12–20 years.[29] The takeaway is that bridging the technology gap may increase efficiency, lower production costs, reduce loss and waste, and therefore may contribute to reduce food imports, but this is not something that will happen in the near term.

The economic power of agricultural science is seen by the rebound in food production that has been greatly augmented by increases in yield per hectare, milk output per cow, and meat yield per cow, results that come from greater use of high-yield seeds and animals. Russia imports most of its high-yield animals at present. To help boost domestic production, Russia's federal government exempted the import of high-yield pedigree cattle from the value-added tax starting in 2016, which was to last to the end of 2020. In November 2020, President Vladimir Putin signed into law an extension for the tax exclusion through 2022.[30]

2.4 Per Capita Income and Value of the Ruble

The value of the ruble against the dollar, which as the international currency is used for most trade transactions, is an influential factor that affects import levels. During 2014–2015, for example, the devaluation of the ruble against the U.S. dollar made imported food more expensive and, combined with a drop in real per capita income, contributed to a decline in the value of Russia's food imports (see Table 1). Russia's aggregate value of food imports will continue to be affected by the value of the ruble and trends in per capita income. If the value of the ruble falls against the dollar, Russian importers face higher import bills and may be cautious due to uncertainty over the ability to sell more expensive products.

2.5 Politicalisation of Food Trade Policy

Recent years have witnessed the politicalisation of Russia's food policy. The Russian government's definition of food security is very narrow, referring to production of several basic commodities. But upon closer examination it becomes obvious that the Russian version of food security, i.e., lessened dependence on imports, is far from reality. Despite official proclamations of food security, Russia imports a high percentage of its seeds; high percentages of farm machinery and equipment are imported; high percentages of pedigree livestock are imported; and foreign agrifirms have a substantial presence in food processing and market share in food retailing. All of these factors are central to a nation's food security, suggesting that the government's narrow fixation on the production of a few commodities does not offer a complete view of Russia's actual food security. In addition, political leaders' expressed concerns over food insecurity have been used as political symbolism rather than an indicator of inadequate food consumption among Russian consumers.[31]

In Russia, the term 'food security' is politicised to justify trade protectionism. Food import policy has been politicised in the form of countersanctions, originally introduced in August 2014 but extended through 2022 by presidential decree in September 2021.[32] This protectionist policy tool has been used to rally nationalist feelings and anti-Western sentiment. Moreover, Russia's food trade in general has been politicised.[33] This occurrence is reflected by numerous temporary import limitations on milk and dairy exports from Belarus, or outright food import bans against former Soviet republics such as Ukraine since 2016, or Uzbekistan in 2020.[34] Russia has also waged a hot and cold 'tomato war' with Turkey that witnessed a ban on tomato imports from November 2015 to November 2017 when the ban was completely lifted (although restrictions were partially lifted starting in fall 2016). From May 2018 the ban was replaced with an import quota on Turkish tomatoes, originally set at 50,000 tonnes during the winter months, but the quota was gradually increased several times.[35] In 2020 a disagreement arose over Turkey's import tariffs on sunflower seed and oil.[36] The point is that 'objective' factors such as the level of food production and population trends are not the sole drivers of Russia's food imports. Objective factors send signals to Russia's food market, but decisions about country origins of food imports and import levels are also based on political calculations.

2.6 *Population and Food Consumption*

A final variable that affects food imports is the size of the population and its demographic characteristics. In Russia's case, according to government estimates, the total population is projected to decline slightly from 147.1 million in 2018 to 146.9 million in 2036, but the urban population will increase from 109.3 million to 114.0 million during that same period.[37] The rising number of urban residents is accompanied by higher levels of per capita food consumption among urban consumers. While the size of the urban working-age cohort is expected to decrease slightly from 62.1 million in 2017 to 61.3 million in 2030, higher food consumption levels may offset the decline.[38] At the same time, Russia's population is aging and life expectancy is not high compared to other developed states. As the Russian population continues to age and a higher percentage becomes too old to work, there will be downward pressure on demand for food imports.

3 Prospects for Sustainability as an Agri-Food Exporter

While Russia has long been a net food importer, its role as a substantial exporter in the international food trade system is relatively new. The Ministry of Agriculture claims that Russia exported its grain to 138 nations in the world in 2020.[39] Russia's rise to significance has been rapid in recent years, leading President Vladimir Putin in 2018 to decree that the dollar value of food exports should reach $45 billion USD by 2024.[40]

A general increase in the dollar value of Russia's food exports has occurred since 2000, as shown in Table 3, and this trend is expected to continue. Data from the Russia's Ministry of Agriculture show that in 2020 Russia's agri-food exports equalled $28.9 billion USD, a 18 percent increase over the same period in 2019. Grain exports accounted for $9.7 billion USD; fish and seafood exports were second at $5.2 billion USD; oilseed was in third place at $4.6 billion USD; and processed foods were in fourth place at $4.1 billion USD. Currently about 6 percent of Russia poultry meat and pork production is exported, but Andrei Dal'nov, an analyst at ***Rossel'khozbank***, believes that meat exports will reach 10 percent of output. If new markets can be opened, meat exports could reach 1 million metric tonnes a year.[41] In 2020, China was the single largest importer of Russia's agri-food products with a value of $3.9 billion USD, with fish and seafood the single largest category at $1.5 billion USD; followed by the European Union at $3.2 billion USD, with fish and seafood the

Table 3 Russia's food exports as percentage of its total exports (billion USD)

	Dollar value of total commodity exports	*Dollar value of Russian food exports*	*Food exports as percentage of total exports (%)*[a]
2000	$103.0 billion	$1.6 billion	1.5
2005	$241.4 billion	$4.4 billion	1.8
2010	$397.0 billion	$9.4 billion	2.4
2012	$524.7 billion	$16.8 billion	3.2
2013	$525.9 billion	$16.2 billion	3.0
2014	$497.3 billion	$19.8 billion	3.9
2015	$343.5 billion	$17.0 billion	4.9
2016	$285.6 billion	$17.8 billion	6.2
2017	$357.7 billion	$21.6 billion	6.0
2018	$449.5 billion	$24.9 billion	5.5
2019	$426.0 billion	$24.8 billion[b]	5.8
2020	$336.3 billion[d]	$30.4 billion[c]	9.0

Notes
[a]Based on dollar value of exports. Percentages have been rounded
[b]Dollar value of food exports in 2019 is from the federal customs agency. The ministry of agriculture's data is a bit higher at $25.6 billion
[c]Dollar value of food exports in 2020 is from the federal customs agency. The ministry of agriculture's data for exports is a bit lower at $28.9 2020 is from the federal customs agency
Sources Rosstat, ***Rossiiskii statisticheskii ezhegodnik***, various years; Ministry of agriculture export data (https://mcx.gov.ru/ministry/departments/departament-informatsionnoy-politiki-i-spetsialnykh-proektov/industry-information/info-operativnaya-statistika/); author's calculations

single largest category at $1 billion USD; and Turkey in third place at $3.0 billion USD, with grains the single largest commodity at $1.7 billion USD.[42] Together, those three countries account for about 36 percent of the total dollar value of Russia's agri-food exports.[43]

The table shows an upward trend in Russia's food exports in dollar value and in percent of total exports, rising from 1.5 percent of total exports in 2000 to 9 percent in 2020 (based on data from the Federal Customs Agency). That said, food exports continue to have a small share in overall export revenue, a theme discussed in more detail in Chapter 3. Oil and gas and other mineral exports will remain Russia's primary generators of revenue from exports for the next decade at least, although Aleksei Kudrin predicts that during the 2030s other Russian exports will become more important due to the decline in global demand for oil and other fossil fuels in the effort to combat climate change.[44] To a significant degree, the increase in the share of agri-food exports is due to a decline in total commodity exports.

To be sure, Putin's $45 billion USD food export target was always as much about political signalling as it was economics. After the May 2018 decree, a political campaign mobilised regional leaders who were expected to draw up plans to increase food exports and to report on fulfilment towards the target. But politics cannot change economic realities and in 2020 Russia's Ministry of Agriculture identified a number of risks and limitations to different branches of production that would affect agri-food exports even in the best of conditions.[45]

Thereafter, the combination of Putin's political goal imposed from above, the COVID-19 pandemic and its economic effects on consumers, and the litany of risks identified by the ministry led to an extension of the deadline to 2030 to reach the $45 billion USD agri-food export goal.[46] The new target is to reach $34 billion USD in agri-food exports by 2024. Going forward, a variety of economic and political factors affect Russia's sustainability as a major food exporter. As with food imports, we discuss several variables that affect the sustainability of Russia's food export levels in alphabetical order.

3.1 Agri-Food Export Policy

Russia's agri-food export policy has become a story of contradictions, torn between two impulses since 2018. The first impulse is to protect domestic consumers from higher prices and possible shortages, thereby reflecting the importance of food security that continues to resonate among top policymakers. The second impulse is to increase food exports, expand to new markets, and deepen market presence in existing markets.

The first impulse was evidenced in previous years by Russia's export ban on wheat exports during August 2010-July 2011 due to drought and severe harvest losses, which led to an export tariff on grain starting February 2015 (subsequently lowered to zero in 2019). The anomaly today is that Russia is more food secure than ever and grain harvests have been strong for several consecutive years, but the government is restricting wheat exports in an effort to maintain stable domestic prices and to prevent shortages as a result of a weak ruble and potential excess exports.

The impulse to protect the domestic population continues to be evident. In 2020, an export quota of 7 million metric tonnes was enacted during the second half of the 2019/2020 agricultural year, from 1 April to the end of June 2020. For the 2020/2021 agricultural year, the Ministry of Agriculture returned to an export quota despite a very strong harvest, originally suggesting a quota of 15 million metric tonnes from 15 February 2021.[47] Wheat exporters pushed back and complained about the monetary losses that they would incur.[48] In response, the ministry increased the quota to 17.5 million metric tonnes effective from 15 February 2021 to 30 June 2021.[49] The size of the quota was allocated among exporters in February 2021, based on their share of grain trade during July-December 2020, a practice that critics allege drives small traders out of business.[50] Without a quota allotment, an export company is unable to access transportation or ports. As it turned out, the quota allotment was in fact highly concentrated. Although a total of 234 companies received an allotment, the top ten wheat exporting companies received 70 percent of the quota.[51] Two grain companies from Rostov-na-Donu were allocated 27.5 percent of the quota.[52] As a further disincentive to export, or to put it differently, keep grain within Russia, an export quota was also levied (see Chapter 1). For the entire 2020/2021 season, Russia's total wheat exports were expected to exceed 40 million metric tonnes, close to the record of 41 million metric tonnes exported in 2017/2018.[53] The concern over too much grain being exported was reflected in President Vladimir Putin's comment in his year-end press conference at which he stated that it had been a mistake for the government to subsidise food exports.[54]

Wheat is not the only commodity that either has been restricted or there are appeals for restrictive measures. In October 2020, Russia's Oilseed Union called for limits on the export of oilseed. In November 2020, animal husbandry unions asked for restrictions on corn exports in order to slow the rise in price of animal feed. Livestock and flour producers in Russia support export tariffs on grain to prevent higher cattle feed prices and higher domestic grain prices for wheat to be milled.[55] In December 2020, the Oilseed Union requested an increase in the export tariff on sunflower seed from 6.5 percent up to 30 percent in order to slow the price increase in sunflower oil.[56] The Union also asked for and received an increase in the export tariff on soybean to 30 percent.

The second impulse, to increase food exports, has been followed since Putin's May 2018 decree on the national development strategy to 2024, which emphasises an increase in the value of agri-food exports. Russian food policy took a turn from food security through protectionism, import substitution, and self-sufficiency to emphasising agri-food exports and an expansion into new markets. A Federal Analytical Center within the Ministry of Agriculture was created to assist exporters to enter markets, produce analyses to help exporters understand foreign demand, and offer guidance about negotiating and concluding contracts (see www.aemcx.ru). A state project on food exports was adopted in late 2018 with its own budget line to facilitate food exports (R400 billion allocation upon inception, which of course is subject to change). In 2019, R38 billion of multidimensional state support was allocated to increase food exports. State support is budgeted at R47 billion in 2021, approximately the same level as in 2020.[57] State support for food exports is scheduled to rise to R69.5 billion in 2022 and R80.8 billion in 2023.[58]

As part of the national project, the number of Russian foreign trade attaches is increasing. There has also been a rise in the number of memoranda of understandings and cooperative agreements in agriculture between Russia and foreign governments (see Chapter 6). In September 2020, as part of the national project on food exports, an information system called 'One Window' was unveiled. The purpose of this information system is to simplify the process between exporting companies on the one hand and ministries and regulatory bodies on the other for the purpose of reducing operating and administrative costs incurred by exporters.[59] The One Window system essentially allows exporting companies to order services they need, from logistics to consulting.[60] In

October 2020 the government extended subsidisation for the certification of products to be exported. Under the new expanded rules, exporters who work through an intermediary are eligible for compensation from the state for the cost of certification for their products.[61] Taken together—the creation of a bureaucratic entity to promote exports, the adoption of a national project attached to money, the increase in foreign attache offices, and the creation of a service provider to exporters—suggest that the Russian government considers food exports to be sustainable.

3.2 Climate Change and Effects on Food Production

The level of food production, particularly crops, is a variable that depends to a large degree on the weather. For the past decade there has been year-to-year fluctuation in Russia's grain output but the overall trend has been upward. Weather and weather-related anomalies play a key role, of course, but so far agricultural output has continued to rise despite frequent drought and flooding in different regions of Russia. A future trend line in which food production declines over several years, however, will set off political concerns about food supplies and generate pressures to increase food imports and decrease exports.

In recent years there are numerous regional examples of weather 'anomalies' that are believed to stem from climate change. Because Russia is so large, the effects of climate change and anomalous weather are felt differently depending on the location of a specific region. Severe flooding in recent years in the Far East, wildfires in Siberia, and rising air temperatures in the Far North are attributed to climate change. Table 4 presents a summary of weather anomalies and their economic cost to the agricultural sector during 2010–2020.

The impact of climate change on Russia's agriculture sector affects prospects for food exports. Climate change could bring lower volumes of grain production in traditional grain-growing regions and more grain production in non-black earth regions where yields are lower and production costs are higher.[62] If Russia's south produces less grain due to climate change, the entire agricultural profile of Russia may shift from being a major grain exporter, thereby putting stress on global grain supplies. The entire structure of grain production would change, and non-black earth regions would become relatively more important. This scenario is problematic for three reasons.

Table 4 Effects of climate change on Russian agriculture, 2010–2020

	Event	*Number of regions affected*	*Land area affected (hectares)*	*Value of monetary loss to agriculture (rubles)*
2010	Drought	43	13 million +	41 billion
2012	Drought	22	5.5 million	21 billion
2013	Flooding	7	458 thousand	8.7 billion
2013	Drought	10	2 million	11.5 billion
2015	Drought	13	9 million	7 billion
2017	Drought	20	489 thousand	3.6 billion
2018	Drought and flooding	27	5.8 million	7.3 billion
2019	Drought	25	3.5 million	13 billion
2020	Drought, flood	12	4.2 million	8 billion

Note 2020 data are through October
Sources Compiled from various reports in the Russian press

First, it raises the prospect of food insecurity for low-income groups as prices rise due to tighter supplies. Non-black earth regions generally are less suitable for agricultural production due to soil composition, a prevalence of forested land, and shorter growing seasons. Two of Russia's Western regions—the Central and Northwest Federal Districts—have marginal farm land that lacks the natural fertility of Russia's south.[63] These two non-black earth districts have experienced significant land abandonment, rural depopulation, and farm closures during the past 30 years, and as a result there are demographic 'black holes'.[64] These black holes in the non-black zone reflect insufficient human capital ***in addition*** to deficiencies in physical infrastructure and poor land quality for agriculture.[65] It would be a monumental task to reverse demographic trends, if it could be accomplished at all, which means that non-black earth regions cannot be depended upon to replace lost food production in the south.

Second, Russia's role in the international food trade system would change. If Russia's dependence on grain production had to shift to non-black earth regions, the country would undoubtedly lose its position as one of the world's top wheat exporters. Grain production in non-black earth regions would become much more expensive with lower yields per hectare and lower volumes of production. Given the fact that federal policymakers have indicated that productive and profitable farms are to receive the most state support, it is not clear how directing more resources to marginal agricultural areas would play out since farms in the south would be unwilling to give up their advantaged position even if their production declined.

A third problem is that if Russia's south becomes hotter, drier, and less productive, Russia's grain exports may decrease which in turn affects world grain supplies. At a time when the global population is increasing and the need for more food production is greater, global reserves would decline and the entire world would be much more vulnerable to spikes in food prices if drought or other weather conditions affected production in the United States, Canada, Australia, or Argentina. There are also international political implications. During 2010–2012, several grain-producing countries curtailed their grain exports which in turn caused global grain shortages and a spike in global commodity prices. In the Middle East, many countries experienced chronic food insecurity, high rates of poverty, high unemployment, and inequality for many years. Russia's grain cutoff of grain exports in 2010–2011 to the Middle East contributed to political instability that led to the Arab Spring and the collapse of regimes in Tunisia and Egypt, and the outbreak of civil war in Syria.[66] Today, among Middle Eastern nations, Turkey, Egypt, Iran, Saudi Arabia, Morocco, and United Arab Emirates are among the biggest buyers of Russian grain (see Chapter 9). In addition, Russia provides food assistance to Syria.

3.3 *Foreign Competition and Russia's Competitiveness*

Wheat will remain Russia's most valuable food commodity export for the foreseeable future. Russia's wheat exports in turn are affected by foreign competitors: the United States, Canada, Australia, France, and Argentina. As a major player in the international grain market, Russia competes for market share. A particularly good harvest for a competitor increases competition for Russia's exporters, just as a poor harvest among one or more competitors creates opportunity. Together, producer countries influence the level of world reserves and international grain prices.

Many variables affect world grain production such as weather, rainfall, and fuel prices, thereby making it difficult to forecast exact production. That said, the FAO determined that global reserves for cereals will increase slightly during the 2020/2021 agricultural year despite the economic effects of COVID-19.[67] Longer-term forecasts are more problematic due to a high degree of variability. The United States

Department of Agriculture (USDA) predicts that world grain prices are likely to decline to 2029 as production and reserves increase, which could create fewer incentives to export depending on the magnitude of decline. Against those trends, the USDA forecasts that Russia will continue to increase production thanks to higher yields, which will lead to higher grain exports but that the growth rate in exports will not match those in the 2010s (see Chapter 2).

On the demand side, the United Nations projects that the world's population will increase from its current 7.7 billion to 9.7 billion by 2050.[68] The fastest population growth rates will be in developing countries where the structure of the diet is oriented towards grain, starches, and carbohydrates, which plays into Russia's strength. To feed the new population, the FAO estimates that cereal production will need to rise by about one-third and annual meat production will need to more than double by 2050.[69] In developing countries, yields of major crops have been dropping, which means that their net imports of cereals will more than double to 300 million metric tonnes by 2050.[70] The expected food situation in developing countries presents an opportunity for grain exporting countries such as Russia.

A second aspect of foreign competition is food trade policy used by other countries. Russia's exports are obviously susceptible to import tariffs and non-tariff barriers that may be used by other states. The World Trade Organisation noted a general rise in trade import restrictions among G20 countries in 2019.[71] In 2020, the number of trade restrictions decreased, but mainly because the spread of COVID-19 reduced the growth rate in international trade.[72] The general rise in protectionism as a result of populist governments may also enhance the general drift towards more restrictions on trade. Furthermore, Russia's grain exports are impacted not only by objective needs in the purchasing country, but also by the presence (or absence) of regional trade agreements that the importing country may have with other states; the status of political relations with the importing country; the comparative quality of Russia's grain; and the actual terms of the deal that is negotiated.

A third factor that affects the competitiveness of Russia's export of food commodities is quality and food safety. The Ministry of Agriculture has made clear that the promotion of Russian food brands requires accurate labelling of food products if Russia is to be successful in expanding its food exports abroad.[73] A favourable reputation is necessary to expand exports because, in the words of Deputy Minister of Agriculture Oksana

Lut, Russia is engaged 'in a competitive battle for consumers throughout the world'.[74] In recent years there have been concerns that Russia's dairy and other milk products may contain unsafe additives or labels may not accurately reflect the content. Falsification of product content is not unique to the post-Soviet food system, but may have become worse since 2014 in the push for food self-sufficiency. In February 2019, *Rospotrebnadzor* raised the possibility of criminal penalties for product falsification by domestic food producers.[75] In March 2019, senators in the Federation Council began to consider changes in penalties for misrepresentation of goods, services, and labour, which had not been revised since 2007. Misrepresentation by companies involving false advertising or mislabelling would see fines increase tenfold to R300,000-R400,000. If the falsification threatens health or lives of humans, plants, or animals, companies could face fines of R500,000-R800,000.[76]

To crack down on counterfeit food, the re-export of food from banned countries through transit countries such as Belarus and Kazakhstan, and to increase consumer confidence in food safety, in May 2019 the government announced the introduction of a system for product certification called 'Merkurii' for packaged milk, yogurt, kefir, and several types of cheeses. Starting 1 July 2019 a pilot system for digital labelling was introduced for sweetened milk and sour cream and different cheeses, not including pasteurised milk products. Obligatory digital labelling for all dairy products was supposed to begin in March 2020 for milk and cream, dry milk and cream, kefir, yogurt, cheeses, butter, tvorog, and other dairy products, but the start date was delayed. Digital labelling of food products allows a product to be traced and tracked. Three ministries (Agriculture, Trade, and Communications), *Rossel'khoznadzor*, *Rospotrebnadzor*, the Federal Customs Agency, and the Federal Security Service (FSB) are responsible for implementation and compliance with labelling regulations.[77] Following several postponements, the Ministry of Trade announced that mandatory digital labelling would be phased in starting in 2021. According to the latest schedule as this chapter is completed, labelling for dairy products was on a voluntary basis starting in January 2021. Beginning in June 2021, mandatory labelling was required for ice cream and cheeses. Starting in September 2021, mandatory labelling was required for dairy products that have an expiration date of more than 40 days. From December 2021, mandatory labelling was required for dairy products that have an expiration date of less than 40 days.[78] Those timeframes obviously are subject to modification as they have since 2019.

By 2024, the government expects digital labelling to expand to other food products besides dairy.

The introduction of digital labelling raised strong objections in the private sector against the government's plan. Dairy producers and processors have raised many complaints, one of which is that digital labelling will impose high costs on producers of dairy products, estimated between R15,000–R35,000 for a small enterprise. But this estimate has been called into question. The General Director of Russia's Milk Union, Artem Belov, implied that cost estimates are too low by pointing out that a company would have to buy a machine capable of reading the digital codes, equipment for applying the codes to product packaging, and would need to integrate digital labelling with the information systems used in the enterprise.[79] For small producers, those added costs could be the difference between profitability and having to close. Other objections included: (1) digital labelling would lead to higher prices for consumers as companies pass on their costs; (2) digital labelling does not stop producers from misrepresenting products' contents; and (3) some dairy processors do not have the equipment to begin digital labelling according to the government's timeline, and therefore interruptions in supplies may occur. For example, the General Director of Russia's Ice Cream Union, Natalia Utkina, asked for digital labelling to be postponed to at least 1 December 2021 because the branch is unprepared to begin labelling by 1 June 2021 and the machinery needed to label ice cream is only available in Italy and Denmark. She indicated that packaging prices would increase by an estimated 40 percent, and that if labelling began in June 2021 production would have to be interrupted during peak demand in order to begin labelling.[80] Finally, (4) digital labelling in Russia may create an opportunity for black marketeers to increase their market share because they can offer lower prices.

The government rejects these arguments, indicating that retail prices are likely to rise only modestly. The head of the Ministry for Industry and Trade, Denis Manturov, argues that he expects a one-time price increase of 1.8 percent for dairy products that are digitally labelled, a price rise that he termed 'hardly even noticeable'. Further, he indicated that producers are eligible for loans with interest rates below 1 percent to help them reduce production costs.[81] In addition, the Ministry of Agriculture does not accept the notion that there will be interruptions in supplies.[82]

The takeaway from this discussion is that the government is interested in building a 'produced in Russia' brand that has a solid reputation abroad. The private milk and dairy sector is concerned about its bottom line. The introduction of obligatory digital labelling presents an interesting case study of the private sector pushing back against a government initiative. Previously, the relationship between the government and agricultural interests had been mostly cooperative and corporatist during the Putin administrations. At the end of the day, it is likely that state interests will 'win'. The state holds powerful policy levers—licensing, subsidies, loans and credit, tax audits—over private companies and can use those levers to force compliance. Moreover, the public and private sectors have a common interest. Private producers benefit from domestic consumers' trust in their products. The Russian state benefits from foreign purchases having faith in the quality of its food exports.

3.4 Regional Foreign Demand Based on Population Trends

Russia is expanding the number of food trade partners by signing regional and free trade agreements, memoranda of agreements, and bilateral trade agreements with other nations (see Chapter 6). Russia's largest export customers are, in order: Asia, Europe, and the Middle East and North Africa (MENA). Population trends in those regions are discussed.

In Asia, Russia's attempts to increase market share in the enormous Chinese market go hand in hand with the geostrategic pivot to China that occurred more than a decade ago. Trade relations are steadily improving and the two countries hope to reach $200 billion USD in total trade turnover by 2024 (see Chapter 7). Bilateral agri-food trade is growing although it remains quite modest in a comparative perspective. Russia's prospects for increasing food exports to China are affected by three demographic realities, one positive and two negative. The first reality is the size of China's middle class, estimated at up to 500 million consumers, who represent a potential base for Russia to increase its market share as consumers' income and preferences change. The second reality is that China faces a looming demographic decline. Its fertility rate has been below the population replacement rate of 2.1 since the early 1990s and presently stands at 1.6 according to the Chinese government. Other estimates place China's fertility rate at 1.4 and in major cities it may be below one child per woman.[83] As a result, China will see its population peak in 2027, after which its working-age population will decrease by 100 million from 2015 to 2040 according to the United States Census Bureau. The working-age population under the age of 30 may decrease by 30 percent during the same time period.[84] A third reality is that China's over-65 population will increase very rapidly, from 135 million in 2015 to at least 325 million in 2040, which means that in 2040 China could have twice as many people over 65 as children under the age of 15.[85] Older people on average need and consume fewer calories per day than working-age people. The effect of the two negative demographic trends on Russia's ability to increase food exports remains to be seen, but Russia's policymakers cannot count on ever-expanding demand for its exports from the Chinese population. Assuming that the political relationship remains friendly, we envision a rise in Russia's food exports to China for the next 10 years or so, then a flattening of the curve, followed by long-term stagnation or even decline.

In Europe, despite Russia's ban against food imports from the European Union, the EU continues to buy Russian food exports, and the value of these exports has actually increased a bit during 2009–2019. That said, Russian food exports to the EU pale in comparison to the sale of its energy and manufactured goods to the EU.[86] In 2019, Russia exported 4 billion euro worth of agri-food products to the EU, compared to 97 billion euro worth of energy.[87] In aggregate, EU members comprise a large food market with almost 448 million consumers who had an average per capita income of more than $37,100 USD in 2019. In other words, on the positive side, the EU is a valuable food market and although many nations within the EU have contracting total populations and working-age populations, food demand will remain strong due to high income. On the negative side, Russia does not have any regional free trade agreements with the EU and thus faces high tariffs on its exports which puts it at a disadvantage vis-à-vis low cost producers who as members of the EU enjoy free trade with other member states. As a result, Russia's food exports to the EU may be expected to grow slowly in coming years.

The population in the Middle East and North Africa is projected to double to more than 650 million people by 2050, thereby exceeding the population of the EU, which means that the size of the food market will be significant. Russia's main food export to MENA is grain. Based on its demographic structure, large numbers of Middle East youth will enter the workforce in the coming years, which means that they will have increased income and higher demand for food because employed individuals require higher caloric intake than unemployed persons. Russia is actively increasing trade ties and agricultural cooperation with Middle

East countries (see Chapter 9). Based on these trends, Russia's agri-food exports to MENA could grow rapidly in the coming years.

4 Outlook

Since 2010, Russia has experienced repeated weather anomalies (see Table 4), a recession, significant devaluations of the ruble in 2014–2015 and 2019–2020, sluggish economic growth, a decline in the price of oil which affects revenue, increasing trade protectionism at home and abroad, and a global pandemic. Through it all, Russia's domestic food production has increased, import substitution has improved food self-sufficiency, and the dollar value of the nation's agri-food exports has almost tripled. As a result, Russia's role in the international agri-food trade system has changed from importer to importer and exporter. A lot has gone right to get Russia to this point, and state food policy appears determined to maintain that positive momentum.

Returning to the original question posed at the beginning of the chapter whether recent trade trends are sustainable, Russia will remain a food importer. For all of the hoopla from the Russian government surrounding progress in food security, import substitution, and rise in self-sufficiency, actual reductions in food imports have occurred for mainly meat products (see Table 2). In the early 2000s, Russia imported 2.5–3 million tonnes of meat annually, now, it is around 600 thousand tonnes thanks to protectionism and increases in domestic production.[88] Russia remains a large importer of milk and dairy products, although the supplier has changed from the EU prior to 2014 to Belarus after 2014. Belarus now accounts for almost 80 percent of Russia's milk and dairy imports. Due to its climate and geographical position, Russia is likely to continue to be an importer of fruits and vegetables.[89] The point is that the structure of imports may continue to evolve, as will trading partners, but Russia will remain a food importer.

Regarding the sustainability of food exports going forward, a lot could go wrong. There could be a long-term economic downturn. Foreign markets could turn drastically more protectionist. The China market may not turn out to be as lucrative as expected or may be arbitrarily closed. Australia serves as an example of the fickleness of the Chinese market. In response to complaints by the Australian government, in 2020 Chinese leaders essentially closed their market to Australian goods: coal was unable to unload; wine sat stranded on the quay in Hong Kong, barley, sugar, timer, lobster, and copper were been banned, and as of early December 2020, a ban on wheat was expected to follow.[90] While Russian–Chinese relations are favourable now, there is always the possibility that a disagreement may arise that will lead China to curtail access or even close its market to Russian food exports.

Other factors that impinge on sustainability of Russia's food exports include: climate anomalies could worsen in severity and duration; domestic food production may not generate the surpluses needed to expand exports; investment in food processing may fall short of plans; and Russia may lose out to other foreign competitors in the Middle East. Moreover, as was documented above, domestic political concerns about food security within Russia can curtail food exports. In short, Russia's food exports do not depend only upon food production and market conditions. Whereas Russia's recent food production trends are positive and support food exports, cautious optimism is warranted about prospects to sustain food exports because the future is unpredictable. The chapters that follow explore in more detail Russia's food trade policies and practices, as well as regional aspects of its food trade.

Notes

1. Lazar Volin, *A Century of Russian Agriculture: From Alexander II to Khrushchev* (Cambridge, MA: Harvard University Press, 1970), 110.
2. TASS, 'V Rossel'khoznadzore otmetili rost chisla pretenzii so storony importerov Rossiiskogo zerna', 19 December 2020. https://agrovesti.net/news/indst/v-rosselkhoznadzore-otmetili-rost-chisla-pretenzij-so-storony-importerov-rossijskogo-zerna.html. Accessed 19 December 2020.
3. Christina L. Davis, *Food Fights over Free Trade: How International Institutions Promote Agricultural Trade Liberalization* (Princeton: Princeton University Press, 2003).
4. United States Department of Agriculture, 'U.S. Food Imports', 17 November 2020. https://www.ers.usda.gov/data-products/us-food-imports/us-food-imports/#All%20tables%20in%20one%20file. Accessed 21 December 2020. According to USDA data, $34 billion USD was from animal products, $81.4 billion USD from plant products, and $21.7 billion USD from beverages.
5. Stephen K. Wegren with Alexander Nikulin and Irina Trotsuk, *Russia's Food Revolution: The Transformation of the Food System* (London and New York: Routledge, 2021), 209–210.
6. Stephen K. Wegren, Alexander Nikulin, and Irina Trotsuk, 'The Russian Variant of Food Security', *Problems of Post-Communism* 64, no. 1 (2017):

47–62; Jennifer Clapp, 'Food Self-Sufficiency: Making Sense of it, and When it Makes Sense', *Food Policy* 66 (2017): 88–96.

7. Tat'iana Kulistikova, 'Lidery rynka ukrepliaiut pozitsii', *Agroinvestor* no. 6 (June 2020): 58–65. Meat ouput in general is highly concentrated in a few companies. In 2019, for example, the top 25 agroholding companies accounted for 50 percent of total meat production (beef, pork, poultry), and their level of production is growing.
8. Elena Maksimova, 'Eksport miasa v 2020 godu prevysit milliard dollarov', 19 October 2020. https://www.agroinvestor.ru/analytics/news/34581-eksport-myasa-v-2020-godu-prevysit-milliard-dollarov/. Accessed 19 October 2020.
9. Ekaterina Shokurova, 'Proizvodstvo svininy v Rossii budet rasti do 2024 goda', 4 December 2020. https://www.agroinvestor.ru/analytics/news/34926-proizvodstva-svininy-v-rossii-budet-rasti-do-2024-goda/. Accessed 4 December 2020.
10. Agrovestnik, 'Import svininy obnulilsia', 30 November 2020. https://agrovesti.net/news/indst/import-svininy-obnulilsya.html. Accessed 30 November 2020.
11. Rossiiskaia gazeta, 'V etom godu vpervye za 30 let Rossiia oboidetsia bez importnoi svininy', 4 December 2020. https://agrovesti.net/news/indst/v-etom-godu-vpervye-za-30-let-rossiya-obojdetsya-bez-importnoj-svininy.html. Accessed 4 December 2020. The same article notes that per capita consumption of pork is 28 kg, or 36 percent of the 77 kg of meat consumption per capita in Russia.
12. RIA Novosti, 'RF k 2025 godu smozhet proizvodit' svinei v 1.5 raza bol'she, chem v 2019 godu', 3 December 2020. https://agrovesti.net/news/indst/rf-k-2025-godu-smozhet-proizvodit-svinej-v-1-5-raza-bol she-chem-v-2019-godu.html. Accessed 3 December 2020.
13. Rosstat, *Sel'skoe khoziaistvo Rossii 2019* (Moscow: Rosstat, 2019), 58.
14. Ekaterina Shokurova, 'Rossiia ne smogla sokratit' import prodovol'stviia do tselevykh pokazatelei', 7 December 2020. https://www.agroinvestor.ru/analytics/news/34940-rossiya-ne-smogla-sokratit-import-prodovols tviya-do-tselevykh-pokazateley/. Accessed 7 December 2020.
15. Finmarket.ru, 'Rossiia v etom godu uvelichit proizvodstvo bol'shinstva vidov produktsii APK', 7 December 2020. https://www.dairynews.ru/news/rossiya-v-etom-godu-uvelichit-proizvodstvo-bolshin.html. Accessed 7 December 2020.
16. 'Ukaz Prezidenta RF ot 21 Ianvaria 2020 g. No. 20 "Ob utverzhdenii Doktriny prodovol'stvennnoi bezopasnosti Rossiiskoi Federatsii",' 22 January 2020. http://www.garant.ru/products/ipo/prime/doc/733 38425/. Accessed 30 Novembrer 2020.

17. Rossaprimavera.ru, 'Rossiia smogla sama obespechit' sebia molokom', 4 December 2020. https://www.dairynews.ru/news/rossiya-smogla-sama-obespechit-sebya-molokom-agrar.html. Accessed 4 December 2020.
18. RIA Novosti, 'RF za 5–6 let dob'etsia polnogo importozameshcneniia po ogurtsam i tomatam', 3 December 2020. https://agrovesti.net/news/indst/rf-za-5-6-let-dobetsya-polnogo-importozameshcheniya-po-ogurtsam-i-tomatam.html. Accessed 3 December 2020.
19. Kommersant, 'Dolia importnykh ovoshchei v Rossii mozhet sokratit'sia do 10% za piat' let', 26 November 2020. https://agrovesti.net/news/indst/dolya-importnykh-ovoshchej-v-rossii-mozhet-sokratitsya-do-10-za-pyat-let.html. Accessed 26 November 2020.
20. Eugenia Serova, 'Challenges for the Development of the Russian Agricultural Sector in the Mid-Term', *Russian Journal of Economics* 6, no. 1 (2020): 3.
21. Tat'iana Karabut, 'Na melioratsiyu nuzhno dobavit', *Agroinvestor* no. 6 (June 2017): 42–47.
22. Ministerstvo sel'skogo khoziaistva Rossiiskoi Federatsii, 'Do 2025 goda v Rossii planiruetsia vvesti v oborot 4 mln ga neispol'zuemoi pashni', 4 June 2020. http://mcx.ru/press-service/news/do-2025-goda-v-rossii-planiruetsya-vvesti-v-oborot-4-mln-ga-neispolzuemoy-pashni/. Accessed 4 June 2020.
23. Food and Agriculture Organisation, *The State of Food and Agriculture 2019: Moving Forward on Food and Waste Reduction* (Rome: FAO, 2019), 4–7.
24. Serova, 'Challenges for the Development of the Russian Agricultural Sector in the Mid-Term', 4.
25. Ibid., 8.
26. Rossiiskaia gazeta, 'Novaia Sistema agrostrakhovaniia dolzhna zarabotat' k seredine 2021 goda', 7 December 2020. https://agrovesti.net/news/indst/novaya-sistema-agrostrakhovaniya-dolzhna-zarabotat-k-seredine-2021-goda.html. Accessed 7 December 2020.
27. RIA Novosti, 'Minsel'khoz RF predlagaet kompensirovat' mykomolam chast' zatrat na pokupku zerna', 5 December 2020. https://agrovesti.net/news/indst/minselkhoz-rf-predlagaet-kompensirovat-mukomolam-chast-zatrat-na-pokupku-zerna.html. Accessed 5 December 2020.
28. Rossiiskaia gazeta, 'Finansirovanie APK v 2021 godu budet umen'sheno', 7 December 2020. https://agrovesti.net/news/indst/finansirovanie-apk-v-2021-godu-budet-umensheno.html. Accessed 7 December 2020.
29. Serova, 'Challenges for the Development of the Russian Agricultural Sector in the Mid-Term', 2.
30. Parlamentskaia gazeta, 'L'goty po NDS na vvoz plemennogo skota prodlili na 2 goda', 24 November 2020. https://kvedomosti.ru/news/

https-www-pnp-ru-economics-lgotu-po-nds-na-vvoz-plemennogo-skota-prodlili-na-2-goda-html.html. Accessed 24 November 2020.
31. Wegren, Nikulin, and Trotsuk, 'The Russian Variant of Food Security', 47–62.
32. TASS, 'Putin prodlil na 2022 god deistvie kontrsanktsii', 20 September 2021. https://kvedomosti.ru/news/https-tass-ru-politika-12457189.html. Accessed 21 September 2021.
33. Stephen K. Wegren and Alexander Nikulin, 'Food and Foreign Policy', in *Putin's Russia: Past Imperfect, Future Uncertain*, ed. Stephen K. Wegren (Lanham, MD: Rowman and Littlefield, 2019), 269–89.
34. TASS, 'V Rossii s 26 Noiabria zapretili vvoz iz Ferganskoi oblasti Uzbekistana tomatov i pertsev', 26 November 2020. https://kvedomosti.ru/news/https-tass-ru-ekonomika-10099705.html. Accessed 26 November 2020.
35. RIA Novosti, 'Minsel'khoz RF rassmotrit izmenenie kvoty na import tomato viz Turtsii posle ee vyborki', 4 December 2020. https://agrovesti.net/news/indst/minselkhoz-rf-rassmotrit-izmenenie-kvoty-na-import-tomatov-iz-turtsii-posle-ee-vyborki.html. Accessed 4 December 2020. In February 2020 the quota was set at 200,000 tonnes. In December 2020 the Ministry of Agriculture suggested increasing the quota to 250,000 tonnes in order to compensate for the ban on imported tomatoes from Azerbaijan, Armenia, and Uzbekistan earlier in the fall, thus showing how trade is subject to political considerations. RIA Novosti, 'Minsel'khoz RF predlozhil uvelichit' kvotu na vvoz tomatorv iz Turtsii do 250 tonn', 16 December 2020. https://agrovesti.net/news/indst/minselkhoz-rf-predlozhil-uvelichit-kvotu-na-vvoz-tomatov-iz-turtsii-do-250-tys-tonn.html. Accessed 16 December 2020.
36. Maslozhirovoi soiuz Rossii, 'Podsolnechnye voiny: Rossiia i Turtsiia', 23 November 2020. https://agrovesti.net/news/indst/podsolnechnye-vojny-rossiya-i-turtsiya.html. Accessed 23 November 2020.
37. Rosstat, *Predpolozhitel'naia chislennost' naseleniia Rossiiskoi Federatsii do 2035 goda* (Moscow: Rosstat, 2017), table 1.1.
38. Rosstat, *Predpolozhitel'naia chislennost' naseleniia Rossiiskoi Federatsii do 2030 goda* (Moscow: Rosstat, 2013), table 1.3.
39. Ministerstvo sel'skogo khoziaistva Rossiiskoi Federatsii, 'Spravochniai informatsiia o rabote po otkrytiiu novykh rynkov po sostoianiiu na 18 Noiabria 2020 goda', November 2020. https://mcx.gov.ru/ministry/departments/departament-informatsionnoy-politiki-i-spetsialnykh-proektov/industry-information/info-otkrytie-zarubezhnykh-rynkov-dlya-rossiyskoy-produktsii-apk/. Accessed 25 November 2020.
40. See Stephen K. Wegren, 'Can Russia's Food Exports Reach $45 Billion in 2024?' *Post-Communist Economies* 32, no. 2 (2020): 147–75.

41. Ibid.
42. Ministerstvo sel'skogo khoziaistva Rossiiskoi Federatsii, 'Operativnyi obzor eksporta produktsii APK', 27 December 2020. www.mcx.gov.ru. Accessed 30 December 2020.
43. Ibid.
44. TASS, 'Kudrin schitaet, shto Rossiia dolzhna budet zamestit' neftianoi eksport drugim v 2030-x godakh', 30 November 2020. https://kvedomosti.ru/news/https-tass-ru-ekonomika-10120963.html. Accessed 30 November 2020.
45. Ministerstvo sel'skogo khoziaistva Rossiiskoi Federatsii, 'Agroeksport 2030: trendy i perspektivy', 5 August 2020. https://mcx.gov.ru/upload/iblock/186/186a255a5aefae001e3d6f1e7a93089d.pdf. Accessed 25 November 2020.
46. Ekaterina Shokurova, 'Minsel'khoz skorrektiroval plany eksporta produktsii APK', 16 November 2020. https://www.agroinvestor.ru/analytics/news/34801-minselkhoz-skorrektiroval-plany-eksporta-produktsii-apk/. Accessed 16 November 2020.
47. RIA Novosti, 'Kvota na eksport zerna is RF vo II pol sezona 2020/21 mozhet sostavit' 15 mln t', 12 November 2020. https://agrovesti.net/news/indst/kvota-na-eksport-zerna-iz-rf-vo-ii-pol-sezona-2020-21-mozhet-sostavit-15-mln-t.html. Accessed 12 November 2020.
48. Kommersant', 'Eksportery pshenitsy predupredili pravitel'stvo o riskakh novykh ogranichenii', 30 November 2020. https://agrovesti.net/news/indst/eksportery-pshenitsy-predupredili-pravitelstvo-o-riskakh-novykh-ogranichenij.html. Accessed 30 November 2020.
49. TASS, 'Pravitel'stvo poruchilo Minsel'khozu raspredelit' kvotu na eksport zerna is RF do 9 Fevralia', 16 December 2020. https://agrovesti.net/news/indst/pravitelstvo-poruchilo-minselkhozu-raspredelit-kvotu-na-eksport-zerna-iz-rf-do-9-fevralya.html. Accessed 16 December 2020.
50. Finam, 'Kvota na eksport zerna iz RF mozhet uskorit' ukhod nebol'shikh treiderov s rynka—analitiki', 26 November 2020. https://agrovesti.net/news/indst/kvota-na-eksport-zerna-iz-rf-mozhet-uskorit-ukhod-nebolshikh-trejderov-s-rynka-analitiki.html. Accessed 26 November 2020.
51. Ekaterina Shokurova, 'Top-10 eksporterov smogut vyvezti 70% zerna po kvote', 8 February 2021. https://www.agroinvestor.ru/markets/news/35249-top-10-eksporterov-smogut-vyvezti-pochti-70-zerna-po-kvote/. Accessed 8 February 2021.
52. Ekspert Iug, 'Dva Rostovskikh zernotreidera poluchili 27.5% Rossiiskoi kvoty na eksport zerna', 11 February 2021. https://agrovesti.net/news/indst/dva-rostovskikh-zernotrejdera-poluchili-27-5-rossijskoj-kvoty-na-eksport-zerna.html. Accessed 11 February 2021.
53. Kommersant', 'Ob'emy eksporta mogut povtorit' proshlogodnii rekord', 25 November 2020. https://agrovesti.net/news/indst/obemy-eksporta-

mogut-povtorit-proshlogodnij-rekord.html. Accessed 25 November 2020; Ekaterina Shokurova, 'Eksport pshenitsy v etom sezone mozhet stat' rekordnuym', 26 November 2020. https://www.agroinvestor.ru/analytics/news/34863-eksport-pshenitsy-v-etom-sezone-mozhet-stat-rekordnym/. Accessed 26 November 2020.
54. Ekaterina Shokurova, 'Vladimir Putin nazval oshibkoi chrezmernuiu podderzhku eksporta', 18 December 2020. https://www.agroinvestor.ru/markets/news/35005-vladimir-putin-nazval-oshibkoy-chrezmernuyu-podderzhku-eksporta/. Accessed 18 December 2020.
55. Ekaterina Shokurova, 'Proizvoditeli miasa i muki prosiat vvesti poshlinu na eksport zernovykh', 23 November 2020. https://www.agroinvestor.ru/markets/news/34835-proizvoditeli-myasa-i-muki-prosyat-vvesti-poshlinu-na-eksport-zernovykh/. Accessed 23 November 2020.
56. Ekaterina Shokurova, 'Eksportnuiu poshlinu na soiu mogut podniat' do 20%', 3 December 2020. https://www.agroinvestor.ru/markets/news/34922-eksportnuyu-poshlinu-na-soyu-mogut-podnyat-do-20/. Accessed 3 December 2020.
57. Shokurova, 'Vladimir Putin nazval oshibkoi chrezmernuiu podderzhku eksporta'.
58. RIA Novosti, 'Podderzhka eksporta APK v 2021 g dolzhna pomoch' vypolnit' tselevye pokazateli', 6 December 2020. https://agrovesti.net/news/indst/podderzhka-eksporta-apk-v-2021-g-dolzhna-pomoch-vypolnit-tselevye-pokazateli.html. Accessed 6 December 2020.
59. TASS, 'Pravitel'stvo planiruet sozdat' instrumentarii podderzhki eksporta', 14 September 2020. https://kvedomosti.ru/news/https-tass-ru-ekonomika-9436709.html. Accessed 14 September 2020.
60. Ibid.
61. Parlamentskaia gazeta, 'Pravitel'stvo rasshirilo podderzhku eksporta sel'khozproduktsii', 28 October 2020. https://kvedomosti.ru/news/https-www-pnp-ru-economics-pravitelstvo-rasshirilo-podderzhku-eksporta-selkhozprodukcii-html.html. Accessed 28 October 2020.
62. N. M. Svetlov, S. O. Siptits, I. A. Romanenko, and N. E. Evdokimova, 'The Effect of Climate Change on the Location of Branches of Agriculture in Russia', *Studies on Russian Economic Development* 30, no. 4 (2019): 411.
63. See Grigory Ioffe and Tatyana Nefedova, 'Areas of Crisis in Russian Agriculture: A Geographic Perspective', *Post-Soviet Geography and Economics* 41, no. 4 (2000): 288–303; and Grigory Ioffe and Tatyana Nefedova, 'Marginal Farmland in European Russia', *Eurasian Geography and Economics* 45, no. 1 (2004): 45–59.
64. Grigory Ioffe, Tatyana Nefedova, and Ilya Zaslavsky, *The End of Peasantry? The Disintegration of Rural Russia* (Pittsburgh: University of Pittsburgh Press, 2006).

65. Ministerstvo sel'skogo khoziaistva Rossiiskoi Federatsii, *O sostoianii sel'skikh territorii v Rossiiskoi Federatsii v 2017 godu: ezhegodnyi doklad po resul'tatam monitoringa* (Moscow: Ministry of Agriculture, 2019).
66. Travis J. Lybbert and Heather R. Morgan, 'Lessons from the Arab Spring: Food Security and Stability in the Middle East and North Africa', in *Food Security and Sociopolitical Stability*, ed. Christopher B. Barrett (Oxford: Oxford University Press, 2013), 357–380.
67. FAO, 'World Food Situation: Cereal Supply and Demand Brief', 5 November 2020. http://www.fao.org/worldfoodsituation/csdb/en/. Accessed 29 November 2020.
68. United Nations, 'Growing at a Slower Pace, World Population is Expected to reach 9.7 billion in 2050', 17 June 2019. https://www.un.org/development/desa/en/news/population/world-population-prospects-2019.html. Accessed 28 November 2020; and United Nations, *World Population Prospects 2019: Data Booklet*, 2019. https://population.un.org/wpp/Publications/Files/WPP2019_DataBooklet.pdf. Accessed 28 November 2020.
69. FAO, 'How to Feed the World in 2050', 24–26 June 2009. http://www.fao.org/fileadmin/templates/wsfs/docs/expert_paper/How_to_Feed_the_World_in_2050.pdf. Accessed 29 November 2020.
70. Ibid.
71. WTO, 'Trade Restrictions Among G20 Economies Remain at Historic Highs', 21 November 2019. https://www.wto.org/english/news_e/news19_e/trdev_21nov19_e.htm. Accessed 28 November 2020.
72. WTO, 'WTO report shows slowdown in G20 trade restrictions as COVID-19 impacts world economy', 18 November 2020. https://www.wto.org/english/news_e/news20_e/trdev_18nov20_e.htm. Accessed 28 November 2020.
73. Ministerstvo sel'skogo khoziaistva Rossiiskoi Federatsii, 'Prodvizhenie Rossiiskikh prodovol'stvennykh brendov sposobstvuet razvitiiu eksporta APK', 26 March 2019. http://mcx.ru/press-service/news/prodvizhenie-rossiyskikh-prodovolstvennykh-brendov-sposobstvuet-razvitiyu-eksporta-apk-/. Accessed 26 March 2019.
74. 'Brend stanet normoi', *Sel'skaia zhizn'*, 18–24 October 2018, 5.
75. Kvedomosti.ru, 'Rospotrebnadzor predlagaet vvesti ugolovnuiu otvetstvennost' za fal'sifikat', 20 February 2019. http://kvedomosti.ru/news/rospotrebnadzor-predlagaet-vvesti-ugolovnuyu-otvetstvennost-za-falsifikat.html. Accessed 20 February 2019.
76. Kvedomosti.ru, 'Shtrafy za obman potrebitelei mogut vyrasti v desiat' raz', 20 March 2019. http://kvedomosti.ru/news/shtrafy-za-obman-potrebitelej-mogut-vyrasti-v-desyat-raz.html. Accessed 20 March 2019.
77. TASS, 'Obiazatel'naia markirovka molochnoi produktsii nachnetsia v Rossii s Marta 2020 goda', 19 July 2019. https://agrovesti.net/news/

indst/obyazatelnaya-markirovka-molochnoj-produktsii-nachnetsya-v-rossii-s-marta-2020-goda.html, accessed 19 July 2019.
78. The Dairy News, 'Markirovka: kto vinovat i chto delat'? 1 December 2020. https://www.dairynews.ru/news/markirovka-kto-vinovat-i-chto-delat.html. Accessed 1 December 2020.
79. Soiuzmoloko, 'Govorit' o minimal'nykh zatratakh na markirovku do okonchaniia eksperimenta prezhdevremenno', 9 July 2020. https://agrovesti.net/news/indst/soyuzmoloko-govorit-o-minimal-nykh-zatratakh-na-markirovku-do-okonchaniya-eksperimenta-prezhdevremenno.html. Accessed 9 July 2020.
80. The Dairy News, 'Morozhenshchiki poprosili otlozhit' zapusk markirovki', 1 December 2020. https://www.dairynews.ru/news/soyuz-morozhenshchikov-rossii-poprosil-otlozhit-za.html. Accessed 1 December 2020.
81. Rossiiskaia gazeta, 'Do 2024 goda planiruetsia rasshirit's spisok tovarov dlia markirovki', 25 September 2020. https://www.dairynews.ru/news/do-2024-goda-planiruetsya-rasshirit-spisok-tovarov.html. Accessed 25 September 2020.
82. Praim, 'Minsel'khoz RF ne ozhidaet pereboev s postavkami molochki posle nachala ee markirovki', 30 September 2020. https://agrovesti.net/news/indst/minselkhoz-rf-ne-ozhidaet-pereboev-s-postavkami-molochki-posle-nachala-ee-markirovki.html. Accessed 30 September 2020.
83. Nicholas Eberstadt, 'With Great Demographics Comes Great Power', *Foreign Affairs* 98, no. 4 (July–August 2019): 149.
84. Ibid., 150.
85. Ibid.
86. Eurostat, 'Russia-EU—International Trade in Goods statistics', March 2020. https://ec.europa.eu/eurostat/statistics-explained/index.Php/Russia-EU_-_international_trade_in_goods_statistics. Accessed 26 November 2020.
87. Ministerstvo sel'skogo khoziaistva Rossiiskoi Federatsii, 'Operativnyi obzor eksporta produktsii APK', 27 December 2020. www.mcx.gov.ru. Accessed 30 December 2020.
88. Shokurova, 'Rossiia ne smogla sokratit' import prodovol'stviia do tselevykh pokazatelei'.
89. Ibid.
90. 'Hurly-barley', *The Economist*, 28 November-4 December 2020, 34.

Selected Bibliography

Clapp, Jennifer. 'Food Self-Sufficiency: Making Sense of it, and When it Makes Sense'. *Food Policy* 66 (2017): 88–96.

Davis, Christina L. *Food Fights over Free Trade: How International Institutions Promote Agricultural Trade Liberalization*. Princeton: Princeton University Press, 2003.

Eberstadt, Nicholas. 'With Great Demographics Comes Great Power'. *Foreign Affairs* 98, no. 4 (July–August 2019): 146–157.

Food and Agriculture Organisation (FAO). *The State of Food and Agriculture 2019: Moving Forward on Food and Waste Reduction*. Rome: FAO, 2019.

Ioffe, Grigory, Tatyana Nefedova, and Ilya Zaslavsky. *The End of Peasantry? The Disintegration of Rural Russia*. Pittsburgh: University of Pittsburgh Press, 2006.

Lybbert, Travis J. and Heather R. Morgan. 'Lessons from the Arab Spring: Food Security and Stability in the Middle East and North Africa'. In *Food Security and Sociopolitical Stability*, ed. Christopher B. Barrett. Oxford: Oxford University Press, 2013, 357–380.

Serova, Eugenia. 'Challenges for the Development of the Russian Agricultural Sector in the Mid-Term'. *Russian Journal of Economics* 6, no. 1 (2020): 1–5.

Svetlov, N. M., S. O. Siptits, I. A. Romanenko, and N. E. Evdokimova. 'The Effect of Climate Change on the Location of Branches of Agriculture in Russia'. *Studies on Russian Economic Development* 30, no. 4 (2019): 406–418.

Volin, Lazar. *A Century of Russian Agriculture: From Alexander II to Khrushchev*. Cambridge, MA: Harvard University Press, 1970.

Wegren, Stephen K. 'Can Russia's Food Exports Reach $45 Billion in 2024?'. *Post-Communist Economies* 32, no. 2 (2020): 147–75.

Wegren, Stephen K. 'Russian Grain Production: Too Much of a Good Thing?'. *Post-Communist Economies* 30, no. 6 (November 2018): 835–46.

Wegren, Stephen K., Alexander Nikulin, and Irina Trotsuk. *Russia's Food Revolution: The Transformation of the Food System*. London and New York: Routledge, 2021.

Wegren, Stephen K., Alexander Nikulin, and Irina Trotsuk. 'The Russian Variant of Food Security'. *Problems of Post-Communism* 64, no. 1 (2017): 47–62.

Wegren, Stephen K. and Christel Elvestad. 'Russia's Food Self-Sufficiency and Food Security: An Assessment'. *Post-Communist Economies* 30, no. 5 (2018): 565–87.

Open Access This chapter is licensed under the terms of the Creative Commons Attribution 4.0 International License (http://creativecommons.org/licenses/by/4.0/), which permits use, sharing, adaptation, distribution and reproduction in any medium or format, as long as you give appropriate credit to the original author(s) and the source, provide a link to the Creative Commons license and indicate if changes were made.

The images or other third party material in this chapter are included in the chapter's Creative Commons license, unless indicated otherwise in a credit line to the material. If material is not included in the chapter's Creative Commons license and your intended use is not permitted by statutory regulation or exceeds the permitted use, you will need to obtain permission directly from the copyright holder.

PART I

Agri-Food Trade Policy and Practice

Chapter 1: Russia's Foreign Food Trade: An Historical Survey

Stephen K. Wegren

1 Introduction

Russia's role in the international food trade system and impact on that system has gone through different phases over time. In the pre-World War I period, Russia was Europe's largest grain exporter, especially wheat. During the Soviet period from the 1970s onward the USSR impacted the international food trade system by entering the global market to purchase grain to compensate for domestic shortfalls. Recently, Russia has returned to its historical place and currently plays a significant role in the international food trade system as a global supplier of wheat. Russia has been the leading wheat exporter in the world during six of the past seven agricultural years, surpassing the United States. Russia's contemporary role as a leading grain exporter is juxtaposed to lingering impressions of the Soviet Union as a grain importer to feed people and cattle. The change in Russia's role in international agricultural trade is attributable to several factors: the liberalisation of the economy after 1992; the emergence of private sector entrepreneurs who propel economic development much

S. K. Wegren (✉)
Southern Methodist University, Dallas, TX, USA
e-mail: swegren@smu.edu

© The Author(s) 2022

S. K. Wegren and F. Nilssen (eds.), *Russia's Role in the Contemporary International Agri-Food Trade System*, Palgrave Advances in Bioeconomy: Economics and Policies,
https://doi.org/10.1007/978-3-030-77451-6_2

as American inventors and investors were driving forces in the American food industry in the early twentieth century; a significant rebound in agricultural production; an increase in the state ambitions for international prestige; and the emergence of mega-farms that are modern, globally competitive, and use advanced technology to achieve high efficiency. These processes work together to produce a food revolution in food supply, distribution, and retailing that has led to unprecedented consumer choice about how and where to obtain food.[1]

The purpose of this chapter is to survey Russia's role in international agricultural trade and how that role has changed over time. The chapter sheds light on three related questions. (1) To what extent has Russia's role as a significant player in the international food trade system changed over time? (2) To what extent has Russia been integrated to world food markets and how has the degree of integration changed over time? (3) What is the significance of those changes? The goal is to provide historical context for the chapters that follow which focus on the contemporary period since 2014.

2 Analytical Framework

Countries engage in food trade for a variety of reasons. History shows that nations engage in food trade because it yields several benefits. In the economic realm, a food exporting country may have a comparative advantage and is able to sell its food at an attractive price, thereby earning foreign currency by meeting demand in another country. Or maybe a country wants to reduce its food surplus and support domestic prices. In the political realm, countries export food to strengthen or maintain friendly relations. Exports may be used to bind other nations to the exporter; in this respect food exports are useful for maintaining alliances and empires. Food exports are also used to build international status and prestige. And food may be exported as aid as a means to expand soft power abroad. In the security realm, food exports may help an ally or withheld to punish an adversary. These motivations are not exclusive and several may be true simultaneously.

Although protectionism throughout the world has been on the rise since 2016, countries may benefit from food imports. For example, a country may have a comparative disadvantage for a given commodity and therefore it saves money by importing. A country may experience chronic or temporary supply shortages and needs to import food to avoid hunger or political instability. A country may import food to benefit consumers by opting for a cheaper alternative to domestic production, or simply to allow consumers more choice. A country may import a commodity or commodities that it cannot produce itself. Or a country may import food as part of an alliance network in which trade serves to maintain that alliance.

My framework to analyse Russia's food trade behaviour consists of four variables, with responses ranging from low to high: (1) *frequency* of entrance into the global food market; (2) *degree* of food trade protectionism; (3) degree of *integration* with Western global trading institutions; and (4) degree of *involvement* in the global food market. The variables are defined as follows. The global food market consists of trading institutions defined and created by the West, such as General Agreement on Trade and Tariffs (GATT) or World Trade Organisation (WTO). Frequency is defined as how often Russia enters the global food market in a given timeframe; the range is periodic to consistent entrance. Degree of protectionism concerns whether food trade protectionism was high or low, encompassing both tariff and non-tariff barriers. Degree of integration refers to whether Russia was a full member of global trading institutions or acted outside of them. Degree of involvement concerns the volume of Russia's food imports and exports with Western nations. Time is overlaid with those variables and the framework is illustrated in Table 1.

The table displays patterns of continuity and change. Since the 1980s, Russia has had high frequency of entrance into the global food market, mostly as a food importer. Its degree of involvement in the global food market has been high as a consistent food importer and recently as a food exporter. Discontinuity since the 1980s is found in the degree of agricultural protectionism, degree of integration with global trade institutions, and Russia's emergence as a significant grain exporter since 2014.

3 Institutions for International Agri-Food Trade

The Soviet Union participated in the Bretton Woods conference in 1944 that led to trading rules established by the 1947 General Agreement on Trade and Tariffs (GATT). Ultimately, the Soviet Union chose not to join GATT or other institutions created out of the conference such as the World Bank or International Monetary Fund (IMF). The GATT allowed

Table 1 Framework for analysis of Russia's food trade behaviour

	1970s	*1980s*	*1990s*	*2000–2013*	*2014–2020*
Frequency of entrance into global food market	Low	High	High	High	High
Agricultural protectionism	High	High	Transition from high to low	Low	Transition from low to selectively high
Degree of integration with Western trade institutions	Low	Low	Low	Transition from low to high	Transition from high to low
Degree of involvement in global food market, including:	Low	High	High	High	High
Food imports	Periodic	Consistent	Consistent	Consistent	Consistent
Food exports	Low	Low	Low	Transition from low to high	High

Source Author's analysis

countries in the developed world to use non-tariff barriers, quotas, tariffs on imports, and export subsidies to protect their agricultural sectors. Soviet participation in GATT was on the table in 1972 when the United States proposed entry as a complement to détente, but the Soviet leadership declined the invitation.[2] The Soviet Union also chose not to participate in the Tokyo Round of negotiations that began in 1973.

The importance of the Soviet Union being outside of GATT was that it allowed non-application countries to be denied most-favoured nation status (MFN). Therefore, the USSR's non-application status meant that the U.S. Congress could extend or withhold MFN for the Soviet Union, which in turn allowed trade to be politicised as was evident with the 1974 Jackson-Vanik Amendment which linked MFN to Jewish emigration from the USSR. When the Soviets balked at this linkage, MFN was denied. Henceforth, MFN would only be granted after annual certification of the Soviet Union's behaviour. It was not until 1992 that post-Communist Russia was given permanent MFN.

The Tokyo Round of negotiations in 1973 revealed three different approaches to agricultural trade among developed countries. First, efficient producers wanted negotiations to lead to freer agricultural trade, while inefficient producers preferred stable markets through regulation and minimum commodity prices. Second, the European Community preferred to negotiate agricultural products separately from industrial products, a disagreement that would not be settled until 1977. Third, the United States favoured a reduction of tariffs on all products, including agriculture, and also supported a prohibition on direct export subsidies for all products. This position was rejected by the European Community.[3]

Meanwhile, the use of trade 'exceptions' by the United States, Western Europe countries, and Japan meant that the general trend in reducing trade barriers as mandated by GATT did not affect agricultural trade. For example, the U.S. Congress pressured GATT members to allow tariffs if imports caused 'domestic injury' to agriculture (Sect. 22), or allowed GATT rules to be suspended if needed in order to preserve health, safety, or national security.[4] Thus, the agricultural sector in developed nations remained more protected than industry and manufacturing. Over time, however, the cost of farm subsidies and protectionism grew onerous, rising to $300 billion annually by the mid-1980s in OECD countries, with around 40 percent of farm income coming from subsidies.[5]

The cost of agricultural protectionism to U.S. taxpayers was also considerable and financial pressures led to support for liberalised agricultural trade. During the 1970s the United States quadrupled the value of its agricultural exports from $6.7 billion USD in fiscal 1970 to over $27 billion USD in fiscal 1978. As a result, the U.S. share of world agricultural trade increased from 13.5 percent in 1970 to 17 percent in 1978. In 1981, U.S. agricultural exports reached $43.8 billion USD; but by 1986 they had declined to $26.3 billion USD. U.S. stockpiles of wheat, corn, and rice grew rapidly. By the mid-1980s, the American farm sector was in crisis due to overproduction and high farm debt, which led to farm closures. Export markets for American products that had been robust in the 1970s contracted as oil price shocks led to tighter monetary policy, higher interest rates, and weakened purchasing power.[6] Thus, the United States was saddled with an expensive farm policy at a time of declining exports. Faced with a domestic farm problem, the U.S. government felt that freer agricultural trade would open new markets and help to alleviate farm surpluses that were driving down domestic prices. This situation served as the background to the Uruguay Round of negotiations.

In September 1986 the eighth round of GATT negotiations began, called the Uruguay Round. The Soviet Union requested to join the negotiations but was denied permission. In 1990, the Soviet Union applied for observer status to GATT but was originally blocked by the United States. The United States subsequently relented following opposition to its stance from other countries. In May 1990 the Soviet Union was granted observer status to GATT, a move that represented the first step in integrating to the world trade system. Observer status allowed Soviet representatives to attend meetings but not to participate in decision-making or dispute resolution.[7]

After several years of negotiations and several failures, in 1994 the Uruguay Round Agreement on Agriculture (AoA) was signed, which focused on improving market access, domestic support, and export subsidies. The Uruguay Round Agreement came into effect in 1995 and improved access to foreign markets for food exporting countries by lowering tariffs and removing quantitative restrictions on imports. Countries agreed to convert quantitative restrictions to tariffs, to be followed by a reduction in tariffs.[8] Developed countries would reduce their agricultural tariffs by an average of one-third over six years while developing countries would reduce their tariffs by an average of 25 percent over ten years.[9] Under the AoA, domestic subsidies to agriculture were also scheduled for reduction. Developed countries were to reduce their domestic subsidies by 20 percent over six years while developing countries would reduce subsidies by 13 percent over ten years.[10] Least developed countries were exempt from any reductions. Domestic subsidies were categorised into different boxes, representing the level of distortion that they caused in trade. Subsidies in the 'amber box' were considered highly trade-distorting and were to be reduced the most. 'Green box' subsidies were considered to have minimal trade-distorting effects and did not require reduction. 'Blue box' subsidies also did not require reductions and were not limited. Finally, the AoA required reductions in export subsidies, the purpose of which was to end agricultural dumping (selling below production cost). Developed countries would reduce their export subsidies by an average of one-third over six years while developing countries would reduce their subsidies by an average of 25 percent over ten years.[11]

Although the AoA represented progress in liberalising agricultural trade, Clapp notes that because the United States and European Union (hereafter EU) moved many of their subsidies into green and blue boxes, their level of subsidies *increased* in comparison to the 1980s. Moreover, as late as 1998 agricultural protection remained high and tariffs averaged 40 percent. Clapp argues that, 'loopholes in the agreement allowed United States and the EU to continue with many of the protectionist practices to which they had become accustomed. As such, the AoA has been criticized as reinforcing already unequal agricultural trade rules'.[12] Davis adds that, 'nontariff barriers remained common in the agricultural sector long after they were eliminated for most industrial goods'.[13] Ironically, developed countries *raised* their level of agricultural protectionism even as the size of the agricultural sector was shrinking in comparison to the rest of the economy.

Until the last two years of its existence, the Soviet Union was virtually a non-entity in Western international trade arrangements. Its primary trade, both agricultural and non-agricultural, was with fellow East bloc nations who comprised the Council for Mutual Economic Assistance (CMEA, sometimes referred to as Comecon, 1949–1991). This bloc of communist economies was not integrated with capitalist economies and instead opted for intra-bloc trade to the widest extent possible. Communist leaders wanted to protect their consumers from global food prices and their producers from Western competition. As a result, Soviet protectionism vis-à-vis Western nations was in line with Western protectionism as described above.

In 1993, Russia's post-Soviet government applied to join GATT, which in 1995 became the World Trade Organisation (WTO). Negotiations over Russia's entry to the WTO would continue for 18 years, cycling through periods of cooperation when membership seemed near and animosity.[14] Negotiations over agriculture were particularly contentious.[15] Finally, a breakthrough occurred in fall 2011 that led to a positive vote to allow Russia's membership. In July 2012 the State Duma ratified the agreement and in August 2012 Russia officially joined the WTO, the 156th country to do so at that time. Accession brought two major changes. First, Russia's membership to the WTO represented integration with the global trading system. Second, Russia's integration into the global institutional trading system brought obligations and responsibilities.[16]

Not long after Russia's WTO accession, however, the 2014 political crisis in Ukraine and Crimea led President Vladimir Putin to suspend some of Russia's commitments by invoking 'protection of national security', allowed by Article XXI in GATT.[17] Since then, Russia has continued to communicate with the WTO concerning issues in food safety, photosanitary standards, and veterinary requirements. Broader trade obligations such as refraining from the use of import quotas or import bans have gone by the wayside. Russia also continues to use various forms of state assistance that may be considered market-distorting, for example, transportation subsidies for grain from point of origin to port. That said, it is useful to review briefly the set of obligations that Russia agreed to when it joined the WTO.

First, Russia's agricultural budget for 'trade-distorting support' was limited to no more than $9 billion (USD) in 2012 and 2013, which dropped to $4.4 billion by 2018. Not limited are expenditures for research, disease control, infrastructure, food security, farm restructuring, and rural development, which are not considered trade distorting.

Second, the average tariff rate for agricultural products after full implementation was scheduled to decline from 13.2 to 10.8 percent.[18] In comparison, the average tariff rate for manufactured goods dropped from 9.5 percent currently to 7.3 percent, so agriculture remained somewhat more protected but less so than in the past. For context, during 2000–2008 Russia's average tariff rate on imported food almost doubled from 10 to 18 percent, which is not especially high by global standards as many nations have much higher tariff rates, including the EU, but it did represent more, not less, protectionism.[19] Thus, entry into the WTO was expected to bring a reduction in Russia's agricultural tariffs.

A third obligation was that one-third of tariff lines were to be reduced on the date of accession, with another one-quarter of tariffs to be reduced within three years. The longest implementation period was to be eight years for pork. Tariff rates for dairy products and cereals were to be reduced by about 5 percent; tariffs for oilseeds, fats, and oils were to decline by about 2 percent.[20] Under the terms of accession, tariffs for agricultural products would decline by more but still be higher than for many other non-agricultural goods. Russia was allowed to continue to use tariff-rate quotas (TRQs) for beef, pork, and chicken. Russia's use of TRQs, which originated in 2003, was adjusted in 2012 following Russia's accession. According to the adjustment, the in-tariff quota for fresh and chilled beef was increased from 30 thousand tonnes to 33 thousand tonnes; the in-tariff quota for fresh and chilled pork was reduced from 472 thousand tonnes to 400 thousand tonnes; and the in-tariff quota for fresh and chilled poultry was raised from 330 thousand tonnes to 341 thousand tonnes. From 2013 through 2019 in-tariff quotas for these products were kept constant: 570 thousand tonnes for fresh, chilled, and frozen beef; 400 thousand tonnes for fresh, chilled, and frozen pork; and

364 thousand tonnes for fresh, chilled, and frozen poultry. In compliance with its promises made to the WTO, starting in 2020 Russia's in-tariff quota for pork was abolished and all pork imports were subject to a 25 percent tariff. Previously, pork imports within the in-tariff quota were taxed at 0 percent and outside the quota at 65 percent.[21] Whether linked to the ending of the TRQ or the rise in domestic pork production, pork imports fell in 2020 to a very low level (see Chapter 4). In late 2020, Russia proposed to the Eurasian Economic Union to replace its TRQ for beef with a flat tariff rate of 27.5 percent. If approved, the change would take effect in January 2022.

4 Russia's Agricultural Trading Behaviour

This section moves from the global trading institutions to Russia's actual trading behaviour over several time periods. The USSR was an irregular player in the international (Western dominated) agri-food trade system prior to the 1970s. The first significant Soviet foray into the international grain market followed poor harvests in 1963 and 1965. During 1964–1966 the Soviet Union was forced to make large grain purchases on the international food market for the first time since World War II. The 1964–1966 period was also the first time that Soviet grain imports exceeded grain exports since the early 1950s.[22]

The Soviet Union's entry into international food markets as a grain importer was driven by several factors: domestic production shortfalls; grain stock building policy; the need for feed grain for cattle; and livestock expansion plans. Soviet food imports were also influenced by weather anomalies during the 1960s–1980s. Arguably, aside from weather, the most important driver for grain imports was the degree to which domestic production could meet consumption needs.[23] Starting in 1971, Soviet leaders decided to improve levels of food consumption *and* to increase livestock inventories which would lead to higher meat production.[24] Henceforth, the so-called 'social contract' between regime and population was based on a commitment to produce more food and increase consumption during each successive Five-Year Plan. Specifically, Soviet leaders wanted to increase output in animal husbandry in order to meet rising consumer demand for meat, milk, cheese, and other animal-based protein. During several five-year plans the goal to increase meat consumption was successful, as annual per capita consumption rose from 47.5 kg in 1970 to 62.4 kg in 1986.[25] These official statistics do not, of course, factor in the quality of production or the time that consumers expended to obtain meat which had an economic cost to productivity. The Soviet social contract based on a more diversified diet was mirrored in Eastern Europe. Deutsch links political stability in Eastern bloc countries with the need to improve food consumption via a 'food revolution', writing that 'rising consumer demands now form the most serious challenge that the socialist system has ever had to meet'.[26]

5 Russia's Trading Behaviour in the 1970s

During the pre-1970s period, the USSR did not play a significant role in the international food system except during 1964–1966 due to exceptional circumstances when grain was imported from the West as noted above. During the 1970s, Russia's frequency of entrance into the global food market was periodic, its integration with global institutions was low, and its degree of involvement with the global food market was low. Soviet entry into the international food system was based on need until the early 1970s. Conversely, its protectionism was high.

The 1970s began with the USSR basically food self-sufficient. In 1970 the Soviet Union was actually a net grain exporter of more than 7 million metric tonnes (mmt). As previously noted, most of Soviet Russia's trade consisted of intra-bloc trade with CMEA nations. This occurrence was an outflow of the economic integration imposed by the Soviet Union on Eastern Europe during the 1950s and 1960s, and by the 1971 Comprehensive Program for Socialist Integration that stressed plan coordination, joint investment projects, and cooperation in long-term programmes.[27] During the first half of the 1970s, trade with the West by CMEA nations accounted for only 30 percent of exports and 37 percent of imports.[28]

The positive food situation in the USSR changed rapidly as poor harvests occurred in 1971–1972, followed by another poor harvest in mid-decade (1975) and at the end of the decade (1979). Actual grain output during 1971–1975 fell significantly below planned levels, and the same was true for the 1976-1980 Five-Year Plan as well.[29] As a result, the Soviet Union became a more significant participant in the global food system, although not on a regular basis. Beginning in 1972, the Soviet Union turned to the West for grain imports and particularly the United States (see Chapter 10). The Soviet Union became a 'burden' on the world food system.[30] As a further irritant, Robert Paarlberg argues that the Soviets 'used its access to western food markets as more than a means to compensate for domestic production shortfall' by re-exporting imported American grain at a higher price.[31]

In 1979, the Soviet Union experienced another poor harvest. The volume of grain available for domestic trade was down about 30 mmt compared to 1978, including a decline of more than 20 mmt of wheat.[32] The USSR again turned to the West, and particularly the United States, to purchase grain. But that effort was stymied following the Soviet Union's December 1979 invasion of Afghanistan after which U.S. President Jimmy Carter imposed an embargo beginning in January 1980 on 17 mmt of wheat sales that had been sold to the Soviet Union. The embargo lasted into April 1981. The Soviet Union started the decade as an irregular and mostly insignificant player in the international food system, but during the 1970s it became a consistent purchaser of Western grain, which means that its entrance into the global food market became more frequent and its degree of involvement with the global food market rose.

6 Russia's Trading Behaviour in the 1980s

During the 1980s, Russia's frequency of entrance into the global food market was high, its protectionism was high, and its degree of involvement with the global food market was high as a consistent grain importer. Its integration with global institutions remained low.

In the 1980s the USSR became a regular participant in the international food system by importing grain due to domestic shortfalls. The 1980s started badly, beginning with three consecutive years of poor harvests, 1980–1982. By 1982, the Soviet Union had a net agricultural trade deficit of $18 billion and had net grain imports of 45 mmt, a very different situation from just a decade earlier. Another very poor harvest came in 1984. During 1980–1985 grain output in the Soviet Union averaged about 182 mmt, far short of the 200 mmt that state planners had anticipated. To be clear, domestic grain production was sufficient to provide the population with bread and grain products and Western analysts recognised that hunger was not a problem in the USSR.[33] Poor harvests created feed grain deficiencies that affected livestock herds that trickled down to affect meat and milk production. The Kremlin's plan to expand livestock herds stalled.

The Soviet Union transformed from a periodic participant in the international food system in the 1970s into a regular buyer of grain during the 1980s who impacted the world food system. In the early 1980s, Western economists warned that Soviet demand for imported grain could 'create disruption in world grain trade with serious consequences for both grain-exporting and grain-deficit countries'.[34] During 1976–1980, the Soviet Union imported an average of 19.9 mmt of grain per year. In the 1981–1985 period, however, average annual grain imports rose to over 40 mmt, of which 12.4 mmt were purchased from the United States.[35] The value of Soviet grain imports from the West averaged $10 billion USD per year during 1981–1984 when hard currency reserves were declining. Moreover, the Soviet Union also became a buyer of meat, fruit, vegetables, vegetable oil, and sugar on the international market.[36] The Soviet Union's largest impact on the international food market, however, remained its grain imports.

The final Soviet leader, Mikhail Gorbachev (1985–1991), frequently spoke about far-reaching reforms in agriculture. He had made his reputation for modest agrarian reforms as First Secretary in Stavropol' krai in the 1970s. After he was brought to Moscow in 1978, he became Party Secretary for agriculture in November 1978, a position for which he was eminently qualified, and he remained in the position for several years (1978–1984). As the secretary in charge of agriculture, he played a large role in drafting the 1982 Food Programme. As General Secretary of the Communist party, Gorbachev targeted agriculture for reform, although space limitations prevent a full discussion of those reforms.[37] Gorbachev first tried to implement some of the goals of the 1982 Food Programme—improving the capital stock of farm machinery and repair facilities, improving storage and transportation, improving rural housing, and upgrading food processing and packaging.[38] After 1987, Gorbachev moved beyond the Food Programme to embrace farm self-financing, farm autonomy and incentives, land leasing, and encouraging a private (non-state) sector. In 1987 foreign trade was partially liberalised although the USSR did not turn into a free trade country. During Gorbachev's early years in power, 1985–1987, the Soviet Union remained highly food protectionist except when needed. After 1988, the Soviet economy opened up and foreign companies entered the Soviet food market in food retailing and restaurants, including the opening of the first McDonald's restaurant in Moscow in 1990.[39]

Despite the fact that there was a short-term rise in food consumption, Gorbachev's reforms did not bring farm autonomy and food losses remained high: as much as 30 percent of the harvest and 50 percent for potatoes and vegetables.[40] The Stalinist procurement system that had existed since the 1930s crumbled in 1990 and 1991 and the *prodnalog* (food tax) proved ineffective for obtaining food to feed the cities and maintain livestock.[41] As a result, grain imports from the West continued to be high. Despite favourable harvests of 211 mmt in 1989 and 235 mmt in 1990, the USSR imported nearly 40 mmt of grain in 1989 and 26 mmt in 1990. In 1991, the last year of the Soviet Union's existence, the harvest was less than 173 mmt and it imported 38 mmt of grain.[42] Gorbachev's agrarian reforms did little to reduce reliance on Western grain, which meant that entrance into the global food market remained frequent and its degree of involvement with the global food market remained high. Its agricultural trade protectionism transitioned from high to low by the end of the decade.

7 Russia's Trading Behaviour in the 1990s

In the 1990s, Russia's frequency of entrance into the global food market was high and its degree of involvement in the global food market was high as the value of imports rose significantly. Post-Soviet protectionism was low during much of the decade although that started to change in mid-decade. The degree of integration with Western global institutions remained low as Russia remained outside of GATT/WTO.

As the country transitioned from a command to a market economy during the 1990s, Russia was a regular participant in the international food trade system as an importer due to the steep decline in its agricultural production. Large farm enterprises traditionally fed the nation, whereas food production from household gardens tended to be consumed by the household, in other words, locally. An index for 1994 estimated agricultural output by agricultural enterprises (large farms) at 57 percent of their 1990 level.[43] To compensate for falling domestic production by large farms, Russia turned to food imports. Calculated in U.S. dollars, the value of Russia's food imports rose from $5.6 billion USD in 1993 to $13.3 billion USD in 1997 before declining in 1998 and 1999 following the financial collapse and devaluation of the ruble that made foreign food very expensive. It is worth noting that the value of food imports exceeded by many times the value of domestic food production. The 1990s witnessed an increase in food imports from the West, which replaced former republics as Russia's primary food trading partner. Up to

1998, the dollar value of food imports from states not in the Commonwealth of Independent States (CIS) exceeded the dollar value of food imports from CIS members by a factor of two or three, depending on the year.[44]

The increase in the value of Russia's food imports accompanied the liberalisation of the economy and foreign trade after 1992. Although still not a member of GATT, the early post-Soviet years witnessed a lowering of Soviet-era barriers and further opening the Russian economy in anticipation of early membership in the WTO. As a result, foreign foodstuffs both raw and processed flooded Russia's marketplace. Within the context of a rising value of food imports, Russia changed from a large importer of grain early in the decade (more than 15 mmt per year during 1990–1992),[45] to a large meat importer by mid-decade, driven by a significant drop in domestic livestock herds. The percentage decline in the number of pigs, beef cattle, and milk cows during the first five years of market reform in the 1990s exceeded the losses during the first five years of Stalin's collectivisation. The decline in livestock herds reflected farm adaptation to new economic conditions: a range of state subsidies disappeared, price increases for domestic feed grain, fuel, and other inputs exceeded farmgate prices. As a consequence, large cities were importing upwards of 70–80 percent of their meat by 1995–1996.[46]

Russia had poor harvests throughout the decade. The first year as a non-communist state started with a good harvest of nearly 107 mmt in 1992. During 1995–1996, however, its grain harvest averaged 66.3 mmt and in 1998–1999 it averaged of just 51.2 mmt per year. Nonetheless, grain imports averaged just 3.74 mmt for 1995–1996 and 3.78 mmt for 1998–1999, far below the levels of the 1980s. The precipitous decrease in the size of livestock herds was one reason why grain consumption plummeted and there was less need for foreign feed grain, as explained by the Lieferts in Chapter 2. In addition, consumers' food consumption patterns changed. As retail food subsidies from the state disappeared after 1992, for most Russian consumers the primary problem during the 1990s was the price of food, not availability.[47] In the grips of a major recession, consumers ate less beef, which put downward pressure on farm incentives to maintain large herds.[48] By 1996–1997 Russian consumers substituted cheap imported poultry for domestic beef, similar to how American consumers turned to chicken during the early 1930s when up to one-half of households had no regular income during the Great Depression. The availability of cheap starches and carbohydrates meant that even with high food inflation and mass poverty, there was no mass hunger even as average caloric intake decreased.[49]

Russia's financial crisis in 1998 led to three occurrences that affected its food imports. First, with the devaluation of the ruble, imported food became very expensive and thus Russian consumers shifted to domestic products. As a result, the dollar value of food imports fell from $13.3 billion USD in 1997 to $7.3 billion USD in 2000. Second, Russian food processors and manufacturers adapted quickly to capitalise on their price advantage and created attractive packaging that mirrored Western brands. Third, Russia's trade policy became more protectionist.

The origins of increased trade protectionism pre-dated Russia's August 1998 financial crisis. By 1996–1997 conservative voices in society and the government were raising alarms about threats to national food security. In December 1997, President Boris Yeltsin approved a document titled 'Conception of the National Security of the Russian Federation', which stated that dependence on food imports and Russia's integration into the world market was not beneficial. Simultaneously, conservative and nationalist groups within Russia complained about the loss of food independence.[50] In April 1998, the law 'On Measures of Protection of Russian Economic Interests in Foreign Trade' was signed that identified poultry, vegetable oil, and meat for protection through an increase in tariffs.[51] In June 1998, a 5 percent increase in tariffs for all food imports was enacted. At this time, Russian leaders were engaged in a delicate balancing act, wanting to protect domestic producers while simultaneously avoiding a large increase in the cost of food to the average family budget, which already was quite high; and in 1998 the Yeltsin administration still held out hope to join the WTO by the end of the year and thus did not want to go too far in protectionist measures.

Following Russia's financial crisis in August 1998, then-Minister of Agriculture Viktor Semenov (April 1998–May 1999) called for a 'new course' in agrarian policy that rested on increased state regulation of the agro-industrial complex and defence of Russia's domestic food market. In particular, Semenov noted that export subsidies in the European Union undercut Russian producers, thus 'easily conquering' Russia's food market.[52] Aleksei Gordeev, who became Minister of Agriculture in August 1999 (to March 2009), was explicit that his 'new agrarian policy' would emphasise strengthening the role of the government in regulating Russia's food market. He also specified that tariff-custom policy would create conditions whereby domestic producers could effectively compete with food imports.[53]

8 Russia's Trading Behaviour in the 2000-2013 Period

During the 2000-2013 period, Russia's frequency of entrance into the global food market was high and its degree of involvement in the global food market was high as the value of food imports and exports rose significantly. Russia's degree of protectionism remained relatively low. The degree of integration was transitional as Russia finally became a member of the WTO in 2012.

Russia remained a consistent participant in the international food trade system as a food importer. The value of Russia's food imports grew substantially as a result of economic recovery, a significant increase in real per capita income, and a strengthening in the ruble that made imports cheaper. Russia's agricultural imports increased from $7.3 billion USD in 2000 to over $35 billion USD in 2008. After a brief decline in food imports in 2009 due to the global financial crisis (Russia's GDP fell by almost 9 percent), the value of food imports began to rise again in 2010 and eventually reached its post-Soviet peak of $43.2 billion USD in 2013. Similar to the 1990s, the largest value of food imports consisted of meat and animal husbandry, not grain, as explained by the Lieferts in Chapter 2. Other main imports included highly processed foods, fruits, and vegetables. During the first decade of the 2000s, Russia became the second largest agricultural importer among emerging markets, trailing only China. It is conceivable that the value of Russia's food imports would have continued to rise had the 2014 Ukrainian crisis not occurred that led to a ban on agri-food imports from major Western nations.

Russia's participation in the international food trade system was also fuelled by a rise in its food exports. The value of Russia's agricultural exports grew from $1.62 billion USD in 2000 to $10 billion USD in 2009 before declining in 2010. Russia's food exports then rose to $12 billion USD in 2011 and reached their pre-Ukrainian crisis high of $18.9 billion USD in 2014. Most of the export growth came from grain (mainly wheat and barley). Grain exports rose from 1.3 mmt in the 2000/2001 agricultural year to 21.8 mmt in the 2009/10 agricultural year before declining in 2010/2011 due to a drought and a subsequent ban on grain exports from August 2010 to July 2011. One the export ban ended, grain exports started to increase again, reaching 22.4 mmt in the 2012/2013 agricultural year. Grain exports generated the most foreign trade revenue among Russia's food exports. Expressed in dollar value, however, the overall impact of Russia's exports on the world food system was low. During 2000–2009, the value for global exports of food commodities averaged $522 billion USD per year.[54] The dollar of Russia's food exports during the same period averaged just $5.14 billion USD.

Foreign food trade protectionism remained low during this time period. In 2003 Russia introduced tariff-rate quotas on beef, poultry, and pork that offered some protection to domestic producers. The Putin administration walked a fine line: on the one hand it wanted to protect domestic large farm enterprises from foreign competition until such time that they could compete effectively, and it wanted to help them recover financially. On the other hand, it wanted to meet rising consumer demand for food and therefore the volume of meat imports continued to climb. If cheaper food imports helped to limit the amount an average household spent on food, all the better.

Government policy began to emphasise food security in 2008 when the combination of high food imports and the dramatic rise in global commodity prices sparked fear of contagion. In 2008, a Food Security Doctrine was drafted and circulated for commentary; it was signed into force in January 2010 by former President Dmitrii Medvedev, the importance of which was to quantify what percentage of different foodstuffs Russia should produce for itself in order to be food secure. Until 2014, Russia's Food Security Doctrine did not translate into higher trade barriers or an increase in food trade protectionism aside from what already existed.

Russia's integration with global food trade institutions transitioned from low to high as Russia finally became a member of the WTO in 2012 after being an observer to the WTO for many years. The debates over whether to integrate with the world trading system appeared to be over.[55] At the time Russia entered the WTO, most of its food trade was with Western nations. In 2000, for example, 72 percent of Russia's food imports came with nations that were not former Soviet republics in the Commonwealth of Independent States (CIS), as did 56 percent of its food exports. Over time, trade with non-CIS nations increased. In 2013, the last full year before the Ukrainian crisis in 2014 and Russia's subsequent food embargo in August 2014, food trade with non-CIS nations accounted for 85 percent of Russia's food imports and 70 percent of its exports.[56]

After the Ukrainian crisis and the first rounds of Western sanctions in 2014, Putin invoked the protection of national security clause in the WTO to relieve Russia from some of its commitments, for instance, not to introduce food bans or treating trading partners differently. Russia continues adhere to other obligations. In 2017 import duties on sunflower oil, water, and cigars were reduced in accordance with commitments made to the WTO. As noted before, in 2020 Russia ended its tariff-rate quotas on pork, replaced by a flat tariff of 25 percent. Whether coincidental to the changed tariff rate or not, Russia's pork imports fell in 2020, attributed to rising investment in the sector, increased output, and the attraction of export possibilities.

9 Russia's Trading Behaviour since 2014

Since 2014, two contradictory impulses in Russia's agri-food trade policy have become discernible. The first impulse is a strong emphasis on food security, import substitution, and food self-sufficiency (see Chapter 4). As Clapp reminds us, self-sufficiency means to produce enough to meet one's own needs, and thus food self-sufficiency is concerned with the origin of food.[57] Self-sufficiency policy implies not just protectionism but a withdrawal from international markets in terms of food imports.[58] The second impulse, which contradicts the first, is an emphasis on expanding food trade, opening new markets, and increasing food exports. Despite a food self-sufficiency policy, Russia has not withdrawn from international food markets, and although the dollar value of its food imports is down from the pre-2014 period, Russia remains a large importer of food. In this respect, Russia's policy of self-sufficiency is not exactly what the literature would assume is true. Further, although Russia's food security policy has economic implications, it should be understood as a political variable that is used in tandem with food trade as an instrument of foreign policy, and as a prop for nationalism. What this means is that Russian leaders definition of 'success' in food security is very narrow, referring mainly to the production of several basic commodities. But if the view of food security is expanded just a bit, it is obvious that the Russian version of food security, i.e., protectionism and lessened dependence on imports, is far from reality. In this respect, one may point to high percentages of seeds that are imported; high percentages of farm imported farm machinery and equipment; high percentages of imported pedigree livestock; and a substantial presence and market share by foreign agri-firms in food processing and food retailing. One might even include the erosion of human capital in rural areas, a result of outmigration, as an aspect of food security.[59] Thus, a narrow fixation on certain commodity production, therefore, does not offer a complete or necessarily accurate view of Russia's food security.

Turning to the four variables that frame the analysis, since 2014 Russia's frequency of entrance into the global food market has been high and its degree of involvement in the global food market is high. Russia regularly enters the global food market as both a food importer and exporter, both of which are valued in the tens of billions of dollars annually. Agri-food trade protectionism became variegated as it transitioned from low protectionist to selectively high towards Western nations while remaining more open to non-Western nations. The degree of integration with Western institutions transitioned from high following entry to the WTO in 2012 to low starting in 2014 and continuing thereafter.

The year 2014 was a watershed year for Russia's role in the international food trade system. The origins of change in Russia's role in international food trade were found in the Ukrainian crisis that witnessed the removal of Ukrainian President Viktor Yanukovych in February 2014, followed by Russia's military involvement in eastern Ukraine and annexation of Crimea in March 2014. Subsequently, Western sanctions were placed on Russia in March and July 2014, and Russia's countersanctions—a food embargo against the West—were announced in August 2014. Russia's countersanctions, often referred to as the food embargo, banned most agri-food imports from the United States, the European Union, Canada, Norway, and Australia from 7 August. The ban has been extended several times since then and currently runs to the end of 2022. In 2015, four other nations were added to the banned list, and in 2016 Ukraine was added. Since 2014, four discontinuities with previous agri-food trade patterns have occurred.

The first discontinuity from the pre-2014 period is a reversal in the upward trend in the dollar value of Russia's food imports. Russia's food imports rose from $30 billion USD in 2009 to over $43 billion USD in 2013. Following the introduction of Russia's food embargo in August 2014 against Western nations, its food imports fell to $26.5 billion in 2015 and then to a low of $25 billion USD in 2016 before starting to rise somewhat in subsequent years, but remaining far below the pre-embargo level. In 2020, the value of food imports was just over $29 billion USD. As noted above, the decline in the value of Russia's food imports was facilitated by policies of import substitution and food self-sufficiency, both of which were actively pursued by the Kremlin (see Chapter 4).

A second discontinuity is a significant rise in the volume and value of food exports, a departure from many years of moderate food exports. The rise in exports is due to a confluence of factors, including favourable weather, state financial assistance that promotes higher grain production, protectionism from competition, and favourable farming practices such as re-mechanisation, digitalisation, and increases in yield per hectare. Russia's wheat exports since the 2014/2015 agricultural year and continuing through the 2019/2020 agricultural year averaged more than 37 mmt. From 2014/2015 through the 2019/2020 agricultural year, Russia led the world in volume of wheat exports in four of the six agricultural years, and ranked second in the other two agricultural seasons. By volume, in the 2016/2017 agriculture year Russia's wheat exports accounted for 14 percent of global wheat trade; in the 2017/2018 agricultural year, Russia's wheat exports accounted for 18 percent of global wheat trade; 19 percent in the 2018/2019 agricultural year; and 18 percent in the 2019/2020 agricultural year.[60]

In 2020, grain exports generated approximately one-third of Russia's total food export revenue ($9.7 billion of $28.9 billion USD), and wheat in particular accounted for more than any other agri-food commodity.[61] In 2020, other main food exports consist of fish and seafood (18 percent of total), fats and oils (16 percent of total), and processed and manufactured foods (14 percent of total). Although Russia will remain a major grain exporter, it is necessary to note in passing that political food security remains an important variable. During the second half of the 2019/2020 agricultural year the government introduced an export quota of 7 mmt to the end of June when a new agricultural year would begin (on 1 July). In reality, the quota was reached prior to the 30 June deadline. Although the quota did not appear to directly reduce grain exports, the existence of the quota affected the willingness of traders to enter into contracts. The purpose of the quota was to ensure that too much grain was not exported, fuelling inflation or causing domestic shortages. For the 2020/2021 agricultural year, the government introduced another export quota of 17.5 mmt 15 February 2021 to 30 June 2021, plus an export tariff. Starting 15 February, the tariff was 25 euro per tonne which doubled to 50 euro per tonne on 1 March. From 2 June 2021, a flexible tariff was used for wheat, corn, and barley sold outside the Eurasian Economic Union (EAEU), equal to 70 percent of the difference between the contract price and the base price of $200 per tonne for wheat and $185 for corn and barley.[62]

A third discontinuity is a partial withdrawal from integration with major Western nations, at least as far was food imports into Russia are concerned, although Russia continues to export to member states of the European Union. Russia has not withdrawn from the WTO, although some voices within Russia have called for doing so. Further, as early as 2015 the United States Trade Representative noted in its annual report about Russia's compliance to its WTO commitments that Russian standards for tetracycline, ractopamine, and other hormones in pork and beef were more stringent than accepted levels. The June 2015 report concluded that 'the United States has become increasingly concerned that Russia may be moving away from the core WTO principle of trade liberalization'.[63] Subsequent reports continued to express concern over Russia's standards, notification of risk assessment, and implementation. The 2018 report, for example, noted that, 'although Russia has put in place the legal framework to allow it to comply with its WTO commitments, its implementation of these commitments remains problematic….Russia does not appear to have implemented fully its commitments to base measurements on international standards, or, where it applies a more stringent standards, to provide a science-based, objectsive risk assessment'.[64] In other words, Russia became increasingly willing to use non-tariff barriers such as sanitation requirements to restrict food imports from the West.

A fourth discontinuity flows from the third and concerns the expansion of trade relations with non-Western partners. Russia has changed its main food trading partners, substituting China and Southeast Asia, the Middle East, and South America for the EU and United States. The discontinuity is seen by the fact that up to 2014 the EU was Russia's primary partner in agricultural trade. Ironically, while most agricultural imports from the EU are banned, the EU remains an important market for Russia's food exports. In 2020, the EU ranked second after China in dollar value of Russia's agri-food exports, accounting for about 11 percent.[65] Following the events in Ukraine in 2014, Russia turned elsewhere to substitute for its lost partner in the EU (see Chapters 5 And 7).

Furthermore, the EAEU, which came into being in January 2015, represents Moscow's efforts to create a regional trade bloc with non-Western nations. Other chapters explore agri-food trade within the EAEU in more detail, but here suffice it to say that since its inception the EAEU has expanded its trading network. In May 2018 China signed a trade agreement with the EAEU that has been touted as a free trade agreement but in reality seems to be something less than that as explained in Chapter 8. In May 2018, Iran signed a provisional free trade agreement with the EAEU that covers a limited number of goods, including agricultural products. The provisional agreement is to last for three years and paves the way to full free trade. In December 2018 the EAEU and Iran established free trade zones. In October 2019, the EAEU and Serbia signed a free trade zone agreement for cheese and alcohol, building on the previous preferential trade agreement.[66] The EAEU had previously agreed to free trade with Vietnam in December 2016, and trade between Russia and Vietnam is explored in Chapter 6. The point is that Russia is using the EAEU to pivot its food trade away from Western nations.

The opening to non-Western trade partners is further witnessed by Russia's bilateral memoranda of understanding (MoU) or statements of cooperation in agriculture with India, Morocco, China, Syria, Mongolia, Japan, and Saudi Arabia during 2017–2019, to name just a few. Egypt, Iran, Bangladesh, and Turkey remain main purchasers of Russian wheat. Food trade with China very likely will increase as Russia's exporters attempt to capture market share lost by American farmers due to the trade war started by President Donald Trump. Russia's food exporters are also eyeing markets in Vietnam and other Southeast Asian nations and the Middle East as discussed in subsequent chapters. In addition to those regions, agricultural trade has expanded with South America since 2014. In particular, Russia became the largest importer of Brazilian meat. Chile has increased its exports of poultry, pork, fish, vegetables, and fruits to Russia. Uruguay also increased meat exports to Russia.

10 Outlook

The future outlook for Russia's agri-food trade behaviour is summarised according to the four variables that comprise the analytical framework. The *frequency* of Russia's entrance into the global food market is likely to remain high as an annual importer and exporter. The Russia's structure of demand for food that suggests an impending large decrease in food imports. Further, Russia's food export ambitions commit the country to continue as a significant food exporter on an annual basis. Russia intends to remain an active participant in global food trade as evidenced by the adoption of an export programme in 2016, followed by the adoption of a national project on food exports in late 2018. The existence of an analytical centre within the Ministry of Agriculture facilitates Russia's food exports by training personnel in contracts and negotiations and providing consultation and legal services to exporting companies. The export project received more than R38 billion in 2019 and is scheduled to receive more than R400 billion during 2019–2024.[67] Under the auspices of the export project, the Ministry of Agriculture is opening attaché offices abroad to establish trade ties in new markets. Russia's role as a food exporter is likely to expand.

Agricultural *protectionism* is likely to remain selectively high, which is to say that there is no end in sight to Russia's countersanctions against the West. Russia's domestic agri-food producers are pleased with the government's protectionism and favour its continuation. The government likes agricultural protectionism because it helps domestic producers and processors whose higher profitability leads to more tax revenue for regional budgets and the federal government. The government also appreciates the prestige that comes from being a large wheat exporter.

The degree of *integration* with Western trade institutions is likely to remain low. As noted above, the trend is for less cooperation with the WTO. Instead, Russia has pivoted to Asia, the Middle East, and other non-Western countries. Engagement with other BRICS nations, the EAEU, and the Shanghai Cooperation Organization (SCO), as well as bilateral trade ties has replaced most food imports from the EU. So far, the pivot has worked well and thus Russia shows little motivation to revert back to ties with the West which would make Russia vulnerable to the whims of Western policy again.

Russia's degree of *involvement* with the global food market is likely to remain high. Russia will continue to import food valued in the tens of billions of dollars annually. As an exporter, Russia is likely to account for a significant portion of global grain trade. A major effort is being made to increase the export of processed and manufactured food products, not just raw commodities. Further, Russia's agricultural sector is generally considered to be a winner during climate change as growing seasons in northern latitutes lengthen. Around the world, water tables are depleted, but Russia has an ample supply of water. In many regions of the world, land is leached of its nutrients, but Russia has tens of millions of unused hectares of agricultural land. Russia is already increasing the cultivation of previously unused or abandoned agricultural land and expects to bring millions of hectares into production by 2025.

Finally, a few words about the impact of the COVID-19 pandemic on food exports. The pandemic created uncertainty for lives and livelihoods around the world, leading to higher unemployment, loss of income, the closure of businesses including restaurants, and disruptions in supply chains. The economic effects, which were initially quite severe—trade turnover in Russia decreased to 35–45 percent in April 2020 and by at least 60 percent at restaurants and cafes—may be shortlived as people get vaccinated and businesses rebound.[68] Through it all, Russia's agricultural sector performed well, with the second largest harvest in the post-Soviet period at 133 mmt of grain after cleaning. Russia's infrastructure for policy as a food exporting state remains strong: high ambition to be a global food power and to benefit from the leverage that accrues from that position; an active state that promotes food exports; and strong political commitment to increase global influence and status. Those factors, combined with a weak ruble, led *Rossel'khozbank* to predict that Russia's role in the world food system will become more significant despite myriad obstacles.[69]

Notes

1. Stephen K. Wegren with Alexander Nikulin and Irina Trotsuk, *Russia's Food Revolution: The Transformation of the Food System* (London and New York: Routledge Publishers, 2021).
2. Craig VanGrasstek, *Trade and American Leadership: The Paradoxes of Power and Wealth from Alexander Hamilton to Donald Trump* (Cambridge: Cambridge University Press, 2019), 289.
3. Jane M. Porter and Douglas E. Bowers, 'A Short History of U.S. Agricultural Trade Negotiations,' Staff Report no. AGES 89–23 (Washington, DC: Economic Research Service, 1989), 12–14.
4. Michael Reed, *International Trade in Agricultural Products* (Scotts Valley, CA: CreateSpace Independent Publishing, 2016), 169.
5. Jennifer Clapp, *Food*, 2nd edition (Cambridge: Polity Press, 2016), 69–70.
6. Porter and Bowers, 'A Short History of U.S. Agricultural Trade Negotiations', 18.
7. Burton Bollag, 'Soviet Union Becomes Observer in Trade Body', *The New York Times*, 17 May 1990. https://www.nytimes.com/1990/05/17/business/soviet-union-becomes-observer-in-trade-body.html. Accessed 3 February 2020.
8. Reed, *International Trade in Agricultural Products*, 174.
9. Clapp, *Food*, 70.

10. Ibid., 71.
11. Ibid., 72.
12. Ibid., 75–76.
13. Christina L. Davis, *Food Fights Over Free Trade: How International Institutions Promote Agricultural Trade Liberalization* (Princeton: Princeton University Press, 2003), 5.
14. William H. Cooper, 'Russia's Accession to the WTO and Implications for the United States', Congressional Research Service Report R42085 (15 June 2012), 3–5.
15. Stephen K. Wegren, 'Russian Agriculture and the WTO', *Problems of Post-Communism* 54, no. 4 (2007): 46–59.
16. This text draws from Stephen K. Wegren, 'The Impact of WTO Accession on Russian Agriculture', *Post-Soviet Affairs* 28 no. 3 (2012): 296–318.
17. Merlinda D. Ingco and John D. Nash, eds., *Agriculture and the WTO: Creating a System for Development* (Washington. DC: The World Bank, 2004), 29.
18. Olga Liefert, William Liefert, and Eric Luebehusen, 'Rising Grain Exports by the Formers Soviet Union Region', Economic Research Service Report WHS-13A-01 (February 2013), 16. https://www.ers.usda.gov/webdocs/publications/39804/34899_whs13a01.pdf?v=0. Accessed 14 February 2020.
19. William Liefert, Olga Liefert, and Matthew Shane, 'Russia's Growing Agricultural Imports: Causes and Outlook', Economic Research Service Report WRS-09–04 (May 2009), 12. https://www.ers.usda.gov/webdocs/publications/40471/9481_wrs0904_1_.pdf?v=0. Accessed 9 February 2020.
20. Cooper, 'Russia's Accession to the WTO and Implications for the United States', 6.
21. IKAR, 'RF s 1 Ianvaria zamenila kvoti na import svininy poshlinoi, vypolniv vse obiazatel'stva pered VTO', 9 January 2020. https://agrovesti.net/news/indst/rf-s-1-yanvarya-zamenila-kvotu-na-import-svininy-poshlinoj-vypolniv-vse-obyazatelstva-pered-vto.html. Accessed 9 January 2020.
22. Alex Nove, 'Soviet grain: Problems and Prospects', *Food Policy* 1, no. 1 (November 1975): 34.
23. Edward C. Cook, 'Have the Soviets Turned the Corner on Grain Imports?' *Food Policy* 12, no. 2 (May 1987): 116–122. This position was not universally shared and Western economists debated other drivers of grain import policy, pointing to adequate reserves of foreign currency to purchase grain; the role of the planning system; and international grain prices. See Padma Desai, 'Soviet Grain and Wheat Import Demands in 1981–1985', *American Journal of Agricultural Economics* 64, no. 2 (May 1982): 312–322; George Allen, 'USSR Grain Imports: Past and Future',

Food Policy 12, no. 2 (May 1987): 90–93; and C. T. Ennew, 'A Model of Import Demand for Grain in the Soviet Union', *Food Policy* 12, no. 2 (May 1987): 106–115.

24. Allen, 'USSR Grain imports: Past and Future', 91.
25. Goskomstat SSSR, *Narodnoe khoziaistvo SSSS za 70 let* (Moscow: Finansy i statistika, 1987), 470.
26. Robert Deutsch, *The Food Revolution in the Soviet Union and Eastern Europe* (Boulder: Westview Press, 1986), 5–6.
27. Paul Marer, 'The Political Economy of Soviet Relations with Eastern Europe', in *Soviet Policy in Eastern Europe*, ed. Sarah Meiklejohn Terry (New Haven: Yale University Press, 1984), 160–62.
28. Benedykt Askanas, Halina Askanas, Friedrich Levcik, and Michel Vale, 'The Foreign Trade of the CMEA Countries in the Second Half of the Seventies', *Eastern European Economics* 17, no. 3 (Spring 1979): 78.
29. D. Gale Johnson and Karen McConnell Brooks, *Prospects for Soviet Agriculture in the 1980s* (Bloomington: Indiana University Press, 1983), 15–16.
30. Paarlberg argues that from the early 1960s to the early 1970s the USSR increased its net grain imports by 18 million tonnes, more than Japan and the European Community who were the largest buyers of American grain at that time. Robert L. Paarlberg, 'The Soviet Burden on the World Food System: Challenge and Response', *Food Policy* 1, no. 5 (November 1976): 393.
31. Ibid.
32. Tsentral'noe statisticheskoe upravlenie SSSR, *Narodnoe khoziaistvo SSSR v 1980 g*. (Moscow: Finansy i statistika, 1981), 207.
33. Karl-Eugen Wadekin, 'Soviet Agriculture's Dependence on the West', *Foreign Affairs* 60, no. 4 (Spring 1982).
34. Desai, 'Soviet Grain and Wheat Import Demands in 1981–1985', 312.
35. Author's calculations from data in Abram S. Becker, *U.S.-Soviet Trade in the 1980s*, Rand Note N-2682RC (Santa Monica: Rand Corporation, 1987), 5. https://www.rand.org/content/dam/rand/pubs/notes/2009/N2682.pdf. Accessed 1 February 2020.
36. Stephen K. Wegren, *Russia's Food Policies and Globalization* (Lanham: Lexington Books, 2005), 48; and Directorate of Intelligence, CIA, 'USSR: The Food Supply Situation'.
37. See Karl-Eugen Wadekin, 'Agriculture', in *The Soviet Union under Gorbachev*, ed. Martin McCauley (New York: St. Martin's Press, 1987), 118–34.
38. Penelope Doolittle and Margaret Hughes, 'Gorbachev's Agricultural Policy: Building on the Brezhnev Food Program', in *Gorbachev's Economic Plans*, vol. 2. Study Papers Submitted to the Joint Economic Committee of the Congress of the United States, Joint Economic Committee, 100th

Congress, 1st session (Washington, DC: Government Printing Office, 1987), 30–33.

39. For a summary of the entrance of Western fast food restaurants into Russia in the late Gorbachev period, see Stephen K. Wegren, Alexander Nikulin and Irina Trotsuk, *Food Policy and Food Security: Putting Food on the Russian Table* (Lanham, MD and London, UK: Lexington Books, 2018), 23–24.
40. William Liefert, 'The Food Problem in the Republics of the Former Soviet Union', in *The 'Farmer Threat': The Political Economy of Agrarian Reform in Post-Soviet Russia*, ed. Don Van Atta (Boulder, CO: Westview, 1993), 28.
41. See Werner Hahn, 'The Farms' Revolt and Grain Shortages in 1991', in *The 'Farmer Threat': The Political Economy of Agrarian Reform in Post-Soviet Russia*, ed. Don Van Atta (Boulder, CO: Westview, 1993), 43–54.
42. World Bank, *Food and Agricultural Policy Reforms in the Former USSR: An Agenda for the Transition* (Washington, DC: The World Bank, 1993), Table 4.5 on p. 188.
43. Goskomstat Rossii, *Rossiiskii statisticheskii ezhegodnik 1995* (Moscow: Goskomstat, 1995), 351.
44. Wegren, *Russia's Food Policies and Globalization*, 134.
45. World Bank, Food and Agricultural Policy Reforms in the Former USSR, 188.
46. A. Altukhov and D. Vermel', 'Prodovol'stvennoe samoobespechenie strany: sostoyanie i perspektivy', *APK: ekonomika, upravlenie* no. 11 (November 1997): 21.
47. William Liefert, 'Food Security in Russia: Economic Growth and Rising Incomes are Reducing Insecurity', in *Food Security Assessment*, GFA-15, Economic Research Service, USDA (Washington, DC: USDA, 2004), 38–40.
48. Ibid., 36–37.
49. David Sedik, Sergey Sotnikov, and Doris Wiesmann, *Food Security in the Russian Federation* (Rome: FAO, 2003), 36–45.
50. Mikhail Maximenko and Michael Fay, 'Agricultural Situation', GAIN Report RS8002, January 14, 1998. http://www.fas.usda.gov/data. Accessed 11 February 2020.
51. Michael Fay and R. Matthewmann, 'Agricultural Situation', GAIN Report RS8025, 29 May 1998. http://www.fas.usda.gov/data. Accessed 11 February, 2020.
52. V. Semenov, 'Novyi kurs agrarnoi politiki', *Economist* no. 1 (January 1999): 14.
53. A. Gordeev, 'Stabil'noe i dinamichnoe razvitie APK—pervostepennaia zadacha', *APK: ekonomika, upravlenie* no. 11 (November 2000): 8–9.

54. Peter Engstrom, 'Unraveling the Complex Web of Global Food Trade', 4 September 2015. http://environment.umn.edu/discovery/gli/unraveling-the-complex-web-of-global-food-trade/. Accessed 22 February 2020.
55. See S. V. Kiselev, ed., *VTO i sel'skoe khoziaistvo Rossii* (Moscow: Teis, 2003), 57–65.
56. Author's calculations from data in Rosstat, *Rossiiskii Statisticheskii ezhegodnik 2015* (Moscow: Rosstat, 2015), 633–34.
57. Jennifer Clapp, 'Food Self-Sufficiency: Making Sense of It, and When it Makes Sense', *Food Policy* 66 (2017): 88–96.
58. Stephen K. Wegren and Christel Elvestad, 'Russia's Food Self-Sufficiency and Food Security: An Assessment', *Post-Communist Economies* 30, no. 5 (2018): 565–87.
59. See for example, S. G. Golovina, I. N. Mikolaichik, L. N. Smirnova, 'Chelovecheskii capital sel'skikh territorii: demograficheskie aspekty', *Ekonomika sel'skokhoziaistvennykh i pererabatyvaiushchikh predpriiatii* no. 8 (August 2020): 72–76.
60. Calculated from data in United States Department of Agriculture, Foreign Agricultural Service, 'Grain: World Markets and Trade', July 2020. https://apps.fas.usda.gov/psdonline/circulars/grain.pdf. Accessed 24 July 2020.
61. Ministry of Agriculture, 'Operativnyi obzor eksporta produktsii APK (dannye po sostoianiiu na 27 Dekabria 2020 goda)' 27 December 2020. http://www.mcx.gov.ru. Accessed 2 January 2021.
62. Ekspert Iug, 'Dva Rostovskikh zernotreidera poluchili 27.5% Rossiiskoi kvoty na eksport zerna', 11 February 2021. https://agrovesti.net/news/indst/dva-rostovskikh-zernotrejdera-poluchili-27-5-rossijskoj-kvoty-na-eksport-zerna.html. Accessed 11 February 2021.
63. United States Trade Representative, 'Report on WTO Enforcement Actions: Russia', June 2015, 10. https://ustr.gov/sites/default/files/2015-Russia-Enforcement-Report.pdf. Accessed 5 March 2020.
64. United States Trade Representative, '2018 Report on the Implementation and Enforcement of Russia's WTO Commitments', February 2019, 21–22. https://ustr.gov/sites/default/files/Russia-2018-WTO-Report.pdf. Accessed 5 March 2020.
65. Ministry of Agriculture, 'Operativnyi obzor eksporta produktsii APK (dannye po sostoianiiu na 27 Dekabria 2020 goda),' 27 December 2020. http://www.mcx.gov.ru. Accessed 2 January 2021.
66. Parlamentskaia gazeta, 'Serbiia smozhet postavliat' v EAES syr i alkogol' bez poshlin', 22 October 2020. https://kvedomosti.ru/news/https-www-pnp-ru-economics-serbiya-smozhet-postavlyat-v-eaes-syr-i-alkogol-bez-poshlin-html.html. Accessed 22 October 2020.
67. Ministry of Agriculture, 'Do 2024 goda na podderzhku eksporta APK budet napravleno svyshe 406 mlrd rublei', 26 December 2018. http://

mcx.ru/press-service/news/do-2024-goda-na-podderzhku-eksporta-apk-budet-napravleno-svyshe-406-mlrd-rubley/. Accessed 26 December 2018.

68. TASS, 'Ekspert: oborot torgovli v Rossii v Aprele upal na 35–45%', 15 May 2020. https://kvedomosti.ru/news/ekspert-oborot-torgovli-v-rossii-v-aprele-upal-na-35-45.html. Accessed 15 May 2020.
69. Elizaveta Litvinova, 'RSKhB prognoziruet uvelichenie doli Rossii na mirovom rynke prodovol'stviia', 14 May 2020. https://www.agroinvestor.ru/analytics/news/33697-rskhb-prognoziruet-uvelichenie-doli-rossii-na-mirovom-rynke-prodovolstviya/. Accessed 14 May 2020.

Selected Bibliography

Allen, George. 'USSR Grain Imports: Past and Future'. *Food Policy* 12, no. 2 (1987): 90–93.

Askanas, Benedykt, Halina Askanas, Friedrich Levcik, and Michel Vale. 'The Foreign Trade of the CMEA Countries in the Second Half of the Seventies'. *Eastern European Economics* 17, no. 3 (1979): 77-87.

Becker, Abram S. *U.S.-Soviet Trade in the 1980s*, Rand Note N-2682RC. Santa Monica: Rand Corporation, 1987.

Clapp, Jennifer. *Food*, 2nd ed. Cambridge: Polity Press, 2016.

Cook, Edward C. 'Have the Soviets Turned the Corner on Grain Imports'? *Food Policy* 12, no. 2 (1987): 116–122.

Cooper, William H. 'Russia's Accession to the WTO and Implications for the United States'. Congressional Research Service Report R42085 (June 15, 2012).

Davis, Christina L. *Food Fights over Free Trade: How International Institutions Promote Agricultural Trade Liberalization*. Princeton: Princeton University Press, 2003.

Desai, Padma. 'Soviet Grain and Wheat Import Demands in 1981–1985'. *American Journal of Agricultural Economics* 64, no. 2 (1982): 312–322.

Deutsch, Robert. *The Food Revolution in the Soviet Union and Eastern Europe*. Boulder: Westview Press, 1986.

Doolittle, Penelope and Margaret Hughes. 'Gorbachev's Agricultural Policy: Building on the Brezhnev Food Program'. In *Gorbachev's Economic Plans*, vol. 2. Study Papers Submitted to the Joint Economic Committee of the Congress of the United States, Joint Economic Committee, 100th Congress, 1st session. Washington, DC: Government Printing Office, 1987, 26–44.

Ennew, C. T. 'A Model of Import Demand for Grain in the Soviet Union'. *Food Policy* 12, no. 2 (1987): 106–115.

Hahn, Werner. 'The Farms' Revolt and Grain Shortages in 1991'. In *The 'Farmer Threat': The Political Economy of Agrarian Reform in Post-Soviet Russia*, ed. Don Van Atta. Boulder: Westview, 1993, 43–54.

Hough, Jerry. *Russia and the West: Gorbachev and the Politics of Reform*, 2nd edn. New York: Touchstone, 1990.

Ingco, Merlinda D., and John D. Nash, eds., *Agriculture and the WTO: Creating a System for Development*. Washington. DC: The World Bank, 2004.

Johnson, D. Gale and Karen McConnell Brooks. *Prospects for Soviet Agriculture in the 1980s*. Bloomington: Indiana University Press, 1983.

Liefert, Olga, William Liefert, and Eric Luebehusen. 'Rising Grain Exports by the Formers Soviet Union Region'. Economic Research Service Report WHS-13A-01 (February 2013). Available at https://www.ers.usda.gov/webdocs/publications/39804/34899_whs13a01.pdf?v=0.

Liefert, William, Olga Liefert, and Matthew Shane. 'Russia's Growing Agricultural Imports: Causes and Outlook'. Economic Research Service Report WRS-09-04 (May 2009). Available at https://www.ers.usda.gov/webdocs/publications/40471/9481_wrs0904_1_.pdf?v=0.

Liefert, William. 'Food Security in Russia: Economic Growth and Rising Incomes are Reducing Insecurity'. In *Food Security Assessment*, GFA-15, Economic Research Service, USDA. Washington, DC: USDA, 2004.

Liefert, William. 'The Food Problem in the Republics of the Former Soviet Union'. In *The 'Farmer Threat': The Political Economy of Agrarian Reform in Post-Soviet Russia*, ed. Don Van Atta. Boulder: Westview, 1993, 25–42.

Marer, Paul. 'The Political Economy of Soviet Relations with Eastern Europe'. In *Soviet Policy in Eastern Europe*, ed. Sarah Meiklejohn Terry. New Haven: Yale University Press, 1984, 155–88.

Nove, Alec. 'Soviet grain: Problems and prospects'. *Food Policy* 1, no. 1 (1975): 32–39.

Paarlberg, Robert L. 'The Soviet Burden on the World Food System: Challenge and Response'. *Food Policy* 1, no. 5 (1976): 392–404.

Porter, Jane M. and Douglas E. Bowers. *A Short History of U.S. Agricultural Trade Negotiations*. Staff Report no. AGES 89–23. Washington, DC: Economic Research Service, 1989. Available at www.ers.usda.gov.

Reed, Michael. *International Trade in Agricultural Products*. Scotts Valley, CA: CreateSpace Independent Publishing, 2016.

Sedik, David, Sergey Sotnikov, and Doris Wiesmann. *Food Security in the Russian Federation*. Rome: FAO, 2003.

VanGrasstek, Craig. *Trade and American Leadership: The Paradoxes of Power and Wealth from Alexander Hamilton to Donald Trump*. Cambridge: Cambridge University Press, 2019.

Wadekin, Karl-Eugen. 'Agriculture'. In *The Soviet Union under Gorbachev*, ed. Martin McCauley. New York: St. Martin's Press, 1987, 118–34.

Wadekin, Karl-Eugen. 'Soviet Agriculture's Dependence on the West'. *Foreign Affairs* 60, no. 4 (Spring 1982).
Wegren, Stephen K. 'The Impact of WTO Accession on Russian Agriculture'. *Post-Soviet Affairs* 28, no. 3 (2012): 296–318.
Wegren, Stephen K. 'Russian Agriculture and the WTO'. *Problems of Post-Communism* 54, no. 4 (2007): 46–59.
Wegren, Stephen K. *Russia's Food Policies and Globalization*. Lanham: Lexington Books, 2005.
Wegren, Stephen K., Alexander Nikulin and Irina Trotsuk. *Food Policy and Food Security: Putting Food on the Russian Table*. Lanham: Lexington Books, 2018.
Wegren, Stephen K. with Alexander Nikulin and Irina Trotsuk. *Russia's Food Revolution: The Transformation of the Food System*. London and New York: Routledge Publishers, 2021.
World Bank. *Food and Agricultural Policy Reforms in the Former USSR: An Agenda for the Transition*. Washington, DC: The World Bank, 1993.

Open Access This chapter is licensed under the terms of the Creative Commons Attribution 4.0 International License (http://creativecommons.org/licenses/by/4.0/), which permits use, sharing, adaptation, distribution and reproduction in any medium or format, as long as you give appropriate credit to the original author(s) and the source, provide a link to the Creative Commons license and indicate if changes were made.

The images or other third party material in this chapter are included in the chapter's Creative Commons license, unless indicated otherwise in a credit line to the material. If material is not included in the chapter's Creative Commons license and your intended use is not permitted by statutory regulation or exceeds the permitted use, you will need to obtain permission directly from the copyright holder.

Chapter 2: Russia's Development as a Top Player in World Grain Trade

William M. Liefert and Olga Liefert

1 Introduction

Since the mid-2000s, Russia has developed into a major grain exporter. The growth in grain exports in the last few years was especially high, with foreign sales rising from the 2011–2015 period to the 2016–2019 period by an annual average of 64 percent, from 27 to 44 million metric tonnes (mmt). The country's main grain export is wheat, and by the late 2010s

---

The authors thank Steven Zahniser for helpful comments. The findings and conclusions in this chapter are those of the authors and should not be construed to represent any official USDA or U.S. Government determination or policy. The research in this article was supported by the intramural research programme of the U.S. Department of Agriculture, Economic Research Service

---

W. M. Liefert (✉) · O. Liefert
Economist, Market and Trade Economics Division of the Economic Research Service, United States Department of Agriculture, Washington, DC, USA
e-mail: wliefert@ers.usda.gov

O. Liefert
e-mail: Olga.Liefert@usda.gov

© The Author(s) 2022

S. K. Wegren and F. Nilssen (eds.), *Russia's Role in the Contemporary International Agri-Food Trade System*, Palgrave Advances in Bioeconomy: Economics and Policies,
https://doi.org/10.1007/978-3-030-77451-6_3

Russia's annual average foreign sales of 35 mmt gave the country around a 20 percent share in world wheat trade.

During the late Soviet period, Russia (along with the Soviet Union as a whole) was a major grain importer rather than exporter. This chapter examines how Russia has flipped its trade balance in grain and emerged as a large wheat exporter. The key causal developments were the extreme downsizing of the country's livestock sector during the 1990s which reduced domestic demand for feed grain, and more importantly, the steady rise in grain production beginning after 2000 that created surpluses for export. The growth in Russian grain output has been driven by an increase in yield (output per hectare). We explain why Russian grain yields have been rising. The chapter also examines the outlook for Russian grain production and exports.

The chapter is structured as follows. The next section discusses Russia's importance in world grain markets, followed by an analysis of the close connection between the Russian grain and livestock sectors. The following section examines why Russian grain production has increased substantially since 2000. The effect on grain production and trade of state policy and changes in the value of the Russian ruble (especially its exchange rate vis-à-vis the U.S. dollar) is also assessed. The last section presents the outlook for the Russian grain economy, in particular the volumes of production and exports. A model of world agriculture and trade developed by the Economic Research Service (ERS) within the United States Department of Agriculture (USDA) is used to project future Russian grain area, yield, production, and exports to the year 2029.

2 Russia in the World Grain Market

During 2016–2019, Russia supplied 10–14 percent of total world grain exports, and about 20 percent of wheat exports (see Fig. 1). In recent years the country has supplanted the United States as the world's top wheat exporter. The country is also a major exporter of barley, with 17 percent world export share in 2016–2019, while Russia's corn export share during that time was 2.7 percent.[1]

During 2016–2019, Russia's total grain exports averaged 44 mmt a year, and exports of wheat 35 mmt. In volume terms, wheat accounted for 79 percent of Russia's total grain exports, while barley and corn both had shares of 10 percent during the same period. Russia currently imports almost no grain.

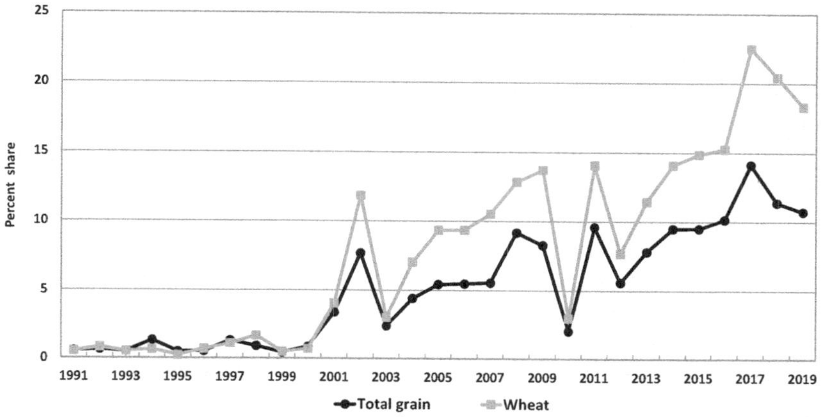

Fig. 1 Russia's share in world grain exports (*Source* USDA Production, Supply, and Distribution Online, accessed 27 July 2020 *Note* Exports are gross)

Currently, the main foreign markets for Russian grain are the Middle East and North Africa (especially Turkey, Egypt, Sudan, Morocco, and Yemen), certain Asian countries (such as Bangladesh and Vietnam), Nigeria, and some countries formerly within the USSR (such as Latvia and Azerbaijan). Most of the wheat exported is of low milling quality used to produce (human) food products, though it can also be used as animal feed.

3 Russia's Grain Economy and the Livestock Sector

Historically, Russia's grain economy has been closely linked to its livestock sector. During the last two decades of the Soviet Union, the main goal of state agricultural policy was to expand the production and consumption of meat and other animal products in order to raise the country's standard of living. Between 1970 and 1990, a policy built on large subsidies to both producers and consumers succeeded in increasing meat production by more than 50 percent.[2] To help supply its livestock sector with animal feed, the Soviet Union became a larger importer of grain, soybeans, and soybean meal, to the benefit of large producers of these bulk crops such as the United States, Canada, and Australia.

The transition from a planned to a market economy in the 1990s led to contraction in the livestock sector. Because of severe financial constraints, the large budget subsidies to agriculture—and especially the previously favoured livestock sector—were mostly terminated. Price reform also ended the indirect subsidies that agriculture had enjoyed during the Soviet period, whereby output prices were set high relative to input prices.[3] Consequently, during the 1990s the terms of trade for Russian agricultural producers (the ratio of output to input prices) fell by about 75 percent. Substantially higher prices for inputs resulted in a large decline in their use, which contributed to the extreme drop in agricultural production, both in ruble value and in volume.

During the 1990s, product output in Russia fell by about a half.[4] As livestock herds declined in size, the demand for animal feed dropped sharply. Russia's large imports of feed grain (as well as soybeans and soybean meal) largely ended, and grain production declined by about a third, from an annual average of 95 mmt during 1987–1991 to 63 mmt during 1996–2000 (see Table 1). Rather than importing a lot of animal feed to maintain a large and costly livestock sector, Russia increased its imports of meat, from an annual average of 1.9 mmt during 1989–1991 to 3.1 mmt during 2006–2010.[5]

The extreme downsizing of agriculture during the 1990s caused severe hardship for producers and was regarded by the Russian government as a disaster. However, the major restructuring of agricultural production and trade during the decade appears to have been an economically rational and necessary correction to the overexpansion of the sector during the last decades of the Soviet period, especially of livestock.

4 Growth in Grain Production

After 2000, Russian grain production began to slowly rise, and then increased more rapidly after 2008. From 1996–2000 to 2016–2019, annual average Russian grain output increased from 63 to 115 mmt (see Table 1). The growth from 2011–2015 to 2016–2019 was especially high, with annual average production over the two periods rising by almost a third. In addition, from 1996–2000 to 2016–2019, the annual production of wheat more than doubled, from 34 to 76 mmt (all output figures are annual averages). Corn output also rose at a fast rate to 13.5 mmt by 2016–2019 (though from a low base). However, the annual production of other coarse grains, including barley, rye, and

Table 1 Russian Grain Production and Trade

	1987–1991	*1992–1995*	*1996–2000*	*2001–2005*	*2006–2010*	*2011–2015*	*2016–2019*
Production				Million tons			
wheat	41.8	38.0	34.3	44.9	52.3	53.2	75.7
barley	23.4	24.2	14.2	17.8	16.6	16.7	18.6
corn	3.3	1.8	1.4	2.2	4.2	10.3	13.5
other grain	26.2	19.7	12.8	11.2	8.8	8.1	7.3
total grain	94.8	83.7	62.7	76.1	81.9	88.3	115.2
Area (harvested)				Million hectares			
wheat	23.8	22.5	21.5	22.9	24.2	23.7	27.0
barley	15.0	14.3	9.1	9.3	8.0	8.0	8.0
corn	1.1	0.6	0.6	0.7	1.2	2.2	2.6
other grain	18.3	13.6	9.2	6.9	5.3	4.9	4.0
total grain	58.2	51.1	40.4	39.8	38.8	38.9	41.6
Yield				Tons per hectare			
wheat	1.76	1.69	1.59	1.96	2.16	2.24	2.80
barley	1.56	1.69	1.57	1.91	2.08	2.07	2.34
corn	3.00	2.82	2.34	3.30	3.42	4.61	5.24
other grain	1.43	1.45	1.39	1.62	1.66	1.64	1.83
total grain	1.63	1.64	1.55	1.91	2.11	2.27	2.77
Exports (gross)				Million tons			
wheat	0.9	0.6	0.9	7.7	12.8	20.0	34.9
barley	0.1	0.8	0.5	2.2	1.8	3.6	4.4
corn	0.3	0.0	0.0	0.0	0.4	3.2	4.5
other grain	0.3	0.3	0.0	0.1	0.0	0.1	0.2
total grain	1.6	1.6	1.4	10.0	15.0	26.9	44.0
				Million tons			
Net trade	– 21.1	– 7.7	– 2.6	8.3	14.3	25.9	43.4

Note Grain excludes rice, buckwheat, and pulses. Figures are annual average over the period identified. Net trade is for total grain; positive values are net exports, negative values net imports

Source USDA Production, Supply, and Distribution Online, and for yield, computed from data from that source

oats, fell collectively from 1987–1991 to 1996–2000 by over half, and to 2016–2019 by a further 43 percent (see Table 1).

Contraction of the livestock sector during the 1990s contributed to the growth in grain exports after 2000 by reducing demand for domestic feed, thereby freeing up output for sale abroad. The downsizing of the livestock sector, replacing of domestically produced livestock products with imports, and rising grain exports after 2000 are consistent with the country's fundamental cost competitiveness (or comparative advantage) in world markets.[6]

Russia's move from being a large grain importer during the late Soviet period to a major exporter has resulted in about 70 mmt of more grain being available on the world market (see Fig. 2). Similar to Russia, both Ukraine and Kazakhstan have experienced a similar restructuring of their grain and livestock economies during their transition from planned to

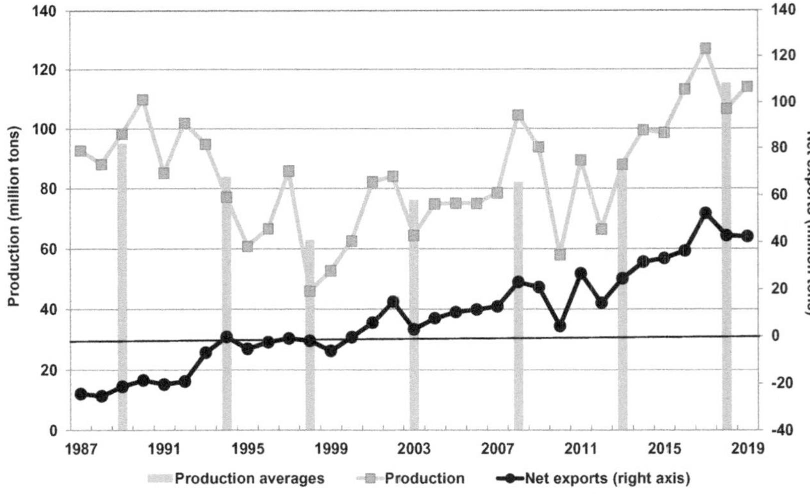

Fig. 2 Russian grain production and net trade (*Source* Russian Federal Service of State Statistics, *Russian Statistical Yearbook*, various issues, accessed 31 July 2020; USDA Production, Supply, and Distribution Online, accessed 27 July 2020. *Note* The bars give average annual grain production over the periods 1987–1991, 1992–1995, 1996–2000, 2001–2005, 2006–2010, 2011–2015, and 2016–2019. Negative net grain exports are net imports)

market economies. If one includes those two countries with Russia, an additional 120 mmt of grain is available on the world market.

4.1 *Grain Area*

Given that grain output can be expressed as grain area times yield, one way of examining why Russian grain production began to rise around 2000 is to focus on these two elements. Russian grain output has been increasing mainly because of growth in yields rather than area. Total Russian grain area (harvested) dropped from 1987–1991 to 1996–2000 by 30 percent, and since that time has remained fairly flat, with an annual average of 42 million hectares during 2016–2019. The main reason Russian grain area has not rebounded from its drop during the 1990s appears to be that much of the abandoned land was in remote regions with high production costs, mainly in the northern and eastern parts of the country, though also in some arid regions in southern European Russia.[7]

However, some switch in area has occurred between the various grain crops, with the changes in area mirroring those in production. From 1987–1991 to 2016–19, the area devoted to wheat increased from 24 to 27 million hectares, while over the same period the area cultivated with corn more than doubled (though from a small base) to 2.6 million hectares. On other hand, area for the other coarse grains (such as barley, rye, and oats) decreased over this period by almost 80 percent (see Table 1).

4.2 *Grain Yield*

In contrast to area, Russian grain yields since 2000 have increased substantially. From 1996–2000 to 2016–2019, total grain yield rose from 1.55 tonnes per hectare (annual average) to 2.77 tonnes per hectare (see Table 1). One reason for the growth was a rebound in fertiliser use, which during the 1990s had declined by around 80 percent (as measured by kilograms of fertiliser used per hectare of sown grain area), as part of the overall decline in agricultural input use discussed earlier. From 2000 to 2018, fertiliser use per hectare of Russian grain tripled, from 20 to 60 kg per sown hectare.[8]

Yields can grow from increasing the amount of inputs (such as fertiliser) used in production, or by raising the productivity of those inputs (measured by units of output per units of input used in production). One way to raise productivity is through technological change. Russian agriculture, including the grain sector, has benefited from such improvement, partly from the use of new and superior inputs (called embodied technological progress). For the grain sector, this has taken the form of new high-quality seed varieties (such as high-yielding hybrid corn seed) and modern machinery, much of it imported. Modern techniques such as soil testing for fertiliser rates have also been adopted. Productivity-enhancing investment and technological change are occurring in Russian agriculture.[9] For example, between 2010 and 2015, investment in machinery and equipment grew by 120 percent in real terms.

Another reason why the Russian agricultural sector in general, and grain yields in particular, improved was that the new market-oriented economy freed farms from the dictates of central planning. Producers, rather than distant planners, could now determine for themselves the mix of goods to produce and the inputs to use in production. Economists call the specific type of gain that can ensue from such changes improvement in *allocative efficiency*, which can have two components.

The first is a gain in the *allocative efficiency in production*, whereby producers/farms determine the optimal mix of inputs to use in making a given volume of output.[10] The second is a gain in the *allocative efficiency in consumption*, whereby in determining the mix and volume of goods to make, producers respond to market demand rather than planners' orders. The market-generated changes in the composition of output raise consumer welfare, and thereby the welfare of the overall economy.[11]

Improvement in allocative efficiency can be difficult to measure. However, the major changes in the mix of specific grain products in total grain area and production since 2000 (more wheat and corn and less other coarse grains) are indicators of likely improvement in allocative efficiency.

An example of an allocative efficiency gain in production within the grain economy that is amenable to some measurement is that since 2000, area has been moving from spring wheat to higher-yielding winter wheat. Between 2000–2002 and 2017–2019, Russian spring wheat area fell from an annual average of 14.2 to 11.6 million hectares, while Russian winter wheat area rose from 8.7 to 15.3 million hectares.[12] Winter wheat is a higher-yielding crop than spring wheat, and after 2000 investment in its production pushed its trend yield up, while spring wheat yields grew only slightly. Figure 3 shows that since 2000, Russian winter wheat yields have

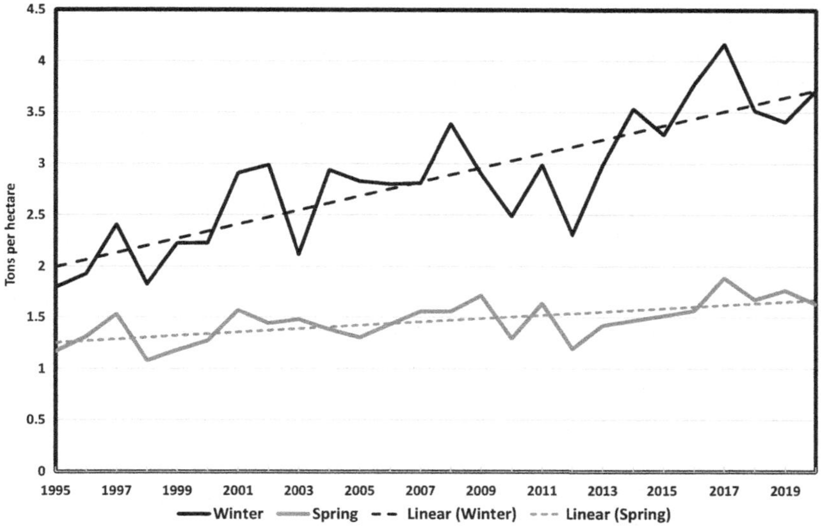

Fig. 3 Russian Winter Versus Spring Wheat Yield (*Source* Calculated from USDA Production, Supply, and Distribution Online, accessed 27 July 2020)

risen at more than twice the rate of spring wheat yields, increasing the yield gap between the two crops. The switch from spring to winter wheat is raising the allocative efficiency of grain production, and thereby overall grain yields and output, by moving resources (in particular land) from producing a less productive type of wheat to a more productive one.

An appeal of allocative efficiency gains that can increase input productivity and output, as well as consumer welfare, is that the benefits achieved do not require technological change. Russia's allocative efficiency gains have been generated by systemic change, whereby market-oriented producers replaced planners in determining the mix of goods produced and the inputs used in their production.[13]

That said, technological change and improvement in allocative efficiency can both increase the productivity of inputs used in production, thereby raising the volume of output produced by a given amount of inputs. Empirical studies find that since 2000 productivity in Russian agriculture has been increasing. From 1999 to 2008, total factor productivity (TFP) in Russian agriculture grew by about a quarter.[14] Other analysts concluded that during 2000–2007, TFP rose even more substantially, by

54 percent.[15] Still others found that from 1998 to 2013, agricultural TFP increased by 72 percent.[16] Productivity growth was highest in southern European Russia, which specialises in grain and oilseeds.

5 Producers

The systemic change of moving from a planned to a market economy allowed agricultural producers to improve allocative efficiency by switching to a more productive mix of inputs and a more consumer-satisfying mix of outputs. Around 2000, another major systemic/institutional change occurred in Russian agriculture whereby a new type of agricultural operator emerged which took advantage of the opportunities offered by the market economy to increase productivity and profit. Before discussing these new operators, we will review the main types of producers in Russian agriculture.

During the 2000s, several types of agricultural producers developed, but in 2000 there were three major types in Russia: (1) the former state and collective farms inherited from the Soviet period; (2) household plots; and (3) new private family farms.[17] The dominant producer has been the former Soviet state and collective farms, which in the 1990s were forced officially to reorganise. Most became corporate, and in particular 'joint stock' enterprises that issued ownership vouchers to their managers and workers, giving them a share in the farm's land and other assets. Individuals could use these vouchers to obtain land and leave the farm to work as private farmers, or they could sell their vouchers to the farm management and remain on the farm as hired labour. Most workers chose the latter option. These farms retained their large size from the Soviet period, typically holding thousands of hectares.

A second type of producer is household plots, also inherited from the Soviet period, where households on the large farms were given small plots to tend (typically only half a hectare). Households tended to produce animal husbandry products, fruit, vegetables (including potatoes), and honey; they contributed less than 1 percent of grain supply. Production from household plots could be consumed by the households themselves or sold in farmers' private markets.[18]

The third type of producer is private family (also called 'peasant') farms. These were created mainly by workers on the new corporate farms using their ownership vouchers to obtain land and break away as independent producers. These farms specialise in producing bulk crops such as grain and oilseeds, and by 2018 they held about held 34 percent of Russian grain area. In that year, they accounted for 29 percent of Russian grain output, a sizeable increase from their share in 2000 of 8 percent.[19]

In the early years of the 2000s, a new type of agricultural producer emerged call 'new operators', agroholdings, which are vertically integrated enterprises that typically combine primary agriculture, processing, distribution, and retail sale.[20]Agroholdings usually acquire a number of existing corporate farms and try to improve them, by cutting waste and reducing production costs, and generally becoming more profit-oriented. Agroholding management typically comes from outside of agriculture, and brings investment, management skills, and technological innovation into the sector (including foreign technology and know-how).

The Russian Federal Service of State Statistics (Rosstat) does not collect separate data about agroholdings. Some authors argue that agroholdings hinder grain production and exports due to management and financial problems, but those conclusions have been shown to be erroneous.[21] However, an emerging literature has revealed other trends that are important to Russia's status as a major grain producer and exporter. The largest agroholdings are several hundred thousand hectares in size, which means that they are many times the size of Soviet-era state and collective farms.[22] Uzun calculated that in 2016 agroholdings held 11 percent of Russia's total arable land and produced 23 percent of the country's grain.[23] Agroholdings are particularly prominent in the Russian grain belt of south-central and southern European Russia, which covers the country's rich black soil region.[24]

Some specialists argue that the new operators, and especially agroholdings, outperform other agricultural producers in terms of productivity, and therefore are a major source of the growth in Russian agricultural production (including grain) since 2000.[25] Uzun and Shagaida show that agroholdings accounted for about 54 percent of all production, 56 percent of gross earnings, and more than 41 percent of total employment among Russia's agricultural enterprises in 2016.[26] Some analysts argue that the agroholdings benefit not from economies of scale but *economies of scope*, given the continued institutional dysfunctionalities of Russian agriculture.[27] Other analysts find that agroholdings are neither more productive nor profitable than other large Russian agricultural enterprises.[28] Perhaps the agroholdings have become so large and unwieldy that they suffer from diseconomies of scale. The data from Uzun and Shagaida, however, cast doubt on these latter lines of argumentation.

To summarise, the causality chain in growing Russian grain exports since 2000 is as follows: systemic change combined with improved farm management motivated both technological progress and gains in allocative efficiency. The resulting increase in input productivity raised grain yields, thereby generating surplus production above domestic needs available for export.

6 State Agricultural and Grain Policy

Russian agricultural policy played mixed role in the post-2000 success of the grain economy. In some ways, agrarian policy facilitated grain production, for example by providing debt relief to large farms that freed up money for investment and increasing production; by establishing a price floor and a state contract system so that in years of good harvests farms would have an outlet for sales at a guaranteed price; by providing access to subsidised seed, fertiliser, fuel, and rail transport. Further, in 2005 the federal government identified agriculture as a national priority area (along with health, education, and housing) that would receive increased funding. From 2005 to 2010, total state support to agriculture rose by 135 percent in real (inflation-adjusted) terms. In other ways, the government impeded rather than promoted grain exports. In the 2000s, the Russian government took strong action to reverse the extreme decline of the livestock sector during the 1990s. As during the Soviet period, state budget subsidies favoured the livestock sector. In 2003, the government also introduced tariff-rate quotas on pork, poultry, and beef, which remained in effect into 2020 except for pork imports. The government also imposed health and sanitary restrictions on imports of meat, a policy that continued after Russia joined the World Trade Organization in 2012.

Russian agricultural and trade policy has promoted the interests of the livestock sector over that of grain. From 1996–2000 to 2016–2019, Russian meat production increased on annual average by 150 percent, from 3.6 to 9.0 mmt.[29] However, by increasing domestic demand for feed, the growth of the livestock sector has the isolated effect of reducing grain exports. Furthermore, when domestic grain supplies have been low, say because of drought or other bad weather, or when grain prices have been high, the Russian government has used an array of policies to restrict grain exports. The controls are intended to help domestic food consumers and the feed-using livestock sector by keeping more grain within the country and lowering grain (and thereby food-related and animal feed) prices. These restrictions have included export taxes, a complete export ban that lasted from August 2010 to July 2011, and taxing and obstructing the transport of grain to exporting ports.[30] In early 2020, Russia imposed a quota on grain exports, this time in response to concerns that the COVID-19 outbreak could disrupt the internal grain market and cause food price inflation. Combined with Russia's climate and volatile weather that can generate poor grain harvests (mainly because of drought but sometimes also because of excessive rainfall during planting or harvesting), such policies lower the country's reliability as a grain exporter.[31]

6.1 Ruble Exchange Rate and Grain Exports

A development that helped Russian grain production and exports in the years immediately following the country's macroeconomic crisis of 1997–1998 was the extreme crisis-generated depreciation of the ruble vis-à-vis the U.S. dollar and other major currencies.[32] During 1997–1999, the ruble depreciated against the dollar in real (inflation-adjusted) terms by 47 percent, which greatly increased the price competitiveness of Russian grain exports on the world market.[33] Currency depreciation also raised the prices received by domestic producers of traded goods, thereby motivating more production.

However, once the Russian economy stabilised after the 1997–1998 crisis and GDP growth resumed, the ruble began steadily *to appreciate in real terms* against the U.S. dollar and other major currencies. From 2000 to 2009, the ruble appreciated in real terms against the dollar by about 150 percent. This real appreciation occurred because renewed growth coincided with domestic price inflation, while the nominal exchange rate remained fairly stable. Inflation in excess of nominal currency depreciation appreciates a country's currency in real terms, thereby making its exports less price competitive on the world market. More intuitively, inflation hurts a country's export price competitiveness and world market share of exported products by raising the prices of its exports to foreign purchasers, and the stable nominal exchange rate does not correct that loss in price competitiveness.

Since the economic crisis of 1997–1998, Russia has experienced a cycle of economic crises that substantially depreciate the currency in real terms, followed by a period of macro stability and growth that appreciate the ruble in real terms against the U.S. dollar). The world financial/economic crisis of 2008–2009 hit the Russian economy and the ruble depreciated against the dollar in 2009 by 12 percent. During 2010–2013, the ruble appreciated in real terms by 19 percent. The economic crisis of 2014–2015, caused in part by geopolitical tensions with the West and Western economic sanctions (stemming from Russia's occupation of the Crimea and eastern parts of Ukraine), generated depreciation of the ruble in 2014–2016 of about 40 percent. That was followed again by ruble appreciation over 2017–2019 of 15 percent. In 2020, the COVID-19 outbreak plunged the Russian economy once again into crisis, with the ruble depreciating against the dollar from mid-January to the beginning of August 2020 by about 18 percent.[34] These macroeconomic-generated jolts to the ruble exchange rate have in turn jolted the country's foreign trade, including grain exports.

7 Outlook

Continued growth in Russian grain exports will require further increases in grain production. Our crystal ball-gazing involves examining the prospects for grain area and yields. For grain area, the question concerns the likelihood of returning to production the grain area removed from grain sowing since the Soviet period. The Ministry of Agriculture has stated its intent to bring back into production as much as 12 million hectares of unused and abandoned farm land by 2024, requiring federal expenditures of hundreds of billions of rubles.[35] According to one study, only 5.3 million hectares of the remaining idled land for all agriculture (not just grain) qualifies for being returned to the plow, if soil and climatic conditions, accessibility, and environmental trade-offs are all considered.[36] Much of Russia's abandoned area is in remote regions in the northern and eastern parts of the country, though also in some arid regions in southern European Russia.[37] Returning the land to the plow requires that world grain prices rise substantially and remain high, to cover both the fixed costs of making the land suitable again for cultivation, and the high variable costs of production.

Studies of the effect of climate change on Russian agriculture argue that rising global temperature could make currently unused land in northern parts of Russia amenable to agricultural use.[38] However, whether or not grain production on the new land would be commercially viable is unclear, given the relative isolation and marginal conditions of production. Another consideration is that some of the grain area lost during the past decades was not abandoned, but rather switched in use from producing grain to sunflower seed, Russia's main oilseed crop. This occurred largely in Russia's major grain and oilseed producing districts in southern and central European Russia.[39]

Russia has made tremendous progress in increasing grain yields since 2000, both in an absolute sense, and in closing the yield gap with major Western producers that also have large endowments of agricultural land, such as the United States and Canada. During 1996–2000, Russian wheat yields (annual average) were 58 percent and 67 percent of the levels in the United States and Canada, respectively. However, by 2016–2019, Russia had closed the yield gap to 84 percent and 83 percent (2.80 tonnes per hectare in Russia, 3.34 in the United States, and 3.39 in Canada.[40] The fact that Russia is narrowing the yield gap with major Western producers, while reaching its limit of switching from spring to higher-yielding winter wheat, suggests that Russian grain yields will continue to grow, though not at the high rate of the 2010s.

Given that Russian agriculture continues to suffer from major problems, the potential exists to raise grain yields further and improve the overall performance of the agricultural economy by correcting (or mitigating) these weaknesses. We mentioned earlier in discussing agroholdings that Russian agriculture continues to endure deficient commercial services and institutional infrastructure to support the sector. A major study on Russian agriculture conducted two decades ago identified those weaknesses as the major problem within the Russian agro-food system.[41] Although progress has certainly been made in the last couple of decades in strengthening the Russian agricultural economy, deficiencies remain (as they do in the agricultural sector of most developed states, so Russia is hardly unique).

Another continued weakness in Russian agricultural operations is the shortage of skilled farm labor, in such jobs as machine operators, technical and production specialists, management, marketing personnel, and financial.[42] The educational and research establishment also remains subpar, suffering from conservatism and institutional rigidity.[43]

Climate change could also affect future Russian grain yields. In the main grain-producing regions of southern and central European Russia, higher temperatures and other climatic changes are predicted to create greater aridity, threaten water supplies, and increase droughts. Climate change is likely to cause grain yields initially to fall.[44] However, if producers adapt to the new conditions, such as by improving irrigation and changing the sowing schedule, grain yields could then rise. On the other hand, although climate change could improve the productivity of grain production in Russia's north and Siberia, it will hurt grain productivity in the main producing regions in the south, with an aggregate net effect for the grain economy.[45]

A model for world agriculture and trade created by the United States Department of Agriculture's Economic Research Service annually makes projections of the volumes of world production and trade for major agricultural commodities out to ten years. The United States Department of Agriculture (USDA) projects that over the next decade world grain prices will fall rather than rise.[46]

We next examine the projections generated by this model for Russian grain production and trade, plus area and yield, to 2029.[47] The model employed is the Country-Commodity Linked (CCL) System, that covers 44 countries and regions, and generates annual volumes of production, consumption/use, and trade, as well as prices, for 24 agricultural commodities. The model is dynamic and partial equilibrium in nature, and consists of supply and demand equations for products that use synthetic (rather than estimated) own and cross-price elasticities. In the following discussion, projected growth to 2029 volumes and levels is relative to the annual average for 2016–2019.

The model projects that by 2029, the average area devoted to grain will grow by only half a percent from 41.6 to 41.8 million hectares (see Table 2). Russia's wheat area is projected to grow by 17 percent to about 28 million hectares.

The projections in Table 2 indicate that although Russian grain production and exports will likely continue to rise in the 2020s, the growth will occur at a slower rate than during the 2010s, again with almost all the increase driven by rising yields. Although production and exports will continue to increase, the rate of high growth in providing grain to the world could be winding down.

According to the USDA model, Russian grain yields are projected to increase to 2029 to almost 3 tonnes per hectare. Wheat yield growth of 7.7 percent will be just slightly below that for total grain of 8 percent. These results are also consistent with our previous discussion that Russian grain yields should continue to grow, but at a lower rate than during 2016–2019.

The projections show that the growth in Russian grain production will be driven almost wholly by rising yields, such that total grain output is

Table 2 USDA Projections for Russia's Grain Economy

	2016–19	*2029 projection*	*Growth (%)*
Production		Million tons	
wheat	75.7	83.5	10.3
barley	18.6	21.4	15.1
corn	13.5	14.0	3.7
total grain	115.2	125.1	8.6
Area (harvested)		Million hectares	
wheat	23.7	27.7	16.9
barley	8.0	8.1	1.3
corn	2.6	2.6	0.0
total grain	41.6	41.8	0.5
Yield		Tons per hectare	
wheat	2.80	3.01	7.7
barley	2.34	2.64	12.9
corn	5.24	5.38	2.8
total grain	2.77	2.99	8.0
Exports (gross)		Million tons	
wheat	34.9	38.8	11.2
barley	4.4	7.3	65.9
corn	4.5	4.9	8.9
total grain	44.0	51.3	16.6
Meat production		Million tons	
beef	1.35	1.23	− 8.9
pork	3.06	3.53	15.4
poultry	4.59	5.26	14.6
total meat	9.00	10.02	11.3
Grain used as feed		Million tons	
wheat	18.0	23.1	28.3
barley	9.6	10.1	5.2
corn	8.1	8.2	1.2
total grain	39.3	44.9	14.2

Note Total grain excludes rice, buckwheat, and pulses, and total meat includes beef, pork, and poultry. Data for 2016–2019 are annual average over the period
Source Same as Table 1

projected to expand to 2029 by 8.6 percent. Production is projected to increase from an annual average of 115 mmt during 2016–2019 to 125 mmt in 2029. Wheat output is projected to rise across the two periods from 76 to 83 mmt.

Growth in the livestock sector cuts into surplus grain production for export by increasing domestic demand for animal feed. The model projects that meat production (beef, pork, and chicken) will grow to 2029 by 11 percent to 10 mmt. Correspondingly, the total amount of grain used as domestic animal feed will rise to 2029 by 14 percent to 45 mmt, and wheat feed use will rise by 28 percent to 23 mmt. The increase in the amount of total grain and wheat used as feed will be 5.6 and 5.1 mmt, respectively.

The model projects that total grain exports will rise between 2016–2019 (annual average) and 2029 from 44 to 51 mmt, and wheat exports from 35 to 39 mmt. Barley exports will increase by two-thirds, although from a much smaller base.

After the surges in world agricultural prices over 2006–2012, some observers argued that the three main grain-producing countries of the former Soviet Union—Russia, Ukraine, and Kazakhstan—had the potential to raise their grain production substantially, by increasing both area and yields (depending on the specific country). The additional grain output would raise world supplies considerably, thereby working to lower grain prices and bolster world food security. Returning abandoned agricultural land in Russia to grain production would help make this three-country region a breadbasket to the world.[48]

Notes

1. See U.S. Department of Agriculture, Foreign Agricultural Service, 'Production, Supply and Distribution Online', n.d. https://apps.fas.usda.gov/psdonline/app/index.html#/app/home; and William M. Liefert and Olga Liefert, 'Russian Agricultural Trade and World Markets', *Russian Journal of Economics* 6, no. 1 (2020): 56–70.
2. William Liefert and Johan Swinnen, 'Changes in Agricultural Markets in Transition Economies', Agricultural Economic Report no. 806 (Washington, DC: Economic Research Service, USDA, 2002).
3. William M. Liefert and Olga Liefert, 'Russian Agriculture During Transition: Performance, Global Impact, and Outlook', *Applied Economic Perspectives and Policy* 34, no. 1 (2012): 37–75.
4. Ibid.
5. United States Department of Agriculture, Foreign Agriculture Service, 'Production, Supply and Demand Online Database'.
6. William M. Liefert, 'Comparative (Dis?) Advantage in Russian Agriculture', *American Journal of Agricultural Economics* 84, no. 3 (2002): 762–767.
7. Vasilii Uzun, Valery Saraikin, Ekaterina Gataulina, Natalya Shagaida, Renata Yanbykh, Sebastien Mary, and Sergio Gomez y Paloma, 'Prospects

of the Farming Sector and Rural Development in View of Food Security: The Case of the Russian Federation', (Luxembourg: European Commission, 2014); and William M. Liefert and Olga Liefert, 'Russia's Potential to Increase Grain Production by Expanding Area', *Eurasian Geography and Economics* 56, no. 5 (2015): 505–523.

8. Rosstat, *Rossiiskii statisticheskii ezhegodnik* (Moscow: Rosstat, various years).
9. L. I. Gokhberg, I. Kuzminov, A. Chulok, and T. Thurner, 'The Future of Russia's Agriculture and Food Industry Between Global Opportunities and Technological Restrictions', *International Journal of Agricultural Sustainability* 15, no. 4 (2017): 457–466; and Ilya Kuzminov, Leonid Gokhberg, Thomas Thurner, and Elena Khabirova, 'The Current State of the Russian Agricultural Sector', *EuroChoices* 17, no. 1 (2018): 52–57.
10. An example of improvement in the allocative efficiency of production is if two producers are using the same two inputs in production, but one is using too much of one input, and the other too much of the other, given the inputs' marginal productivity. If the two producers exchange among themselves some of their overused input for their underused one, both could increase their volume of output.
11. Although the focus of this discussion is on improvement in the allocative efficiency of grain production and yields, the major changes in the structure of Russian agricultural production since 2000 suggest that huge gains have been made in the allocative efficiency of consumption/use throughout the Russian agricultural economy. Poultry/chicken was a neglected livestock product during the Soviet planned period. However, between 2000 and 2019 production has skyrocketed, rising by over 450 percent from 0.81 to 4.67 mmt, as the market responded to strong demand for this relatively inexpensive meat (compared to beef and pork). The production of oilseeds was also neglected during the Soviet period. From 1996–2000 to 2016–2019, output of Russia's main oilseed, sunflowerseed, increased by an average of 275 percent to 12.3 mmt a year. Russia has also started to expand the production of soybeans, with output averaging 3.8 mmt during 2016–2019. All data from United States Department of Agriculture, Foreign Agriculture Service, 'Production, Supply and Demand Online Database'.
12. United States Department of Agriculture, Foreign Agriculture Service, 'Production, Supply and Demand Online Database'.
13. Trade based on comparative advantage is related to allocative efficiency, in that it is an extension of allocative efficiency decision-making involving production and market exchange to include foreign trade.
14. Raushan Bokusheva, Heinrich Hockmann, and Subal C. Kumbhakar, 'Dynamics of Productivity and Technical Efficiency in Russian Agriculture', *European Review of Agricultural Economics* 39, no. 4 (2011):

611–37. Total factor productivity for a sector such as agriculture is computed by dividing total agricultural output by the weighted average of all inputs used in production.

15. Johan F. M. Swinnen, Kristine Van Herck and Liesbet Vranken, 'Agricultural Productivity Paths in Central and Eastern European Countries and the Former Soviet Union: The Role of Reforms, Initial Conditions and Induced Technological Change', in *Productivity Growth in Agriculture: An International Perspective*, eds. Keith O. Fuglie, Sun Ling Wang, and V. Eldon Ball (Oxfordshire, UK: CABI International, 2012), 127–44.
16. Nicholas Rada, William M. Liefert, and Olga Liefert, 'Productivity Growth and the Revival of Russian Agriculture', Economic Research Report no. 228 (Washington, DC: Economic Research Service, USDA, 2017).
17. See Natalya Shagaida and Zvi Lerman, 'Land Reform and Development of Land Markets', in *Russia's Agriculture in Transition: Factor Markets and Constraints on Growth*, ed. Zvi Lerman (Lanham, MD: Lexington Books, 2008), 137–183; and Stephen K. Wegren, 'Land Reform in Russia: What Went Wrong?' *Post-Soviet Affairs* 24, no. 2 (2008): 121–147.
18. Although using a small share of total farmland during both the Soviet and post-Soviet periods, household plots have produced a disproportionate share of the total ruble value of Russian agricultural output—around 50 percent in 2000, though by 2020 the value was less than 30 percent. Historically, plots produce mostly high value goods such as meat, dairy, vegetables, and fruit, although during the past decade animal husbandry has declined due to disease, regional limitations, and a growing unwillingness to raise animals.
19. Rosstat, *Rossiia v tsifrakh 2020* (Moscow: Rosstat, 2020), 356.
20. Dmitri Rylko, Irina Khramova, Vasilii Uzun, and Robert Jolly, 'Agroholdings: Russia's New Agricultural Operators', in *Russia's Agriculture in Transition: Factor Markets and Constraints on Growth*, ed. Zvi Lerman (Lanham, MD: Lexington Books, 2008), 95–133.
21. Oane Visser, Max Spoor, and Natalya Mamonova, 'Is Russia the Emerging Global "Breadbasket"? Recultivation, Agroholdings and Grain Production', *Europe-Asia Studies* 66, no. 10 (2014): 1589–1610.
22. See Stephen K. Wegren, Alexander M. Nikulin, and Irina Trotsuk, *Food Policy and Food Security: Putting Food on the Russian Table* (Lanham, MD: Lexington Books, 2018), 16–20.
23. Vasilii Uzun, Natalya Shagaida, and Zvi Lerman, 'Russian Agriculture: Growth and Institutional Challenges', *Land Use Policy* 83 (2019): 475–487.
24. FAO, *Russian Federation: Analysis of the Agribusiness Sector in Southern Russia* (Rome: FAO, 2009); and David Epshtein, Konstantin Hahlbrock, and Jurgen Wandel, 'Why Are Agroholdings so Pervasive in Russia's

Belgorod Oblast'? Evidence from Case Studies and Farm-Level Data', *Post-Communist Economics* 25, no. 1 (2013): 59–81.

25. Rylko, Khramova, Uzun, and Jolly, 'Agroholdings: Russia's New Agricultural Operators'; FAO, *Russian Federation: Analysis of the Agribusiness Sector in Southern Russia*; and V. Ia. Uzun and N. I. Shagaida, *Agrariaia reforma v postsovetskoi Rossii: mekhanizmy i resul'taty* (Moscow: Delo: 2015), 174–82.
26. V. Ia. Uzun and N. I. Shagaida, 'Razvitie sel'skogo khoziaistva: ot krupnogo importera do eksportera', in *Ekonomicheskaia politika Rossii*, eds. V. S. Gurevich et al. (Moscow: Delo, 2020), 427.
27. I. Davydova and J. R. Franks, 'The Rise of Large Farms: Why Agroholdings Dominate Russia's Agricultural Sector', *Journal of the National Research University Higher School of Economics* 24, no. 3 (2015): 133–159.
28. E. A. Gataulina, V. Ia. Uzun, A. V. Petrikov, and R. G. Yanbykh, 'Vertical Integration in an Agroindustrial Complex: Agrofirms and Agroholdings in Russia', in *The Dynamics of Vertical Coordination in Agrifood Chains in Eastern Europe and Central Asia, Case Studies*, ed. Johan F. M. Swinnen, Working Paper no. 42 (Washington, DC: World Bank, 2005), 45–71; and Heinrich Hockmann, Raushan Bokusheva, and Irina Bezlepkina, 'Agroholding Membership: Does That Make a Difference in Performance?' *Quarterly Journal of International Agriculture* 48, no. 1 (2009): 25–46.
29. United States Department of Agriculture, Foreign Agriculture Service, 'Production, Supply and Demand Online Database'.
30. Olga Liefert, William M. Liefert, and Eric Luebehusen, 'Rising Grain Exports by the Former Soviet Union Region', Outlook Report WHS-13A-01 (Washington, DC: Economic Research Service, USDA, 2013).
31. The close relationship between fluctuation in Russian annual grain production and exports shows how weather-driven downturns in output generate export volatility.
32. Suchada Langley, 'International Agriculture and Trade Reports. International Financial Crises and Agriculture', Report WRS-99–3 (Washington, DC: Economic Research Service, U.S. Dept. of Agriculture, 2000).
33. Unless otherwise identified, all data on changes in the ruble exchange rate are from or computed from ERS International Macroeconomic Database.
34. Trading Economics, 'Russia Inflation Rate', n.d. https://tradingeconomics.com/russia/inflation-cpi. Accessed 17 August 2020.
35. Tat'iana Kulistikova, 'Minsel'khoz razrabotal gosprogrammu vovlencheniia v oborot sel'khozzemel'. 9 January 2020. https://www.agroinvestor.ru/analytics/news/33051-minselkhoz-razrabotal-gosprogrammu-vovlecheniya-v-oborot-selkhozzemel/. Accessed 8 October 2020.

36. Patrick Meyfroidt, Florian Schierhorn, Alexander V. Prishchepov, Daniel Müller, and Tobias Kuemmerle, 'Drivers, Constraints and Trade-offs Associated with Recultivating Abandoned Cropland in Russia, Ukraine and Kazakhstan', *Global Environmental Change* 37 (2016): 1–15.
37. Uzun et al., 'Prospects of the Farming Sector and Rural Development in View of Food Security'; and Liefert and Liefert, 'Russia's Potential to Increase Grain Production by Expanding Area', 505–523.
38. See Sergei Kiselev, Roman Romashkin, Gerald C. Nelson, Daniel Mason-D'Croz, and Amanda Palazzo, 'Russia's Food Security and Climate Change: Looking into the Future', *Economics E-Journal* 7 (2013–39): 1–66.
39. William M. Liefert and Olga Liefert, 'Changing Crop Area in the Former Soviet Union Region', Outlook Report FDS17b-01 (Washington, DC: Economic Research Service, USDA, 2017).
40. United States Department of Agriculture, Foreign Agriculture Service, 'Production, Supply and Demand Online Database'.
41. Peter Wehrheim, Klaus Frohberg, Eugenia Serova, and Joachim von Braun, eds. *Russia's Agro-food Sector: Towards Truly Functioning Markets* (Dordrecht, Netherlands: Kluwer Academic Publishers, 2000).
42. Stephen K. Wegren, Alexander M. Nikulin, and Irina Trotsuk, 'Russian Agriculture During Putin's Fourth Term: A SWOT Analysis', *Post-Communist Economies* 31, no. 4 (2019): 419–50.
43. Gokhberg, Kuzminov, Chulok, and Thurner, 'The Future of Russia's Agriculture and Food Industry Between Global Opportunities and Technological Restrictions'.
44. Simo Leppanen, Markku Ollikainen, and Liisa Saikkonen, 'Impact of Climate Change on CerealGrain Production in Russia', in *Agricultural Goods and Bads: Essays on Agriculture and Environmental Externalities* (Helsinki: University of Helsinki, 2019).
45. Maria Belyaeva and Raushan Bokusheva, 'Will Climate Change Benefit or Hurt Russian Grain Production? A Statistical Evidence from a Panel Approach', *Climatic Change* 149 (2018): 205–17.
46. U.S. Department of Agriculture, 'USDA Agricultural Projections to 2029', Long-term Projections Report OCE-2020-1 (Washington, DC: USDA, 2020).
47. Ibid.
48. V. V. Rau, 'Grain Market in Russia: From Crisis to Revival', *Studies in Russian Economic Development* 23, no. 1 (2012): 48–56.

Selected Bibliography

Belyaeva, Maria and Raushan Bokusheva. 'Will Climate Change Benefit or Hurt Russian Grain Production? A Statistical Evidence from a Panel Approach'. *Climatic Change* 149 (2018): 205–17.

Bokusheva, Raushan, Heinrich Hockmann, and Subal C. Kumbhakar. 'Dynamics of Productivity and Technical Efficiency in Russian Agriculture'. *European Review of Agricultural Economics* 39, no. 4 (2011): 611–37.

Davydova, I. and J. R. Franks. 'The Rise of Large Farms: Why Agroholdings Dominate Russia's Agricultural Sector'. *Journal of the National Research University Higher School of Economics* 24, no. 3 (2015): 133–159.

Epshtein, David, Konstantin Hahlbrock, and Jurgen Wandel. 'Why Are Agroholdings so Pervasive in Russia's "Belgorod Oblast"? Evidence from Case Studies and Farm-level Data'. *Post-Communist Economics* 25, no. 1 (2013): 59–81.

Food and Agriculture Organization (FAO). *Russian Federation: Analysis of the Agribusiness Sector in Southern Russia*. Rome: FAO, 2009.

Gataulina, E. A., V. Ia. Uzun, A. V. Petrikov and R. G. Yanbykh. 'Vertical Integration in an Agroindustrial Complex: Agrofirms and Agroholdings in Russia'. In *The Dynamics of Vertical Coordination in Agrifood Chains in Eastern Europe and Central Asia, Case Studies*, ed. Johan F.M. Swinnen. Working Paper No. 42. Washington, DC: World Bank, 2005, 45–71.

Gokhberg, L., I. Kuzminov, A. Chulok, and T. Thurner. 'The Future of Russia's Agriculture and Food Industry Between Global Opportunities and Technological Restrictions'. *International Journal of Agricultural Sustainability* 15, no. 4 (2017): 457–466.

Hockmann, Heinrich, Raushan Bokusheva, and Irina Bezlepkina. 'Agroholding Membership:Does that Make a Difference in Performance?' *Quarterly Journal of International Agriculture* 48, no. 1 (2009): 25–46.

Kiselev, Sergei, Roman Romashkin, Gerald C. Nelson, Daniel Mason-D'Croz and Amanda Palazzo. 'Russia's Food Security and Climate Change: Looking into the Future'. *Economics E-Journal* 7 (2013–39): 1–66.

Kuzminov, Ilya, Leonid Gokhberg, Thomas Thurner, and Elena Khabirova. 'The Current State of the Russian Agricultural Sector'. *EuroChoices* 17, no. 1 (2018): 52–57.

Langley, Suchada (ed.). 'International Agriculture and Trade Reports. International Financial Crises and Agriculture'. Report WRS-99–3. Washington, DC: Economic Research Service, U.S. Dept. of Agriculture, 2000.

Leppänen, Simo, Liisa Saikkonen, and Markku Ollikainen. 'Impact of Climate Change on Cereal Grain Production in Russia'. In *Agricultural Goods and Bads: Essays on Agriculture and Environmental Externalities*. Helsinki: University of Helsinki, 2019.

Liefert, William M. 'Comparative (Dis?) Advantage in Russian Agriculture'. *American Journal of Agricultural Economics* 84, no. 3 (2002): 762–767.

Liefert, William M. and Johan Swinnen. 'Changes in Agricultural Markets in Transition Economies'. Agricultural Economic Report No. 806. Washington, DC: Economic Research Service, USDA, 2002.

Liefert, William M. and Olga Liefert. 'Russian Agriculture During Transition: Performance, Global Impact, and Outlook'. *Applied Economic Perspectives and Policy* 34, no. 1 (2012): 37–75.

Liefert, William M. and Olga Liefert. 'Russia's Potential to Increase Grain Production by Expanding Area'. *Eurasian Geography and Economics* 56, no. 5 (2015): 505–523.

Liefert, William M. and Olga Liefert. 'Changing Crop Area in the Former Soviet Union Region'. Outlook Report FDS17b-01. Washington, DC: Economic Research Service, U.S. Dept. of Agriculture, 2017.

Liefert, William M. and Olga Liefert. 'Russian Agricultural Trade and World Markets'. *Russian Journal of Economics* 6, no. 1 (2020): 56–70.

Liefert, Olga, William M. Liefert, and Eric Luebehusen. 'Rising Grain Exports by the Former Soviet Union Region'. Outlook Report WHS-13A-01. Washington, DC: Economic Research Service, U.S. Dept. of Agriculture, 2013.

Meyfroidt, Patrick, Florian Schierhorn, Alexander V. Prishchepov, Daniel Müller, and Tobias Kuemmerle. 'Drivers, Constraints and Trade-offs Associated with Recultivating Abandoned Cropland in Russia, Ukraine and Kazakhstan'. *Global Environmental Change* 37 (2016): 1–15.

Rada, Nicholas, William M. Liefert, and Olga Liefert. *Productivity Growth and the Revival of Russian Agriculture*. Economic Research Report no. 228. Washington, DC: Economic Research Service, U.S. Dept. of Agriculture, 2017.

Rau, V. V. 'Grain Market in Russia: From Crisis to Revival'. *Studies in Russian Economic Development* 23, no. 1 (2012): 48–56.

Rosstat. *Rossiia v tsifrakh 2020*. Moscow: Rosstat.

Rylko, Dmitri, Irina Khramova, Vasilii Uzun, and Robert Jolly. 'Agroholdings: Russia's New Agricultural Operators'. In *Russia's Agriculture in Transition: Factor Markets and Constraints on Growth*, ed. Zvi Lerman. Lanham, MD: Lexington Books, 2008, 95–133.

Shagaida, Natalya and Zvi Lerman. 'Land Reform and Development of Land Markets'. In *Russia's Agriculture in Transition: Factor Markets and Constraints on Growth*, ed. Zvi Lerman. Lanham, MD: Lexington Books, 2008, 137–183.

Swinnen, Johan F. M., Kristine Van Herck and Liesbet Vranken. 'Agricultural Productivity Paths in Central and Eastern European Countries and the Former Soviet Union: The Role of Reforms, Initial Conditions and Induced

Technological Change'. In *Productivity Growth in Agriculture: An International Perspective*, eds. Keith O. Fuglie, Sun Ling Wang, and V. Eldon Ball. Oxfordshire, UK: CABI International, 2012, 127–44.

U. S. Department of Agriculture. 'USDA Agricultural Projections to 2029'. Long-term Projections Report OCE-2020–1. Washington, DC: USDA, 2020.

Uzun, V. Ia. and N. I. Shagaida. 'Razvitie sel'skogo khoziaistva: ot krupnogo importera do eksportera.' In *Ekonomicheskaia politika Rossii*, eds. V. S. Gurevich et al. Moscow: Delo, 2020.

Uzun, V. Ia. and N. I. Shagaida. *Agrariaia reforma v postsovetskoi Rossii: mekhanizmy i resul'taty*. Moscow: Delo, 2015.

Uzun, Vasilii, Natalya Shagaida, and Zvi Lerman. 'Russian Agriculture: Growth and Institutional Challenges'. *Land Use Policy* 83 (2019): 475–487.

Uzun, Vasilii, Valery Saraikin, Ekaterina Gataulina, Natalya Shagayda, Renata Yanbykh, Sebastien Mary, and Sergio Gomez y Paloma. 'Prospects of the Farming Sector and Rural Development in View of Food Security: The Case of the Russian Federation'. Luxembourg: European Commission, 2014.

Visser, Oane, Max Spoor, and Natalia Mamonova. 'Is Russia the Emerging Global 'Breadbasket'? Recultivation, Agroholdings and Grain Production'. *Europe-Asia Studies* 66, no. 10 (2014): 1589–1610.

Wegren, Stephen K. 'Land Reform in Russia: What Went Wrong?' *Post-Soviet Affairs* 24, no. 2 (2008): 121–147.

Wegren, Stephen K., Alexander M. Nikulin and Irina Trotsuk. 'Russian Agriculture during Putin's Fourth Term: A SWOT Analysis'. *Post-Communist Economies* 31, no. 4 (2019): 419–50.

Wegren, Stephen K., Alexander M. Nikulin, and Irina Trotsuk. *Food Policy and Food Security: Putting Food on the Russian Table*. Lanham, MD: Lexington Books, 2018.

Wehrheim, Peter, Klaus Frohberg, Eugenia Serova, and Joachim von Braun, eds. *Russia's Agro-food Sector: Towards Truly Functioning Markets*. Dordrecht, Netherlands: Kluwer Academic Publishers, 2000.

Open Access This chapter is licensed under the terms of the Creative Commons Attribution 4.0 International License (http://creativecommons.org/licenses/by/4.0/), which permits use, sharing, adaptation, distribution and reproduction in any medium or format, as long as you give appropriate credit to the original author(s) and the source, provide a link to the Creative Commons license and indicate if changes were made.

The images or other third party material in this chapter are included in the chapter's Creative Commons license, unless indicated otherwise in a credit line to the material. If material is not included in the chapter's Creative Commons license and your intended use is not permitted by statutory regulation or exceeds the permitted use, you will need to obtain permission directly from the copyright holder.

Chapter 3: The Role of Food Exports in Russia's Economy

Nikolai M. Svetlov

1 Introduction

The impressive increase in Russia's agri-food exports makes this chapter possible and gives it significance. Twenty years ago, Russia was not an important food exporter; today it is. Because Russia's food exports have become more significant, the chapter explores the role of food exports in Russia's national economy from different perspectives. In the 1980s, the USSR was a large grain importer and exported small amounts of agricultural and food products to its allies in Eastern Europe. In the post-Soviet 1990s, Russia's agricultural production plummeted during the transition to a market economy, and it reduced grain imports but became a large meat importer (see Chapters 1 and 2). Further, Russia's position in the 1990s was unfavourable because it produced low-quality wheat which did not have high global demand. Moreover, in general the country did not have capacity for large-scale food export. The claims of some experts that this situation could change relatively soon were not well-grounded.

N. M. Svetlov (✉)
All-Russian Institute for Agrarian Problems and Informatics A. A. Nikonov, Moscow, Russia
e-mail: svetlov-nm@ranepa.ru

© The Author(s) 2022

S. K. Wegren and F. Nilssen (eds.), *Russia's Role in the Contemporary International Agri-Food Trade System*, Palgrave Advances in Bioeconomy: Economics and Policies,
https://doi.org/10.1007/978-3-030-77451-6_4

The inability to become a large food exporter was rooted not only in the dramatic fall of agricultural production in Russia after the crash of the USSR, but also in the structure of the Soviet economy in its last decades. After many political efforts to become a top agrarian power in the world (the campaign on developing virgin lands in Southwest Siberia and North Kazakhstan is a well-known example), the last years of the Soviet era witnessed the country having to trade oil and gas in exchange for buying food abroad.

During the past 20 years Russia's agricultural sector has rebounded and as noted by several authors in this book, the country has emerged as a major grain exporter. The existing literature related to Russia's food exports is not large but is growing and contributes to our understanding of the development of Russia's agricultural export capacity. Petrenko and his colleagues provide a brief historical review of food regulation in the Eurasian Economic Community.[1] Russia inherited important principles that earlier had been implemented by the World Trade Organisation (WTO), the Organisation for Economic Co-operation and Development (OECD), and the European Union (EU), and adjusted those processes to the institutional and technical heritage of the Soviet agricultural sector. Taking this pathway made it possible to establish stable and sufficiently working institutions. These, on one hand, made it worthy for producers to learn how to trade abroad; on another hand, secured food sufficiency and safety in domestic markets. Rau explores the quantitative characteristic of how the integration process changed agriculture and trade in the Eurasian Economic Union during the first decade of its operation.[2] Forecasts by Visser et al. and Liefert et al. that Russia could only be a moderate grain exporter has not played out in reality as Russia has achieved a significant share in global markets for grain and sunflower oil.[3] More recently, other analysts have explored the impact of Russia's food security policy on food exports and prospects for a significant expansion of food exports to 2024 as posited by President Vladimir Putin.[4] Currently, the Russian government is pursuing larger market shares for fish and seafood, vegetable oils, animal products, and processed food.[5]

Other macro-level debates raise other questions about Russia's food exports. For one, the resources and capacities of Russia, either alone or as part of the Eurasian Economic Union, have led many Russian-speaking researchers to optimistic views on the future of Russia's expansion of food exports and the food sector. However, Russia's food sector still suffers from institutional shortcomings, obsolete habits, excess risk aversion, paternalism, poor management of human resources, and deficits in working capital. A different question asks whether agricultural exports can contribute to the welfare of people living in Russia. Ksenofontov warns that an increase in world grain prices creates incentives for increasing exports, possibly with damage to consumers if domestic prices increase as well.[6] Others, however, conclude that risks to national food security arising from international food trade are minor.[7] In either case, it is clear that certain political risks exist that could affect Russia's agri-food exports.[8]

Why does Russia export grain? Russia's grain exports are necessary when the yields are high. Liefert analysed border and domestic prices and concluded that the price transmission into domestic Russian markets is incomplete, and second, is due to the underdeveloped market infrastructure.[9] Uzun and his colleagues show that the grain export volumes are weakly sensitive to price gaps between border and domestic prices, but very sensitive to current grain production with a delay of up to two months.[10] Thus, exports are caused by the limited grain storage capacity within the country during large harvests, and this shortcoming limits the country's ability to benefit from favourable prices in the international grain market. Krylatykh and Belova, as well as Uzun and Lerman, argue that Russia can benefit from increased consumption of grain even while reducing its export, and instead entering the global market for animal products.[11]

The purpose of this chapter is to examine from an economic perspective the significance of Russia's agri-food exports. It addresses two main questions: (1) what contribution do food exports make to the national economy and specifically the agricultural sector?; and (2) what contribution do food exports make to the national budget? The chapter is organised as follows. Section 2 uses national statistics and estimates from the available literature to explore the contribution of food exports to the national economy and the agricultural sector. Section 3 studies the expected consequences of various policy interventions primarily to figure out whether (and how) the role of agricultural export in Russia's economy can be increased by policy measures. Section 4 concludes with an outlook for Russia's food exports.

2 The Contribution of Russia's Agri-Food Exports to the National Economy

Despite the impressive gains in the value of food exports during the last two decades, agri-food exports are far from a dominating share in Russia's overall exports. Popkova and Sukhodolov indicate the share of food products and agricultural raw materials in Russia's total exports measured in USD: 1.8 percent in 1995, 1.6 percent in 2000, 1.9 percent in 2005, 2.2 percent in 2010, and 3.8 percent in 2014.[12] In 2016, the share of agri-food exports amounted to 5 percent of total exports according to Rosstat.[13] Agriculture exports alone accounted for only 1.81 percent of Russia's national exports in 2016. To compare, the export of oil and gas contributed nearly 19 percent of total national exports and about 5 percent of Russia's GDP. These data suggest that food exports play a secondary, if not tertiary, role in the Russian economy, although their role is steadily growing. That said, it is necessary to point out the record harvest in 2017 and the second highest harvest in post-Soviet Russia's history in 2020, including the higher levels of wheat output, help to account for a higher percentage of total exports than in 2016.

The agri-food sector largely relies on exports for its development, especially in recent years, thus suggesting the emergence of an export-led development strategy. Russia's agri-food exports grew annually by an average of more than 18 percent from 2001 to 2018. The fastest rate, 56.4 percent, was achieved in 2011 due to recovery after the drought of 2010 (see Table 1). The growth of food and agricultural export outstrips Russia's growth in total exports. After Russia's accession to the World Trade Organization in August 2012, the rate of export growth became lower, with an average rate of only 0.5 percent for the period from 2012 to 2016. This slowdown was caused by the high base from 2012. Nonetheless, the role of agricultural exports as a source of foreign currency inflows to Russia's economy is significant, although still far from the topmost.

Although Russia's agri-food sector is small in comparison to the whole national economy (as measured in the monetary value of output), it still influences the lives of more than 37 million rural dwellers as an employer, supplier, buyer, and taxpayer. The sector's capacity to contribute to family or municipal income is directly related to its export capacity. While the Russian economy has numerous sources of foreign currency, there exist millions of workers whose budgets and welfare are very sensitive to the

Table 1 Russian agri-food exports in comparison to other national indicators

Year	*Total exports of agri-food products*				*Grain and legumes exports*			
	Billion USD	*Increase compared to the previous year*	*Percent of gross Russia's export*	*Percent of gross agricultural production*	*Billion USD*[a]		*Increase compared to the previous year*	*Percent of gross agricultural production*
2001	1.460	...	1.46	4.64	0.3		...	0.95
2002	2.177	1.49	2.04	7.05	1.0		3.3	3.24
2003	2.690	1.24	2.01	7.67	1.1		1.1	3.13
2004	2.479	0.92	1.37	5.70	0.7		0.6	1.61
2005	3.881	1.57	1.61	7.96	1.4		2.0	2.87
2006	4.849	1.25	1.61	8.38	1.6		1.1	2.76
2007	8.257	1.70	2.35	11.34	4.1		2.6	5.63
2008	8.389	1.02	1.79	8.86	3.3		0.8	3.49
2009	9.281	1.11	3.08	12.34	3.5		1.1	4.65
2010	7.250	0.78	1.83	8.94	2.4		0.7	2.96
2011	11.337	1.56	2.19	10.75	4.6		1.9	4.36
2012	16.738	1.48	3.19	16.46	6.6	6.252	1.4	6.49
2013	16.227	0.97	3.09	14.97	4.9	4.752	0.7	4.52
2014	18.981	1.17	3.82	18.18	7.3	7.060	1.5	6.99
2015	16.181	0.85	4.71	20.69	6.0	5.651	0.8	7.67
2016	17.045	1.05	5.97	22.28	6.0	5.610	1.0	7.84
2017	20.706	1.21	5.79	23.63	7.9	7.490	1.3	9.01
2018	24.885	1.20	5.54	29.28	10.8	10.464	1.4	12.71

[a]Values printed in small font relate to grain export
Source Author's calculations based on Rosstat data

success and failure of agri-food exports. In 2001, the agri-food sector sent less than 5 percent of its production abroad, so revenues almost exclusively depended on the domestic market. By 2010, as Table 1 shows, the share of production exported abroad was about 10 percent, but by 2018 the share increased to about 30 percent. In other words, exports account for a substantial portion of growth within the agricultural sector. Thus, Russia's contemporary agri-food sector largely depends on exports, first, from the viewpoint of ability to reach foreign markets, and second, from the viewpoint of monetary inflows.

Among food exports, the export of grain (including a small share of legumes) is the most important (see Chapter 2). Since 2005, grain exports account for at least 30 percent of gross agri-food export. The average annual growth rate for the exports of grain and legumes during 2001–2018 is almost 23.5 percent, a high number that is due mostly to a very low base in 2001. Because gross grain yields and weather conditions in a specific year have a significant impact on grain exports, it would be more correct to compare the averages of two nine-year periods, 2001–2009 and 2010–2018. In the 2001–2009 period, mean exports of grain and legume amounted to $1.9 billion USD. In the 2010–2018 period, mean exports of grain and legume increased to $6.3 billion USD. The nine-year growth has an average annual rate of 14.3 percent. The average annual growth rate for agricultural and food exports amounts to 14.7 percent, so the share of grain remains relatively stable in the long run. In comparison to gross agricultural production, the value of grain export reached 12.7 percent of total agricultural production by 2018. The value of grain exports in 2019 fell to $7.928 billion USD, with grain and legumes exports valued at $8.3 billion USD, which equals about 9 percent of gross agricultural production.

2.1 The Contribution of Agri-Food Exports to Agricultural Production[14]

Russian agriculture is meeting internal needs and import substitution, witnessed by the fact that domestic consumption per capita has approached the standards recommended by the Ministry of Health. At the same time, Russia's agrarian sector has significant potential and opportunities to increase its efficiency. Russia accounts for about 4.5 percent of the world's agricultural land and has only 2 percent of the global population. Under these conditions, exports play an increasingly important role in the growth of agricultural and food production.

Gross agricultural output from 2000 to 2018 increased by almost one and a half times. Crop and livestock production grew at approximately equal rates. The highest growth rates in production were observed in poultry meat farming (by 5.9 times), sugar beets and oilseeds (by 2.9 times), and in pig farming (by 2.2 times). During the same time period, the production of potatoes and forage crops decreased by 24 and 30 percent, respectively, as did beef and milk production by 16 and 5 percent respectively. The most significant contribution to the growth of gross agricultural production was made by grain farming and poultry meat farming: together their share accounted for more than 50 percent of gross growth

(26 percent for grain and almost 29 percent for poultry meat). Contributions to the growth of gross output were also high due to the growth in the production of oilseeds and pig breeding (more than 19 percent), as well as vegetables (8 percent) and sugar beet (4 percent).[15]

In parallel with the growth of agricultural production, the value of agri-food exports increased (see Table 1). During the period 2000–2018, the share of agri-food exports from crop production increased from 3 to 27 percent, while the share of export from livestock production remained low. The largest increase in exports was from the gross production of oilseeds and grain. In 2018, more than three-quarters of oilseed production was exported, including the export of sunflower oil. During 2012–2018, 31.5 percent of all grain production (including legumes) was exported. During the same period, the share of exported fruits (including berries and nuts) and poultry meat was 5.2 and 2.2 percent of production. For comparison, during 2000–2005 these shares were 10.4 percent for grain and legumes, 3.8 percent for fruits, berries, and nuts, and only 0.1 percent for poultry meat.[16]

According to calculations by this author, the growth in exports influences an increase in production. Exports in effect spurred sectoral growth during 2000–2018. Calculations show that for the period 2000–2018, the estimated contribution of exports to the incremental production of grain and legumes is 79 percent. A similar estimate for oilseeds shows that exports accounted for 61 percent; 56 percent for sunflower; and 78.5 percent for rapeseed. Conversely, the contribution of exports to livestock production appears very small, reaching only 0.9 percent for livestock (including poultry) and 2.4 percent for eggs during the same period. The contribution of exports to the production of cattle, milk, and wool approximates zero. In total, the growth of agri-food exports during 2000–2018 caused about 34 percent of the growth in gross agricultural output.

In conclusion, since 2000 exports have stimulated growth for a significant part of gross agricultural production. The contribution of exports to growth in the agri-food sector is positive and statistically significant for products that by 2018 accounted for 43 percent of gross agricultural production. Although the rate of growth in agri-food exports from the past two decades may not be duplicated in coming years, it can be projected that exports will remain a main source of growth in the agricultural sector. This projection is based on the satisfaction of consumption demand by domestic production and a stabilisation in the volume of agri-food imports.

2.2 *Budgetary Inflows from Agri-Food Exports Compared to Overall Budget Inflow*

Due to the diversity of budgetary transfers and institutions reporting them, it normally is very difficult to assess the contribution of the agricultural sector as a taxpayer into the national budget from exports. Unfortunately, input–output tables are published seldom and differ from each other in how they aggregate economic activities. For 2016, however, a set of sufficiently detailed input–output tables for the Russian economy is available from Rosstat, which makes it possible to understand the role of agri-food exports in the national budget. The discussion below is based on this author's calculations from available input–output data. To start, I refer the reader to Table 2, which shows net taxes paid by different sectors of the economy.[17]

A main conclusion from Table 2 is that the boom in Russia's agri-food exports brings almost nothing to the consolidated budget. This conclusion is based on two considerations. First, the oil and gas industries provide more than one-third of overall net tax inflows and, if we limit the analysis to the tax inflows from exports only, more than 97 percent of the total. Thus, any other tax revenue from exporting businesses is minuscule for the national budget in comparison. Second, agri-food exports are taxed 5.2 times lower than household consumption, accumulation, and other internal uses. The rate of net taxation for exported agricultural output is 0.65 percent and for the remaining part it is 3.4 percent. Both rates are quite low, inasmuch as part of taxes are returned to agricultural producers via various subsidies. It becomes evident that the exported part of total agricultural output is taxed lower, and this helps Russia's agricultural exporters to increase their shares in international markets. Lower taxes also positively influence the welfare of the rural population, but lower taxes barely make a contribution to the consolidated national budget. While it is true that the large harvests in 2017 and 2020 generate somewhat more tax revenue, it remains true that in terms of net input–output much of even higher tax revenue is returned to agriculture in the form of myriad subsidies.

Table 2 Net taxes from selected sectors of Russian economy

Sector	*Net taxes from exported production, million USD*	*Net taxes from exported production percent of national total*	*Net taxes from gross production, million USD*	*Net taxes from gross production, percent of national total*	*Net taxes from exported production, percent of those from gross production*
Agricultural products	14.7	0.04	980.2	0.89	1.50
Food and agricultural products	39.3	0.12	15,856.1	14.34	0.25
Food (excluding fish) and agricultural products	37.3	0.11	15,854.2	14.34	0.24
Total of national economy	33,106.3	100	110,535.4	100	29.95
Oil, oil-based products and natural gas	32,187.7	97.23	41,427.0	37.48	77.70

Sources Rosstat; author's calculations

The main takeaway of this subsection is that Russia's agri-food export is not a significant source for Russia's national budget. The positive contribution from agri-food exports to the national economy falls into the hands of private actors. Subsequently, revenue is redistributed between various economic agents through a network of contract relations, including employment contracts.

3 How Sensitive Are Agri-Food Exports to Trade Policies?

State financial support to agriculture in various forms has increased substantially since 2006, helping to boost food production. That part of the story has been well told.[18] This section explores the impact of national policy on Russia's agri-food exports. The section examines through modelling the extent to which agri-food exports are sensitive to trade policy.

3.1 Methodology

At a policy level, scholars and analysts have known for many years that trade policy affects the level of exports through such instruments as export subsidies, export quotas, or outright export bans. Russia does not use direct export subsidies but did ban wheat exports in 2010–2011 and introduced the option to enact export quotas for the second half of agricultural years starting in January 2020. While it is generally true that national trade policy impacts agri-food exports, this section is unique in that it attempts to measure the sensitivity of agri-food exports to different policies. To measure sensitivity, the section employs a mathematical model called the 'production frontier plus partial equilibrium'.[19] The mathematical principle of combining the production frontier with partial equilibrium equations is developed in Central Economics and Mathematics Institute (Moscow). This principle was used in an analysis of the impact of climate change on Russia's agricultural markets, taking into account spatial differences.[20] The purpose of the model is to quantify the effects of policy change based on four scenarios.[21]

The 'base scenario' simulates the policies that were in force during the model's base period 2013–2017. The differences between the base scenario and reality are twofold. The first difference is that the base scenario assumes that each region consumes each of five products that is sufficient to comply the with food consumption norms recommended by Russia's Ministry of Health. The second difference is that the scenario presumes equilibriums in all the markets which, in general, is not the case in reality. Four alternative scenarios are compared to this base scenario. All the four inherit the conditions of the base scenario with some specific change.

The first alternative scenario imposes some effective regulation that increases the export of five products in total by at least 10 percent compared to the base scenario. In this scenario, 'the government' permits the producers to meet food consumption norms at least 95 percent of the recommended levels instead of 100 percent in the base scenario. This scenario describes partial redistribution of sales from domestic to foreign markets. The second scenario relates to when the country rejects the regulations of the World Trade Organisation. The scenario imposes 10 percent export subsidies on the five products. Other conditions do not differ from the base scenario. The third scenario relates to forcing national agribusinesses to use a larger share of their grain production as fodder internally instead of exporting it.[22] The scenario imposes a 10 percent export tax on wheat and grain while leaving other conditions of the base scenario unchanged. The fourth scenario is 'populistic'. It imposes a 10 percent export tax on the export of the five products, a step that would partly lock in the supply for the domestic market, resulting in lower domestic prices for producers if during good harvest years.

3.2 Results

The major economic indicators for the entire agricultural sector under the four scenarios are summarised in Table 3. In the case of the first scenario, the growth of the gross margin is fully due to the opportunity to reduce food supply to regions with low demand, while in the second scenario it is due to the considerable export subsidy inflows. The second and third scenarios promote exports, increase production, reduce domestic sales and import, slightly raise domestic prices, and increase the sectoral gross margin.

Table 3 Models of agricultural production under different trade policies (billion USD)

Indicator	*Scenario*				
	0. Base	*1. Export + 10%, food security rate −5%*	*2. Export subsidy + 10%*	*3. Grain export tax +10%*	*4. Export tax +10%*
Production	80.09	81.12	81.12	79.93	79.92
Domestic sales	89.27	88.13	88.26	89.25	89.24
Import	21.60	19.90	19.90	21.58	21.56
Export	9.89	10.87	10.87	9.81	9.79
Farm gate price index to the base scenario	×	1.014	1.014	0.997	0.997
Gross margin	8.51	10.14	10.27	7.70	7.45

Source Author's calculations

In the third and fourth scenarios, exports account for less agricultural production in comparison to the base scenario and also in domestic sales, although this effect is small. The reason is a lower margin on sales, which makes it unprofitable to supply food above the set food consumption rates in some regions. The decline in the gross margin is caused by lower domestic prices, lower exports, and larger imports.

In general, we conclude that the policy has a weak impact on the outcomes of policy. The overall outcome of the export promoting policy is clearly to the favour of agricultural producers, yet at the expense of domestic consumers, who experience a bit lower consumption and a bit higher prices, and taxpayers (in the case of the export subsidising scenario).

Thus, it can be concluded that purely economic considerations do not support any systematic change in the agricultural and trade policy from the base period. In the view of this, large policy changes are not very likely, unless they would be driven by non-economic considerations, and even if that occurs, they will not make important changes in the domestic production and markets.

4 Outlook

It is essential to distinguish the role of agri-food exports in Russia's national economy and in its national food economy. In the national economy, the role is still minor, while in latter the role is very important. This chapter has shown that the percentage of agri-food production is now exported, but the agri-food sector does not contribute much to the national economy or to the national budget, although exports do spur development in the agricultural sector and do provide some welfare to the rural population. For these reasons, the short-run outlook for an expansion in Russia's agri-food exports will likely be driven from commercial interests. Over the longer term, one can ask whether agricultural export can one day become a factor of importance for the welfare of the whole nation.

As for now, Russia has a wide choice on what to export in the future, depending on its successes or failures in frontier research, global demand for oil and gas, the consequences of climate change,[23] and its political willingness to join international food production chains. Even with comparative advantages due to climate change, Russia's agricultural sector is unlikely to become one of the topmost sectors of the national economy unless severe crises occur in other sectors that currently fund the national economy and budget. In addition, scenario modelling makes it evident that in the short run there is a very small likelihood for raising the role of agricultural exports in the national economy through trade policy instruments. Sanctions and countersanctions between the European Union and Russia constrain exports.[24] Sanctions in general slow down further Russia's achievements in international agricultural trade.

That said, Russia's agri-food exports face both obstacles and opportunities in the years ahead.[25] My feeling is that agri-food exports are more likely than not to keep growing in the coming years, although the rate of growth may decrease. Two factors favour an increase in production that may fuel higher exports: progress in technology as well as overcoming existing inefficiencies; and, to a smaller extent, an abundance of unused land suitable for cultivation.[26] In the long run, Russia's large water resources became an important additional factor contributing to the competitiveness of crop production in the country compared to increasing aridity around the world.[27] Thus, the role of agricultural export in overall Russia's economy is likely to gradually increase, but within the constraints and limitations that have been examined in this chapter.

Notes

1. Alexei Petrenko, Anatoly Kutyshenko and Victor Tutelyan, 'Food Regulation in the Customs Union of Belarus, Kazakhstan and Russia', in *International Food Law and Policy,* eds. Gabriela Steier and Kiran K. Patel. (Cham: Switzerland: Springer, 2016), 1379–407.
2. Vladimir V. Rau, 'Russia in the Customs Union: The Agrarian Aspect', *Studies on Russian Economic Development* 24, no. 1 (2013): 77–83.
3. William M. Liefert, Stefan R. Osborne, Olga Liefert and Michael A. Trueblood, 'Can Russia Be Competitive in Agriculture?' *EuroChoices* 2, no. 3 (2003): 18–23; Oane Visser, Max Spoor, and Natalia Mamonova, 'Is Russia the Emerging Global 'Breadbasket'? Recultivation, Agroholdings and Grain Production', *Europe-Asia Studies* 66, no. 10 (2014): 1589–610.
4. See Stephen K. Wegren, Frode Nilssen, and Christel Elvestad, 'The Impact of Russian Food Security Policy on the Performance of the Food System', *Eurasian Geography and Economics* 57, no. 6 (2016): 671–99; Stephen K. Wegren and Christel Elvestad, 'Russia's Self-Sufficiency and Food Security: An Assessment', *Post-Communist Economies* 30, no. 5 (2018): 565–87; Stephen K. Wegren, 'Grain Production in Russia: Too Much of a Good Thing?" *Post-Communist Economies* 30, no. 6 (2018): 835–46;

Stephen K. Wegren, Alexander Nikulin, and Irina Trotsuk, *Food Policy and Food Security: Putting Food on the Russian Table* (Lanham, MD: Lexington Press, 2018); and Stephen K. Wegren, 'Can Russia's Food Exports Reach $45 Billion in 2024?' *Post-Communist Economies* 32, no. 2 (2020): 147–75.
5. Ministry of Agriculture of the Russian Federation, 'Russia to Allocate Over R406 Billion by 2024 to Support Agricultural Exports', 26 December 2018. https://mcx.gov.ru/en/news/Russia_allocate_over_406_billion_rubles/. Accessed 1 August 2020.
6. M.Y. Ksenofontov, D.A. Polzikov, I.A. Gol'denberg and and P. V. Sitnikov, 'Methodological Problems of the Formation of the Concept of Food Security in Russia', *Studies on Russian Economic Development* 29, no. 5 (2018): 551–57.
7. Y. S. Pappe, N.S. Antonenko and D.A. Polzikov, 'Modern Approach to the Food Security of Russia', *Studies on Russian Economic Development* 28, no. 3 (2017): 286–95.
8. Nikolai M. Svetlov, Denis S. Ternovskiy, Vasily Ya. Uzun, Natalia I. Shagaida, Ekaterina A. Shishkina, *Vliianie eksporta na sel'khozproizvoditelei i potrebitelei v Rossii* (Moscow: Delo, 2020), 42–51.
9. William M. Liefert, 'Decomposing Changes in Agricultural Price Gaps: An Application to Russia', *Agricultural Economics* 40 (2009): 15–28.
10. Vasilii Ia. Uzun, Nikolai M. Svetlov, Natalia I. Shagaida, Daria A. Loginova, and Ekaterina A. Shishkina, *Sovershenstvovanie mekhanizmov gosudarstvennogo regulirovaniia Rossiiskogo rynka zerna* (Moscow: IPEI RANEPA, 2016), 69.
11. Elmira N. Krylatykh and Tat'iana N. Belova, 'Eksport Rossiiskogo zerna v kontekste formirovaniia regional'noi ekonomicheskoi politiki', *Ekonomika regiona* 14, no. 3 (2018): 778–90; Vasilii Uzun and Zvi Lerman, 'Outcomes of Agrarian Reform in Russia', in *The Eurasian Wheat Belt and Food Security: Global and Regional Aspects*, eds. M. Keyzer and M. Merbis (Seville, Spain: IPTS JRC, 2017), 81–101.
12. Elena G. Popkova and Yakov A. Sukhodolov, *Foreign Trade as a Factor of Economic Growth: Russian-Chinese Foreign Trade Cooperation* (Cham: Switzerland: Springer, 2017), 50.
13. This figure encompasses the production of agriculture, services provided to agriculture (excluding veterinary), hunting and breeding wild animals, fishery, all kinds of food products, beverages and tobacco.
14. The subsection is based on the earlier quantitative study carried out at the Russian Presidential Academy of National Economy and Public Administration (RANEPA) with the participation of the author of this chapter. Nikolai M. Svetlov, Denis S. Ternovskii, Vasili Ia. Uzun, Natalia I. Shagaida, Ekaterina A. Shishkina, *Vliianie eksporta na sel'khozproizvoditelei i potrebitelei v Rossii* (Moscow: Izdatel'skiy dom Delo, 2020), 17–25. The

methodology is developed by Professor Vasili Ia. Uzun in cooperation with Professor Denis S. Ternovskii.

15. The largest negative contribution in gross production was due to the decline in potato growing (by 6.7 percent) followed by the decline in the production of forage crops (by 3.8 percent), cattle for slaughter (3.9 percent) and milk (2.7 percent).
16. A methodological issue arises while quantifying the contribution of export in the growth of agricultural production. Ultimately, the role of exports is defined as its contribution to the indicators of growth in gross output. However, the use of the traditional approach, which provides for the calculation of the ratio of incremental export to incremental production, in the case of the analysis of agricultural exports is difficult for the following reasons. First, the dynamics of exports are not solely provided by production change, but also by changes in stocks, consumption and imports. Second, export volumes, as a rule, tend to be stable over time because of the need to secure the occupied share of the international markets, even in a situation of a short-term or cyclical reduction in production. Taking into account the above, the contribution of exports to the growth of gross output for an individual agricultural product is calculated in the RANEPA study as the ratio of the average absolute increment of its export to the average absolute increment of its production. Furthermore, both increments are computed from the parameter estimates of functions that approximate the original time series, provided that these estimates are unidirectional for both export and production and statistically significant. In turn, the average estimate of the contribution of exports to the output of any product aggregate is calculated as the average weighted by the share of the incremental production of each product in the incremental output of gross agricultural production for 2000–2018. See Svetlov, Ternovskii, *Uzun, Shagaida, and Shishkina, Vliianie eksporta na sel'khozproizvoditelei i potrebitelei v Rossii.*
17. The calculations are based on Rosstat's input–output tables spreadsheet accessed March 1, 2020 from https://rosstat.gov.ru/storage/mediabank/baz-tzv-2016.xlsx. One of sheets in this file contains data on net tax (i.e. tax less subsidies) transfers to the consolidated (i.e. federal, regional and local in total) national budget, distributed among products and sectors. The row 'Agricultural products' in Table 2 sums up rows in the source sheet coded 001 to 008 and 010 to 017. The row 'Food and agricultural products', adds to the list above rows coded 022, 036 to 046 and 049 to 055. The next row 'Food (excluding fish) and agricultural products' excludes the code 022 from the bundle of codes for the previous row. The row 'Total of national economy' comes from code 207. Finally, the row 'oil, its products and gas' sums up rows 025, 026 and

079. Column 'Net taxes from exported production' comes from column coded 109 in the source and column 'Net taxes from gross production' from column coded 111. Then all the transfers are converted into million USD.

18. Wegren, Nikulin, and Trotsuk, *Food Policy and Food Security*, 54–76.
19. Nikolai M. Svetlov, 'Neparametricheskaia granitsa proizvodstvennykh vozmozhnostei v vychislimoi modeli chastichnogo ravnovesiia', *Ekonomika i matematicheskie metody* 56, no. 4 (2019): 104–16.
20. Nikolai M. Svetlov and Ekaterina A. Shishkina, 'Innovatsionnaia model' chastichnogo ravnovesiia v prilozhenii k analizu effektov izmeneniia klimata', *Mezhdunarodnyi sel'skokhoziaystvennyi zhurnal* 5 (2019): 58–63.
21. The model operates with six products: wheat, other grain, sunflower, milk, meat (in liveweight measure) and the remaining agricultural production. The products are measured in 1000 tonnes, except for the latter, for which the monetary measure is used. The model allows inter-regional transportation (along with import and export) and calculates revenues using prices of the region where the product is consumed, again excluding the remaining production: its transportation (both within the country and across its borders) is not modelled and the prices to calculate revenue from its sales are whose of the producing region. For simplicity, it is assumed that the products are always transported in kind and processed at the place of consumption.

    The production frontier is defined as the following set of resources: labour resources; arable land; all agricultural land; value of fixed assets used in agricultural production; the resource of mechanical power; herd population (derived to the number of cows); working capital. This frontier differs on 12 natural agricultural zones defined with respect to climate and soil conditions and on the year-specific conditions modelled from five distinct year of the period 2013–2017. The modelled unit (region) is a Russia's federal subject. In total, the model includes 82 regions, of which 80 are agricultural producers and two remaining regions are cities (Moscow and Saint Petersburg). Crimea and Sevastopol are not included in the current version of the model.
22. Elmira N. Krylatykh and Tat'iana N. Belova, 'Eksport Rossiiskogo zerna v kontekste formirovaniia regional'noi ekonomicheskoi politiki', 778–90.
23. Nikolai M. Svetlov, Stanislav O. Siptits, Irina A. Romanenko and Natalia E. Evdokimova, 'The effect of climate change on the location of branches of agriculture in Russia', *Studies on Russian Economic Development* 30, no. 4 (2019): 406–18; M.Y. Ksenofontov and D. A. Polzikov, 'On the Issue of the Impact of Climate Change on the Development of Russian Agriculture in the Long Term', *Studies on Russian Economic Development* 31, no. 3 (2020): 304–11.

24. Mark Baimbridge, Ioannis Litsios, Karen Jackson and Uih Ran Lee, *The Segmentation of Europe* (London: Palgrave Macmillan, 2017), 208–15.
25. Wegren, 'Can Russia's Food Exports Reach $45 Billion in 2024?'.
26. Nikolai M. Svetlov, 'Land use projections for Southern Non-Black-Earth regions of Russia: coping with uncertainty', paper presented at IAMO Forum, 21–23 June 2017, Halle (Saale), Germany; https://ssrn.com/abstract=3240669, 10–11.
27. Anastasia Likhacheva, 'Global Water Challenge and Prospects for Russian Agenda', in *Russia in a Changing World*, eds. Glenn Diesen and Alexander Lukin (Singapore: Palgrave Macmillan, 2020), 161–78.

Selected Bibliography

Acemoglu, Daron and Simon Johnson. 'Unbundling Institutions'. NBER Working Paper 9934. Cambridge, MA, USA: National bureau of economic research, August 2003. https://www.nber.org/papers/w9934.pdf.

Baimbridge, Mark, Ioannis Litsios, Karen Jackson and Uih Ran Lee. *The Segmentation of Europe*. London: Palgrave Macmillan, 2017.

Karpova, Olga and Igor Mayburov. 'Comparison of VAT Systems in Russia and China'. *The Turkish Online Journal of Design, Art and Communication* (September 2018): 1115–20.

Ksenofontov, M. Y. and D. A. Polzikov. 'On the Issue of the Impact of Climate Change on the Development of Russian Agriculture in the Long Term'. *Studies on Russian Economic Development* 31, no. 3 (2020): 304–11.

Ksenofontov, M. Y., D. A. Polzikov and A. V. Urus. 'Food Security and Grain Market Regulation in Russia'. *Studies on Russian Economic Development* 30, no. 6 (2019): 606–13.

Ksenofontov, M. Y., D. A. Polzikov, I. A. Gol'denberg and and P. V. Sitnikov. 'Methodological Problems of the Formation of the Concept of Food Security in Russia'. *Studies on Russian Economic Development* 29, no. 5 (2018): 551–7.

Liefert, William M. 'Decomposing Changes in Agricultural Price Gaps: An Application to Russia'. *Agricultural Economics* 40 (2009): 15–28.

Liefert, William M., Stefan R. Osborne, Olga Liefert and Michael A. Trueblood. 'Can Russia be Competitive in Agriculture?' *EuroChoices* 2, no. 3 (2003): 18–23.

Pappe, Y. S., N. S. Antonenko and D. A. Polzikov. 'Modern Approach to the Food Security of Russia'. *Studies on Russian Economic Development* 28, no. 3 (2017): 286–95.

Petrenko, Alexei, Anatoly Kutyshenko and Victor Tutelyan. 'Food Regulation in the Customs Union of Belarus, Kazakhstan and Russia'. In *International Food Law and Policy*, ed. Gabriela Steier and Kiran K. Patel. Cham: Switzerland: Springer, 2016, 1379–407.

Popkova, Elena G. and Yakov A. Sukhodolov. *Foreign Trade as a Factor of Economic Growth: Russian-Chinese Foreign Trade Cooperation*. Cham: Switzerland: Springer, 2017.

Rau, Vladimir V. 'Russia in the Customs Union: The Agrarian Aspect'. *Studies on Russian Economic Development* 24, no. 1 (2013): 77–83.

Svetlov, Nikolai M. 'Land use projections for Southern Non-Black-Earth Regions of Russia: Coping with Uncertainty'. Paper presented at IAMO Forum, 21–23 June 2017. Halle (Saale), Germany. https://ssrn.com/abstract=3240669.

Svetlov, Nikolai M., Denis S. Ternovskii, Vasilii Ia. Uzun, Natalia I. Shagaida, Ekaterina A. Shishkina. *Vliianie eksporta na sel'khozproizvoditelei i potrebiteliy v Rossii*. Moscow: Delo, 2020.

Svetlov, Nikolai M., Stanislav O. Siptits, Irina A. Romanenko and Natalia E. Evdokimova. 'The Effect of Climate Change on the Location of Branches of Agriculture in Russia'. *Studies on Russian economic development* 30, no. 4 (2019): 406–18.

Ushachev, Ivan G., Andrei G. Paptsov, Aleksandr F. Serkov, Vlada V. Maslova, Vyacheslav S. Chekalin, Natalia F. Zaruk, Aleksandr I. Amosov, et al. *Razvitie eksportnogo potentsiala APK Rossii: tsenovoi aspect*. Moscow: FGBNU Rosagrotekh, 2019.

Uzun, Vasilii Ia., Nikolai M. Svetlov, Natalia I. Shagaida, Daria A. Loginova and Ekaterina A. Shishkina. *Sovershenstvovanie mekhanizmov gosudarstvennogo regulirovaniia rossiiskogo rynka zerna*. Moscow: IPEI RANEPA, 2016.

Uzun, Vasilii and Zvi Lerman. 'Outcomes of agrarian reform in Russia'. In *The Eurasian Wheat Belt and Food Security: Global and Regional Aspects*, eds. M. Keyzer and M. Merbis, 81–101. Seville, Spain: IPTS JRC, 2017.

Visser, Oane, Max Spoor, and Natalia Mamonova. 'Is Russia the Emerging Global 'Breadbasket'? Recultivation, Agroholdings and Grain Production', *Europe-Asia Studies* 66, no. 10 (2014): 1589–610.

Wegren, Stephen K. 'Can Russia's Food Exports Reach $45 Billion in 2024?' *Post-Communist Economies* 32, no. 2 (2020): 147–75.

Wegren, Stephen K., 'Grain Production in Russia: Too Much of a Good Thing?" *Post-Communist Economies* 30, no. 6 (2018): 835–46.

Wegren, Stephen K., Alexander Nikulin, and Irina Trotsuk, *Food Policy and Food Security: Putting Food on the Russian Table*. Lanham, MD: Lexington Press, 2018.

Wegren, Stephen K. and Christel Elvestad, 'Russia's Self-Sufficiency and Food Security: An Assessment'. *Post-Communist Economies* 30, no. 5 (2018): 565–87.

Wegren, Stephen K., Frode Nilssen, and Christel Elvestad, 'The Impact of Russian Food Security Policy on the Performance of the Food System'. *Eurasian Geography and Economics* 57, no. 6 (2016): 671–99.

Open Access This chapter is licensed under the terms of the Creative Commons Attribution 4.0 International License (http://creativecommons.org/licenses/by/4.0/), which permits use, sharing, adaptation, distribution and reproduction in any medium or format, as long as you give appropriate credit to the original author(s) and the source, provide a link to the Creative Commons license and indicate if changes were made.

The images or other third party material in this chapter are included in the chapter's Creative Commons license, unless indicated otherwise in a credit line to the material. If material is not included in the chapter's Creative Commons license and your intended use is not permitted by statutory regulation or exceeds the permitted use, you will need to obtain permission directly from the copyright holder.

Chapter 4: Russia's Food Security and Impact on Agri-Food Trade

Linde Götz, Maximilian Heigermoser, and Tinoush Jamali Jaghdani

1 Introduction

The emergence of food security as a core component of Russia's food policy and as a political priority is important because it affects domestic food production and the way in which Russia interacts with the international agri-food market. Whereas the Soviet period witnessed Russia as a large grain importer, in the 1990s Russia changed to a meat importer. In both periods, Russia's role as an importer meant that Russia was a significant player in the international food market (see Chapter 1). Since 2000,

L. Götz (✉) · M. Heigermoser · T. J. Jaghdani
Leibniz-Institute of Agricultural Development in Transition Economies (IAMO), Halle, Germany
e-mail: Goetz@iamo.de

M. Heigermoser
e-mail: heigermoser@iamo.de

T. J. Jaghdani
e-mail: jaghdani@iamo.de

© The Author(s) 2022
S. K. Wegren and F. Nilssen (eds.), *Russia's Role in the Contemporary International Agri-Food Trade System*, Palgrave Advances in Bioeconomy: Economics and Policies,
https://doi.org/10.1007/978-3-030-77451-6_5

Russia's food and agrarian policy has prioritised less dependence on food imports.

Essentially, Russia's contemporary food policy entails a trifecta of sub-policies, all of which are located at the protectionist end of the trade policy continuum: (1) food security policy, which has a variety of dimensions including reducing dependence on food imports; food security in the traditional sense, referring to consumption norms and nutrition; food safety; product tracing; and truth in labelling; (2) food self-sufficiency, which refers to the effort to increase agricultural production to meet domestic needs for certain basic commodities; and (3) import substitution policy, which refers to the attempt to substitute domestic production for imports where possible. As imports are substituted with domestically produced foods, consumers often face higher food prices.[1]

To achieve these goals of food policy and its subcomponents, Russian policymakers have different instruments to choose from: import taxes, non-tariff barriers, export quotas, and import bans against companies and countries. The subcomponents of food policy and the instruments used are united in trying to reduce the presence of agri-food imports in Russia's domestic food market. This protectionism provides incentives for domestic producers to increase their production. Protectionism has been combined with higher investments in the domestic agricultural sector through comprehensive financial subsidies.[2]

Russia's food policy frames the way in which Russia interacts with other states in agri-food trade with carry over effects to other dimensions as well. Through food security, self-sufficiency, and import substitution, the Russian government aims not only to decrease Russia's food import dependency and to increase its food self-sufficiency, but also to consolidate Russia as a large agri-food exporting country, a feature explicitly discussed in the Food Security Doctrine adopted in 2020. Previously, in May 2018, President Vladimir Putin signed a decree instructing that the dollar value of Russia's agricultural exports reach $45 billion by 2024.[3] In late 2020, Russia's Ministry of Agriculture extended the date by which that target value of exports would be reached to 2030.

The purpose of this chapter is to examine the impact of food policy on Russia's domestic production and its role in the international food trade system. The chapter will explore the domestic ramifications of food security as well as the international implications through imports and exports. Section 2 below presents a brief review of Russia's food security policy, noting that policy has evolved from an import substitution policy towards a policy that also generates agricultural and food exports. Section 3 presents an overview of the domestic ramifications of import substitution policy, focusing on pork, poultry, beef, raw milk, and fruit and vegetables. Section 4 looks at the international implications of Russia's protectionism, using pork and wheat as case studies. Section 5 provides an outlook to how Russia's food security policy, self-sufficiency, and import substitution will affect its role in the international agri-food system in the medium-term future.

2 Food Security, Self-Sufficiency, and Import Substitution

This section provides an overview of Russia's food security policy, which has changed from import protectionism and food self-sufficiency exclusively to also generating agri-food exports for international markets. It is important to emphasise that Russia's food security policy does not signify a withdrawal from international food markets, and this theme will be further elaborated. Food security does signify a change in Russia's role in the international food trade system from mainly a food importer to an importer and exporter, and it does signify a change in trading partners in terms of countries and regions.

2.1 Russia's Food Security Doctrines

In reaction to the spike in world food prices in 2007–2008, food security emerged as a significant economic and political variable in Russia that affects food trade policy, international relations, and domestic agrarian policy.[4] The emergence of food security as a core component of food policy and as a political priority is important because it affects the way in which Russia interacts with the international agri-food market. Whereas during the Soviet period Russia was a large grain importer, in the 1990s Russia changed to a meat importer. In both periods, Russia's role as an importer was significant. Since 2000, food and agrarian policy has prioritised less dependence on food imports.

In Russia, the concept of food security extends beyond the generally accepted definition of 'food access, availability, food use and stability' as stated by the 1996 World Food Summit.[5] Specifically, food security does *not* refer to the origin of food as opposed to self-sufficiency which is sensitive to where food originates.[6] Rather, Russian policymakers place particular emphasis on reducing food import dependency and therefore use the terms food security and food self-sufficiency synonymously.[7] Whereas many countries are protectionist on agricultural imports, and several nations have explicit food security policies, Russia is unique in that food security and food self-sufficiency are conflated, whereas in the literature the two terms are distinct.[8] Also unique is that since at least 2009 Russia's food security has explicit connections to national security, more so than in Western countries.[9]

An indicator of the seriousness with which Russian policymakers approach food security was evidenced by the signing of Russia's first Food Security Doctrine in January 2010. The doctrine established specific self-sufficiency targets for several basic agricultural and food products, defined as the percentage of domestic production in the total supply of commodities. The original Food Security Doctrine was more than mere rhetoric, as policymakers repeatedly referred to the doctrine and its standards for self-sufficiency to guide food and agrarian policy. That said, the Food Security Doctrine was not hard protectionism, as the dollar value of food imports into Russia continued to increase during 2010–2013. The original doctrine acquired extra importance when, on 7 August 2014, Russia implemented a food import ban on a wide range of agri-food products from the European Union (EU), the United States of America (USA), Norway, Canada, and Australia. The original ban was renewed several times and in late 2021 was extended through 2022. The food import 'countersanctions' were implemented by Russia in retaliation to Western sanctions over the Ukrainian crisis. It is important to note that countersanctions did *not* signal the end of Russia as a food importer. Instead, Russia changed food trade partners and began to trade more with China (see Chapter 7), within the Eurasian Economic Union (see Chapters 6 and 8), and the Middle East (see Chapter 9). Countersanctions did, however, bring decreased food trade between Russia and the European Union, and between Russia and the United States (see Chapter 10). Thus, neither the Food Security Doctrine nor the food embargo signalled Russia's withdrawal from the global food market, but rather a change with whom it traded.

The impact of the original Food Security Doctrine and countersanctions are beyond the scope of this chapter but have been discussed elsewhere.[10] The success of the original doctrine, plus the impressive growth in domestic food production, led to the signing of a new Food

Security Doctrine by President Putin in January 2020.[11] The new 2020 Doctrine explicitly mentions the expansion of agri-food exports, which marks a significant change in Russia's role in the international food system compared to the period leading up to 2018.[12] In addition to agricultural products, Russia is also among the major global producers of fish from wild fisheries and aquaculture. The development of the fishery and aquaculture sectors is supported by the 'Strategy for Development of Agriculture and Fisheries Through 2030', which was approved by Prime Minister Mikhail Mishustin and published in April 2020.[13]

The Food Security Doctrine and various strategies for different commodities and products should be understood as having economic importance in that they impact domestic food production, and political importance in that they frame food trade interactions with other states. In terms of the theme of this book, these political acts define the nature of economic interactions and the underlying strategy of those interactions. Food security, self-sufficiency, and import substitution did not just occur accidentally or organically. They were deliberate policy choices by policymakers. Their decision reflected a calculation to enhance national security and as an appeal to rising nationalism in Russia. Those decisions impact Russia's international interactions and role in the global food system.

3 Domestic Ramifications of Food Security Policy

Food policy and its subcomponents have domestic and international dimensions. This section focuses on the domestic ramifications and provides an overview of the main agricultural import sectors which are targeted by Russia's food security policy. In particular, poultry, pork, beef, and raw milk are protected by Russia's food import ban against competition from producers in Western countries, while investments in those products are subsidised by the government. We also cover fruit and vegetables since they receive greater attention within the 2020 Food Security Doctrine. The basic takeaway is that for countersanctions and trade protectionism to work, domestic food production needs to increase, and the country needs to maintain or increase self-sufficiency for basic food groups.

3.1 Domestic Structure of Production

We start with a brief discussion of the structure of food production. The change in the structure of production relates to food security because Russia has become increasingly dependent on output from agricultural organisations and agroholdings. This dependence in turn means that organisations and agroholdings receive most of the investment credit and subsidies from the state. Policymakers have an interest in a strong, vibrant large farm sector, both for domestic food production and export potential. The emergence of agroholdings has also led to a concentration of production in just a few companies for several commodities. In 2019, for example, the top 25 companies accounted for one-half of total meat production in the country, and 63 percent of meat production coming from agricultural organisations.[14] The rate of growth in meat production among the top 25 companies is nearly four times as fast as the rate of growth in meat production in general.

While not a direct outcome of food security policy, one of the notable characteristics in Russia's agrarian system is a change in the structure of production during the 2000s compared to the 1990s. Russia has three categories of food producers: agricultural enterprises (also called organisations), which have subcategories; households, again with different subcategories; and private farms. Whereas agricultural organisations were in decline during the 1990s, since 2000 there has been a clear and unmistakable trend towards dominance by agricultural organisations. In particular, among agricultural organisations, a specific subset of farms organisations called agroholdings is the largest, representing mega-farms often with several hundred thousand hectares each.[15] Agroholdings use industrial methods of production and are characterised by high vertical integration, reflecting that they own several stages of the supply chain. In some cases, agroholdings have full control over the whole food supply chain. During the 1990s, households accounted for more than 50 percent of the ruble value of agricultural production. Household production declined in volume and relative contribution after 2000, however, and by 2019 agricultural organisations accounted for 58 percent of Russia's agricultural production, while the contribution from household production decreased to 28 percent (based on ruble value). Overall, during the 2000–2019 period, the ruble value of agricultural production increased more than fivefold, with the value of production from agricultural organisations leading the way. Thus, a distinct positive is increased volume and value of production from agricultural organisations; on the other hand, food security and food self-sufficiency have increased vulnerability to the financial and production health of agricultural organisations.

Turning to specific commodities, poultry production has always been dominated by large agricultural organisations who have on average about 320,000 chickens per organisation.[16] Organisations' share in production increased since 1996 from 60 percent up to 92 percent in 2019, thereby decreasing the importance of households, which have, on average, 33 chickens. Concurrently, national poultry production increased from about 1 million tonnes to 6.7 million tonnes. Of particular note is the extreme concentration of production by a handful of agroholding companies. In 2018, for example, the top 20 poultry companies accounted for two-thirds of the production of Russia's broilers.[17]

Pork production is also dominated by agricultural organisations. By 2019, 87 percent of organisations had more than 10,000 pigs, while households have an average of 4.5 pigs (and a significant number of households have no pigs at all). Similar to poultry, the increasing importance of agricultural organisations in the pork sector led to strong growth in production, rising from 2 million tonnes in 1999 to 5 million tonnes in 2019. Similar to poultry, there is significant concentration. In 2018, the top 20 pig raising companies accounted for 56 percent of the nation's pork production.[18] There has also been a geographical structural shift. The expansion of domestic pork production was accompanied by a regional shift from the Southern Federal District to the Central Federal District. Since 2006, pork production has been increasingly concentrated in Belgorod, an oblast about 600 km south of Moscow that accounts for almost 20 percent of Russia's total pork production today. On the other hand, pork production in Krasnodar Krai and Rostov Oblast in the Southern Federal District has decreased significantly, two regions that previously were leading pork producers.

The production structure is different in the beef and milk sectors. Households average five cattle, of which three are typically milk cows; while medium-sized private farmers and individual entrepreneurs average 62 cattle, of which 32 are typically milk cows. Overall, households accounted for 54 percent of beef and 37 percent of raw milk production in 2019, although these percentages have been steadily decreasing in recent years.[19] Agricultural organisations average 785 cattle per farm, of which 330 are milk cows, accounting for 54 percent of raw milk and 36 percent of beef production in 2019. Total raw milk production has stagnated at around 30–31 million tonnes for many years, the share of raw milk produced by commercial farms has been increasing especially since 2014, accounting for 63 percent of production in 2019.[20]

Since the Russian government now includes vegetables and fruit in the 2020 Food Security Doctrine, we take a closer look at the structure of production for these two sectors. Unlike the meat sector, the production of fruit and vegetables did not experience a comparably strong decline during the early post-Soviet years. This occurrence might be explained by the high share of production from households, who did not experience the declines that large farms did, although more recently households' share is decreasing similar to meat production. Households accounted for about 60 percent of open ground/field vegetable production in 2019, while the share from agricultural organisations was 20 percent. Vegetable production from private farmers and individual entrepreneurs has also increased, reaching 20 percent of total production in 2019. The primary vegetable producing areas are located in the Southern Federal District and Central Federal District. These two districts account for about 50 percent of Russia's total area devoted to vegetable production. In contrast to open field vegetable production that is dominated by household production, large agricultural organisations dominate vegetable production in greenhouses. With the strong production growth observed since 2014, the share from agricultural organisations amounted to 70 percent of greenhouse vegetable production in 2019. Overall, greenhouse vegetable production has slightly increased in the recent years, accounting for about 14 percent of total vegetable production in 2019. The situation for fruit production is similar to open ground vegetable production. In 2019 households accounted for 65 percent of production, while agricultural organisations produced 28 percent.

3.2 Food Self-Sufficiency

The domestic dimension of Russia's food security includes a quest to improve food self-sufficiency. Figure 1 presents data on production, trade, and self-sufficiency for several commodities (see Fig. 1). First, for poultry and pork, self-sufficiency (calculated as the share of domestic production in consumption) has increased since 2010 due to higher production, while imports have decreased. According to Russian government data, the country attained self-sufficiency of 97 percent for poultry and 100

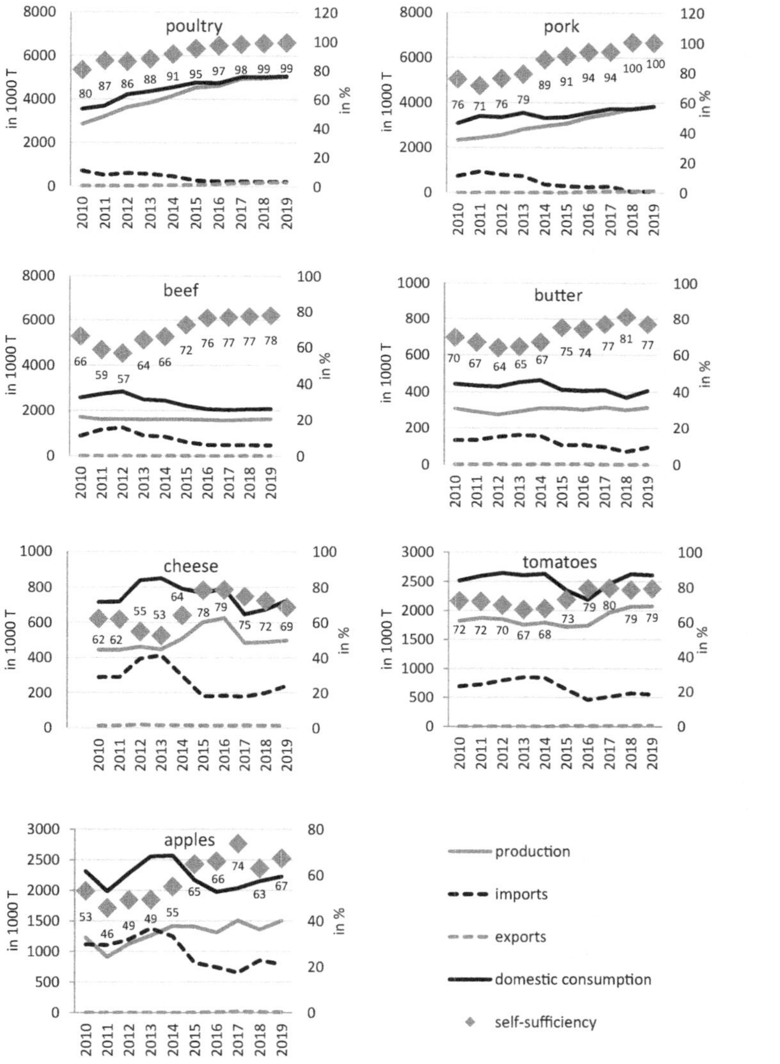

Fig. 1 Development of production, trade, and self-sufficiency for selected commodities (*Note* Production of poultry, pork, and beef refers to the production of slaughtered meat as only slaughtered meat is traded. *Sources* Authors' calculations from Rosstat data, various years; data from EMISS Gosudarstvennaia statistika, https://www.fedstat.ru/, accessed 20 August 2020; United States Department of Agriculture, Foreign Agricultural Service, 'PS&D: Production, Supply, and Distribution', https://apps.fas.usda.gov/psdonline/app/index.html#/app/advQuery, accessed 20 August 2020)

percent for pork despite a simultaneous increase in domestic consumption. Russia is on the cusp of turning into a net exporter for poultry and pork. Even though beef production has been in long-term decline, self-sufficiency for beef increased to 78 percent in 2019, the result of lower consumption and substitution by consumers. There is some evidence that beef production has started to slightly increase recently. Russia remains a net importer of beef, although imports are declining thanks to higher yields from pedigree animals.

Similar to beef, self-sufficiency for butter increased to 77 percent in 2019. Production remained constant, but domestic consumption decreased. In addition, the Russian market for dairy products (except cheese) was increasingly supplied by Belarus, which, as a member of the Eurasian Economic Union, has tax-free access to the Russian market. Despite Russia's recurrent temporary bans on the import of milk and dairy products originating from Belarus, (e.g. on milk in bulk from April 2018 until May 2019), evidence points to a continuing lively black trade of dairy products between Belarus and Russia.[21]

Unlike the butter market, Russia's cheese market was heavily affected by the import ban implemented in 2014, which led to the strong decrease in cheese imports. In contrast, the Russian cheese market could not be supplied by Belarus, and consequently domestic consumption of cheese in Russia decreased. Although the domestic production of cheese strongly increased in the aftermath of the food ban against Western countries, it soon started to decrease again, which was accompanied by strong decreases in domestic cheese consumption as well. Thus, self-sufficiency of cheese varies substantially, amounting to between 70 and 80 percent. Those developments could be linked to the well-known problems with cheese quality, resulting specifically from the use of vegetable fats as a substitute for milk fat, which is not sufficiently available in Russia. This prompted the Russian government to take measures to reduce the mixing of vegetable oils with dairy products. In particular, the reduced tax for palm oil was abolished and the value-added tax was increased to 20 percent in July 2019. In addition, new labelling rules were implemented, requiring information on the use of vegetable fats, especially palm oil, to be provided on the packaging.

Self-sufficiency in fresh apples, the most popular fruit in Russia, rose to about 80 percent in 2019. Apple imports heavily declined following the 2014 Russian food import ban, as large amounts of apples originating from Poland could no longer be supplied to the Russian market. We also observe a strong increase in the self-sufficiency of tomatoes, rising to about 80 percent in 2019. Tomatoes are among the most commonly consumed vegetables in Russia, boosted by output from greenhouses. As domestic tomato production has risen, tomato imports from Turkey have decreased, and since 2016 Russia has placed a quota on the volume of tomato imports from Turkey.

The point of this discussion is that for several basic commodities, domestic production increased and the level of self-sufficiency rose. In that respect, the food self-sufficiency policy has been successful, although we note that those basic commodities do not represent the full spectrum of consumer demand. It is, therefore, a rather narrow definition of success. Further, and more important as far as this book is concerned, an increase in self-sufficiency does not mean that Russia has withdrawn from the global food market. We turn next to the international dimension of food security in the section below.

4 International Ramifications of Food Security Policy

The fact that food security (in the Russian variant), food self-sufficiency, and import substitution lie at the protectionist end of the trade spectrum does not mean that Russia has withdrawn from being a significant player in the global food trade system. Russia continues to play an important role as a food importer, and despite food security policy the dollar value of its agri-food imports exceeded the dollar value of its agri-food exports until 2020. Chapter 1 in this book explains how Russia remains active in the global food market, and Chapters 6, 7, 8, and 9 show that Russia's agri-food trade is increasing vis-à-vis several different regions of the world as well as individual (non-western) countries. Further, as noted above, Putin's May 2018 decree and the 2020 Food Security Doctrine aspire to increase Russia's role as an agri-food exporter. Russia already has led the world in wheat exports in six of the seven agricultural years since 2014. That said, there is no doubt that food security policy has affected Russia's foreign food trade, indicated at the macro-level by a decrease in the dollar value of food imports since 2014 and the introduction of the food ban. Some of the reduction is due to the 2014–2015 recession, and since then lower import values are due to changes in consumers' buying habits and preferences, the importation of food from lower-cost nations, as well as import substitution. The purpose of this section is to explore in more detail the impact of food security policy on foreign food trade. We use pork as a case study for imports, and grain as a case study for exports.

4.1 *Imports: Pork Trade*

Russia's pork sector illustrates the way in which food security and its protectionism along with import substitution affect trade relations and more broadly Russia's role in the international food trade system.[22] For pork, increased domestic production, concerns over sanitary and health conditions and additives, and political considerations have led to a significant decrease in pork imports. Not only has the volume of pork decreased, but the composition of the countries of Russian pork imports has changed significantly as the country's pork import policy was modified (see Fig. 2).

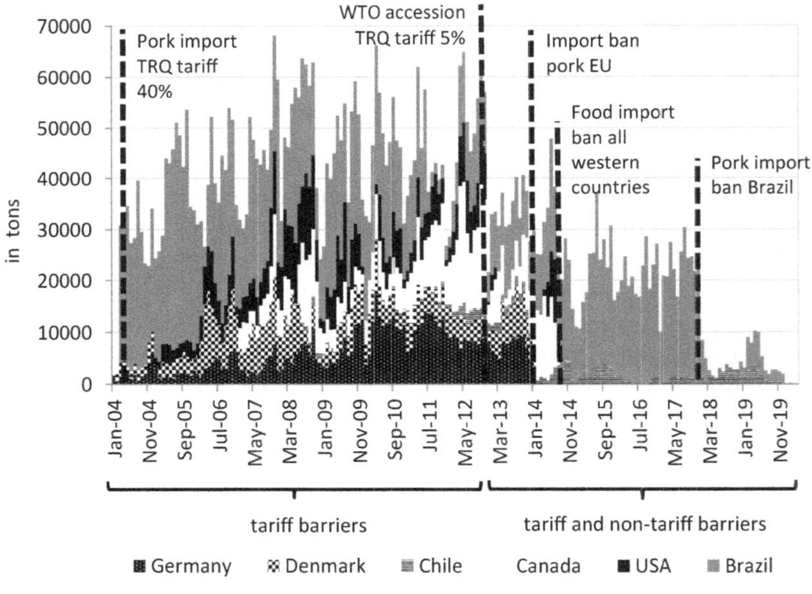

Fig. 2 Structure of Russia's pork imports and trade policies (*Sources* Linde Götz and Tinoush Jaghdani, 'Russia's agricultural import substitution policy: Price volatility effects on the pork supply chain', 57th Annual Conference of the German Association of Agricultural Economists, München, Germany, 13–15 September 2017; ITC, 'Trade Map', n.d. https://www.trademap.org/, accessed 20 August 2020)

Protectionism for the pork sector began in 2003 with the introduction of a tariff-rate quota (TRQ), with an in-quota tariff of 40 percent and a prohibitive out-of-quota tariff of 68 percent. Poultry and beef were also subject to TRQs. For pork, the TRQ began at 500,000 tonnes although it was marginally reduced over time, falling to 472,000 tonnes in 2011. This policy was in effect until August 2012, when the in-quota tariff was reduced to 0 percent and the out-of-quota tariff to 65 percent, while the quota was reduced to 400,000 tonnes (exclusive of trimmings, which add another 30,000 tonnes) as a condition of Russia's accession to the World Trade Organization (WTO).[23] During this time, Russia's pork imports primarily originated from Germany, Denmark, Canada, the United States, and Brazil.

The reduction in Russia's in-tariff quota and the rise in domestic production led to a decrease in pork imports following entry into the WTO. In addition, non-tariff barriers, such as sanitary and phytosanitary measures and technical barriers to trade, were increasingly applied to reduce pork imports. As an example, since December 2012, selected pork exporting companies in Germany were banned by the Russian government and were no longer allowed to export pork to Russia. This ban was extended to all companies located in Bavaria, North Rhine-Westphalia, and Lower Saxony in February 2013. *Rossel'khoznador*, Russia's Federal Service for Veterinary and Phytosanitary Surveillance, justified these interventions by pointing to non-compliance with Russia's phytosanitary and hygiene standards.

In January 2014, pork exports from the European Union to Russia were completely banned due to the outbreak of the African swine fever in the Baltic countries.[24] In addition, pork imports from Germany and Denmark completely stopped. Then, in August 2014, pork exports from all Western countries to Russia were banned as a result of the agricultural import ban imposed as countersanctions because of the Ukrainian crisis. Consequently, pork imports from Canada and the United States were blocked as well and Russia replaced those suppliers by importing almost exclusively from Brazil and small quantities from Chile. In December 2017, Russia imposed a ban on pork imports originating from Brazil. *Rossel'khoznadzor* justified those restrictions by citing food safety concerns resulting from the reported presence of the feed additive ractopamine.[25] Although the import ban against Brazil was lifted in November 2018, selected pork production plants in Brazil remained banned.[26] Subsequently, pork imports from Brazil did not recover to the pre-ban level.

Since 2014, Russia's agricultural import ban against Western countries has been extended several times and is currently valid until the end of 2022. As a result, Russia's pork imports from Western nations decreased to zero.

In 2020, the tariff rate quota for pork was abandoned altogether and replaced by a flat 25 percent tariff on all pork imports. The combination of higher domestic production and the import tariff led to an overall decline in pork imports. During 2018–2019, Russia imported about 100,000 tonnes of pork annually, but during the first half of 2020 the volume of imported pork declined to just over 1,000 tonnes.[27] Thus, Russia's global role as a pork importer has changed. A similar situation occurred with poultry, although we do not discuss that commodity here, but the same dynamics were at work: food security and protectionism, import substitution, and a healthy dose of politicised trade, all of which contributed to self-sufficiency and a significant decline in poultry imports.

4.2 Exports: Grain Trade

Perhaps the best example of Russia's new role in the international agri-food trade system is its emergence as a major grain exporter. Through the 2019/2020 agricultural year, Russia led the world in the volume of wheat exports in five of the past six years and was on track to lead again in the 2020/2021 agricultural year on the strength of the second largest harvest in post-Soviet history. An overview of grain production, imports and exports, and export share is shown in Fig. 3.

In contrast to pork and other meat products, Russia's grain sector is not protected by food security or trade policies. Grain imports have decreased to almost nothing (see Chapters 2 and 10 in this book). But concerns over food security continue to influence grain trade policy nonetheless through wheat export restrictions, which is to say that Russia is not a completely free trader. Its trade restrictions on grain trade at various times point to the fact that Russia's international role in global grain trade is subject to domestic food security concerns.

Russia has a history of restricting wheat exports as a crisis policy measure that aims to stabilise domestic prices, counteract food price inflation, and dampen feed prices. In response to the spike in global commodity prices in 2007–2008, the Russian government restricted grain exports through an export tax of up to 40 percent over concerns that exports would try to maximise their profits at the cost to domestic food

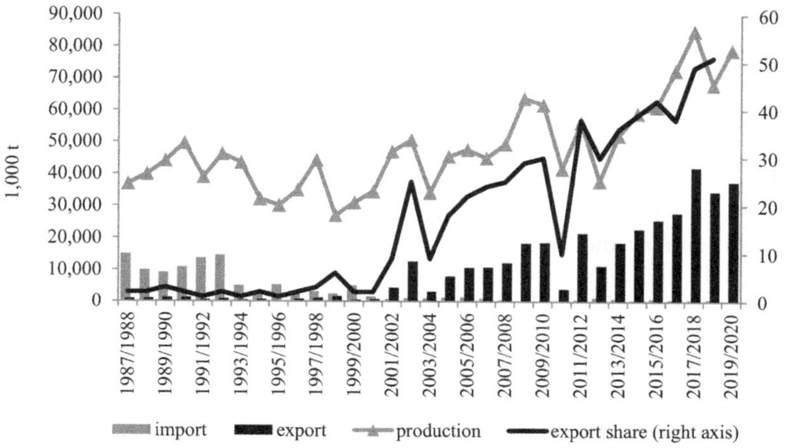

Fig. 3 Production, imports, exports, and export share for wheat in Russia (*Note* Until 1991 wheat production of the Russian Socialist Federative Soviet Republic. The values for 2019/2020 represent predictions (*Source* United States Department of Agriculture, Foreign Agricultural Service, 'PS&D: Production, Supply, and Distribution', https://apps.fas.usda.gov/psdonline/app/index.html#/app/advQuery, accessed 20 August 2020)

security. When Russia's wheat production was hit by serious drought and heat in 2010, leading to a loss of 30 percent of the harvest on average, a complete ban on grain exports was implemented from August 2010 to July 2011. In 2015, the devaluation of the ruble during 2014–2015 prompted the Russian government to establish a grain export tax of 15 percent with an additional payment of 7.5 Euro per tonne in order to prevent a surge in wheat exports. The intent was to prevent domestic shortages and high food inflation.

Finally, in January 2020 the government announced that going forward it may implement a grain export quota during the second half of an agricultural year (January–June), depending on conditions. Russia is not the only country to use export quotas, and ordinarily governments would not be concerned about food shortages in the midst of the second largest harvest in post-Soviet history.[28] Therefore, the export quota suggests that concerns over food insecurity may be more political than physiological.[29] For 2020, Russia's grain export quota was set at

7 million tonnes starting in April, limiting the export of grain to non-member states of the Eurasian Economic Union to June 2020.[30] The export quota was not well received by grain exporters who complained about the loss of revenue. In addition, the Russian government placed export bans on sunflower seed, rice, barley, and corn starting in April 2020 to the end of June countries outside the EAEU, even though no domestic shortages were reported. In 2021, the export quota on wheat began in January and extended to the end of June.

5 Outlook

Food security policy, self-sufficiency, and import substitution have guided domestic food policy for more than a decade. They are unlikely to go away anytime soon, as witnessed by the adoption of the 2020 Food Security Doctrine. Further, food security considerations affect agri-food imports and exports as the discussion in the previous section illuminated. Thus, food security frames international interactions, influences trade partners and relations with them, and defines the role that Russia plays in the international food system.

Going forward, we may expect continued emphasis on self-sufficiency. Russia is essentially self-sufficient in pork and poultry, while continuing as a net importer of beef and butter, as well as fruit and vegetables. The future development of those sectors strongly depends on whether their markets will continuously be shielded from international competition by Russia's food import ban. If the food import ban against Western countries would be removed, it can be expected that imports of beef and dairy products, as well as fruit and vegetables, would increase. If the food import ban remains and continues to protect domestic producers vis-à-vis international competition, production growth in those sectors can be expected to be more dynamic. However, Russia's food security policy is an element of foreign policy, and geopolitics will decide whether the Russian food import ban is sustained or abolished.[31]

In terms of food exports, short of catastrophic events such as megadrought or years of anomalous heat, we expect Russia to remain a strong wheat exporter.[32] That said, Russia's wheat market remains challenged by large distances between the grain-producing regions and access points to the world market at the Black Sea and also the Pacific Ocean.[33] Although Russia has significant potential to increase grain production, the question is to what extent additional grain production can be mobilised and transformed into grain export supply on the world market. Since grains, and in particular wheat, is the primary agricultural export product, the political will to catalyse the mobilisation of grain exports by financing investments in transport and port infrastructure and subsidising the recultivation of land is high. However, growing livestock production will increase domestic demand for grains and thus reduce the grain export potential. Nonetheless, given the large additional grain production potential, a rather weak ruble, and strong political support for upscaling grain transport infrastructure for domestic and international trade, it can be expected that wheat exports will further increase, and Russia will continue to be among the dominant wheat exporters in the world. However, continuing restrictions of wheat exports by the Russian government, and increasing domestic livestock production may moderate wheat export growth.

The bottom line is that food security has not prevented Russia from playing a major role in the international food trade system, and that is likely to remain true. We expect Russia to continue its role as an importer of certain raw products for which it may not attain self-sufficiency (as well as the importation of packaged and processed foods ready for immediate consumption). And we expect Russia to maintain and expand its role as an agri-food exporter to more than 100 countries in the world. Russia as a player in the global food system is here to stay, even with protectionist food security policies.

Notes

1. Tleubayev Alisher, Tinoush Jaghdani, Linde Götz, and Miranda Svanidze, 'The effects of trade policy on domestic dairy market: the case of Russian food import ban on regional cheese market integration in Russia', International Conference of Agricultural Economists, 28 July–2 August 2018, Vancouver, Canada. Available at https://ageconsearch.umn.edu/record/277373?ln=en.
2. See Vasyl Kvartiuk and Thomas Herzfeld, 'Redistributive Politics in Russia: The Political Economy of Agricultural Subsidies', *Comparative Economic Studies*, https://doi.org/10.1057/s41294-020-00131-2, August 2020. Accessed at https://link.springer.com/content/pdf/10.1057/s41294-020-00131-2.pdf. Accessed 2 November 2020.
3. See Stephen K. Wegren, 'Can Russia's Food Exports Reach $45 Billion in 2024? *Post-Communist Economies* 32, no. 2 (2020): 147–75.

4. See Stephen K. Wegren, Alexander Nikulin, and Irina Trotsuk, *Food Policy and Food Security: Putting Food on the Russian Table* (Lanham, MD and London, UK: Lexington Books, 2018).
5. Food and Agriculture Organisation, 'Rome Declaration on World Food Security and World Food Summit Plan of Action', World Food Summit, 13–17 November 1996. http://www.fao.org/3/w3613e/w3613e00.htm. Accessed 2 November 2020.
6. Stephen K. Wegren and Christel Elvestad. 'Russia's Food Self-Sufficiency and Food Security', *Post-Communist Economies* 30, no. 5 (2018): 565–87.
7. Stephen K. Wegren, Alexander Nikulin, and Irina Trotsuk, 'The Russian Variant of Food Security', *Problems of Post-Communism* 64, no. 1 (2017): 47–62; and Stephen K. Wegren, Frode Nilssen, and Christel Elvestad, 'The Impact of Russian Food Security Policy on the Performance of the Food System', *Eurasian Geography and Economics* 57, no. 6 (2016): 671–99.
8. Jennifer Clapp, 'Food Self-Sufficiency: Making Sense of It, and When It Makes Sense', *Food Policy* 66 (2017): 88–96.
9. Stephen K. Wegren, 'Russia's Food Policies and Foreign Policy', *Demokratizatsiya: The Journal of Post-Soviet Democratization* 18, no. 3 (2010): 189–207.
10. Wegren and Elvestad, 'Russia's Food Self-Sufficiency and Food Security: An Assessment'; Wegren, Nilssen, and Elvestad, 'The Impact of Russian Food Security Policy on the Performance of the Food System'; and Stephen K. Wegren, 'Effects of Russia's Food Embargo After 5 Years', *Russian Analytical Digest* no. 241 (November 2019): 6–10.
11. United States Department of Agriculture, Foreign Agricultural Service, 'New Food Security Doctrine Adopted', GAIN Report RS2020-0003. 4 February 2020. www.fas.usda.gov/data. Accessed 18 August 2020. The food self-sufficiency targets in the 2020 Food Security Doctrine were slightly increased from 80 to 90 percent for sugar and vegetable oils, and from 80 to 85 percent for fish products compared to the 2010 Food Security Doctrine. In addition, food security targets were introduced for vegetables, melons, and gourds (90 percent), fruit and berries (60 percent), and seeds of key domestic agricultural crops (75 percent). The food security targets defined in the Food Security Doctrine 2020 had already been reached for the majority of products in 2019. Exceptions were milk and dairy products (82 percent achieved versus the 90 percent target), fruit and berries (34 percent versus the 60 percent target), and seeds of key agricultural crops (85 percent of the target fulfilled for grain seeds).
12. These objectives are in line with the presidential decree 'On the National Goals and Strategic Tasks of the Development of the Russian Federation for the Period up to 2024'. Announced by President Putin in May

2018, the decree communicates the goal of increasing Russia's agricultural exports to $45 billion USD in 2024. 'Presidential Decree on national objectives and strategic tasks of Russian Federation's development in the period up to 2024'. 7 May 2018. http://extwprlegs1.fao.org/docs/pdf/rus182356E.pdf. Accessed 18 August 2020.

13. United States Department of Agriculture, Foreign Agricultural Service, 'Strategy for Development of Agriculture and Fisheries Through 2030', GAIN Report RS2020-0026, 14 May 2020. www.fas.usda.gov/data. Accessed 1 November 2020.
14. Tat'iana Kulistikova, 'Lidery rynka ukrepliaiut pozitsii', *Agroinvestor*, no. 6 (June 2020): 59.
15. For a discussion of the origins and operation of agroholdings, see Dmitri Rylko, Irina Khramova, Vasilii Uzun, and Robert Jolly, 'Agroholdings: Russia's New Agricultural Operators', in *Russia's Agriculture in Transition: Factor Markets and Constraints on Growth*, ed. Zvi Lerman (Lanham, MD: Lexington Books, 2008), 95–133; V. Ia. Uzun and N. I. Shagaida, *Agrarnaia reforma v postsovetskoi Rossii: Mekhanizmy i resul'taty* (Moscow: Delo, 2015), 174–82; Wegren, Nikulin, and Trotsuk, *Food Policy and Food Security: Putting Food on the Russian Table*, 16–20; and Stephen K. Wegren with Alexander Nikulin and Irina Trotsuk, *Russia's Food Revolution: The Transformation of the Food System* (London and New York: Routledge, 2021), 62–70.
16. Dmitry Prikhodko and Albert Davleyev, *Russian Federation: Meat Sector Review* (Rome, Italy: FAO, 2014). http://www.fao.org/3/a-i3533e.pdf. Accessed 18 August 2020.
17. Wegren, Nikulin, and Trotsuk, *Russia's Food Revolution*, 68.
18. Ibid.
19. See Stephen K. Wegren, 'Understanding the Decline of Smallholders in Contemporary Russia', *Outlook on Agriculture*, https://doi.org/10.1177/0030727020969201, October 2020.
20. Petrick and Götz identify access to value chains for milk marketing as a decisive factor for on-farm herd growth. Small household farms especially do not often have access to value chains that connect small producers with spatially dispersed consumers. Thus, household producers are restricted to milk marketing directly to end consumers, which is of rather limited size, and does not provide opportunities for herd growth. See Martin Petrick and Linde Götz, 'Herd Growth, Farm Organisation and Subsidies in the Dairy Sector of Russia and Kazakhstan', *Journal of Agricultural Economics* 70, no. 3 (2019): 789–811.
21. See Wegren, Nikulin, and Trotsuk, *Food Policy and Food Security: Putting Food on the Russian Table*, 160–62.
22. See Linde Götz and Tinoush Jaghdani, 'Russia's agricultural import substitution policy: Price volatility effects on the pork supply chain',

57th Annual Conference of the German Association of Agricultural Economists, München, Germany, 13–15 September 2017. Available at https://econpapers.repec.org/paper/agsgewi17/262003.htm.

23. United States Department of Agriculture, Foreign Agricultural Service, 'Customs Union Announces 2012 Meat and Poultry TRQs', GAIN Report RS1159, 28 December 2011. www.fas.usda.gov/data. Accessed 1 November 2020; United States Department of Agriculture, Foreign Agricultural Service, 'Russia 2018 Livestock and Products Annual', GAIN Report RS1828, 29 October 2018. www.fas.usda.gov/data. Accessed 1 November 2020.
24. In August 2016 the WTO declared that the Russian import ban on pork from the EU was illegal since it violates the WTO Agreement on the Application of Sanitary and Phytosanitary Measures.
25. Jose Roberto Gomes, 'Russia ban on Brazil meat exports may soon be reversed: ABPA', 21 November 2017. https://www.reuters.com/article/us-russia-brazil-livestock-idUSKBN1DL1B6. Accessed 2 November 2020.
26. Reuters, 'Russia removes restrictions on two Brazilian beef plants – regulator', 29 November 2019. https://cn.reuters.com/article/brazil-russia-meat-idINL1N2890HL. Accessed 2 November 2020.
27. Kommersant, 'Import svininy upal do minimal'nykh znachenii', 29 July 2020. https://agrovesti.net/news/indst/import-svininy-upal-do-minimal-nykh-znachenij.html. Accessed 1 November 2020.
28. See Linde Götz, Feng Qiu, Jean-Philippe Gervais, and Thomas Glauben, 'Export Restrictions and Smooth Transition Cointegration: Export Quotas for Wheat in Ukraine', *Journal of Agricultural Economics* 67, no. 2 (2016): 398–419.
29. The argument that concerns over food security may be manufactured for political purposes was first made in Wegren, Nikulin, and Trotsuk, 'The Russian Variant of Food Security'.
30. Ministry of Agriculture of the Russian Federation, 'The Russian Government approved the Ministry's of Agriculture initiative on the grain export quota', 3 April 2020. www.mcx.gov.ru/en/news/Russian-Government-approved-the-grain-export-quota/. Accessed 1 November 2020.
31. Stephen K. Wegren, Frode Nilssen, and Christel Elvestad, 'The Impact of Russian Food Security Policy on the Performance of the Food System', 671–99.
32. See Linde Götz, Ivan Duric, and Oleg Nivievskyi, 'Regional Price Effects of Extreme Weather Events and Wheat Export Controls in Russia and Ukraine', *Journal of Agricultural Economics* 67, no. 3 (2016): 741–63.
33. See Miranda Svanidze and Linde Götz, 'Determinants of spatial market efficiency of grain markets in Russia', *Food Policy* 89 (2019). https://doi.org/10.1016/j.foodpol.2019.101769; and Miranda Svanidze and Linde

Götz, 'Spatial market efficiency of grain markets in Russia: Implications of high trade costs for export potential', *Global Food Security* 21 (2019): 60–68.

Selected Bibliography

Clapp, Jennifer. 'Food Self-Sufficiency: Making Sense of It, and When It Makes Sense'. *Food Policy* 66 (2017): 88–96.

Götz Linde, Ivan Duric, and Oleg Nivievskyi. 'Regional Price Effects of Extreme Weather Events and Wheat Export Controls in Russia and Ukraine'. *Journal of Agricultural Economics* 67, no. 3 (2016): 741–63.

Götz, Linde, Feng Qiu, Jean-Philippe Gervais, and Thomas Glauben. 'Export Restrictions and Smooth Transition Cointegration: Export Quotas for Wheat in Ukraine'. *Journal of Agricultural Economics* 67 no. 2 (2016): 398–419.

Götz, Linde and Tinoush Jaghdani. 'Russia's Agricultural Import Substitution Policy: Price Volatility Effects on the Pork Supply Chain'. 57th Annual Conference of the German Association of Agricultural Economists, München, Germany, 13–15 September 2017. https://econpapers.repec.org/paper/ags gewi17/262003.htm.

Kvartiuk, Vasyl and Thomas Herzfeld. 'Redistributive Politics in Russia: The Political Economy of Agricultural Subsidies'. *Comparative Economic Studies*, https://doi.org/10.1057/s41294-020-00131-2, August 2020. https://link.springer.com/content/pdf/10.1057/s41294-020-00131-2.pdf.

Petrick, Martin and Linde Götz. 'Herd Growth, Farm Organisation and Subsidies in the Dairy Sector of Russia and Kazakhstan'. *Journal of Agricultural Economics* 70, no. 3 (2019): 789–811.

Prikhodko, Dmitry and Albert Davleyev. *Russian Federation: Meat Sector Review.* Rome, Italy: FAO, 2014.

Rylko, Dmitri, Irina Khramova, Vasilii Uzun, and Robert Jolly. 'Agroholdings: Russia's New Agricultural Operators'. In *Russia's Agriculture in Transition: Factor Markets and Constraints on Growth*, ed. Zvi Lerman. Lanham, MD: Lexington Books, 2008, 95–133

Svanidze, Miranda and Linde Götz. 'Determinants of Spatial Market Efficiency of Grain Markets in Russia'. *Food Policy* 89 (2019). https://doi.org/10.1016/j.foodpol.2019.101769.

Svanidze, Miranda and Linde Götz. 'Spatial Market Efficiency of Grain Markets in Russia: Implications of High Trade Costs for Export Potential'. *Global Food Security* 21 (2019): 60–8.

Tleubayev, Alisher, Tinoush Jaghdani, Linde Götz, and Miranda Svanidze. 'The Effects of Trade Policy on Domestic Dairy Market: The Case of Russian Food Import Ban on Regional Cheese Market Integration in Russia'. International

Conference of Agricultural Economists, 28 July-2 August 2018, Vancouver, Canada. https://ageconsearch.umn.edu/record/277373?ln=en.
United States Department of Agriculture, Foreign Agricultural Service, 'Strategy for Development of Agriculture and Fisheries Through 2030'. GAIN Report RS2020–0026, 14 May 2020.
United States Department of Agriculture, Foreign Agricultural Service, 'New Food Security Doctrine Adopted'. GAIN Report RS2020-0003, 4 February 2020.
United States Department of Agriculture, Foreign Agricultural Service, 'Russia 2018 Livestock and Products Annual'. GAIN Report RS1828, 29 October 2018.
United States Department of Agriculture, Foreign Agricultural Service, 'Customs Union Announces 2012 Meat and Poultry TRQs'. GAIN Report RS1159, 28 December 2011.
United States Department of Agriculture, Foreign Agricultural Service, 'Food Security Doctrine Adopted'. GAIN Report RS1008, 11 February 2010.
Wegren, Stephen K. 'Understanding the Decline of Smallholders in Contemporary Russia', *Outlook on Agriculture*, https://doi.org/10.1177/0030727020969201, October 2020.
Wegren, Stephen K. 'Can Russia's Food Exports Reach $45 Billion in 2024?'. *Post-Communist Economies* 32, no. 2 (2020): 147–75.
Wegren, Stephen K. 'Russia's Food Policies and Foreign Policy'. *Demokratizatsiya: The Journal of Post-Soviet Democratization* 18, no. 3 (2010): 189–207.
Wegren, Stephen K., Alexander Nikulin and Irina Trotsuk. *Russia's Food Revolution: The Transformation of the Food System*. London and New York: Routledge, 2021.
Wegren, Stephen K., Alexander Nikulin, and Irina Trotsuk. *Food Policy and Food Security: Putting Food on the Russian Table*. Lanham, MD and London, UK: Lexington Books, 2018.
Wegren, Stephen K., Alexander Nikulin, and Irina Trotsuk. 'The Russian Variant of Food Security', *Problems of Post-Communism* 64, no. 1 (2017): 47–62.
Wegren, Stephen K. and Christel Elvestad. 'Russia's food self-sufficiency and food security: an assessment'. *Post-Communist Economies* 30, no. 5 (2018): 565–87.
Wegren, Stephen K., Frode Nilssen and Christel Elvestad. 'The Impact of Russian Food Security Policy on the Performance of the Food System'. *Eurasian Geography and Economics* 57, no. 6 (2016): 671–99.

Open Access This chapter is licensed under the terms of the Creative Commons Attribution 4.0 International License (http://creativecommons.org/licenses/by/4.0/), which permits use, sharing, adaptation, distribution and reproduction in any medium or format, as long as you give appropriate credit to the original author(s) and the source, provide a link to the Creative Commons license and indicate if changes were made.

The images or other third party material in this chapter are included in the chapter's Creative Commons license, unless indicated otherwise in a credit line to the material. If material is not included in the chapter's Creative Commons license and your intended use is not permitted by statutory regulation or exceeds the permitted use, you will need to obtain permission directly from the copyright holder.

Chapter 5: Russia's Role in International Fish and Seafood Trade

Frode Nilssen

1 Introduction

This chapter examines Russia's role in the global seafood trade system over time and concludes with perspectives on its future role.[1] The chapter examines three periods of Russia's seafood production and trade: (1) the development of Soviet fishing industry; (2) the early post-Soviet period (1991–2001); and (3) the Putin period of consolidation. The last section of the chapter presents an outlook for the future role of Russia in global seafood trade. My analysis fits into the larger literature on the Russian government's dual concern for food security in the domestic market on the one hand and a desire for Western currency from export earnings on the other.[2] A key question is how Russia balances the tension between food security concerns and business interests related to foreign trade.

During the past 20 years Russia's seafood trade policy has emphasised both exports and a concern that domestic supplies are sufficient. During the presidency of Dmitrii Medvedev (2008–2012), some noticeable changes in seafood import policy were made following the introduction

F. Nilssen (✉)
Nord University Business School, Bodø, Norway
e-mail: frode.nilssen@nord.no

© The Author(s) 2022

S. K. Wegren and F. Nilssen (eds.), *Russia's Role in the Contemporary International Agri-Food Trade System*, Palgrave Advances in Bioeconomy: Economics and Policies,
https://doi.org/10.1007/978-3-030-77451-6_6

of the Food Security Doctrine in 2010. For example, during his presidency, the government increased control over the import of foodstuffs to Russia. Russia's seafood imports had grown substantially during 2000–2008. Under Medvedev, *Rossel'khoznadzor* developed a tight system of control over registered foreign food export companies and increased inspections of them. At the same time, new regulations and incentives related to control of seafood exports were introduced. Since Vladimir Putin reassumed the presidency of Russia in 2012, Russia's export of fish and seafood has been steadily growing. Both commercial interests and the Russian government have recently advocated for even higher levels of seafood exports.[3] In particular, Russia's seafood exports play an important role in the trade with the neighbouring regions such as the European Union (EU) and Asia. For example, through 27 December 2020, Russia exported $3.2 billion USD in food to the EU, of which fish and seafood accounted for $1.1 billion. To the same date, Russia exported $3.9 billion USD of food to China, of which $1.6 billion USD was fish and seafood.[4]

2 The Development of the Soviet-Russian Seafood Industry

Seafood has always represented an important dimension of the Russian food system. Looking at Russia as a whole, there are two main geographical areas for catches and one region for seafood trading. For seafood catches, the two areas are: (1) The Northwest Russian fishing industry, which focuses on cod fisheries in the Barents Sea and Northeast Atlantic. This industry exports seafood to Norway and other European countries such as Portugal, UK, Spain, and Germany. (2) In the Russian Far East, the main exportable seafood is Alaskan pollack to China, Japan, South Korea, and Vietnam. In the Far East, Russia has exclusive fishing rights to huge fish stocks, in particular Alaskan pollock. Pollock is one of the world's largest fisheries, with annual harvests ranging from 4 to 7 million metric tonnes annually in the North Pacific over the past decade. Management of this wild fish resource in the Pacific is a joint responsibility between the surrounding coastal states, the United States and Russia, although China, the Republic of Korea, Japan, and Poland also take part in the annual commission meetings as stakeholders.[5] Seafood imports to the Russian Far East region are modest, explained by the huge fish resources that Russia manages and controls in the area. Domestic demand for seafood in the Russian Far East is also limited by its relatively sparse population, just over 8.1 million people in 2019 in an area that spans more than 6.9 million square kilometres.[6]

(3) For seafood trading, traders in the European part of Russia import seafood, exploiting the supply void that was left by the former Soviet fishing industry. The main import business is centred around Moscow and St. Petersburg where large processing industries have evolved and thrived. Again, geographical proximity is an important factor for the choice of suppliers. A large amount of the seafood, primarily herring, mackerel, and farmed Atlantic salmon, was supplied by Norway while other northern European countries filled in with other seafood species and smaller amounts of salmon and herring.

During the first few decades of the Soviet period, the total seafood catch was relatively modest but there was a steady growth over the years, reaching 6.7 million tonnes of seafood in 1968, an increase of more than 600 percent compared to the 1 million tonne catch in 1913. The big increase came with the industrialisation of the fishing industry, characterised by massive building and use of large factory trawlers with large extractive and storage capacity.[7] Another important factor that enabled the huge growth in the fishing industry was extensive fishing in the open sea. As a result, the Soviet Union experienced an increase in its fish catch to more than 11 million metric tonnes at the apex of the Soviet fishing industry in the 1980s. The entire system was designed to support the Soviet home market, so seafood exports were very limited. The institutional setup was based on the Soviet planned economic principles. The whole industrial complex was one holistic entity structured into five huge seafood general directorates which complied with Gosplan's requirements for output.[8] There was, however, some minor trade of seafood, mainly shellfish (cold water prawns), and caviar that was sold by Soviet state trade organisations, often through foreign subsidiaries in selected countries. This institutional arrangement was coherent, albeit it involved a few faults, the most conspicuous of which was an emphasis on quantity over quality. Fishing vessels were awarded for fulfilling their plan obligation. Any additional delivery that exceeded the plan generated extra benefits for the fishermen and particularly the manager. The Soviet bonus system stimulated an emphasis on volumes rather than quality of the fish, a practice that today would make it difficult to engage in international trade. The primary goals of Soviet seafood policy were to reach per capita consumption of 25 kg of seafood and to support the needs of the Soviet military.

2.1 *The Early Post-Soviet Period (1991–2001)*

After the Soviet Union fell apart, the fishing industry in post-Soviet Russia changed substantially. In terms of structure there was almost total fragmentation, with fishing companies the most heavily affected. Russia's annual seafood harvest fell dramatically to between 3 and 5 million metric tonnes, although the total seafood catch increased gradually since the mid-1990s and continuing to 2019.[9] In the early post-Soviet period, the main geographical areas for the Russian fishing industry were: (1) the Russian Far East with the Sea of Okhotsk and Pacific ocean; (2) northwest Russia with the Bering Sea and Northeast Atlantic; and (3) the open high seas. Over the past ten years, the average volumes of the Russian seafood catch come from the Russian Far East (66 percent); Northwest Russia (12.5 percent); and high seas fisheries (14.4 percent).[10]

Being a coastal state represents an important prerequisite for the ability to balance the trade of fish on the global market. The United Nations Convention on the Law of the Sea paved the way for the establishment of 200-mile Exclusive Economic Zones (EEZ) for coastal states. According to this legal institution, most coastal states were given sovereign rights to exploit the most productive parts of the sea. The rights are defined by their geographical coastline. For Russia, this meant access to two of the most productive sea areas on the globe. In the Northwest, Russia shares sovereign rights to exploit the Atlantic cod fish stock with Norway. The management and quota distribution are made through the Joint Norwegian-Russian Fisheries Commission. The commission has a 50-year record of successful collaboration.

Most of the reduction in Russia's seafood catch during the early post-Soviet period can be explained by changes in the use of open seas fishing areas. The reason why distant fisheries were used less is due to the 200-mile EEZ, which excluded foreign countries from accessing these fishing grounds. As a consequence, many of the distant fishing grounds that Russia used to exploit earlier became significantly less accessible.[11] There are a few exceptions though, where some coastal states contract out parts of their quotas and receive a part of the catch in exchange. Russia has, notwithstanding, seen a large decrease in its fishing industry. In addition to the introduction of the EEZs by coastal states, many of the fish stocks in the open seas have decreased in size as a consequence of over-fishing.

In addition to reduced access to previous fisheries in open waters, during the early post-Soviet period the fishing industry struggled with low effectiveness and problems in the value chain in the Russian market. The institutions, or external working conditions of the fishing industry (the laws, regulations, economic institutions/banks etc.), changed dramatically compared to the Soviet planned system. Since institutions regulate and influence the behaviour of companies, institutional change also influences production and the flow of goods.[12] For example, price reform made operations incredibly expensive for newly privatised companies. Fuel costs increased more than ten times compared to the costs in the late Soviet period. Few incentives were established for fishermen to deliver their catch to the Russian market, and no barriers to export were established.

At the same time, Russian fish companies had incentives to deliver their seafood to nearby harbours. The incentives to export were found in the fact that Russia's land-based industry had problems finding money to pay for deliveries of seafood. Foreign fish buyers paid for fish upfront in Western currency, which was yet another attraction for the Russian fishing companies to export. This led to a situation where large amounts of high-value seafood were delivered directly to foreign ports in adjacent areas to the fishing grounds.

The alteration of behaviour among the fishing companies in the North-west Russian fishing complex illustrates the cumulative effect caused by changes in the use of distant fisheries. Over a ten-year period, from 1990 to 2000, Russian companies shifted their strategy almost 100 percent. While around 85 percent of their total catch was taken from the high seas in 1990, only 6 percent was caught in these areas in 2000. Russia's fish catch to harvesting in fishing grounds close to EEZ waters close to harbours. Russia's fish catch from the Northeast Atlantic increased from about 15 percent of the catch in 1990 to 94 percent in 2000. Table 1 shows the distribution of Russia's fish catch by fishing area and the volume of catches during 1990–2000.

There are two aspects of particular interest to the decrease of the distant fisheries. The first was an increase in Russia's seafood exports, and the second was a direct result of the sudden transition from state-owned to privately-held fishing companies. The newly established, privately-held companies needed quick earnings and lower expenditures on fuel and other significant operating costs. These needs combined with few restrictions on trade.[13] The same situation was present in the Russian Far East, where the new private companies exported large volumes of white fish to Japan, China, and Korea at the expense of deliveries to the Russian home market.[14]

Table 1 Changes in Russia's fishing pattern: High seas and other non-Russian areas vs. regional Russian EEZ Waters

	1990	*1991*	*1992*	*1993*	*1994*	*1995*	*1996*	*1997*	*1998*	*1999*	*2000*
Catches in other fishing grounds (%)	85.3	56.8	28.8	21.9	21.7	11.1	7.8	9.2	8.3	11.7	6.0
Catches in the NE Atlantic (%)	14.7	43.2	71.2	78.1	78.3	88.9	92.2	90.8	91.7	88.3	94.0
Catches in other fishing grounds	1,359	831	347	198	157	73.4	52	57,3	48	85	50.8
Catches in the NE Atlantic	234	633	858	707	568	589	617	566	529	639	792.2
Total catches by the Northwest Russian fleet	1,593	1,464	1,205	905	725	662.4	669	623.3	577	724	843

Note Catches are in thousand tonnes
Sources Data from "Sevryba", Russian Academy of Sciences; *Rosrybolovstvo*, various years; and author's compilation

Other obstacles also affected Russia's fishing industry. Fuel was expensive and in short supply. Russia's fishing fleet was old and very inefficient. According to Deputy Minister Ilya Shestakov, the head of *Rosrybalovstvo*, Russia's federal fishing agency, more than 80 percent of the fishing fleet is older than 20 years. The fuel consumption of old Soviet trawlers was around three times higher compared to a typical Western trawler. Therefore, it became important for newly privatised Russian fishing companies to reduce idle transportation as much as possible. In sum, the privatisation of the fishing industry in Russia drove some of the fishermen towards deliveries to Western markets, in particular in Russia's Northwest and the Russian Far East.[15]

While Russia's privately-held fishing companies searched for alternative solutions to renew and modernise their fleets, investors from Western countries were ready to offer a solution. A special leasing arrangement, called the bareboat charter (BBC), was introduced. BBC arrangements are generally a leasing contract with an option to buy the vessel at the end of the contract period. A key aspect of the BBC contracts is that they are managed by the Western management company who controls all transactions related to the leased vessel. As it applied to Russia, in order to maintain the control of cash flow the leased fishing vessel was required to deliver all its catches to designated processors in the West (including Norway). The Western management company was then responsible for paying the lease in line with the contract requirements, as well as paying for operating expenses in accordance with the bilateral agreement. At the end of the lease, the Russian company could purchase the vessel. Western sellers saw the BBC contracts as the best way of selling fishing vessels to Russian fishing companies. In practice, the BBC contract was organised as an instalment-based purchase arrangement. As the number of BBC contracts increased gradually from 1994 onwards, and as more of seafood catches were delivered to Western processors the volumes of seafood deliveries to Russia's domestic market sank gradually for the next 10 years or so to around 3.2 million tonnes.

The problem for Russia's political and administrative bodies at the regional and the federal level was that deliveries of fish from the BBC vessels were locked into Western buyers by contract. The consequence was that a large percentage of attractive fish catches from Northwest Russian and the Russian Far East fishing fleets were delivered directly to nearby foreign markets. This was basically the export of valuable whitefish—Atlantic cod in the Northwest and Alaska Pollack in the Far East.

The operation provided no benefit for the Russian government in terms of taxes or foreign currency. At the same time, the domestic supply of seafood decreased sharply, and prices increased, thus reducing demand even more.

While domestic deliveries decreased, Russia's seafood exports remained stable at around 1.2 million tonnes. The deficiency in domestic supplies of seafood opened an opportunity for foreign exporters who could sell to Russia. As a consequence, Russia's annual import of seafood more than doubled from 424 thousand tonnes in 1990 to 979 thousand tonnes in 2005, when it stabilised at around 1 million tonnes through 2013.[16] The majority of the imported fish was whole frozen, but the import of fresh fish (mainly farmed Atlantic salmon from Norway) also increased. A corresponding new Russian processing industry thrived on seafood imports. Seafood imports did not, however, manage to compensate fully for the shortage in deliveries to the domestic market. Total supplies to the domestic market dropped from about 3.3 million tonnes in the mid-1990s to a record low level of 2.5 million tonnes in 2005. As a rough estimate, this volume translates to an average per capita seafood consumption of around 17.5 kg. The estimate is based on round weight data of the fish, which means that the actual average consumption was much lower, maybe around 14–15 kg per capita.[17]

Russia's role in the international seafood trade system during the early post-Soviet period was affected by the absence of trade protectionism. The main characteristics of Russia's engagement in the global seafood system may rather be seen as two detached arms: one dealing with the export of valuable whitefish to geographically close markets. The other arm was dealing with the import of seafood, taking advantage of the market demand for high-quality seafood. The Russian food market in the European part of Russia revealed a large demand for seafood that was traditional in the Russian diet, primarily herring and mackerel and later substantial amounts of farmed Atlantic salmon.

2.2 *The Putin Period of Consolidation*

When Vladimir Putin assumed the presidency of Russia in March 2000, emphasis was placed on consolidation and strengthening the central government and Russia itself. One of the priorities was addressing the food situation.[18] During the 1990s, the volume and value of national food production had decreased substantially. At the same time, both the value and volume of food imports—mostly meat and meat products—increased significantly during the decade. Food imports declined in 1998–2000 due to severe devaluation of the ruble before starting to increase again in 2001 (see Chapter 1).[19] Likewise, imports of seafood rose as well. For Russia's fishing industry, the value of seafood imports rose from $209.8 million USD in 2001 to $956.9 million USD in 2005. Interestingly, the majority of Russia's imported seafood came from Norway, a small neighbouring country that has only 5 million inhabitants and an annual seafood production of 2.75 million tonnes. Norway has exclusive rights to a long and sheltered coastline and adjacent 200-mile EEZ. The EEZ is one of the most productive sea areas, which explains Norway's production capacity and why the country is one of the world's largest seafood exporters. During 1991–2005, Norway supplied about 45–50 percent of Russia's seafood imports.

One of the species that increased the value of Norway's seafood exports to Russia was farmed Atlantic salmon. The volume of Norwegian salmon exported to the European part of Russia increased significantly from 9 tonnes in 1998 to 50 tonnes in 2005, and reached a record high of 182 tonnes in 2012.[20] Overall, the value of Russia's seafood imports from Norway grew from $96.8 million USD in 2001, to $450.3 million USD in 2005, and to $1.1 billion USD in 2013.[21] Imports of high-value fish like salmon have a larger impact on import statistics in value than volume, naturally. Frozen herring, a low-priced and highly nutritional fish that is popular in all social strata in Russia, constitute the largest share of frozen imported fish in terms of volume. This situation is neither intended nor seen as desirable from the Russian government's point of view. The political intention remains to reduce seafood imports and lower Russia's dependency on Western countries.

For reasons already explored, seafood exports are difficult to control but from January 2009 a prohibition was enacted on bareboat charter arrangements (BBC) in the Russian EEZ.[22] In January 2010, the Food Security Doctrine defined and gave direction to food independence and food security for the Russian Federation.[23] In the doctrine, food independence and food security refer to Russian sufficiency and economic availability of safe foodstuffs for every citizen. Both independence from international supplies and availability of fish for the average Russian are both important dimensions for Russian food policy and as a basis for the development plans for the fisheries and agricultural complexes.[24] The doctrine defines how much of supply should be supplied to the Russian market from domestic production. According to the 2010 doctrine, Russia's fish catch should account for no less than 80 percent of total consumption of seafood.[25]

Two other important measures were introduced to develop the Russian fishing industry and secure a high level of self-sufficiency. The first was a 'Concept for the Development of the Fishing Industry of the Russian Federation to 2020'. The Concept was approved by governmental order No. 1518 on 8 September 2003. The Concept laid out the principles for how the Russian fishing industry should develop in order to regain an important role as a pillar in the food system.

The second measure was a Federal State Program entitled the 'Development of the Fisheries Complex', approved by the government on 15 April 2014 by Resolution No. 314.[26] The 2014 programme was subsequently amended and revised in March 2018 (Resolution No. 380) and March 2019 (Resolution No. 324). In March 2020, the most recent version of the state programme for the development of fisheries was adopted (Resolution No. 394).[27]

Similar to agriculture and other branches of the economy, a 'Concept' carries more long-term and macro goals, leaving specifics to the state programme. Thus, the state programme was more operational and contained monetary allocations for various policy goals. According to the 2020 version, the programme will run through 2024 and it envisions expenditures of more than R70 billion from 2020 through 2024. During the entire duration of the state programme, 2013–2024, more than R154 billion will be spent. In addition, domestic production should meet 85 percent of demand, and annual per capita seafood consumption should reach 23.1 kg by 2024.

The programme postulated other goals as well. One goal was directed towards the renewal of the fishing fleet and land-based processing industry by introducing an investment fishery quota. The fishery quota is an arrangement whereby a relative share of the total fishing quota for more valuable species is allocated to actors on the condition that they actually carry out renewal projects in the fishing industry. Basically, Russia's government is allocating 20 percent of the total allowable catch (TAC) for companies willing to invest in new vessels, which must be built in domestic shipyards.[28] The total allowable catch (TAC) is a restricting factor because it sets an upper limit for a country's maximum catch of wild fish species. The establishment of a TAC (which is an annual process) is based on recommendations from ICES (International Council for the

Exploration of the Sea), and a joint decision between the stakeholders (different states).

The initiative from *Rosrybolovstvo* for the investment quota has encouraged fishing companies to spend their money in Russia, that is, to use Russian fishing wharfs for construction of new fishing vessels, and to increase the effectiveness and capacity of the Russian fishing industry and fleet. This is considered as an important dimension of the social and economic contribution to Russia from the fisheries sector. A large part of the fishing fleet is still old and obsolete, and a renewal is necessary. From the perspective of Russia's policymakers, it is desirable that fishing companies invest in Russia, and also that they deliver their catch to Russian processing companies. Together, these key federal support systems, along with a substantial number of other governmental measures, were introduced to improve the productivity of the Russian fishing industry and to secure a much-needed renewal for both the land-based processing industry and the fishing fleet.

In a broad sense, from the perspective of the Russian government, the state programme since 2013 has been successful. The overarching goal—to secure stable and sufficient supplies of seafood to the domestic market without becoming too dependent on any one foreign supplier country or organisation—was achieved. A reduction in seafood imports was further amplified by the food embargo in 2014. At the same time, Russia's seafood exports have continued to grow substantially as illustrated in Fig. 1. The explanation for the increase in exports is twofold: (1) Russia's seafood catch has grown gradually and has generated a surplus that allows for an increase in exports; and (2) Russia's fishing companies have focused on key target markets in the Far East such as China, the Republic of Korea, and Japan. Figure 1 indicates trends in Russia's total catch, seafood imports and exports, domestic supply balance during 2000–2019.

3 The Food Embargo and Its Impact on Russia's Global Seafood Trade

Following the introduction of the Food Security Doctrine in 2010, Russia started to govern seafood imports and exports more systematically. The key goals proceeded along two lines: (1) to reduce dependence on large volumes of seafood from a few, dominating countries; and (2) to achieve the goal of self-sufficiency for seafood, defined by the Russian government

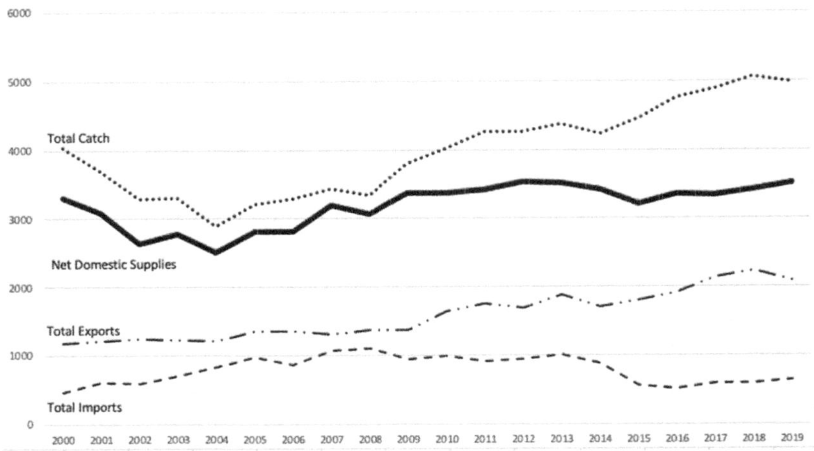

Fig. 1 Russia's total catch, trade, and domestic supply balance, 2000–2019 (1,000 Tonnes) (*Sources* Author's compilation based on data from *Rosrybolovstvo* and Rosstat)

as no less than 80 percent of domestic consumption should be supplied by Russian fishermen and the domestic seafood industry. The 2020 Food Security Doctrine and the State Programme for the Development of Fishing increased the threshold to 85 percent. The first point has concrete implications for the supply structure, that is, who may supply seafood to Russia's domestic market. The 2010 Food Security Doctrine gave power to *Rossel'khoznadzor*, the Russian food safety authority, along with three important power bases: legitimacy, expertise, and coercive power.[29] *Rossel'khoznadzor* has formal independence as an executive expert and has control over the veterinary field, including over aquatic resources.[30]

Rossel'khoznadzor was established in 2004 and immediately started the process of looking into critical issues related to suppliers' (countries) structure and capacity. As the main foreign supplier of seafood to Russia, Norwegian authorities received a letter from *Rossel'khoznadzor* already in 2005, requesting a wide range of information about production systems, capacity, and technical food safety regimes in Norway. By the end of 2007, the number of approved Norwegian exporters was reduced significantly, even as the volume of seafood exports continued to rise. The 2010 Food Security Doctrine provided a formal instrument for Russian authorities to curtail the dominant position that several food exporting countries had in the Russian market, but more time to achieve actual results was evidently required. In 2012, for example, Norway alone had a 45 percent market share in seafood exports to Russia. According to the head of *Rossel'khoznadzor*, Sergei Dankvert, reliance on one supplier is an unacceptable situation for Russia.[31]

Subsequent to the 2010 food doctrine, Russia became a member of the World Trade Organization (WTO) on 22 August 2012. By taking this step, there was an expectation that Russia would join the liberal global trading order and that barriers to entry to the Russian food market would be lowered. In the run-up to formal acceptance into the WTO, Russia had modified its laws and customs policies, made promises about reducing tariffs and non-tariff barriers, agreed to limit its subsidies to agriculture, and indicated a willingness to open certain sectors of its economy to competition (banking, insurance, automobiles).

The expected trade liberalisation from Russia's accession to the WTO, however, had little chance to become reality. Almost exactly two years later, on 6 August 2014, Russia introduced an import ban on agri-food products from selected Western countries as a response to their sanctions which had targeted certain sectors of Russia's economy. Russia's food embargo (countersanctions) towards the EU did not include seafood but focused on agri-food. Prior to the food embargo, Russia had been the second most important destination for EU agricultural products, trailing only the United States. The main agricultural products from the EU that were affected by Russia's countersanctions were pork exports (58.9 percent of Russia's total imports); milk and milk products (37.4 percent of Russia's total imports); and vegetables and fruits (31.9 and 23.5 percent of Russia's total imports), respectively.[32]

Norway, however, was targeted by countersanctions even though it is not part of the EU, and as a consequence its seafood exports to Russia were affected. As shown in Table 2, Russia's import of seafood from Norway terminated almost instantly after countersanctions were introduced. Norway's drop from being the dominating supplier with around 45–50 percent market share in Russia's seafood imports to almost zero overnight was dramatic. To replace Norwegian seafood, Russia needed to find other suppliers. The decline in Russia's seafood imports in 2015 and 2016 reflects initial challenges securing alternative suppliers (as well as the devaluation of the ruble and an economic recession). Eventually, three smaller, but still substantial, producers of farmed Atlantic salmon and

Table 2 Market share by main suppliers of Russia's seafood imports, 2001–2019

	2001	*2005*	*2010*	*2011*	*2012*	*2013*	*2014*	*2015*	*2016*	*2017*	*2018*	*2019*
Norway (%)	45.8	47.1	44.2	41.3	44.8	39.9	22.1	0.6	0	0	0.6	1.0
Chile (%)	1.2	3.1	3.8	0.5	4.9	10.4	16.0	24.3	23.5	20.2	25.6	21.5
China (%)	1.2	4.0	9.5	1.1	9.6	9.2	12.0	12.2	15.5	14.6	1.5	14.9
Vietnam (%)	0.1	2.4	3.7	4.2	3.3	2.8	3.6	5.6	6.4	6.2	4.8	6.0
Argentina (%)	0	3.2	1.0	1.3	0.9	0.8	1.4	1.5	2.2	3.4	3.5	4.7
India (%)	0	0.1	0.1	1.3	1.2	1.4	2.9	2.3	4.2	4.2	4.9	5.4
Greenland, Faroe Isl.,Turkey (%)	0	0.4	1.5	2.3	4.2	5.2	10.1	28.0	28.3	31.6	26.6	25.2
Belarus (%)	0	0	0	0	0.8	2.2	4.3	7.1	7.4	7.2	6.5	6.6
Sum (%)	48.3	60.3	63.7	51.8	69.6	71.9	72.2	81.7	87.5	87.5	73.9	85.4

Note Percentages are based on dollar value of imports
Source Trade statistics for international business development, https://www.trademap.org/

other farm-raised fish from Europe entered the Russian market: Greenland, Faroe Islands, and Turkey. In addition, Chile significantly increased its market share compared to the period before the sanctions. Greenland, Faroe Islands (EU), and Chile are suppliers of farmed Atlantic salmon, while Turkey is a new supplier of farmed whitefish such as sea bass and seabream. In addition, some Norwegian farmed salmon found its way to the Russian market through Belarus, although the volumes were marginal compared to previous direct exports to Russia. Norway was not the only country from which seafood transited through Belarus, which became a kind of trading hub for seafood from sanctioned countries. Table 2 indicates the country of origin for Russia's seafood imports from 2001 to 2019.

The table demonstrates three notable dimensions related to the change in seafood trade in the aftermath of the 2014 embargo. First, there was a change from one dominating supplier to Russia to a higher number of suppliers, each of which exported lower volumes of seafood to Russia than the one dominating supplier had in the pre-embargo period. In particular, Norway went from being the dominant supplier in 2013 to virtual irrelevance, with seafood exports to Russia falling to 1 percent of market share in 2019. Second, after countersanctions were introduced, the combination of main suppliers captured a much higher share of Russia's total seafood imports. Taken together, the group of main suppliers increased their market share from 72 percent in 2013 to 85 percent in 2019. Third, main seafood suppliers to Russia were distributed across a wider spectrum of geographical regions, including Asia, South America, and Europe. Chile in particular increased its market share from 10 percent in 2013 to almost 22 percent in 2019; China's share rose too, from 9 percent in 2013 to nearly 15 percent in 2019. That said, countersanctions contributed to a decline in the value of Russia's imported seafood, which dropped from $2.8 billion USD in 2013 to around $1.6 billion USD in 2018 (the value includes fresh and frozen fish and seafood).[33] The reduction in seafood imports is explained by the combination of reduced import volumes and the purchase of less expensive seafood, i.e. the volume of farmed salmon declined.

In the aftermath of Russia's 2014 countersanctions, Russian seafood exports did not experience the same change as occurred with imports. On the contrary, the primary purchasers of Russia's seafood have remained stable, with the Asian countries by far representing the largest Russian export market. In particular, China, the Republic of Korea, and Japan have been quite stable markets, buying 70–80 percent of the total Russian seafood exports. The volume of seafood exports to Asia coincides with the Russia's seafood resource base, which is by far the largest in the Russian Far East. These three Asian countries buy large quantities of Alaska pollack, salmon, and pelagic species (mackerel and herring). In Europe, the classical customers (Norway, Germany, Denmark, and the UK) are purchasers of Northeast Atlantic cod. Compared to the seafood trade in the Russian Far East, the value is quite small, but is stable and did not change much as a result of countersanctions. Since 2013, the Netherlands has become a relatively large consumer for Russia's seafood, increasing its share from about 10 percent in 2013 to over 17 percent in 2019. In total, European markets received about 20 percent of Russia's seafood exports during 2017–2019. The distribution of Russia's seafood exports by main buyers is indicated in Table 3.

The Putin period of consolidation also brought attempts to establish an institutional setup for the governance of Russia's role in the global seafood trade. The federal government has tried to establish a system of incentives to provide control over seafood exports as a valuable asset. Russia's export of fish has been an important binder in relations with large trade partners in the Far East. Russia seems to have succeeded with the strategy of assuming some control of the export. It is evident that Russia's government intends to remain involved in seafood trade as part of its overall food security strategy. In January 2020, President Putin signed a new Food Security Doctrine to replace the 2010 version. Of note is the fact that the target for self-sufficiency in seafood was raised from 80 to 85 percent (in live weight). In the 2020 version, under the chapter of 'Strategic Goal and Key Objectives of Ensuring Food Security', the doctrine stated:

> The strategic goal of ensuring food security is to provide the country's population with safe, quality and affordable farm products, raw materials and food in the quantities that satisfy balanced food consumption. Based on food independence requirements, the major sources of foodstuffs are products of agricultural, forestry, fishery and hunting sectors, as well as food industry products. The agricultural, fishery and food industries play central role in the food security assurance.[34]

Table 3 Distribution of Russia's seafood exports to main buyers, 2001–2019

	2001	*2005*	*2010*	*2011*	*2012*	*2013*	*2014*	*2015*	*2016*	*2017*	*2018*	*2019*
China (%)	18.8	27.9	41.4	39.6	37.2	36.0	31.9	35.3	34.2	31.3	34.9	36.2
Korea, Republic of (%)	26.8	1.9	3.8	38.5	40.3	39.5	36.4	34.8	33.6	34.2	32.0	3.8
Japan (%)	27.3	20.8	9.1	8.2	10.0	7.2	7.4	9.4	9.1	7.3	8.2	6.2
Netherlands (%)	1.9	1.7	6.1	7.1	.0	9.9	16.4	13.2	14.3	19.7	16.1	17.1
EU countries and Norway (%)	13	13	2	2	2	1	1	1	1	2	2	3
Belarus (%)	0	0	0	0	1.1	1.9	2.5	1.7	0.2	1.6	1.5	1.4
United States of America (%)	0.5	2.4	0.7	0.1	0.1	0.1	0.1	0.2	0.2	0	0.4	0.4
Sum (%)	88.3	67.5	63.1	95.8	95.4	95.7	96.0	95.8	92.5	95.7	95.3	95.9

Note Percentage of exports based on dollar value of exports
Source Trade statistics for international business development, https://www.trademap.org/

Not only does the new Food Security Doctrine provide more detail than the previous 2010 version, it also contains several strategic measures and directions for the desired future development in the food sector.

In addition, a governmental order (*razporiazhenie*) in April 2020 (No. 993-r) laid out a new 'Strategy for Development of the Agribusiness and Fishery Sectors of the Russian Federation to 2030'.[35] The strategy considers economic models for development and is closely tied to the new Food Security Doctrine and other official programmes related to the strategic development of the food sector in general. Some of the goals are to increase the share of value-added products and make them available to Russian consumers, and to increase the exports of food products to at least $45 billion USD annually, a goal that subsequently was modified to $34 billion USD by 2024 instead. To increase exports, the order advocates the elimination of trade barriers, stimulation of export-oriented businesses, and to promote Russia's agriculture and fish products in export markets.[36]

4 Outlook

Russia's role in global seafood trade has changed over time. The first change is as a seafood importer. Russia has stabilised as a less prominent actor as an importer in the global seafood market. The overarching element in the Russia's seafood trade after 2000 has been self-sufficiency, that is, to produce enough to meet Russia's own needs. The early post-Soviet era was characterised by heavy importation of low-value seafood and export of high-value seafood. After 2010, Russia now has net production that exceeds domestic demand and consumption. Over the past decade and, in particular after the 2014 embargo, Russia decreased the value of food imports in general, with the dollar value of food imports falling from a post-Soviet high of $43 billion USD in 2013 to less than $25 billion USD in 2016.[37] The dollar value of Russia's food imports has increased since 2016 but has not come close to the pre-2014 level. The dollar value of seafood imports also fell due to countersanctions, although since 2017 have stabilised (see Fig. 1). The 2020 food security doctrine prescribes more self-sufficiency in seafood.

Seafood imports from Europe fell dramatically as a consequence of the food embargo and has reinforced Russia's reduced role as a seafood importer. The major seafood trade inflows most affected by the ban are imports of Atlantic salmon, herring, and trout from Norway and cold water shrimp from Canada. Even if the import ban against the EU has been compensated somewhat with imports from other countries, the big picture is still a reduction in seafood imports.[38] A parallel trend in Russia's seafood import is the gradual shift from European to Asian countries where China has maintained its position as the second largest foreign supplier of seafood to Russia, with the volume increasing by 23 percent during 2010–2016 (see Table 2). Other states that have appeared as newcomers among the top ten exporters of seafood to Russia are Vietnam, Peru, Morocco, Thailand, and India, thereby strengthening the trend for Russia to distance itself from trade with Western countries.[39]

Russian food security issue is clearly a political ambition strongly related to the independence of seafood imports in order to self-supply the domestic market. As indicated above, the Russian model of food security places emphasis on national vulnerability from foreign sources.[40] On the other hand, the Russian economy benefits from a trade surplus in one sector in order to bolster sectors that have a negative trade surplus (such as the agriculture sector). Based on statements by government leaders, official documents and plans, institutional arrangements, and business interests within Russia, I expect that Russia's role as a seafood importer to remain stable and its global ranking as an importer not to change significantly.

The second change is as a seafood exporter. Russia's export of seafood has increased steadily. During the past 15 years, Russia's role as a dominant global seafood exporter has grown. In 2003, Russia ranked 35th globally in dollar value of seafood exports. In 2019, Russia advanced to 7th place as a seafood exporting country, exceeded only by traditionally large seafood exporting countries such as China, Norway, USA, Chile, and India. Russia's ranking as seafood importer and exporter during 2003–2019 is shown in Table 4.

There is an aspiration to further develop seafood exports. In October 2018, then-Russian Prime Minister Dmitrii Medvedev announced a goal of achieving $8 billion USD in revenue from annual seafood exports by 2024. In 2018, Russia exported seafood valued at $4 billion USD.[41] The head of *Rosrybolovstvo*, Ilya Shestakov, indicated that Russia's fish catch is projected to rise by only 500,000 metric tonnes by 2030, so a rise in export value has to come from an increase in high-value fish.[42] He suggested moving from supplying primarily whole fish to selling value-added products such as fillets that come from processing. The move to exports of value-added products was reflected as well in governmental

Table 4 Ranking of Russia's place in global seafood trade

	2003	*2007*	*2010*	*2015*	*2019*
Ranking of eight largest seafood ***exporting*** *countries*					
1	China	Norway	China	China	China
2	Norway	China	Norway	Norway	Norway
3	USA	USA	Vietnam	USA	Vietnam
4	Vietnam	Vietnam	USA	Vietnam	India
5	India	Canada	Canada	India	Chile
6	Canada	Chile	Thailand	Canada	USA
7	Chile	Spain	Spain	Chile	**Russia (7)**
8	Sweden	Thailand	Chile	Sweden	Sweden
	Russia (10)	**Russia (35)**	**Russia (12)**	**Russia (10)**	
Ranking of eight largest seafood ***importing*** *countries*					
1	Japan	Japan	Japan	USA	USA
2	USA	USA	USA	Japan	China
3	Spain	Spain	Spain	China	Spain
4	France	China	France	Spain	Spain
5	Italy	France	China	France	France
6	China	Italy	Italy	France	France
7	Sweden	Germany	Germany	Sweden	Sweden
8	Hong Kong	Rep. of Korea	Sweden	Germany	Korea repub
	Russia (21)	**Russia (14)**	**Russia (11)**	**Russia (19)**	**Russia (18)**

Note Ranking is based on U.S. dollar value
Sources International Trade Statistics; Federal Customs Service, Russia; Rosstat; and UN Comtrade

order from November 2019 (No. 2798-r), also entitled 'Strategy for Development of the Fisheries Sector to 2030'. In this document, a clear ambition was expressed to strengthen the export of white fish and stimulate increased exports of processed fish.[43] This order is specific to the fishing industry although it shares the same name with the April 2020 order that was mentioned above. According to order No. 2798-r from November 2019, to reach export goals Russia should focus on the export of large-volume, valuable white fish species.

Going forward, the room for manoeuvre for Russia as a global actor in seafood trade is affected by resource accessibility, organisational behaviour, and state political aims, goals, and institutional capabilities. Russia's government has made clear its intentions to play a direct role in seafood exports. Since 2000 a whole range of different economic and institutional measures have been implemented. Legal institutions, regulations, and various incentive measures have been introduced together with the transfer of power to various federal control organs such as the Federal Customs Service, *Rossel'khoznadzor*, and other more sector-specific organs that give the state the ability to move seafood exports in desired directions. With regard to seafood exports, there is little to suggest a pull back in Russia's export orientation. Stable and high levels of the fishing quotas will continue Russia's role as a prominent actor in global seafood trade.

Notes

1. Throughout this chapter, the term 'seafood' is shorthand for fish and seafood.
2. Stephen K. Wegren, Alexander Nikulin and Irina Trotsuk. *Food Policy and Food Security: Putting Food on the Russian Table* (Lanham: Lexington Books, 2018).
3. Ivan Stupachenko, 'Russia Wants to Double Revenues from Seafood Exports by 2024', 12 February 2019. https://www.seafoodsource.com/news/supply-trade/russia-wants-to-double-revenues-from-seafood-exports-by-2024. Accessed 12 November 2020.
4. Ministry of Agriculture, 'Operativnyi obzor eksporta produktsii APK', 27 December 2020. www.mcx.gov.ru. Accessed 10 January 2021.
5. K. M. Bailey, T. J. Quinn II, R. Bentzen, and W. S. Grant, 'Population Structure and Dynamics of Walleye Pollock, Theragra Chalcogramma', *Advances in Marine Biology* 37 (1999): 179–255.
6. Rosstat, *Regiony Rossii 2019* (Moscow: Rosstat, 2019), 22, 44.
7. Nikolai P. Sysoev, *Ekonomika Rybnoi Promyshlennosti SSSR*. Moscow: Izdatelstvo Pichevaia Promyshlennost. Translated by the Israeli programme for scientific translation (Jerusalem, 1974).
8. Ibid.
9. Geir Hønneland and Frode Nilssen, 'Comanagement in Northwest Russian Fisheries', *Society & Natural Resources* 13, no. 7 (2000): 635–648.
10. Author's compilation based on data from *Rosrybolovstvo*, the Federal Russian Fisheries Agency. http://www.fish.gov.ru/ob-agentstve/kollegiya-rosrybolovstva.
11. Frode Nilssen and Geir Hønneland, 'Institutional Change and Problems of Restructuring the Russian Fishing Industry', *Post-Communist Economies* 13, no. 3 (2001): 314–329.
12. Jiangyong Lu, Bin Xu, and Xiaohui Liu, 'The Effects of Corporate Governance and Institutional Environments on Export Behavior in Emerging

Economies: Evidence from China'. *Management International Review* 49 (2009): 455–478.

13. Frode Nilssen, 'Economic Co-operation in the Barents Region: Russian-Norwegian Trade in the Fishing Industry', in *The NEBI Yearbook 2003. North European and Baltic Sea Integration*, eds. Lars Hedegaard, Bjarne Lindstrom, Pertti Joenniemi, Heikki Eskelinen, Karin Peschel, and Carl-Einar Stalvant (Berlin: Springer Verlag, 2003), 151–164.
14. Vladimir I. Radchenko, 'Russian Fisheries Management System Performance', North Pacific Anadromous Fish Commission (NPAFC), Vancouver, Canada, 2017. http://russianpollock.com/upload/iblock/221/russian-fisheries-management-system-performance-report-final.pdf.
15. Geir Hønneland, Lyumila Ivanova, and Frode Nilssen, 'Russia's Northern Fishery Basin: Trends in Regulation, Fleet, and Industry', *Polar Geography* 27, no. 3 (2003): 225–239.
16. FAO, *Russian Federation: Review of the Fisheries Sector*, Report series-N.12 (September 2008). http://www.fao.org/publications/card/ru/c/773afbff-3d2d-5826-abbb-14d74ad7b449/.
17. Christel Elvestad, 'A Sustainable Russian Fishing Industry: Feeding Russia with (Russian) Seafood?' *Russian Analytical Digest*, no. 204 (December 2017): 14–16.
18. For an early analysis, see Stephen K. Wegren, 'Russian Agrarian Policy Under Putin', *Post-Soviet Geography and Economics* 43, no. 1 (2002): 26–40.
19. Luboš Smutka, Mansoor Maitah, and Miroslav Svatoš, 'Policy Impacts on the EU-Russian Trade Performance: The Case of Agri-Food Trade', *Journal of International Studies* 12, no. 2 (2019): 82–98.
20. Author's calculations from raw data at Statistics Norway, Foreign trade, https://www.ssb.no/statbank/table/08809/ (in Norwegian).
21. Data from trade statistics for international business development, https://www.trademap.org/Country_SelProductCountry_TS.aspx?nvpm=1%7c643%7c%7c%7c%7c03%7c%7c%7c2%7c1%7c1%7c1%7c2%7c1%7c2%7c1%7c1%7c1.
22. Radchenko, 'Russian Fisheries Management System Performance'.
23. Stephen K. Wegren, Frode Nilssen, and Christel Elvestad, 'The Impact of Russian Food Security Policy on the Performance of the Food System', *Eurasian Geography and Economics*, 57, no. 6 (2016): 671–699.
24. 'Ukaz Prezidenta Rossiiskoi Federatsii ot 30 Ianvaria 2010 g. N 120 "Ob utverzhdenii Doktriny prodovol'stvennoi bezopasnosti Rossiikoi Federatsii'", 3 February 2010. https://rg.ru/2010/02/03/prod-dok.html. Accessed 12 January 2021.
25. 'Ukaz Prezidenta Rossiiskoi Federatsii. Ob Utverzhdenii Doktriny prodovolstvennoi bezopastnosti Rossiiskoi Federatsii', Moskva, Kreml, 30

Ianvieria 2010 goda, No. 210. https://www.prlib.ru/item/354145. Accessed 12 January 2021.
26. Pravitel'stvo Rossiiskoi Federatsii, 'Postanovlenie ot 15 Aprelia 2014 g., No. 314, Ob utverzhdenii gosudarstvennoi programmy Rossiiskoi Federtatsii "Razvitie Rybokhoziaistvennovo Kompleksa'", 15 April 2014. http://extwprlegs1.fao.org/docs/pdf/rus189742.pdf. Accessed 12 January 2021.
27. The versions of the programme are available at mcx.gov.ru.s.
28. Federal'noe agentstvo po rybolovstvu, 'Prikaz ot 30 marta 2009 g. N 246, "Ob utverzhdenii Strategii razvitiia rybokhoziaistvennogo kompleksa Rossiiskoi Federatsii na period do 2020 goda', 30 March 2009. http://extwprlegs1.fao.org/docs/pdf/rus179598.pdf. Accessed 12 January 2021.
29. R. Anthony Turner and Kira F. Schabram, 'The Bases of Power Revisited: An Interpersonal Perceptions Perspective', *Journal of Organizational Psychology* 12, no. 1 (2012): 9–18.
30. According to its official site, *Rossel'khoznadzor* is a 'federal executive body carrying out functions on control and supervision in the veterinary field: establishment and lifting of phytosanitary quarantine zones, control of pesticide and agrochemical application, maintenance of soil fertility, cultivation achievements, protection, reproduction and use of animal objects (hunting resources) and aquatic biological resources, and protection of humans from animal infectious diseases'. See https://fsvps.gov.ru/fsvps/main.html?_language=en. Accessed 11 January 2021.
31. Personal communication with author, 10 June 2006.
32. Susanne Kraats, 'The Russian Embargo: Impact on the Economic and Employment Situation in the EU', European Parliament Policy Briefing PE 536.291, 12 October 2014. Available at: http://doi.org/10.2861/73046 (pdf).
33. Rosstat, *Rossiiskii statisticheskii ezhegodnik 2019* (Moscow: Rosstat, 2019), 607.
34. 'Ukaz Prezidenta Rossiiskoi Federatsii ot 21.01.2020 g. No. 20. Ob utverzhdenii Doktrina prodovol'stvennoi bezapastnosti Rossiiskoi Federatsii', 21 January 2020. http://kremlin.ru/acts/bank/45106. Accessed 12 January 2021.
35. Pravitel'stvo Rossiiskoi Federatsii, 'Rasporiazhenie ot 12 Aprelia 2020 g. N 993-r, Strategii razvitiia agropromyshlennogo i rybokhoziaistvennogo kompleksov Rossiiskoi Federatsii na period do 2030 goda'. 12 April 2020. http://extwprlegs1.fao.org/docs/pdf/rus195965original.pdf. Accessed 12 January 2021.
36. Domestic fisheries (commercially farmed fish) are seen to hold great potential for increasing production of aquatic resources, the reason being that the wild catch at sea is limited and has natural cyclical fluctuations

over time. That said, commercial aquaculture will continue to play an insignificant role in the production and economics of the fishery sector, even though its average annual production growth rate has been about 15 percent. Commercial aquaculture is a part of the total fish production that is possible to control and increase. Current output from this industry is, however, modest and not subject to export.

37. Stephen K. Wegren and Christel Elvestad, 'Russia's Food Self-Sufficiency and Food Security: An Assessment', *Post-Communist Economies* 30, no. 5 (2018): 565–587.
38. Arina Motova and Fabrizio Natale, 'Impacts of the 2014 Russian Trade Ban on Seafood'. European Commission, JRC Science and Policy Report 94726 (2015). https://publications.jrc.ec.europa.eu/repository/bitstream/JRC94726/lbna27113enn.pdf.
39. Wegren and Elvestad, 'Russia's Food Self-Sufficiency and Food Security: An Assessment', 565–587.
40. Stephen K. Wegren, Alexander M. Nikulin, and Irina Trotsuk, 'The Russian Variant of Food Security', *Problems of Post-Communism* 64, no. 1 (2017): 47–62.
41. Ivan Stupachenko, 'Russia Wants to Double Revenues from Seafood Exports by 2024', 12 February 2019. https://www.seafoodsource.com/news/supply-trade/russia-wants-to-double-revenues-from-seafood-exports-by-2024. Accessed 12 December 2020.
42. Ibid.
43. Pravitel'stvo Rossiiskoi Federatsii, 'Strategiia razvitiia rybokhozi-aistvennogo kompleksa Rossiiskoi Federatsii na period do 2030 goda', 26 November 2019. http://government.ru/docs/38448/. Accessed 12 January 2021.

Selected Bibliography

Elvestad, Christel. 'A Sustainable Russian Fishing Industry: Feeding Russia with (Russian) Seafood?' *Russian Analytical Digest* no. 204 (December 2017): 14–16.

Hønneland, Geir and Frode Nilssen. 'Comanagement in Northwest Russian Fisheries'. *Society & Natural Resources* 13, no. 7 (2000): 635–648.

Hønneland, Geir, Lyudmila Ivanova and Frode Nilssen. 'Russia's Northern Fishery Basin: Trends in Regulation, Fleet, and Industry'. *Polar Geography* 27, no. 3 (2003): 225–239.

Motova, Arina and Fabrizio Natale. 'Impacts of the 2014 Russian Trade Ban on Seafood'. European Commission, JRC Science and Policy Report 94726, 2015. https://publications.jrc.ec.europa.eu/repository/bitstream/JRC94726/lbna27113enn.pdf.

Nilssen, Frode and G. Hønneland. 'Institutional Change and Problems of Restructuring the Russian Fishing Industry'. *Post-Communist Economies* 13, no. 3 (2001): 314–329.

Nilssen, Frode. 'Economic Co-operation in the Barents region: Russian-Norwegian Trade in the Fishing Industry'. In *The NEBI Yearbook 2003. North European and Baltic Sea Integration*, eds. Lars Hedegaard, Bjarne Lindstrom, Pertti Joenniemi, Heikki Eskelinen, Karin Peschel, and Carl-Einar Stalvant. Berlin: Springer Verlag, 2003, 151–164.

Radchenko, Vladimir I. 'Russian Fisheries Management System Performance'. Report to the North Pacific Anadromous Fish Commission (NPAFC). Vancouver, Canada, 2017. http://russianpollock.com/upload/iblock/221/russian-fisheries-management-system-performance-report-final.pdf.

Smutka, Luboš, Mansoor Maitah, and Miroslav Svatoš. 'Policy Impacts on the EU-Russian Trade Performance: The Case of Agri-Food Trade'. *Journal of International Studies* 12, no. 2 (2019): 82–98.

Sysoev, Nikolai P. *Ekonomika Rybnoi Promyshlennosti SSSR*. Moscow: Izdatelstvo Pichevaia Promyshlennost. Translated by the Israeli programme for scientific translation, Jerusalem, 1974.

Turner, R. Anthony and Kira F. Schabram. 'The Bases of Power Revisited: An Interpersonal Perceptions Perspective'. *Journal of Organizational Psychology* 12, no. 1 (2012): 9–18.

Wegren, Stephen K. 'Russian Agrarian Policy Under Putin'. *Post-Soviet Geography and Economics* 43, no. 1 (2002): 26–40.

Wegren, Stephen K., Alexander Nikulin and Irina Trotsuk. *Food Policy and Food Security: Putting Food on the Russian Table*. Lanham: Lexington Books, 2018.

Wegren, Stephen K., Alexander M. Nikulin, and Irina Trotsuk. 'The Russian Variant of Food Security'. *Problems of Post-Communism* 64, no. 1 (2017): 47-62.

Wegren, Stephen K. and Christel Elvestad. 'Russia's Food Self-Sufficiency and Food Security: An Assessment'. *Journal of Post-Communist Economies* 30, no. 5 (2018): 565–587.

Wegren, Stephen K., Frode Nilssen, and Christel Elvestad. 'The Impact of Russian food Security Policy on the Performance of the Food System'. *Eurasian Geography and Economics*, 57, no. 6 (2016): 671–699.

Open Access This chapter is licensed under the terms of the Creative Commons Attribution 4.0 International License (http://creativecommons.org/licenses/by/4.0/), which permits use, sharing, adaptation, distribution and reproduction in any medium or format, as long as you give appropriate credit to the original author(s) and the source, provide a link to the Creative Commons license and indicate if changes were made.

The images or other third party material in this chapter are included in the chapter's Creative Commons license, unless indicated otherwise in a credit line to the material. If material is not included in the chapter's Creative Commons license and your intended use is not permitted by statutory regulation or exceeds the permitted use, you will need to obtain permission directly from the copyright holder.

PART II

Russia's Regional Agri-Food Trade

Chapter 6: Russia's Regional Free Trade Agreements and Agri-Food Trade After 2014

Christel Elvestad and Tatiana Isachenko

1 Introduction

Recent years have witnessed the rise of populism and economic nationalism. International trade in general is attacked from the political left and political right. In the United States, the Trump administration has led the way in attacking free trade. The political left points to rising inequality, loss of jobs, and stagnant incomes for the working class. The political right points to high trade deficits. On the political left, critics argue that trade agreements favour the interests of corporations over workers. On the political right, critics maintain that agreements put international interests above national interests.[1] Both sides blame trade. A contrary trend, however, has been an increase in the popularity of regional trade agreements, (RTAs).[2] Some RTAs are narrow in range, focusing mainly on reducing tariffs for specific types of goods. However, modern RTAs often

C. Elvestad (✉)
Nord University Business School, Bodø, Norway
e-mail: christel.elvestad@nord.no

T. Isachenko
Department of International Economic Relations and Foreign Economic Ties, MGIMO University of the Ministry of Foreign Affairs, Moscow, Russia

© The Author(s) 2022

S. K. Wegren and F. Nilssen (eds.), *Russia's Role in the Contemporary International Agri-Food Trade System*, Palgrave Advances in Bioeconomy: Economics and Policies,
https://doi.org/10.1007/978-3-030-77451-6_7

include a wider range of areas such as trade in goods, services, investments, public procurement, competition, and intellectual property rights. There are over 300 RTAs in force and there is an expanding worldwide RTA network.

Russia started to negotiate regional free agreements later than other countries, but since 2015 it has been an active player. This chapter is important because although Russia has pursued a specific variant of food security since the 2008–2010 period, a variant that emphasises trade protectionism, the story is more nuanced than commonly portrayed. While it is true that food self-sufficiency and import substitution have dominated Russia's food policies since 2014, trade patterns show not a withdrawal from international food markets but rather an adjustment and recalibration of partners. Thus, this chapter sheds light on how Russia's regional trade policies and agri-food trade patterns have changed after the introduction of countersanctions in 2014.

The purpose of this chapter is to: (1) examine Russia's regional trade strategies as the driving force of Eurasian regional trade integration, focusing on agri-food policies as a key component; (2) review Russia's free trade agreements through the Eurasian Economic Union; and (3) access the role of agri-food trade in signed and upcoming agreements, as well as how food trade relations have changed in the period after sanctions were introduced in 2014. The final section provides a look into the future of Russia's free trade agreements and agri-food trade.

2 International Context

Regional and preferential economic cooperation has attracted increasing attention as free trade agreements have expanded in number and scope and become an important part of the global trading system.[3] The proliferation of RTAs is important for most countries regardless of their level of economic development. Because RTAs allow for more favourable terms of trade, the share of global trade between members of RTAs has been steadily growing in recent decades.

In addition to an increase in the number of RTAs, from about 50 agreements in the 1990s to over 300 agreements in 2020, RTAs are becoming more complex.[4] Modern RTAs often go beyond tariff reduction in certain sectors and products, instead covering a wide range of policy areas. There have been a stronger emphasis on reducing and removing non-tariff barriers to trade such as unnecessary or overly bureaucratic technical regulations and procedures that can hinder or even stop trade completely.[5] There is also a growing trend for RTAs to not just liberalise trade in goods, but also to liberalise services, investment, and areas such as intellectual property rights, government procurement, competition policy, and issues like environmental and labour standards.[6]

Furthermore, RTAs can be concluded between countries located within or across regions (inter- or intra-regional agreements). Bilateral agreements are still common, but RTAs can also include a multiple countries, for instance the Trans-Pacific Partnership (TPP 11) or the Regional Comprehensive Economic Partnership (RCEP).[7] In some cases, the agreements are signed between regional trade blocks, for example between the European Union (EU) and the Southern Common Market encompassing Brazil, Argentina, Uruguay, and Paraguay (MERCOSUR).[8] Furthermore, regional trade blocs often coordinate at the multilateral level to try to increase their influence in relevant international organisations. For instance, the EU has suggested a comprehensive approach to push forward modernisation of the Word Trade Organization (WTO).[9]

Why do countries sign RTAs? The classic answer from the economic literature is the benefit of net welfare gain that such trade agreements provide. By removing or reducing trade barriers, transaction costs are lowered and economic growth through internationalisation can be realised. The international political economy literature provides an analytical framework with four categories of motives behind RTAs, following a political–economical dimension and a domestic–international dimension.

The first category 'International Economic Motives' refers to the use of RTAs as a strategy to accommodate and shape the international environment, making it fit the country's economic ambitions in the international arena. Since RTAs provide for better terms of trade, it gives a competitive edge and potential 'first mover' advantages. Another important motive can be the need to cover a new issue that is missing in WTO/multilateral negotiations.[10] A negative view is that it is a mistake to put all efforts on new free trade agreements instead of focusing on multilateralism and thus supporting the World Trade Organization.[11] However, to negotiate RTAs can alternatively be viewed as a constructive response to the lack of progress at the multilateral level. RTAs may not pose a threat but may function as building blocks of trade liberalisation to be multilateralised at a later stage.[12] The typical example of this is the desire to include investment in RTAs, since an agreement is still lacking in this area at the multilateral level. Another variant of international economic motives behind RTAs is the desire to extend domestic reforms to the international level using RTAs as reform anchors to test and benchmark reforms on a wider scale of economic integration.[13]

A second category, 'International Political Motives', refers to ambitions to create new coalitions or to strengthen existing ties between countries. Sometimes economic reasons are not decisive and regional agreements arise as a result of politically motivated efforts emphasising the geographical or historical characteristics of the relationship. For instance, the initial motivation of the United States under former President Obama was to make the Trans-Pacific-Partnership (TPP) the centrepiece of its strategic axis to the Asia–Pacific region.[14] In other words, there can be a strong geopolitical motivation behind RTAs, emphasising and strengthening relationships between countries in and across regions. Furthermore, actors at the national level will try to influence RTA negotiations to fit their interests, and negotiators will try to absorb and take into consideration what outcomes can be accepted by domestic interest groups.[15]

A third category 'Domestic Economic Motives' refers to the quest for better market access for goods and services in order to satisfy the interests of national competitive industries. A classic motivation is to use RTAs as an instrument to promote its export-oriented sectors by opening relevant export markets. In other words, RTAs are used to liberalise trade in order to meet national trade interests.

The fourth category, 'Domestic Political Motives', on the other hand, refers to the use of RTAs in a way that is designed to maintain barriers or even put up new barriers to trade in order to defend national trade interests. A way to protect sectors that are not competitive is to treat the entire sector or specific goods as off-limits to liberalisation in RTAs. Typically, this type of protectionist strategy restricts agricultural concessions in RTAs. Agri-food is a so-called sensitive sector for many countries and as a result, trade liberalisation in the agricultural sector is more limited.[16] Agriculture has only undergone one round of negotiations through the Uruguay Round the WTO. The Doha Round, started in 1997, was supposed to deal with agriculture but negotiations ended in 2008 and never restarted, thereby leaving agricultural tariffs generally high.[17] The lack of agreement on agricultural goods is important because generally RTAs can help lower trade tariffs and barriers. We see that the share of global agri-food trade between countries with RTAs rose from about 20 percent in 1998 to nearly 40 percent in 2009.[18]

Thus, RTAs reflect both domestic and international interests, and for each of the countries involved economic and political interests can come into play. Furthermore, the interests between the negotiation parties may coincide or be contrary to each other, making negotiation of RTAs a complex balancing act. Regarding Russia, one may discern elements of each of the four categories of motives, although during 2014–2018 the primary impulses have been domestic economic and domestic political. Starting in 2019, however, international economic and political motives have gained in importance. The earliest international motivations, however, may be traced to the creation of the Eurasian Economic Union (EAEU) to which we turn below.

3 Russia and the EAEU

This section examines Russia's role as the dominant partner and driving force of Eurasian regional integration. Agri-food policies have been a key component of Russia's trade strategies. One of the most notable features of Russia's modern trade policy is the search for the best possible model of regional partnerships.[19] During the last decade, Russia has tried to revive integration projects with the Commonwealth of Independent States (CIS), as well as to sign trade agreements by drawing from best practices in international trade relations.

In 1994, CIS countries took measures to transition to a common free trade regime to ensure stability in the region. However, the parties failed to agree on a general list of exemptions. Therefore, the 1999 'Protocol on Amendments and Additions to the Agreement on the Establishment of a Free Trade Area' allowed for temporary exemptions from the free trade regime on a bilateral basis. Starting from the early 2000s, Russia initiated negotiations on a new CIS free trade agreement which was finally ratified in 2012 by Russia, Belarus, Kazakhstan, Armenia, Kyrgyzstan, Tajikistan, Moldova, and Ukraine.[20] This phase of post-Soviet integration has been labelled a case of 'holding-together regionalism' of countries originally forming a single political entity struggling to find an effective form of cooperation.[21]

The establishment of the Eurasian Economic Union in January 2015 brought together Russia, Belarus, Kazakhstan, Armenia, and Kyrgyzstan (see Chapter 8 for more institutional detail). Prior to the establishment of the EAEU, Russia, Belarus, and Kazakhstan formed a Customs Union that existed during 2010–2011.[22] A Single Economic Space replaced the

Customs Union during 2012–2014. The Eurasian Economic Treaty was signed in May 2014 which became effective in January 2015, thereby bringing the EAEU into existence. By design, the EAEU is a type of regional integration, featuring free trade between the member states, a common external tariff and suppression of internal customs controls (Customs Union), and further integration into a single market for all the 'four freedoms', for goods, services, labour, and capital. In fact, however, the EAEU has some features of an FTA and some of a Custom's Union.[23]

That said, there are several shortcomings in the EAEU.[24] One problem is that the Eurasian Economic Commission as the executive body and the Supreme Eurasian Council as a legislative body adopt and approve decisions, but both bodies have little power to regulate controversial situations or settle disagreements between members. This situation points to the fact that Russia wanted to form the Union in order to integrate post-Soviet states, but having done so, does not appear committed to making the organisation work and certainly is not willing to cede much sovereignty to the Union.[25]

A second problem is disagreement on several key issues which brings to light the limited ability to resolve intra-EAEU disputes among EAEU members. Armenia and Belarus disagreed with Russia about gas transportation prices within the EAEU.[26] In 2014, Belarussian President Alexander Lukashenko did not support Russia's position during the Ukrainian crisis, for example, refusing to recognise Russia's annexation of Crimea, and for the next several years the two nations engaged in a so-called 'milk war'. The contested situation after the presidential election in Belarus in August 2020 also created tensions among EAEU members. Armenia's recent doubts about participation in the EAEU further complicate the integration process, despite the fact that the most of Armenian agricultural exports are directed to Russia.[27]

A third area of concern encompasses carry over effects from Russia's 2014 food embargo against the West. Several examples are discussed. First, during the formation of the Customs Union between Russia, Belarus, and Kazakhstan, negotiations on free trade agreements with foreign countries outside the CIS were subject to coordination with Customs Union partners. Since the creation of Eurasian Economic Union in 2015, all trade agreements are to be signed on behalf of the block. However, before 2014, Russia negotiated free trade agreements with a wide range of partners. But most of those negotiations were either frozen or suspended or did not enter an active phase, which means that they never rose to the level of including other EAEU members.

Second, the legal basis for economic relations between the EU and Russia is the Partnership and Cooperation Agreement (PCA), which was originally signed in 1997 and ran for ten years. It expired in 2007 and was renewed annually after then. In 2007 the EU and Russia entered into negotiations on a New Agreement. Russia proposed the creation of a free trade area but this idea was not embraced by the EU.[28] The New Agreement was to provide a comprehensive framework for bilateral relations and would have been built on the basis of WTO rules and would have included stable, predictable, and balanced rules for bilateral trade and investment relations. Negotiations started in 2008, but they were stopped in 2010 because no progress was made in the Trade and Investment part.[29] Following the 2014 Ukrainian crisis, the negotiations were suspended. Since 2014, the relationship between Russia and the EU are sporadic and fragmented. The contact between the parties should have be transferred to the EAEU level, but the EU has not been ready to accept this position and deals with EAEU member countries on a bilateral basis.[30]

Third, there were eleven rounds of negotiations between The European Free Trade Association (EFTA) and Russia, Belarus, and Kazakhstan since 2011, but these negotiations were suspended in March 2014 over the Ukrainian crisis.[31] There have also been several attempts to negotiate preferential terms of trade with countries in the Asia-Pacific Economic Cooperation (APEC), like with New Zealand. The access to New Zealand as a part of the APEC market was very important for Russia, but the agreement faced opposition from Belarus who believed that free access for New Zealand products to the EAEU market and the Russian market would put its agricultural exports at risk. The negotiations with New Zealand started in 2013, but they were suspended in 2014 because of the West's sanctions and Russia's countersanctions.

Fourth, the Ukrainian crisis of 2014 and Russia's countersanctions led to the banning of food products from the United States, the EU, Canada, Australia, Norway, Iceland, Liechtenstein, Albania, and Montenegro, including meat, fish, milk, vegetables, fruits, and nuts. Russia's countersanctions have been extended several times and in late 2021 were extended through 2022. Russia's food embargo has led to a reduction in food imports in general as consumers buy more domestic food products; and agri-food trading partners have changed. Domestic food products now account for more than 80 percent of was is sold in retail outlets, compared to 60 percent before the sanctions regime was implemented in 2014.[32] However, when countersanctions were introduced in August 2014, Belarus and Kazakhstan refused to join the ban against Western products.[33] As a result, Russia's import substitution programmes were implemented exclusively in Russia, outside the Eurasian context, and without any use of the resources and capabilities of the EAEU countries. Belarus was, for instance, not in a position to participate in the import substitution programmes, even though Belarus products have traditionally had been approved for import substitution to Russia.[34]

The upshot is that at present, there is no comprehensive agricultural policy among EAEU members, although they do have a common agreement on tariff-rate quotas (TRQs) for meat imports into the EAEU.[35] Further, there is evidence of movement towards greater cooperation and coordination. When speaking about agricultural policy among EAEU members, Russian President Vladimir Putin stated that, 'We foresee large reserves in expanding mutual supplies of food. It is hardly logical to import vegetables, fruit, milk, and meat products from distant countries, placing orders with foreign suppliers when our own producers are ready and willing to work and enter a common Eurasian market with products that are not inferior and, in fact, often superior in quality'.[36]

In August 2020, the Eurasian Economic Commission and Russia's Ministry of Agriculture discussed the creation of a single internal market for agricultural products. This integration project is in its infancy, aiming to foster cooperation in agricultural science, training of agricultural workforce, and exchange of experience and knowledge in agriculture. There is also in the works a treaty on creating a single market for organic agricultural products within the EAEU. The purpose of the proactive approach towards a common agricultural policy for organics is to maximise export potential to meet growing global demand.[37] The heads of the EAEU states created 'The Council for EAEU Agro-Industrial Policy' to ensure effective interaction between the ministries of agriculture of the member countries and to coordinate their policies. In addition, the Council has discussed food security in response to the coronavirus pandemic. A comprehensive act is being drafted that will define general principles and approaches to ensuring food security for the EAEU countries. The minister in charge of the industry and agricultural sector in the Eurasian Economic Commission, Artak Kamalyan, noted that, 'in the context of the coronavirus pandemic, issues of stable saturation of the market with food products are becoming increasingly acute and urgent. In addition to maintaining the stable and uninterrupted functioning of the Union's internal agri-food market, we must join our efforts and take concerted action to find new export niches'.[38]

4 Trade Agreements

Within the framework of the EAEU, Russia has concluded free trade agreements with a number of countries: Vietnam, Serbia, Iran, and Singapore, with other negotiations ongoing. The first such agreement has been in effect since October 2016 between the EAEU and Vietnam, and in the first year about half of all import custom duties were set to zero. Within ten years, 90 percent of goods will be duty-free. For trade in general, Russia has not been able to increase its exports to Vietnam as much as Vietnam increased its exports to Russia, and thus Russia runs a trade deficit with Vietnam.[39]

The FTA between the EAEU and Serbia was originally signed in October 2019 and it was ratified by Russia's Federation Council in October 2020, with the agreement taking effect in November 2020.[40] The FTA with Serbia fully harmonises trade terms with Russia, Belarus, and Kazakhstan and establishes the same terms of trade for agriculture with Armenia and Kyrgyzstan. However, Serbia excluded items like some sugar, tobacco, and undenatured alcohol items and some tariff quotas like for processed cheese and some spirits and tobacco products for the EAEU countries except Russia. The EAEU excluded some poultry items, processed cheese, sparkling wine, undenatured alcohol, and tobacco items. Furthermore, EAEU will apply tariff quotas for some cheese, spirits, and tobacco products, but will allow a limited amount of these goods to be imported duty-free from Serbia.

In October 2019 a Temporary Agreement on Free Trade between the EAEU and Iran was signed. The temporary agreement with Iran was expected to be replaced with a permanent free trade agreement by the end of 2020.[41] The FTA with Iran includes reductions on import duties on 360 Iranian commodities and 502 commodities from the EAEU. Concerning agri-food trade, Iran will reduce import duties on commodities such as beef, mutton, legumes, and vegetable oils. The EAEU gives trade preferences to Iran on products such as cheese, plant items, nuts and fruits, fresh vegetables, processed vegetables and fruits, confectionary, and bakery items.[42] The EAEU-Iran agreement has benefited Russia–Iran agri-food trade. In 2018, Iran was number eight on Russia's top list of export destinations for agricultural products. Unlike the United States and the European Union, Russia has not imposed sanctions on Iran and has aimed for buying up to 500,000 barrels a day of Iranian oil in exchange for Russian equipment and goods.[43]

In addition, a Framework Agreement on Comprehensive Economic Partnership between the EAEU and Singapore was signed in October 2019.[44] Press coverage of the agreement noted that agreement with Singapore 'provides for duty-free trade in almost all the types of goods except for the list of sensitive items from the EAEU member states....[and] will also regulate the existing trade ties and will expand the opportunities for cooperation'.[45] The FTA with Singapore allows all goods from the EAEU countries to Singapore duty-free. After a transition period ranging from three to ten years depending on the product, 87 percent of goods from Singapore will be exempted from duties to the EAEU. Market access for food products is especially important to Singapore, as the country has no agricultural sector. But Singapore cannot supply the EAEU/Russian food market as it is fully dependent on food imports. It is interesting to note that Singapore has made substantial investments in the Russian agricultural sector by investing in grain manufacturing.[46] A list of free trade agreements between the EAEU and other countries is presented in Table 1.

Generally, Russia is shifting its attention to the East in the search for new FTA partners.[47] Negotiations are ongoing between the EAEU and India, Egypt, Indonesia, Brunei, and Cambodia (see Table 2).

In addition, FTA negotiations have been opened with Israel. The ability to increase its influence in the Middle East has been one of Russia's motives for starting FTA negotiations with Israel, from which Russia will be the main beneficiary. According to Israeli Charge d'Affaires in Russia, the deal could be completed by the end of 2020.[48] Since the collapse of the USSR, Russia and Israel have developed closer relations and not only in trade, indicated by Putin's visit to Israel in January 2020 during which Israeli Prime Minister Netanyahu referred to Putin as a 'great friend' and said that he and his wife are 'pleased to host you again at our home here in Jerusalem'.[49] Another country in North Africa that is a long-term trading partner for Russia is Egypt (see Chapter 9), with whom negotiations for a FTA started in 2017. Although there is no official information about the negotiations, it is assumed that a traditional FTA is on the table.

Table 1 EAEU-third country free trade agreements

Trade partners	*Type of agreement*	*Year/status*	*Comments on scope/coverage*
Vietnam	Free trade agreement—FTA	2016	FTA including a wide range of sectors/areas
Iran	FTA	2019	FTA limited in scope (50% of mutual trade), interim agreement until 2021
Serbia	FTA	2019	FTA including a wide range of sectors/areas
China	Trade and Economic Agreement	2019	Non-preferential agreement, focus on technical regulations and Intellectual Property Rights
Singapore	FTA (Memorandum of Understanding, 2016)	2019	Investment, trade in goods and services

Source EAEU, http://www.eaeunion.org/

Table 2 EAEU-third country free trade agreements and memoranda of understanding/FTAs under negotiation

Trade partner(s)	*Year/status*
India	MoU 2017, FTA negotiations
Israel	MoU 2015, FTA negotiations
Egypt	MoU 2016, FTA negotiations
Indonesia	MoU 2019, FTA negotiations
Cambodia	MoU 2016, FTA negotiations
Brunei	MoU negotiations
Peru	MoU 2015
Chile	MoU 2015
South Korea	MoU 2016
Faroe Islands	MoU 2018
Morocco	MoU 2017
Cuba	MoU 2018
Greece	MoU 2017
Moldova	MoU 2017
Jordan	MoU 2017
Mongolia	MoU 2015
Bangladesh	MoU 2019
Thailand	MoU 2018
Mongolia	MoU 2015
Argentine	MoU 2019
Ecuador	MoU 2017

Source EAEU, http://www.eaeunion.org/

Even without a FTA, Egypt is a large purchaser of Russian wheat on an annual basis. In 2014 Egypt ranked third in dollar value for imports of Russian food exports, rising to second place in 2018 at more than $2.1 billion USD. In November 2020, Russia received permission to export dairy and fish products to Egypt.[50] Once a FTA is concluded it may be expected that the value of Russian agri-food exports will increase, perhaps challenging China for first place.

In addition to the ongoing negotiations with the aforementioned countries, there is a list of more than 20 Memoranda of Understanding (MoUs) with individual countries (see Table 2). The EAEU has also established MoUs with other trade blocks including ASEAN (2018), Mercosur (2018), the Andean Community (2019), the Pacific Alliance (2019), and the African Union (2019). MoUs are not binding international agreements, but declarations of intent to promote cooperation and increase trade and investment between the parties. A typical MoU includes areas of cooperation related to trade liberalisation and economic integration with specific chapters on issues like trade facilitation, customs, technical regulations, sanitary and phytosanitary measures, government procurement, and sector-specific provisions such as cooperation between the parties in the area of agriculture. All of the MoUs made publicly available by the Eurasian Economic Commission have specific sections on agriculture. Thus, liberalisation of agricultural trade is or will be an important part of the free trade agreements between the EAEU and these countries. We now assess the role of agri-food trade in current free trade agreements and how agri-food trade relations have changed after 2014.

4.1 Agri-Food Trade

Russia's list of top trading partners for agricultural imports and exports has changed considerably after 2014, a result of Russia turning away from the West.[51] Regarding nations that exported agri-food products to Russia in 2014, the top ten list of countries included Belarus, Brazil, Ukraine, Germany, Turkey, China, Poland, United States, The Netherlands, and France. In 2018, Belarus was still number one, while China advanced from number six to number two on the list. The United States dropped out of the top ten between 2014 and 2018 (see Chapter 10). Ecuador, Indonesia, and Azerbaijan were newcomers to the 2018 list, but some European countries remained important agricultural suppliers despite Russia's countersanctions. For instance, even though the total value of Italy's agricultural exports to Russia has declined, Italy is still on the top ten list of countries supplying Russia with agricultural products. The reason is simply that there is a strong demand in Russia for Italian food products like wine, pasta, peeled and pulp tomatoes, and food oils, as well as other products not covered by Russia's countersanctions.[52] The top ten agri-food exporting nations to Russia in 2014 and 2018 are shown in Table 3.

Belarus, being on Russia's border and a former Soviet republic, has a long-standing trade relationship with Russia. Belarus accounts for a large percentage of Russia's milk and dairy imports, as much as 80 percent according to some calculations. In 2014–2015, the press in Russia humorously noted that Belarus had become famous for its seafood exports to Russia, even though the country is landlocked. For the Russian government, however, the serious issue was that Belarus served as a transit country for banned food products from the West, a fact that has been a sore point in the relationship since 2014. Russia has also accused Belarus of exporting more apples to Russia than it grows, implying that banned apples from Poland are being re-exported. The food trade relationship between the two has turned quite contentious, with periodic Russian bans on Belarussian milk and dairy, as well as Russia's *Rossel'khoznadzor*

Table 3 Top 10 countries of origin for export of agri-food products to Russia in 2014 and 2018 (million USD)

2014 Rank	*Country*	*Total agricultural exports*	*2018 Rank*	*Country*	*Total agricultural exports*
1	Belarus	3,750.2	1	Belarus	4,046.9
2	Brazil	3,593.9	2	China	1,901.2
3	China	1,917.1	3	Germany	1,409.4
4	Turkey	1,765.3	4	Brazil	1,361.4
5	The Netherlands	1,571.6	5	Ecuador	1,288.6
6	Germany	1,547.8	6	Turkey	1,144.5
7	United States	1,394.3	7	Italy	1,118.4
8	Italy	1,303.1	8	Indonesia	896.8
9	France	1,290.7	9	France	850.7
10	Ecuador	1,240.5	10	Azerbaijan	526.2

Source Author's calculations based on data from World Integrated Trade Solutions by the World Bank, https://wits.worldbank.org

essentially insisting on control over Belarussian dairy factories. The re-export of banned food, unsafe additives, and counterfeit labelling has been major drivers behind Russia's push for digital labelling, truth in content labelling, and the tracing of the origins of products, including for grain.[53]

Turning to Russia's agri-food exports, by 2018 China had become Russia's number one export market (see Table 4). The importance of China for Russian trade will most likely continue to grow, as the Chinese economy is growing and the conflict with the West continues.[54] Russia's turn to the East also has clear geopolitical motivations. Considering first total bilateral trade between Russia and China, we can see that it has grown significantly since 2014. In 2014, gross bilateral trade turnover between Russia and China was $90 billion USD, which fell to $64 billion USD in 2015 as a result of the downturn in the Russian economy. In 2017 total trade turnover rose to $87 billion USD. In 2018, Russia–China trade turnover exceeded $108 billion USD, of which $56 billion USD was Russian export. In 2019 Russia–China trade turnover surpassed $110 billion USD, with Russia exporting nearly $57 billion USD to China. In September 2019, the two countries signed agreements to increase bilateral trade to $200 billion USD by 2024. The agreements

Table 4 Top 10 destinations for Russian agri-food exports in 2014 and 2018 (million USD)

2014 Rank	*Country*	*Russia's total agricultural exports*	*2018 Rank*	*Country*	*Russia's total agricultural exports*
1	Turkey	2,372.9	1	China	2,521.6
2	Kazakhstan	1,692.7	2	Egypt	2,147.4
3	Egypt	1,386.6	3	Turkey	1,860.9
4	Korea	1,192.0	4	Korea	1,584.9
5	China	1,095.0	5	Kazakhstan	1,524.6
6	Belarus	1,007.9	6	Belarus	1,253.5
7	Azerbajian	772.3	7	The Netherlands	869.8
8	Netherlands	649.7	8	Iran	791.3
9	Ukraine	584.8	9	Ukraine	671.8
10	Georgia	367.9	10	Vietnam	576.0

Source Author's calculations based on data from World Integrated Trade Solutions by the World Bank, https://wits.worldbank.org

encompass trade, economic cooperation, aviation, infrastructure, agriculture, and science and technology.[55] For context, $200 billion USD in trade turnover for these countries is not particularly large, but it does represent movement in the desired direction. In comparison, for example, American-Chinese trade turnover exceeded $659.8 billion in 2018 and that was despite an ongoing trade war.

Russia's goal to increase its agri-food exports will be greatly enhanced if Russia continues to expand agricultural trade with China. Bilateral agricultural trade turnover between Russia and China has risen since 2014. Russian agri-food exports to China increased from less than $500 million USD in 2000 to $1.1 billion USD in 2014. An important milestone was reached in 2015 when the two sides signed an agreement that opened the Chinese market to Russian wheat and soybean.[56] Agricultural trade began to increase steadily after 2015. By 2018, total bilateral agricultural trade turnover reached about $4.5 billion USD, with Russian exports totaling $2.5 billion USD. In 2019 bilateral agricultural trade turnover exceeded $5 billion USD for the first time. During the first ten months of 2020, Russia exported 3.7 million metric tonnes of agri-food products to China, valued at $3.2 billion USD.[57] The top ten list of nations to which Russia exports agri-food products is shown in Table 4.

Going forward, from the Russian perspective there are several opportunities to increase agricultural trade with China even without a FTA between the EAEU and China (see also Chapter 7). One opportunity to increase agricultural trade is the general economic development of the Russian Far East (RFE). From the Russian side, the Director of the Institute of Agricultural Market Conditions, Dmitry Ryl'ko, is quite optimistic that RFE can increase its food exports to China. He indicated that 'theoretically' soybean exports could expand to 1.5–2 million metric tonnes, up from 1 million tonnes that are currently exported from the region. While admitting that climatic conditions in the Russian Far East make the expansion of crop products modest, Ryl'ko maintains that the export of poultry and pork to China has a 'large potential' and good growth prospects, particularly of chicken feet and wings that are highly valued by Chinese consumers and for which Russia does not face much competition from Brazil or the EU.[58]

A second opportunity for Russian exporters is the enormous demand for food from China's urban middle class. No one knows exactly the size of China's urban middle class other than it is large and growing. At the low end, the Economist Intelligence Unit estimates that 10 percent of the population is middle class, or about 132 million people.[59] At the high end, a different set of authors estimate that 50 percent of all urban households may be in the middle class, or more than 500 million people.[60] Whatever its size, the gradual lowering of trade barriers following China's accession to the WTO was accompanied by rising income and living standards as well as changes in consumption habits. By 2013, China was importing nearly $26 billion USD in agricultural products from the United States alone.[61] During 2016–2018, China averaged more than 15 percent of total U.S. agricultural exports, more than any single country.[62] Since then, China has become the world's largest agricultural importer by dollar value, with total annual agricultural imports reaching almost $140 billion USD in 2017 and 2018. Thus, there is an enormous opportunity for Russian food exporters to increase their market share.

As Chinese consumers' incomes rise, their preferences gravitate towards higher-cost animal husbandry products and it is for that reason that Russian animal husbandry exports will be more valuable than crop exports. Pork is traditionally one of the most popular sources of protein in the Chinese diet and China is the world's largest producer and consumer of pork. In 2019, China's pork imports are estimated to have ranged between 3.1 and 3.3 million metric tonnes in 2019 with projections to reach 4.6 million metric tonnes in 2020.[63] Against this context, Russia's pork production has increased substantially in the past decade, rising from 2.6 million tonnes in 2008 to 4.7 million tonnes in 2018 (all categories of farms). Within this overall rise, the number of pigs and pork production from households declined while pork production on corporate farms rose and in 2018 comprised 61 percent of total production.[64]

The opportunity for Russian exporters to increase their share in China's pork market is supported not only by rising Russian output but also by outbreaks of swine flu in China since 2016. In 2019 alone, the number of pigs in China contracted by more than 50 percent, from nearly 5 million pigs in January 2019 to fewer than 2.5 million pigs by late 2019; and pork production plummeted from 60 million tonnes to less than 30 million tonnes during that same period.[65] That said, the opportunity created by falling domestic pork production in China is offset by shifting consumer preferences away from pork due to health concerns and more towards poultry and eggs.[66]

A final opportunity for Russia's exporters grows out of the U.S.–China trade war that during 2019 and into 2020 decimated American exports of soybean to China. Although Russia will not be able to fill the void completely, the Foreign Agricultural Service forecasts total Russian soy exports rising from 930 thousand metric tonnes in 2019/2020 agricultural year to 1 million metric tonnes in the 2020/2021 agricultural year, of which somewhere between one-half to three-quarters will be sold to China.[67]

In addition to food trade with China, trade with Vietnam has also expanded significantly. Above we noted that for total trade Russia runs a deficit vis-à-vis Vietnam, but if agri-food trade is considered the picture is more positive. Data from the World Bank show that there has been a sharp increase in Russia's agricultural exports to Vietnam after the FTA entered into force.[68] In 2018, Vietnam was number ten on Russia's top list of export destinations for its agricultural products, (see Table 4). Prior to the FTA between Russia and Vietnam, agri-food trade was minimal, less than $1 million USD a year in 2000 and there was not much improvement over time. Once the FTA was signed in 2016, however, Russia's agri-food exports to Vietnam increased quickly to $400 million USD in 2017, and since 2017 Russia's exports have surpassed the value of agri-food imports from Vietnam. Overall, Russia's agri-food exports grew from less than $1 million USD in 2008 to almost $600 million USD in 2018.[69]

5 Outlook

Taking a long view of Russia's agri-food trade policy and partners reveals a high degree of resilience on the part of Russia to changing geopolitical and geoeconomic conditions. Since the 1980s, Russia has gone through at least three iterations in trading partners since 1992. The first iteration was the change from a concentration on intra-bloc trade in the Soviet period—nations that would become CIS members in 1992—to the development of trading relations with the West, most notably the EU, although that relationship was based neither on RTAs nor FTAs. During the 1990s agri-food trade with the EU overtook that with CIS members despite the latter having integrative advantages that continued from the Soviet period. The EU in particular became Russia's most important trading partner by volume and value, including agricultural and non-agricultural goods. That trade relationship continued during the 1990s up to 2014.

The second iteration dates from the introduction of Russia's countersanctions against Western nations in August 2014. This period is marked by Russia's turn away from agri-food imports with the West and the EU, although Russia continues to export food to EU members. Flowing from the second iteration, a third iteration has been the expansion of trade partners and actual trade beyond the EAEU, beyond the EU, and encompassing new partners in the Middle East and Asia, especially China. This third iteration is characterised by RTAs and FTAs that were examined in this chapter. The composition of countries in the third iteration—non-Western, some developing economies—is important because it reflects new political alignments. The composition also reflects the consolidation of trade relations with non-Western nations, which raises the question of not just when but whether Russia-Western trade can ever be revitalised. Further, the composition of trade partners in the third iteration holds importance for Russia's food security in that imports from developing nations are cheaper, thus benefiting consumers, but also may raise food safety and phytosanitary concerns, which obviously is not good for Russian consumers.

Across all three iterations, Russia has been an active participant in the global agri-food trade system as both an importer and exporter. Going forward, we do not expect Russia's role in the international food trade system to decrease in the years ahead. Although Russia is a relative latecomer to RTAs and FTAs, it has been active since 2014. Russian officials claim that the EAEU has received more than 50 proposals from various countries to establish or expand trade and economic relations. With a large number of MoUs, plus ongoing negotiations with Egypt, Ecuador, and Indonesia, we expect Russia to continue to expand its RTA profile.

In essence, Russia's trade resilience entails a three-part strategy since 2014. First, Russia has not severed relations with the WTO and continues to make periodic reports about its phytosanitary standards and other information as required by WTO rules. But agri-food trade with the West has diminished considerably, even to the point of irrelevance in the case of the United States (see Chapter 10). Second, Russia has increased the number of RTAs and FTAs that it participates in, whether temporary or permanent, preferential or non-preferential, and we expect the number to continue to grow. Third, Russia is committed to using the EAEU as an instrument to increase trade and various agreements, although it also is trying to increase bilateral ties as well. In this regard, analysts claim that the EAEU as well as EAEU external trade agreements primarily serve Russia's geopolitical agenda.[70]

All of the above is notable because a decade ago one would have expected that if Russia increased its RTAs and FTAs, it would be with the Western nations. Today, we know that is no longer true and Russia is putting most of its energy in developing trade with non-Western nations. While it is true that the EU is still Russia's most important trade partner as a recipient of Russia's exports (mainly energy), a free trade agreement is unlikely in the foreseeable future. At the same time, Russia's turn to the East holds major implications for its trade relations, the volume and direction of its agri-food trade, and the overall global geostrategic balance.

Notes

1. Kimberly Clausing, 'The Progressive Case Against Protectionism', *Foreign Affairs* 98, no. 6 (November–December 2019): 109–20.
2. Similar to free trade agreements, these types of agreements are referred to as trade preference agreements (PTAs), since trade liberalisation between the parties can go further without extending the privileges to other members of the World Trade Organization (WTO). Preferential free trade agreements can be bilateral or include more parties on a regional or intra-regional scale.
3. Claudia Hofmann, Alberto Osnago and Michele Ruta, 'The Content of Preferential Trade Agreements', *World Trade Review* 18, no. 3 (2018): 365–98.
4. For an updated overview of RTAs in force in 2020, see 'WTO Regional Trade Agreements Database', n.d. http://rtais.wto.org/UI/PublicMaintainRTAHome.aspx. Accessed 23 September 2020.
5. Timothy Josling and Stefan Tangermann, *Transatlantic Food and Agricultural Trade Policy: 50 Years of Conflict and Convergence* (Cheltenham, UK and Northampton, MA: Edward Elgar Publishing, 2015); and Edmond McGovern, *International Trade Regulation* (Exeter, UK: Globefield Press, 2008).
6. Rochini Acharya, 'Regional Trade Agreements: Challenges and Opportunities', *International Trade Forum* no. 4 (2018): 24–5.
7. Membership in the TPP 11 includes Australia, Brunei, Canada, Chile, Japan, Malaysia, Mexico, New Zealand, Peru, Singapore, and Vietnam. The agreement evolved from the Trans-Pacific Partnership (TPP), which never entered into force due to the withdrawal of the United States. The RCEP agreement is under negotiation between Brunei, Cambodia, Indonesia, Laos, Malaysia, Myanmar, the Philippines, Singapore, Thailand, and Vietnam, and five of their FTA partners—Australia, China, Japan, New Zealand, and South Korea.
8. Members of Mercosur, or the Southern Common Market, are Argentina, Brazil, Paraguay, and Uruguay.

9. European Commission, 'European Commission Presents Comprehensive Approach for the Modernisaton of the World Trade Organization', Press Release, 18 September 2018. http://trade.ec.europa.eu/doclib/press/index.cfm?id=1908. Accessed 6 November 2020.
10. Andrew G. Brown and Robert M. Stern, 'Free Trade Agreements and Governance of the Global Trading System', *The World Economy* 34, no. 3 (2011): 331–54.
11. Jagdish Bhagwati and Anne O. Krueger, 'US Trade Policy: The Infatuation with Free Trade Agreements', in *The Dangerous Drift to Preferential Trade Agreements*, eds. Jagdish Bhagwati and Anne O. Krueger (Washington, DC: AEI Press, 1995).
12. Richard E. Baldwin, 'Multilateralising Regionalism: Spaghetti Bowls as Building Blocks on the Path to Global Free Trade', *The World Economy* 29 (2006): 1451–518.
13. Bernard Hoekman, 'Open Plurilateral Agreements, Global Spillovers and the Multilateral Trading System', Working paper for the Bertelsmann Stiftung, 25 March 2020. https://www.bertelsmann-stiftung.de/fileadmin/files/user_upload/MT_OPA_Paper_2020_ENG.pdf. Accessed 6 November 2020.
14. Council on Foreign Relations, 'What Is the Trans-Pacific-Partnership (TPP)?', 4 January 2019. https://www.cfr.org/backgrounder/what-trans-pacific-partnership-tpp. Accessed 20 September 2020.
15. Robert D. Putnam, 'Diplomacy and Domestic Politics: The Logic of Two-Level Games', *International Organization* 42, no. 3 (1988): 427–60.
16. See Christina L. Davis, *Food Fights Over Free Trade* (Princeton: Princeton University Press, 2003).
17. Kimberly Ann Elliott, *Delivering on Doha: Farm Trade and the Poor* (Washington, DC: Institute for International Economics, 2006), 3–9; Jennifer Clapp, *Food*, 2nd ed. (Cambridge, UK: Polity Press, 2016), 67–82.
18. OECD, 'The Impact of Regional Trade Agreements on Trade in Agricultural Products', OECD Food, Agriculture and Fisheries Papers no. 65, 2013. https://www.oecd-ilibrary.org/agriculture-and-food/the-impact-of-regional-trade-agreements-on-trade-in-agricultural-products_5k3xznkz60vk-en. Accessed 7 November 2020.
19. Tatiana Isashenko, 'The Trade Policy of Russia: Latest Developments and Main Priorities', *Rivista di Studi Politici Internationzionali* 80, no. 3 (2013), 347–60.
20. Azerbaijan and Turkmenistan did not sign the agreement, and the participation of Uzbekistan was initially regulated by a special protocol. Russia signed bilateral FTAs with Georgia, Armenia, and Serbia.

21. Alexander Libman and Evgeny Vinokurov, *Holding-Together Regionalism: Twenty Years of Post-Soviet Integration* (London: Palgrave Macmillan, 2012).
22. See V. V. Rau, 'Russia in the Customs Union: The Agrarian Aspect', *Studies on Russian Economic Development* 24, no. 1 (2013): 77–83.
23. Veronika Movchan and Michael Emerson, 'The Eurasian Economic Union's Problematic Customs Union', 11 January 2018. Institute for Economic Research and Policy Consulting, Sweden, http://www.3dcftas.eu/. Accessed 11 November 2020.
24. See Seljan Verdiyeva, 'The Eurasian Economic Union: Problems and Prospects', *The Journal of World Investment and Trade* 19, no. 4 (2018): 722–49.
25. See Rilka Dragneva-Lewers and Kataryna Wolczuk, 'The Eurasian Economic Union: Deals, Rules, and the Exercise of Power' (London: Chatham House, 2017).
26. Anadolu Agency, 'Russia Disputes with Armenia, Belarus on Gas Prices', 19 May 2020. https://www.aa.com.tr/en/economy/russia-disputes-with-armenia-belarus-on-gas-prices/1846465. Accessed 15 September 2020.
27. Samuel Stolton, 'Armenia's EU Accession Could Be a "Question for the People"', 15 October 2019. https://www.euractiv.com/section/armenia/news/armenias-eu-accession-could-be-a-question-for-the-people-deputy-pm-says/. Accessed 14 September 2020.
28. Azimzhan Khitakhumnov and Bulat Mukhamediyev, 'Eurasian Economic Union: Present and Future Perspectives', *Economic Change and Restructuring* 50 (2017): 59–77.
29. European Union, 'The European Union and the Russian Federation', 25 February 2020. https://eeas.europa.eu/headquarters/headquarters-homepage/35939/european-union-and-russian-federation_en. Accessed 11 November 2020.
30. Tatiana Isachenko, 'The European Context of Russian Trade Policy', in *Russian Trade Policy, Achievements, Challenges and Prospects*, eds. Sergei Sutryn, Olga Y. Trofimenko and Alexandra Koval (London: Routledge, 2019), 165–80.
31. EFTA, 'Russia/Belarus/Kazakhstan. Negotiations Currently on Hold', n.d. https://www.efta.int/free-trade/ongoing-negotiations-talks/russia-belarus-kazakhstan. Accessed 15 September 2020.
32. United States Department of Agriculture, Foreign Agricultural Service, 'Retail Foods', GAIN Report RS2020-0036, 6 August 2020. https://apps.fas.usda.gov/newgainapi/api/Report/DownloadReportByFileName?fileName=Retail%20Foods_Moscow%20ATO_Russian%20Federation_06-30-2020. Accessed 6 November 2020.

33. Rilka Dragneva-Lewers and Kataryna Wolczuk, 'Trade and Geopolitics: Should the EU Engage with the Eurasian Economic Union?', European Policy Centre Policy Brief, 2 April 2015. https://css.ethz.ch/en/services/digital-library/publications/publication.html/189983. Accessed 5 September 2020.
34. Ksenia S. Volnistaya, 'Five Years of the Eurasian Economic Union—Results and New Benchmarks for Belarus', 2019. https://elib.bsu.by/bitstream/123456789/221587/1/81-85.pdf. Accessed 12 September 2020.
35. United States Department of Agriculture, Foreign Agricultural Service, 'Eurasian Economic Commission Published 2021 TRQs', GAIN Report no. RS2020-0041, 28 August 2020. www.fas.usda.gov/data. Accessed 12 November 2020.
36. Eurasian Economic Commission, 'Agroindustrial Policy of the Eurasian Economic Union', 2015, 4. http://www.eurasiancommission.org/ru/Documents/APK_ing_n.pdf. Accessed 7 November 2020.
37. Eurasian Economic Commission, 'EEC and Minselkhoz of Russia Discussed Prospects for Developing Integration in Agricultural Sector', 19 August 2020. http://www.eurasiancommission.org/en/nae/news/Pages/19.08.2020-1.aspx. Accessed 6 November 2020.
38. Eurasian Economic Commission, 'EAEU Agriculture Ministers Discussed Food Security in Conditions of Coronavirus Pandemic', 19 May 2020. http://www.eurasiancommission.org/en/nae/news/Pages/19-05-2020-1.aspx. Accessed 16 September 2020.
39. Vladimir Mazyrin, 'The Impact of the EAEU—Vietnam FTA on Bilateral Trade', 25 March 2019. http://greater-europe.org/archives/6636. Accessed 16 September 2020.
40. Parlamentaskaia gazeta, 'Soglashenie o svobodnoi torgovle mezhdu EAES i Serbiei rassmotriat senstory', 4 November 2020. https://kvedomosti.ru/news/https-www-pnp-ru-economics-soglashenie-o-svobodnoy-torgovle-mezhdu-eaes-i-serbiey-rassmotryat-senatory-html.html. Accessed 4 November 2020.
41. TASS, 'Iran i EAES mogut sozdat' postoiannuiu zonu svobodnoi torgovli do kontsa goda', 2 November 2020. https://www.dairynews.ru/news/iran-i-eaes-mogut-sozdat-postoyannuyu-zonu-svobodn.html. Accessed 2 November 2020.
42. Fakhri Vakilov, 'Kazakhstan, Other EAEU Countries to Reduce Import Duties on Iran on 502 Goods', 26 April 2019. https://www.bilaterals.org/?kazakhstan-other-eaeu-countries-to. Accessed 7 November 2020.
43. Aljazeera America, 'Iran and Russia Closing in on Trade Agreement', 10 January 2014. http://america.aljazeera.com/articles/2014/1/10/sources-iran-andrussiaclosinginontradearrangement.html. Accessed 2 September 2020.

44. Eurasian Economic Commission, 'Framework Agreement on Comprehensive Economic Cooperation Between the Eurasian Economic Union and Its Member States, of the One Part, and the Republic of Singapore, of the Other Part', October 2019. http://www.eurasiancommission.org/ru/act/trade/dotp/sogl_torg/Documents/Сингапур/EAEU-Singapore%20Framework%20Agreement.pdf. Accessed 11 November 2020.
45. Bilaterals.org, 'EAEU-Singapore Free Trade Agreement Signed in Yerevan', 1 October 2019. https://www.bilaterals.org/?eaeu-singapore-free-trade. Accessed 11 November 2020.
46. Dmitrii Bokarev, 'FTZ with Singapore—A New Bridge Between EAEU and ASEAN', 23 January 2020. https://journal-neo.org/2020/01/23/ftz-with-singapore-a-new-bridge-between-eaeu-and-asean/. Accessed 16 September 2020.
47. Ekaterina Y. Arapova and Tatiana M. Isaschenko, 'Russian Trade Policy: Main Trends and Impact on Bilateral Trade Flows', *International Journal of Economic Policy in Emerging Economies* 12, no. 1 (2019): 26–48.
48. Yurii Sizov, 'EAEU i Izrail' gotoviatsia k zakliucheniiu soglasheniia o zone svobodnoi torgovli', 3 July 2020. https://rg.ru/2020/07/03/eaes-i-izrail-gotoviatsia-k-zakliucheniiu-soglasheniia-o-zone-svobodnoj-torgovli.html. Accessed 21 August 2020.
49. Israel Ministry of Foreign Affairs, 'PM Netanyahu Meets with Russian President Vladimir Putin in Jerusalem', 23 January 2020. https://mfa.gov.il/MFA/AboutTheMinistry/Conferences-Seminars/World_Holocaust_Forum_2020/Pages/PM-Netanyahu-meets-with-Russian-President-Vladimir-Putin-in-Jerusalem--23-January-2020.aspx. Accessed 11 November 2020.
50. TASS, 'Rossiia poluchila pravo postavki molochnoi i rybnoi produktsii v Egipet', 13 November 2020. https://kvedomosti.ru/news/https-tass-ru-ekonomika-9981907.html. Accessed 13 November 2020.
51. The EAEU reported that in 2014 the top consumers of its food products were CIS countries (20.3%), EU countries (14.8%), Turkey (12.6%), Egypt (7.2%) and China (6.3%). Also, Iran (5.2%) and Korea (4.7%) were important consumer of food from EAEU countries. Eurasian Economic Commission, 'Agroindustrial Policy of the Eurasian Economic Union', 49–50.
52. Italian Food News Net, 'Italian Food Exports to Russia Have Lost 1 bn Euro', 6 August 2019. https://news.italianfood.net/2019/08/06/italian-food-exports-to-russia-have-lost-1-bn-euro/. Accessed 5 October 2020.
53. Ekaterina Shokurova, 'Pravitel'stvennaia komissiia podderzhala sozdanie gossistemy proslezhivaieosti zerna', 12 November 2020. https://www.agroinvestor.ru/analytics/news/34788-pravitelstvennaya-komissiya-pod

derzhala-sozdanie-gossistemy-proslezhivaemosti-zerna/. Accessed 12 November 2020.

54. Vienna Institute for International Economic Studies, 'Trade Reorientation in Russia: Will China Replace the EU?', 10 July 2018. https://wiiw.ac.at/trade-reorientation-in-russia-will-china-replace-the-eu--n-327.html. Accessed 2 September 2020.
55. Kvedomosti.ru, 'Kitai i Rossiia podpishut document o merakh po uvelicheniiu tovarooborota do $200 mlrd', 10 September 2019. https://kvedomosti.ru/news/kitaj-i-rossiya-podpishut-dokument-o-merax-po-uvelicheniyu-tovarooborota-do-200-mlrd.html. Accessed 12 November 2020.
56. Inna Ganenko, 'Terra inkognita dlia Rossiiskogo agroexporta', *Agroinvestor*, no. 5 (May 2019): 19.
57. The Dairy News, 'Eksport Rossiiskoi produktsii APK v Kitai vyros na 24%', 6 November 2020. https://www.dairynews.ru/news/eksport-rossiyskoy-produktsii-apk-v-kitay-vyros-na11.html. Accessed 6 November 2020.
58. See Anatoly Medetsky, 'Russia's Newest Ambition in China Is Selling More Chicken Wings', 22 May 2019. https://www.bloomberg.com/news/articles/2019-05-22/russia-s-newest-ambition-in-china-is-selling-more-chicken-wings. Accessed 12 November, 2020; and Sin'khua, 'Sotrudnichestvo v oblasti APK—novaia tochka rosta v torgovo-ekonomicheskom vzaimodeistvii Rossii i Kitaia', 27 November 2019. https://agrovesti.net/news/indst/sotrudnichestvo-v-oblasti-apk-novaya-tochka-rosta-v-torgovo-ekonomicheskom-vzaimodejstvii-rossii-i-kitaya.html. Accessed 13 November 2020.
59. Economist Intelligence Unit, *The Chinese Consumer in 2030* (London: Economist Intelligence Unit, 2016).
60. These authors use an expansive definition for China's middle class that encompasses not only income but also education and occupation. See Celine Bonnefond, Matthieu Clement, and Francois Combarnous, 'In Search of the Elusive Chinese Urban Middle Class: An Exploratory Analysis', *Post-Communist Economies* 27, no. 1 (2015): 41–59.
61. Fred Gale, James Hansen, and Michael Jewison, 'China's Growing Demand for Agricultural Imports', *Economic Research Service Bulletin*, no. 136 (February 2015): 3–4.
62. Kamron Daugherty and Hi Jiang, 'Outlook for U.S. Agricultural Trade', Economic Research Service Situation and Outlook Report AES-108 (30 May 2019): 5. The value of U.S. agricultural exports to China decreased as a result of the trade war between the two countries, to about $24 billion USD in 2017 and to only $9.3 billion USD in 2018.
63. Reuters, 'China's Pork Imports May Hit Record 4.6 Million Tonnes in 2020: Rabobank', 8 November 2019. https://www.reuters.com/art

icle/us-china-swinefever-pork-imports/chinas-pork-imports-may-hit-record-4-6-million-tonnes-in-2020-rabobank-idUSKBN1XI0ZI. Accessed 13 November 2020.

64. Ministerstvo sel'skogo khoziaistva Rossiiskoi Federatsii, *National'nyi doklad: O khode i resul'tatakh realizatsii v 2010 godu gosudarstvennoi programmy razvitiia sel'skogo khozyaistva i regulirovaniia rynkov sel'skokhoziaistvennoi produktsii, syr'ia i prodovol'stviia na 2008–2012* (Moscow: Ministry of Agriculture, 2011), 42–3; and Ministerstvo sel'skogo khoziaistva Rossiiskoi Federatsii, *National'nyi doklad: O khode i resul'tatakh realizatsii v 2018 godu gosudarstvennoi programmy razvitiia sel'skogo khozyaistva i regulirovaniia rynkov sel'skokhoziaistvennoi produktsii, syr'ia i prodovol'stviia na 2013–2020* (Moscow: Ministry of Agriculture, 2019), 54.
65. Liubov Savkina, 'Kogda svinina poedet v Kitai', *Agroinvestor*, no. 2 (February 2020): 39–40.
66. Ibid., 40.
67. United States Department of Agriculture, Foreign Agricultural Service, 'Oilseeds and Production Annual', GAIN Report RS2020-0023, 27 April 2020. www.fas.usda.gov/data. Accessed 13 November 2020.
68. Author's calculations based on data from World Integrated Trade Solutions by the World Bank, https://wits.worldbank.org. The category of agricultural products is the sum total of «Animal» (HS01, 02, 03, 04 and 05), «Vegetables» (HS06, 07, 08, 09, 10, 11, 12, 13, 14 and 15, and «Food Products» (HS16, 17, 18, 19, 20, 21, 22, 23 and 24).
69. Author's calculations based on data from World Integrated Trade Solutions by the World Bank, https://wits.worldbank.org. The category of agricultural products is the sum total of Animal (HS01, 02, 03, 04 and 05), Vegetables (HS06, 07, 08, 09, 10, 11, 12, 13, 14 and 15, and Food Products (HS16, 17, 18, 19, 20, 21, 22, 23 and 24).
70. Dragneva-Lewers and Wolczuk, 'Trade and Geopolitics: Should the EU Engage with the Eurasian Economic Union?'.

Selected Bibliography

Arapova, Ekaterina and Tatiana Isachenko. 'Russian Trade Policy: Main Trends and Impact on Bilateral Trade Flows'. *International Journal. of Economic Policy in Emerging Economies* 12, no. 1 (2019): 26–48.

Baldwin, Richard E. 'Multilateralising Regionalism: Spaghetti Bowls as Building Blocks on the Path to Global Free Trade'. *The World Economy* 29 (2006): 1451–518.

Bhagwati, Jagdish and Anne O. Krueger. 'US Trade Policy: The Infatuation with Free Trade Agreements'. In *The Dangerous Drift to Preferential Trade Agreements*. Washington, DC: AEI Press, 1995.

Brown, Andrew G. and Robert M. Stern. 'Free Trade Agreements and Governance of the Global Trading System'. *The World Economy* 34, no. 3 (2011): 331–54.

Clapp, Jennifer. *Food*, 2nd ed. Cambridge, UK: Polity Press, 2016.

Clausing, Kimberly. 'The Progressive Case Against Protectionism'. *Foreign Affairs* 98, no. 6 (November–December 2019): 109–20.

Davis, Christina L. *Food Fights Over Free Trade*. Princeton: Princeton University Press, 2003.

Dragneva-Lewers, Rilka and Kataryna Wolczuk. 'The Eurasian Economic Union: Deals, Rules, and the Exercise of Power'. London: Chatham House, 2017.

Elliott, Kimberly Ann. *Delivering on Doha: Farm Trade and the Poor*. Washington, DC: Institute for International Economics, 2006.

Hofmann, Claudia, Alberto Osnago and Michele Ruta. 'The Content of Preferential Trade Agreements'. *World Trade Review* 18, no. 3 (2018): 365–98.

Isachenko, Tatiana. 'The trade policy of Russia: Latest Developments and Main Priorities'. *Rivista di Studi Politici Internazionali* 80, no. 3 (2013): 347–60.

Isachenko, Tatiana. 'The European Context of Russian Trade Policy'. In *Russian Trade Policy. Achievements, Challenges and Prospects*, eds. Sergei Sutyrin, Olga Y. Trofimenko, and Alexandra Koval. London: Routledge, 2019, 165–80.

Josling, Timothy and Stefan Tangermann. *Transatlantic Food and Agricultural Trade Policy: 50 Years of Conflict and Convergence*. Cheltenham, UK and Northampton, MA: Edward Elgar Publishing, 2015.

Khitakhumnov, Azimzhan and Bulat Mukhamediyev. 'Eurasian Economic Union: Present and Future Perspectives'. *Economic Change and Restructuring* 50 (2017): 59–77.

Libman, Alexander and Evgeny Vinokurov. *Holding-Together Regionalism: Twenty Years of Post-Soviet Integration*. London: Palgrave Macmillan, 2012.

McGovern, Edmond. *International Trade Regulation*. Exeter, UK: Globefield Press, 2008.

Putnam, Robert. D. 'Diplomacy and Domestic Politics: The Logic of Two-Level Games'. *International Organization* 42, no. 3 (1988): 427–60.

Rau, V. V. 'Russia in the Customs Union: The Agrarian Aspect'. *Studies on Russian Economic Development* 24, no. 1 (2013): 77–83.

Verdiyeva, Seljan, 'The Eurasian Economic Union: Problems and Prospects'. *The Journal of World Investment and Trade* 19, no. 4 (2018): 722–49.

Wegren, Stephen K. and Christel Elvestad. 'Russia's Food Self-sufficiency and Food Security: An Assessment'. *Post-Communist Economies* 30, no. 5 (2018): 565–87.

Open Access This chapter is licensed under the terms of the Creative Commons Attribution 4.0 International License (http://creativecommons.org/licenses/by/4.0/), which permits use, sharing, adaptation, distribution and reproduction in any medium or format, as long as you give appropriate credit to the original author(s) and the source, provide a link to the Creative Commons license and indicate if changes were made.

The images or other third party material in this chapter are included in the chapter's Creative Commons license, unless indicated otherwise in a credit line to the material. If material is not included in the chapter's Creative Commons license and your intended use is not permitted by statutory regulation or exceeds the permitted use, you will need to obtain permission directly from the copyright holder.

Chapter 7: Prospects for Agri-Food Trade Between Russia and China

Jiayi Zhou

1 Introduction

Amidst the backdrop of ever heightening tensions between the United States and China, a June 2019 meeting of the Russian and Chinese presidents witnessed their bilateral relationship upgraded to a 'comprehensive strategic partnership of coordination in a new era'. In the summit's joint statement, Russia and China agreed to expand bilateral agricultural cooperation, including for soybean trade. President Vladimir Putin later that year would remark that the U.S.–China dispute offered a window of opportunity for Russian producers to fill gaps in the Chinese market, a market from which he claimed the United States had 'voluntarily withdrawn'.[1]

The China–U.S. trade war paused in the beginning of 2020 with the signing of the Phase One economic and trade agreement. However, questions remain as to how the shifting geopolitical landscape is impacting trade in general, and food trade in particular. Indeed, the politicisation if not weaponisation of food trade among the great powers is

J. Zhou (✉)
Stockholm International Peace Research Institute (SIPRI), Stockholm, Sweden
e-mail: zhou@sipri.org

© The Author(s) 2022

S. K. Wegren and F. Nilssen (eds.), *Russia's Role in the Contemporary International Agri-Food Trade System*, Palgrave Advances in Bioeconomy: Economics and Policies,
https://doi.org/10.1007/978-3-030-77451-6_8

evidenced not only by the China–U.S. soybean battle, but also by Russia's ongoing countersanctions against Western food imports. Unsurprisingly, Russia–China agricultural cooperation is framed and interpreted within the broader context of both countries' tensions with the West.[2]

This chapter explores Russia–China agri-food trade as part of that context, as part of a relationship marked by increasingly close rapprochement if not entente. However, in agricultural trade as in the broader political relationship, high-level declarative cooperation is tempered by the countries' respective national and domestic priorities, which are not always aligned. China is and will remain an important trade partner for Russia to reach its main export goals for 2024. However, the chapter thus cautions there are a number of technical as well as political hurdles to enhance trade cooperation.

The chapter proceeds with an overview of Russia–China economic relations, before turning to agri-food trade relations in particular—which has only recently begun to feature as a priority in that relationship. The chapter then turns to their respective national priorities in the agricultural trade sector. On the Russian side, priorities are marked by ambitious export-oriented targets as well as a broader economic turn to the (Far) East. On the Chinese side, authorities emphasise self-sufficiency and prioritise domestic production, particularly in terms of grain. However, China has also become irreversibly dependent on foreign markets, and is also interested in mitigating overseas supply chain risks through the diversification of its agricultural trade partners. The fourth section outlines the prospects and challenges of deepened trade cooperation in specific agricultural commodity and product groups, with an emphasis on Russian exporters' access to Chinese markets. The chapter finally turns to a number of broader structural barriers to deepened bilateral agri-food trade, before concluding with a medium-term outlook.

2 Bilateral Relations

In the more than three decades since the normalisation of diplomatic relations between the Soviet Union and the People's Republic of China, relations between the neighbouring powers have grown to become a constitutive feature of international relations.[3] Long-standing territorial and border demarcation issues were worked out throughout the 1990s, and definitely resolved in 2005. Already by 1996, the relationship had formally become a 'strategic partnership', entailing the establishment of annual meetings of prime ministers with policy consultation along with a number of issue domains. And in 2001, at the beginning of Putin's first term, a Russia–China 'Treaty of Good Neighbourliness, Friendship and Cooperation' was signed, which also included a number of strategic provisions, including strengthened bilateral military cooperation as well mutual defence consultation.

The two powers have, over the past three decades, aligned in their criticism against Western military interventionism, and become outspoken proponents of a 'multipolar' world order. They often hold joint positions on key global issues—including as permanent members of the UN Security Council. The two also have common if not shared foreign policy emphases on state sovereignty and similar threat perceptions, as well as domestic political governance models antithetical to the Western liberal democratic norms. There is a considerable amount of speculation and analysis as to whether a formal alliance is in the cards for the future: though officials' statements suggest that it is not (indeed, this would violate basic tenets of China's non-alignment foreign policy).[4] But there also remains a degree of ambivalence regarding the nature of the relationship. Throughout the early 2000s, Russian foreign and economic policy was oriented towards the West rather than East. Russia policymakers exhibited concerns over sensitive technology transfers, Chinese migration in the Russian Far East, as well as Chinese encroachment in the broader post-Soviet space. Meanwhile, China's own priorities centred around maintaining a stable external environment for domestic economic growth; its foreign policy attention was therefore primarily oriented towards its main trade and investment partners in the United States and other developed countries. Many aspects of the relationship thus remained declarative: high-level, but with limited operational substance.

By the late 2000s, however, it was increasingly clear that Russia's experiment with the Western integration had reached a limit. A pivot to the East took shape, one that coincided with the emergence of China as economic powerhouse. Since the 2014 crisis in Ukraine, Russia's drive to improve ties with China has intensified. Previous ideas that the relationship with China constituted an 'axis of convenience' rather than a strategic priority for Moscow, have become less relevant.[5] Indeed, previous stumbling blocks in the bilateral relationship have since been resolved. In addition to the 2014 signing of a long-term gas deal, Russia has also begun selling its most advanced weapons systems the S-400 anti-aircraft system and its Su-35 fighter jets to China.[6] Russia invited China to participate in Vostok-2018, held in the Russian Far East and its largest military exercise since 1981, and the two have conducted joint air patrols since.[7] In 2015, their respective flagship foreign economic initiatives, the Russia-led Eurasian Economic Union (EAEU) and China's Belt and Road Initiative (BRI) also signed a cooperation agreement.

On the Chinese side, economic and political tensions with the United States have visibly worsened since 2018, which have likewise stimulated a desire for deepened cooperation with Russia. In declarative terms, the relationship between the two countries had by 2011 already been upgraded to a 'comprehensive strategic partnership of cooperation', a singular category in China's foreign relations that applies to Russia alone.[8] President Xi Jinping, who came to power in 2012, has embarked on more state visits to Russia than any other country.[9] On his state visit to Moscow in June 2019, Xi referred to Putin as 'my closest foreign colleague, and best friend', while Putin referred to the relationship as a 'truly comprehensive partnership and strategic interaction' and as having reached an 'unprecedentedly high level'.[10]

At the same time, however, the high-level pronouncements by Moscow and Beijing are belied by more anaemic cooperation on the ground. This is particularly the case in the economic realm where programmes and plans usually face disappointing follow-up and delivery in practice.[11] Latent tensions remain, including Sinophobia and concerns over territorial sovereignty.[12] Economic relations have long been asymmetric, with Russia frequently referred to as the 'junior partner' in the relationship: the Chinese economy has only grown and improved while Russia's is stagnant and remains largely based on extractive commodities. Indeed, while China has been the largest trade partner for Russia outside of the European Union (EU) since 2010, Russia ranked only 10th among China's trade partners in 2019, rising from just 0.8 percent in 2018 to just under 3 percent of China's overall trade turnover.[13] Meanwhile, China accounted for about 15.8 percent of Russia's total trade turnover in 2018, at about $108.2 billion USD. For comparison, U.S.–Chinese trade exceeded $659.8 billion USD in 2018, over six times the Russia–China level. Russia, moreover, largely supplies the Chinese economy with raw materials, with Russia becoming China's largest supplier of crude oil in 2018.

Meanwhile, the extent and success of Putin's pivot eastwards have been debated, given unmet expectations that China would be able to fill the gap of Western investors and trade partners.[14] Russian actors also tend to emphasise that their pivot eastwards is not limited to China, but is also oriented towards strengthening partnerships with Asian governments including South Korea and Japan. Concerns of overreliance and becoming outcompeted domestically, are present for both Russian policymakers and in EAEU-BRI negotiations regarding free trade.[15] Nevertheless, enhancing trade is a policy goal on both sides. At the September 2019 Heads of Government meeting in St. Petersburg, the countries agreed to nearly double the current level of trade, to a targeted $200 billion USD by 2024.

2.1 Bilateral Agricultural Trade Relations

During the first half of the 1990s, up to 1997, Russia was a net importer of agricultural goods from China. The agricultural trade balance began to even out in the rest of the decade, but the overall volume remained low, peaking at just over $1 billion USD in 1993.[16] From the 2000s onwards, however, the volumes of agri-food trade have seen steady growth in both directions, increasing approximately 16 percent annually between 2000 and 2014—when the bilateral agricultural trade volume reached $3.85 billion USD. Prior to the Ukraine crisis, Russia counted as China's 15th largest agricultural trade partner, amounting to approximately 2 percent of China's agricultural trade.[17] In terms of agricultural commodities, Russian trade with China has been relatively balanced (see Fig. 1).

Agri-food exports from Russia to China show a steady increase since 2014, and then a big jump in 2018 to just under $3 billion USD, a result of Russian opportunism during the U.S.–China trade war (see Fig. 2). While China is the largest export market for Russian agri-food products, Russia accounted for only 2 percent of China's agricultural imports in 2018, reflecting the overall direction of economic dependency.[18] Moreover, agriculture still represents a rather small proportion of Russian exports to China, amounting to only 4.5 percent of the total in 2018.[19] In the first half of 2020, Russian exports increased to $1.9 billion USD worth of agricultural products, a pace that would lead to a record level if maintained for the duration of 2020.[20] Going forward, there is ambition by both sides to raise the level of agricultural trade and cooperation as part of the broader economic, political, and strategic relationship under a so-called 'new era' of bilateral cooperation between China and Russia. Given the attention of the highest political leadership, this means that

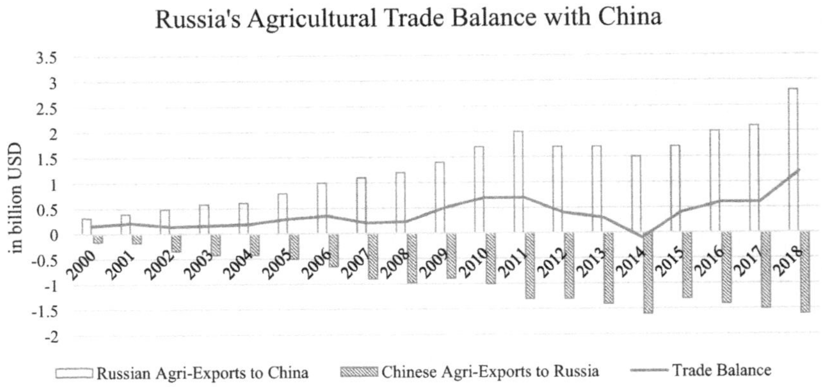

Fig. 1 Russia-China agricultural trade balance (*Source* Author's rendition from data in Chatham House, 'Exploring Interdependencies in Global Resource Trade', 2018. http://resourcetrade.earth/, accessed 29 October 2020)

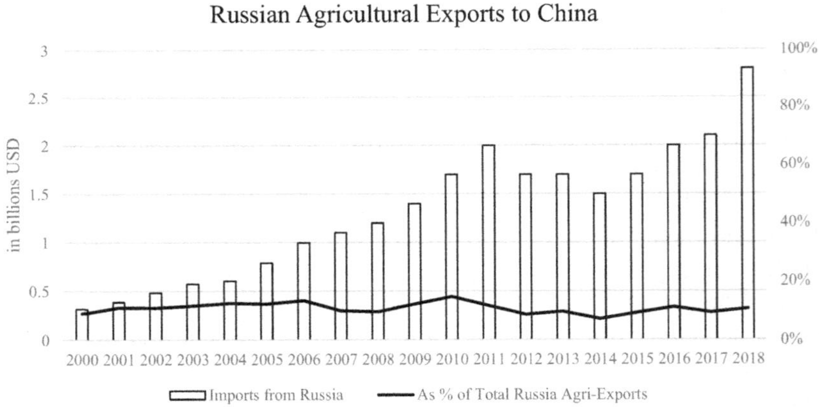

Fig. 2 Russian agricultural exports to China (*Source* Author's rendition from data in Chatham House, 'Exploring Interdependencies in Global Resource Trade', 2018. http://resourcetrade.earth/, accessed 29 October 2020)

there is likely to be increased policy support for enhanced cooperation in agricultural trade.

The main Russian agricultural export to China during the past two decades has consistently been fish and seafood. Exported largely as raw materials for Chinese processing, these products consisted of up to over 90 percent of Russian agricultural exports to China up until the early 2010s.[21] Since then, there has since then been some diversification in the structure of Russian agri-food exports to China, particularly in the direction of oilseeds and fat products as well as some processed foodstuffs. In 2018, fish and crustaceans accounted for 59 percent of agri-food exports to China; oilseed and oilseed products 15 percent; and higher-value-added processed food products at 13 percent.[22] Russian imports of Chinese agricultural goods, on the other hand, have strongly reflected Chinese comparative strengths in labour-intensive goods such as vegetables and fruits. In 2018, those two categories accounted for nearly half of Chinese exports to Russia.

3 Respective National Priorities

There are important domestic drivers for agricultural cooperation on both sides. At the same time, however, those self-same national domestic priorities also create certain limiting conditions for the future. For example, it is important to note that both Russian and Chinese agri-food policies are marked by strategic considerations, in particular, national self-sufficiency. Since at least the early 2010s, the Russian state has embarked on an ambitious import substitution campaign, of which agriculture features prominently.[23] Contours of this policy were outlined in the 2010 Food Security Doctrine, which set self-sufficiency targets in various agricultural product categories. These were made more stringent in a 2020 update. Russia's import ban against Western agricultural products in 2014 was also framed as contribution to those goals; the Russian Ministry of Agriculture has celebrated the reduction of agricultural imports by one-third since the ban was imposed.[24] In short, Russian leadership, while reorienting its trade relations away from the West, has simultaneously endeavoured to limit imports more generally. At the same time, there are ambitious agri-export targets, as exemplified by Putin's statement in 2012, that 'in the next four to five years we must fully ensure our independence in all major types of food production, and Russia must then become the world's largest producer of food'.[25]

China has likewise held a long-standing policy of self-sufficiency in staple grain products, including wheat, corn, and rice, since the mid-1990s.[26] These priorities limit the complementarily of the two markets, given that the current structure of Russian agricultural exports is concentrated in grain. However, Chinese remains a significant agricultural importer outside of the grain category, and demand is growing. China is actively seeking to diversify its suppliers for key agricultural commodities, as well as seeking further agricultural investment opportunities and markets abroad, not least due to the trade tensions with the West. The following subsection describes their respective policies and priorities in greater detail, focusing on Russia's export strategy as it relates to China as well as its vision for internal agricultural development, for which China is seen as a key partner. It also details Chinese policy priorities in this regard.

3.1 Russian Export Targets and RFE Development Priorities

Current Russian export goals are defined by the 2018 Executive Order 'On national goals and strategic objectives for the development of the Russian Federation for the period up to 2024'. This tasks the Russian government with increasing the volume of exports of non-primary non-energy goods to $250 billion USD by 2024. Specific sub-targets include increasing exports of agricultural products to $45 billion USD, more than double the export value in 2017.[27] In late 2020, Russia's Ministry of Agriculture acknowledged that the $45 billion USD goal was unlikely to be reached and the deadline needed to be extended, although the general trend in agri-food exports was upwards. As defined by the Ministry of Agriculture's plan 'Exports of AIC [agro-industrial complex] Products (2018–2024)', agri-exports of all categories should grow, but with a reduction in the proportion of grain exports towards meat and dairy, oilseed products, and processed goods.[28] The plan also sets a target for agricultural exports to China to increase to $7.7 billion USD by 2024, and China also features as an explicit target market in individual product categories.[29]

Related to these ambitious export targets, a priority for the Russian state is agricultural development in the Russian Far East (RFE), which borders China. While the underdevelopment of the RFE has been a historic issue for authorities in Moscow, it began to receive more sustained attention alongside the broader pivot eastwards.[30] A specialised Ministry for the Development of the Far East was established in 2012, and Putin would highlight the development of Siberia and the Russian Far East as a 'national priority for the entire twenty-first century'.[31] This has been recently reconfirmed at, among other venues, the 2018 Eastern Economic Forum (EEF) during which Putin reiterated that 'the development of the Far East is an absolute priority' and part of a 'consistent, long-term policy for the country'. He also singled out agriculture as a particular sector for investment as well as part of the region's comparative advantage.[32] A follow-up draft 'National programme for the development of the Far East for the period up to 2025 and to 2035' was developed in 2019.[33] The Russian government plans to increase agricultural exports from the RFE from $3.8 billion USD to $5.9 billion USD by 2024.[34] Much of that increase is expected to come from fish, seafood, and soybean, whose production is concentrated in the RFE. However, whether those goals will be reached substantially depends on whether promised levels of federal funding and support will be dispersed. RFE development programmes have a habitual tendency to be underfunded; during a 2019 Presidium, it was noted by RFE regional officials that such programmes very often do not have sufficient implementation mechanisms, and that sources of funding have in the past been dispersed only at the level of 10–20 percent level of original promises.[35]

To facilitate development, foreign direct investment into the RFE has long been sought, particularly from Northeast Asian partners and not limited to China.[36] However, Chinese investment in the region is most notable, and still is considered critical. In 2016, for example, a Russia-Chinese Agro-Industrial Development Fund of $10 billion USD was announced, of which nearly 90 percent of the capital was to be provided by Chinese investors.[37] At the 2018 EEF—a forum set up to attract foreign investors—Putin estimated that the Chinese were involved in around 30 ongoing projects in the RFE, with an investment volume of approximately $200 billion USD.[38] However, it is important to note that data about foreign investments tend to be incomplete, with underreporting across both Russian and Chinese governmental departments and agencies.[39]

Agriculture has featured in bilateral regional development plans, including the Program of Cooperation between the Regions of the Far East and Eastern Siberia and the Northeast of the People's Republic of China (2009–2018), the first long-term regional cooperation plan to include agriculture.[40] The Sino-Russian Cooperation and Development Plan in Russia's Far East Region (2018–2024) also contains provisions on agriculture. The document recognises that the lower food self-sufficiency of the RFE creates opportunities for increased Chinese investment, while also aimed at increasing RFE agricultural exports to China.[41]

In addition to providing investment, Chinese individuals and companies also farm a significant amount of RFE territory.[42] Much of China's agricultural activity in Russia is concentrated along those border regions, and there are estimates that this constitutes anywhere from 350,000 hectares to 400,000 hectares of farmland. There is some uncertainty due to the informal nature of some leasing arrangements: the governor of the Jewish Autonomous Oblast, where Chinese presence is purported to be the largest, notes that official land titles do not reflect the reality of Chinese production, due to informal leasing practices.[43]

Thus, Russia's desire for development in the RFE for which both Chinese capital and labour are critical, juxtaposes with concerns about economic overreliance as well as the encroachment of Chinese nationals on domestic territory. Agriculture-specific concerns also include putative predative exploitation by Chinese farmers, and possible longer-term reduction of soil fertility due to intensive agricultural practices and use of chemical fertilisers.[44] This leads to a fickle and uncertain policy environment for Chinese investors.[45] For example, the aforementioned bilateral agreements to enhance imports from China contradict other domestic guidelines to make the region *less* reliant on imports from China.[46]

4 Prospects for Increasing Russian Exports

As noted in Fig. 2, since 2014 there has been significant growth in the volume of agricultural trade between Russia and China, and in particular in the volume of Russian agricultural exports to China. One important driver of the increase has been the devaluation of the ruble.[47] But the increase also reflects that Russia has now gained access to the Chinese market in key product categories, with the clearing of important phytosanitary hurdles in the past five years when protocols for grain, soybeans, poultry, beef, and dairy, and other items have been signed. This certainly bodes well for the future of Russia–China agricultural trade. However, it is worth pointing out that the current increase is from a negligible baseline.

Separate from market access is a question of market competitiveness, for which according to Karlova and Serova Russia's advantages are 'fairly limited'.[48] As officials in Russia's Ministry of Agriculture acknowledge, 'China is the country to which all export-oriented countries want to supply their products. We are no exception'.[49] Rising living standards and changing dietary patterns in China will continue provide to Russia opportunities to increase food exports. But Russia faces competition against already-dominant exporters of soybeans, oilseeds, meat, and dairy, as well as from emerging markets with whom China has been concurrently cultivating closer agricultural trade ties in recent years. The westernisation of Chinese consumption entails greater demand for higher-value products—with a commensurate focus on quality—which are not historically Russian strengths although that situation is changing.

In addition, the Chinese economy is not only marked by significant demand. China also dominates in the global production of many agricultural commodities. Besides being the world's largest single producer of grain, it is also one of the world's largest exporters of fruits and vegetables, and fish and seafood. The latter it exports at twice the level of Russia, even while serving as Russia's largest buyer. Further, for a number of sensitive commodities, including by not limited to wheat, corn, rice, sugar, and wool, China applies strict tariff-rate quotas (TRQs). In the long run, this puts an upper limit on what Russian producers can hope to export. Given these considerations, the following analysis discusses Russian prospects for increasing the presence of the Chinese market in a few important product categories. I then return to broader structure barriers to enhancing agri-food trade.

- Grain: The Chinese market was closed to Russian wheat export since 1997 due to discovery of karnal and dwarf bunt pathogens. However, phytosanitary barriers were resolved in 2015 after the two sides signed a protocol for wheat, corn, rice, soybeans, and rapeseed.[50] As of 2020, wheat exports are allowed from seven Russian regions, including Chelyabinsk, Novosibirsk, Omsk, Amur, Krasnoyarsk, Altai, and Kurgan.[51] Current volumes of export are limited. In 2018, Chinese imports amounted to a mere 86.7 thousand tonnes. Corn imports were equally limited at 40 thousand tonnes.[52] However, in general more and more grain categories are open for Russian exporters. In 2018, a protocol on allowing Russian exports also of buckwheat, oats and oatmeal, millet, as well as other products including semolina and rye flour to China.[53]

China regulates grain trade through TRQs. Within quota tariffs for edible grains are set at a low 1 percent but outside the quota tariffs are a prohibitive 65 percent, and with limited licences that usually go to the major Chinese state-owned enterprises.[54] What imports do arrive are usually of very high quality and for a niche market. There is little indication that Chinese authorities will loosen their food security principles. At the same time, basic staple commodities such as corn, rice, wheat, are also becoming less important for the Chinese diet. Thus, according to Arkady Zlochevsky, the president of the Russian Grain Union, 'there are no particular prospects for the growth of grain sales'.[55]

- Fish and seafood: One of the areas where Russia has a strong foothold in the Chinese market is fish and seafood and these have comprised the bulk of Russian agricultural exports to China for a long time. In 2018, China accounted for 47 percent of Russia's fish and seafood exports, with an export value of $1.2 billion USD. China serves as Russia's main fish and seafood market, meanwhile Russia serves as China's largest foreign source of frozen fish. Russian fish exports to China are dominated by frozen pollock, approximately half the supply, as well as crabs. However, currently these Russian exports are for the most part unprocessed and low value added.
- Meat: China is one of the world's largest meat producers as well as importers.[56] Pork is the main source of animal protein in the Chinese diet, for which China has historically been more or less self-sufficient. But starting from 2018, the African Swine Flu (ASF) and decimation of China's pig stocks have led it to turn more to international markets, as well as to alternative meats. China has only recently opened as a destination for Russian meat exports, but as of the first half of 2020 it has already become the main destination.[57] At a September 2019 Russian Ministry of Agriculture meeting dedicated to the export of meat products, China was identified as one of the most promising markets, with an emphasis on poultry.[58] Poultry indeed exports currently comprise the bulk of meat exports to China.

After being banned in 2005 due to outbreaks of avian influenza, the two countries signed a protocol for mutual trade of frozen poultry in November 2018. In February 2019, the first shipment of 54 tonnes came from the Russian company Miratorg.[59] The company Cherkizovo, Russia's largest poultry producer, also began exporting chicken in May 2019.[60] By the end of 2019, Russia had exported approximately 62 thousand tonnes, worth $143.4 million USD, to China. Currently, chicken wings as well as chicken feet are primary parts being sold, in light of competition against dominant poultry exporters for parts for which Russia is not competitive. A number of requirements unique to the Chinese market, including on the processing side, however, remain to be met across the poultry industry.[61] Despite being the second largest producer in the world, China's poultry consumption and its imports are also expected to continue to grow.[62]

In January 2020, Cherkizovo also began to export turkey meat to China with an initial volume of 27 tonnes. In terms of beef, China has become one of the world's fastest growing markets: from a low starting point of 20,000 tonnes of beef imports in 2011, China imported nearly 1.7 million tonnes in 2019 and is now the world's second largest importer behind the United States.[63] In 2020, the companies Miratorg and Zarechnoe were provided licences to export beef to China, and a first shipment of 21.4 tonnes arrived in Shanghai in May.[64] Chinese imports of Russian beef will certainly grow from such a small baseline. However, Russian beef production is currently not produced at a competitive price, and in scale it is unlikely to challenge Brazil, Argentina, Uruguay, and Australia for any significant share of the Chinese market.

Growth in Chinese demand for poultry and beef is partly due to a substitution effect. ASF had decimated China's pig stocks by at least half (one-quarter of the world's production) by the end of 2019.[65] China's pork imports rose that year to 2.11 million metric tonnes and were expected to peak in 2020 before domestic production can recover.[66] Whether and how much the crisis-induced diversification towards other meat products will continue long-term remains to be seen. However, it is notable that even in 2018, analysts were predicting that China had reached 'peak pork', due both to a switch to alternatives in beef and poultry, but also due to government emphasis and consumer interest in reducing meat intake in general.[67]

As of mid-2020, Russia does not export any pork to China; pork exports to China were banned in 2008 due to ASF concerns. Russia's comparative advantages against larger exporters like the EU, Brazil, and Canada that are interested to taking advantage of the increased demand are also not obvious.[68] Nevertheless, projections by the Chinese Ministry of Agriculture are that meat imports will continue to increase during the next decade.[69] To the extent that Russian meat production keeps pace, the Chinese market will continue to represent an opportunity for growth.

- Dairy: Since 2010, China has also been the world's largest importer of dairy products, amounting to over one-fifth of the global market.[70] At the end of 2018, an agreement on the import of 22 categories of Russian dairy products was also reached. Until then, ice cream was the only dairy product entering into the Chinese market. However, due to logistical factors including cold storage, high transport costs, quality control issues, as well as consumer preferences, traditional dairy products such as milk or yogurts from Russia are less competitive.[71] However, more processed dairy products may have room for growth—though falsification and quality control here remains an issue.[72]
- Soybean and oilseeds: A category of significant attention by policymakers on both sides is soybeans, largely imported for animal feed in China. Since China abolished its import quota system for soybeans as part of its WTO accession commitments, it has become the world's leading importer and accounts for two-thirds of the international market. Due to insufficient if not diminishing arable land, water, and other resource constraints, dependence on foreign soybeans is viewed as largely irreversible. In mid-2018, China placed an effective ban on soybean imports from one of its largest suppliers. Since then, Chinese authorities and state-owned enterprises have been explicit about the need to diversify China's soybeans import structure, to involve more South American states, Canada, as well as the Black Sea region encompassing Russia and Ukraine, as well as Kazakhstan also.[73] As the president of state-owned China Oil and Foodstuffs Corporation (COFCO), China's largest grain trader and food processing company Yu Xubo stated, longer-term supply diversification of soybeans will present a 'historic opportunity for other countries'.[74]

Five Russian provinces were allowed to export soybeans to China in 2015, after phytosanitary approval by Chinese authorities. That year was the first in which any meaningful volumes were exported by Russia to China; by 2018 the volume reached 817 thousand tonnes. During Xi's visit to Moscow in June 2019 the two sides signed a 'Plan for Deepening Cooperation between Russia and China in Soybeans' according to which the goal is for China to import 3.7 million metric tonnes of Russian soybean by 2024.[75] This has since been connected to the larger project of reaching $200 billion USD in total bilateral trade by 2024.[76] In July 2019, the Chinese General Administration of Customs approved imports of soybeans from all territories of Russia, as well as expanding modes of transport to include sea shipping.[77]

China is the primary buyer of Russia's soybean crop. The volume, however, is notably small when compared to China's overall imports of 88 million metric tonnes. Russian targets are expected to more than double the value of soybean exports from 2018, to $600 million USD by 2024.[78] Estimates regarding the potential of soybean export vary, however. Some experts are sceptical that 3.7 million metric tonnes to China can even be reached considering climate, geographic factors, and the scarcity of available arable land.[79] According to Dmitry Ryl'ko, head of the Institute for Agricultural Market Studies, the RFE's potential for soybean is already 'practically exhausted' and a maximum of 2 million metric tonnes is more likely.[80] Finally, Russian soybeans are non-GMO. There are also advantages to this (see below), but among other issues, including pests and lower yields, Russian soybeans are not competitively priced against other major exporters.[81] Thus, while there are prospects for growth, it is likely that Russian soybeans will remain a negligible part of China's overall demand.[82]

As for other oilseeds and oilseed products, sunflower oil has notably been competitive in the Chinese market. Sunflower oil is a relatively niche product, viewed as a healthier alternative to standard cooking oils. Different packaging standards and expectations—for example litre size—however, can limit its appeal.[83] Moreover, Russia faces high competition from Ukraine, including due to infrastructural issues and port capacity.[84] Regarding other intermediary products, a 2019 protocol for Russian export of soybean, rapeseed, sunflower meal was also signed.[85]

- Ecological products: Genetically modified (GM) foods are seen in a negative light by a substantial proportion of Chinese consumers. Since GM production was banned in Russia in 2016, an opportunity exists for Russia to expand its non-GMO exports to China.[86] For example, soybean imports are suitable for niche 'ecological' markets, in particular for non-animal feed uses of soybean.[87] Other niche markets include processed products such as soy milk, soy sauce, tofu, and other seasonings. Non-GMO food presents an advantage for the marketing of healthy products for higher-end markets. Russian legislation including the 2020 federal law 'On Organic Products' on this should assist with labelling and quality standards in this regard.[88] Notably, the development and marketing of ecological products is also a part of Russian export strategy.

- Higher value-added products: Russian leadership is quite clear about the need to move up the supply chain, towards processed and value-added products rather than raw agricultural materials and bulk commodities export. In this area, Russia's chocolate confectionary products have a strong showing on the Chinese market, comprising $112.6 million USD of $438 million USD total Chinese imports of chocolate products in 2019.[89] Russian brands of beer and ice cream have also made inroads into the Chinese market.[90]

Overall, to reach its export targets for 2024, Russia's exports will need to move beyond bulk commodities and raw agricultural materials exports. This requires not only domestic processing, but also vertical integration both at industrial and regulatory levels, across the wider value chain. This includes quality control, monitoring, and inspection, but also packaging, product promotion, and retail, in order to raise the profile, reputation, and overall competitiveness of Russian products on the Chinese market.[91]

5 Agri-Food Trade in Context: Remaining Obstacles

It is clear that the agricultural trade relationship between the two countries is deepening. At the same time, however, declarative statements from officials, such as the putative bilateral 'soybean industry alliance', belie the fact that cooperation is proceeding from an extremely low starting point. The removal of phytosanitary barriers for a range of products is very recent. This might invite some speculation that the opening of the Chinese market is motivated by geopolitical factors. However, negotiations and groundwork for such agreements take place over several years, the fruits of which are only now starting to be realised. Russian producers and distributors themselves point to growth being driven by their better understanding of the 'rules of the game', and their adaptation to Chinese demands over a longer period of time.[92] Finally, any increased accommodation and policy facilitation for Russian exporters should be placed also in the context of China's opening towards a broader range of countries. In 2019 alone, China expanded access to its market to meat imports for an additional 16 countries.[93] Moreover, it is ironically under conditions of strained U.S.–China relations that China has been locked increased vastly increased purchases of U.S. agricultural products under the Phase One trade deal. However, Russian exporters will not be substantially affected due to dissimilar trade profiles vis-à-vis the United States.[94]

Indeed, Russia–China agri-food trade over the last several years has more been marked by the removal of existing political and technical bottlenecks to the point of more normalised market-based relations. Thus, while wider geopolitical dynamics and any broader Russia–China entente are not irrelevant to the agri-food trade, other factors loom larger. These include, for the medium if not long term, obstacles including broader policy misalignment, market dynamics, as well as operational barriers of both hard and soft infrastructure.

At a basic level, Russian export strengths are not necessarily well aligned with Chinese demand due to China's grain self-sufficiency policies. The 'Export of AIC Products (2018–2024)' plan also explicitly notes the difficulty of gaining access to the Chinese market due to domestic protectionism. But similar policies on the Russian side also limit the prospects for increasing Chinese exports to Russia, where there has been increasing focus on substituting imports of fruits and vegetables. And despite other Russian statements to the contrary, Chinese demand for unprocessed soybeans is also potentially misaligned with Russian goals to increase the export of higher-value products, as Russian Minister of Agriculture Dmitrii Patrushev has noted.[95]

Non-tariff barriers also hinder trade. According to a joint report by authors from the Russian International Affairs Council and Chinese Academy of Social Sciences, these 'have the greatest negative impact on mutual trade in agricultural products'.[96] Sanitary and phytosanitary measures for export to China are extremely strict. Though new protocols have been signed, in many cases Russian companies still need to obtain individual export licences. China follows the principle of regionalisation for some product categories. While this is better than wholesale bans, it also means that individual Russian regions need to be cleared for export. Other categories are on the whole not allowed into the Chinese market. Russian exporters must also comply with tough technical regulations regarding quality certification, specific packaging and labelling requirements, as well as complicated customs formalities.[97] This goes both ways: in 2019 and 2020 alone, there were a number of restriction imposed on Chinese agricultural exports to Russia, including a ban on stone fruits from China in August 2019, and in January 2020 restrictions on citrus fruits as well as certain fish and seafood products. During early 2020, many Russian food retailers also suspended Chinese agricultural supplies due to concerns over COVID-19.[98]

On the market side, China is often idealised as having unlimited absorptive capacity, but it is also among the 'most demanding' markets in the world not only to penetrate but also navigate.[99] Understanding if not meeting specialised Chinese tastes and consumer preferences requires investment in baseline market analytics. As Patrushev has admitted, 'the Chinese are a difficult people, it takes a very long time to convince them that our products are better. They are picky and, of course, self-interested'.[100] In terms of competitiveness in higher-value products, particularly in the oilseeds, livestock, and dairy sectors, Russia lags well behind established players.[101] Russia must also compete with as well as emergent agricultural players and fellow CIS countries such as Ukraine, Kazakhstan, as well as a range of other countries that are seeking to increase agricultural exports to China in areas where Russia has advantage. Meanwhile, growing consumer emphasis is on the quality of food, to include food safety, healthiness, as well as organic production.[102] Quality control including resolving issues with counterfeit products for eco-brands or dairy will be important.[103] How much Chinese consumption will continue to grow in volume is another question. Most recently, Xi Jinping's August 2020 directives which place responsibility on individual citizens to cut (wasteful) food consumption, may also soon be reflected in the market.[104]

Another important obstacle is infrastructure. The bulk of Russian agricultural production is currently concentrated in the European part of the country. Transport either proceeds via freight, which is quicker but more expensive, through the body of the continent, or via marine shipping from the West passing Europe, Africa, and the Indian Ocean. From the western part of Russia, it can take up to 60 days for products to reach their destination in China's eastern seaports.[105] The Ministry of Agriculture's export plan entails an additional R30 billion of development of 'transport-oriented agricultural logistics' by 2024. For the time being, however, even RFE's proximity to China does not necessarily translate to cheaper or more efficient logistics. Lack of, or underdeveloped infrastructure, including grain terminals and port facilities, makes a range of investment, development, storage as well transport activities more expensive.[106] Current vehicle-based transport modalities, slow customs procedures, and outdated facilities in the RFE add to the inefficiency. Lengthy customs procedures can hinder the transport of perishable products.[107]

Finally, RFE agricultural development in general continues to face deep challenges, with or without Chinese capital.[108] There has been a long-term shortage of local labour in the region, and although the region has depended on Chinese immigrants for labour, their contribution was waning even before the COVID pandemic.[109] During the COVID-19 pandemic, the Minister of Agriculture for Primorskii krai, Andrei Bronz, reported that due to the lack of Chinese and other foreign migrants usually engaged in vegetable cultivation, alternative labour was found through the use of students and convicts.[110] This practice also affects soy cultivation.[111] Finally, extreme weather events, including massive floods in the RFE in 2013 and again in 2019, which took tens of thousands of hectares of farmland out of commission and decreased crop yields, may increase as consequences of climate change worsen.[112]

6 Outlook

While there are elements of market complementarity between the two markets, overall trade is strongly shaped by domestic political priorities on both sides, which are not always aligned. The evolution from adversaries to strategic partners in recent years means that politics continue to influence trade in general and agricultural trade, both directly and indirectly. Moreover, self-sufficiency policies are unlikely to change on either side. Russian officials are less interested in the level of bilateral trade than they are in increasing exports. And it means that there is limited scope for expanding grain (soy) exports to China. So far, Russia does not yet feature as a significant player in Chinese agri-food markets outside of fish, seafood, and chocolate confectionaries.

Nevertheless, with the recent opening of the Chinese market to a range of Russian products, prospects are certain that agri-food trade value will grow in long if not medium term, and in the export-oriented direction in which Russian policymakers are seeking. Whether the current trajectory is sufficient to help meet the 2024 export target of the Russian government remains to be seen. On the Chinese side, its demand for Russian soy will surely be influenced by trade relations with the United States and the fulfillment of the Phase One Trade Deal. On the Russian side, funding for overcoming the range of obstacles to enhance agri-food trade listed in this chapter, including infrastructure, will be necessary. Finally, beyond accessing the Chinese market, the broader competitiveness of Russian agri-food products on the Chinese market will also require substantial work by Russian industry players themselves.

Notes

1. Kremlin, 'Russia Calling! Investment Forum', 28 November. http://en.kremlin.ru/events/president/news/59216#sel=57:1:D33,57:32:pnj. Accessed 10 September 2020.
2. Thomas Grove and Anatoly Kurmanaev, 'A Surprise Winner from the U.S.-China Trade Spat: Russian Soybean Farmers', *Wall Street Journal*, 21 February 2019. https://www.wsj.com/articles/russia-exploits-u-s-china-trade-tensions-to-sell-more-soybeans-11550745001. Accessed 29 September 2020.
3. Paul Bolt and Sharyl Cross, *China, Russia, and Twenty-First Century Global Geopolitics* (Oxford: Oxford University Press, 2018).
4. TASS, 'Russia, China Not Seeking Military Alliance—Lavrov', 2 November 2019. https://tass.com/politics/1086654. Accessed 29 September 2020.
5. Bobo Lo, *Axis of Convenience: Moscow: Beijing, and the New Geopolitics* (London: Chatham House, 2008); Alexander Gabuev, 'China and Russia: Friends with Strategic Benefits', The Lowy Interpreter, 7 April 2017. https://www.lowyinstitute.org/the-interpreter/china-and-russia-friends-strategic-benefits. Accessed 11 October 2020.
6. Charles Clover, 'Russia Resumes Advanced Weapons Sales to China', *Financial Times*, 3 November 2016.
7. Artyom Lukin, 'The Russia-China Entente and Its Future', *International Politics* (2020). https://doi.org/10.1057/s41311-020-00251-7.
8. Jonathan E. Hillman, 'China and Russia: Economic Unequals', Center for Strategic and International Studies, July 2020. https://www.csis.org/analysis/china-and-russia-economic-unequals. Accessed 11 October 2020; Ivan Zuenko, 'A Milestone, Not a Turning Point: How China Will Develop the Russian Far East', Carnegie Moscow Center, 8 November 2018. https://carnegie.ru/commentary/77671. Accessed 11 October 2020.
9. *People's Daily*, 'Zhongguo you naxie houban guanxi', 31 March 2014. http://world.people.com.cn/n/2014/0331/c1002-24778739.html. Accessed 31 July 2020.

10. Kremlin, 'Press Statements Following Russian-Chinese Talks', 5 June 2019. http://en.kremlin.ru/events/president/news/60672. Accessed 31 July 2020; and Sina, 'Pujing zongtong shi wo zui hao de zhixin pengyou', 5 June 2019. https://finance.sina.com.cn/china/gncj/2019-06-05/doc-ihvhiews6855269.shtml. Accessed 3 August 2020.
11. Zuenko, 'A Milestone'.
12. Neil MacFarquhar, 'As Chinese Flock to Siberia's Lake Baikal, Local Russians Growl', *New York Times*, 2 May 2019. https://www.nytimes.com/2019/05/02/world/europe/chinese-lake-baikal-tourism-russia.html?searchResultPosition=1. Accessed 4 November 2020.
13. PRC Ministry of Commerce, 'Yi jidu zhong e maoyi e zengzhang 3.4%', 26 April 2020. http://ru.mofcom.gov.cn/article/jmxw/202004/20200402959212.shtml. Accessed 30 July 2020.
14. Alexander Lukin, 'Russia's Pivot to Asia: Myth or Reality?', *Strategic Analysis* 40, no. 6 (2016): 573–89; and Alexander Gabuev, 'A Pivot to Nowhere: The Realities of Russia's Asia Policy', Carnegie Moscow Center, 22 April 2016. https://carnegie.ru/commentary/63408. Accessed 11 October 2020.
15. Elena Kuzmina, 'Free Trade Zones Within the EAEU', 31 October 2019. https://russiancouncil.ru/en/analytics-and-comments/analytics/free-trade-zones-with-the-eaeu/. Accessed October 11, 2020.
16. Tong Guangji and Shi Lei, 'Zhong e nongchanpin maoyi ji qi bijiao youshi, hubu xing yanbian qushi', *Journal of South China Agricultural University* 15, no. 5 (2016): 110–22.
17. Yu Min, Jiang Minglun and Geng Jianzhong, 'Zhong e nongye hezuo xin jiyu ji duice yanjiu', *World Agriculture*, no. 8 (2015): 4–9. (Original title of journal in Chinese.)
18. *People's Daily*, 'Zhong e nongye hezuo 'xin shidai' laile ma?', 16 August 2020. http://world.people.com.cn/n1/2019/0816/c1002-31300848.html. Accessed 29 September 2020.
19. A. Y. Osinina, Sun Polin and Jiang Jing, 'Rossiisko-Kitaiskoe sotrudnichestvo v oblasti sel'skogo khoziaistva: sostoianie i perspektivy', May 2019. https://russiancouncil.ru/papers/Russia-China-Agriculture-Policybrief21-Ru.pdf. Accessed 5 November 2020.
20. Elena Sukhorukova, 'Kitai stal krupneishim pokupatelem Rossiiskogo miasa', 28 July 2020. https://www.rbc.ru/business/28/07/2020/5f1ea7a19a79472749e49b3c. Accessed 29 September 2020.
21. Yu Min, et al., 'Zhong e nongye'.
22. Osinina et al., 'Rossiisko-Kitaiskoe sotrudnichestvo'.
23. Stephen K. Wegren, Alexander Nikulin and Irina Trotsuk, *Food Policy and Food Security: Putting Food on the Russian Table* (Lanham, MD and London, UK: Lexington Books, 2018); and Russian Government, 'First Meeting of the Government Commission on Import Substitution',

11 August 2015. http://government.ru/en/news/19246/. Accessed 8 September 2020.
24. Russian Ministry of Agriculture, 'Za poslednie 5 let Rossiia sokratila import prodovol'stviia na tret', 5 August 2019. https://mcx.gov.ru/press-service/news/za-poslednie-5-let-rossiya-sokratila-import-prodovolstviya-na-tret/. Accessed 18 September 2020.
25. Kremlin, 'Address to the Federal Assembly', 12 December 2012. http://en.kremlin.ru/events/president/news/17118. Accessed 29 September 2020.
26. PRC State Council, 'Zhongguo de liangshi wenti,' 1996. http://www.scio.gov.cn/zfbps/ndhf/1996/Document/307978/307978.htm. Accessed 3 February 2016; and PRC State Council, 'Food Security in China,' 2019. http://www.scio.gov.cn/zfbps/32832/Document/1666228/1666228.htm. Accessed 29 September 2020.
27. See Stephen K. Wegren, 'Can Russia's Food Exports Reach $45 Billion in 2024?', *Post-Communist Economies* 32, no. 2 (2020): 147–75.
28. Russian Export Center, 'Natsional'nyy proyekt "Mezhdunarodnaia kooperatsiia i eksport"', n.d., https://www.exportcenter.ru/company/international-cooperation/priority/. Accessed 28 September 2020.
29. Natalia Karlova and Eugenia Serova, 'Prospects of the Chinese Market for Russian Agri-Food Exports', *Russian Journal of Economics* 6, no. 1 (2020): 71–90; and Russian Ministry of Agriculture, 'Agroeksport 2030: trendy i perspektivy', 2020. https://mcx.gov.ru/upload/iblock/186/186a255a5aefae001e3d6f1e7a93089d.pdf. Accessed 20 September 2020.
30. Stephen K. Wegren, Alexander M. Nikulin and Irina Trotsuk, 'Russia's Tilt to Asia and Implications for Agriculture', *Eurasian Geography and Economics* 56, no. 2 (2015): 127–49.
31. Kremlin, 'Plenarnoe zasedanie Vostochnogo ekonomicheskogo foruma', 12 September 2018. http://kremlin.ru/events/president/news/58537. Accessed 29 September 2020.
32. Ibid.
33. Kremlin, 'Zasedanie prezidiuma Gossoveta', 4 September 2019. http://kremlin.ru/events/president/news/61443. Accessed 29 September 2020.
34. Anna Bondarenko, 'Za schet ryby i soi', 28 March 2019. https://rg.ru/2019/03/28/reg-dfo/k-2024-godu-eksport-selhozprodukcii-iz-dfo-vyrastet-v-16-raza.html. Accessed 4 September 2020.
35. Kremlin, 'Zasedanie prezidiuma Gossoveta'.
36. Kremlin, 'Plenarnoe zasedanie'.
37. Far East Development Fund, 'Russia-China Agricultural Fund Is Going to Invest up to 10 bln USD', n.d. https://www.fondvostok.ru/en/press/press_release/russia-china-agricultural-fund-is-going-to-inv

est-up-to-10-bln-usd-into-agricultural-projects-under-/. Accessed 28 September 2020.
38. Kremlin, 'Plenarnoe zasedanie'.
39. Zuenko, 'A Milestone'.
40. Xu Zhenbao and Li Zhemin, 'Yidai yilu zhanlue xia zhongguo yu eluosi nonye hezuo tanxi', 192–6.
41. PRC Ministry of Commerce, 'Zhong e zai eluosi yuandong diqu hezuo fazhan guihua (2018–2024 nian)', 2018. http://images.mofcom.gov.cn/www/201811/20181115164728217.pdf. Accessed 11 October 2020.
42. Jiayi Zhou, 'Chinese Agrarian Capitalism in the Russian Far East', *Third World Thematics: A TWQ Journal* 1, no. 5 (2016): 612–32.
43. Andrey Zakharov and Anastasiya Napalkova, 'Uyedut kitaitsy—vse zarastet: kak fermery iz KNR osvaivaiut Rossiiskii Dal'nii Vostok', 21 October 2019. https://www.bbc.com/russian/features-49978027. Accessed 20 September 2020.
44. Osinina et al., 'Rossiisko-Kitaiskoe sotrudnichestvo'.
45. Yu et al., 'Zhong e nongye'.
46. China-Russia Information Network, 'E zhongli; bixu jiangdi yuandong diqu dui jinkou shuchai yilai', 1 September 2020. http://www.chinaru.info/zhongejmyw/zhongemaoyi/61712.shtml. Accessed 1 October 2020.
47. Inna Ganenko, 'Terra inkognita dlia Rossiiskogo agroeksporta. Kakovy perspektivy vyvoza prodovol'stviia v Kitai', 7 May 2019. https://www.agroinvestor.ru/markets/article/31685-terra-inkognita/. Accessed 29 September 2020.
48. Karlova and Serova, 'Prospects of the Chinese Market'.
49. RIA Novosti, 'Dmitrii Patrushev: sel'skoe khoziaistvo—uzhe ne chernaia dyra i ne ssylka', 21 December 2018. https://ria.ru/20181221/1548381117.html. Accessed 29 September 2020.
50. *Sina*, 'Zhong e ni qianshu youguan eluosi xiang zhongguo chukou liangshi yidingshu', 17 October 2020. http://finance.sina.com.cn/world/20151017/160123502990.shtml. Accessed 4 August 2020.
51. PRC Ministry of Commerce, 'Zhonghua remin gongheguo haiguan zong shu gonggao 2019 nian di 141 hao', 23 September 2019. http://www.mofcom.gov.cn/article/b/g/201909/20190902901102.shtml. Accessed 31 July 2020.
52. Ganenko, 'Terra inkognita'.
53. Osinina et al., 'Rossisko-Kitaiskoe sotrudnichestvo'.
54. Ibid.
55. Ganenko, 'Terra inkognita'.
56. Fred Gale, James Hansen and Michael Jewison, 'China's Growing Demand for Agricultural Imports', Economic Research Service,

Economic Information Bulletin 136, February 2015, p. 7. https://www.ers.usda.gov/webdocs/publications/43939/eib-136.pdf?v=0. Accessed 12 October 2020.
57. Sukhorukova, 'Kitai stal krupneishim'.
58. Russian Ministry of Agriculture, 'V 2019 godu eksport miasa ptitsy v Kitai mozhet prevysit' 100 mln dollarov', 9 September 2019. https://mcx.gov.ru/press-service/news/v-2019-godu-eksport-myasa-ptitsy-v-kitay-mozhet-prevysit-100-mln-dollarov/. Accessed 29 September 2020.
59. Ekaterina Diatlovskaia, 'Miratorg pervym otpravil miaso ptitsy v Kitai', 4 March 2019. https://www.agroinvestor.ru/regions/news/31333-miratorg-pervym-otpravil-myaso-ptitsy-v-kitay/. Accessed 29 September 2020.
60. Ekaterina Diatlovskaia, 'Minsel'khoz: v 2019 godu Rossiia postavit v KNR miasa ptitsy na $100 mln', 9 September 2019. https://www.agroinvestor.ru/markets/news/32385-rossiya-postavit-v-knr-myasa-ptitsy-na-100-mln/. Accessed 29 September 2020.
61. China-Russia Information Network, 'Xuqiu juda eluosi ji zhua yao kou kai zhongguo shichang damen', 24 June 2019. http://chinaru.info/zhongejmyw/zhongemaoyi/57563.shtml. Accessed 29 September 2020; and Sukhorukova, 'Kitay stal krupneyshim'.
62. United States Department of Agriculture, Foreign Agricultural Service, 'China—Poultry and Products Annual', GAIN Report CH19048, 31 July 2019. https://apps.fas.usda.gov/newgainapi/api/report/downloadreportbyfilename?filename=Poultry%20and%20Products%20Annual_Beijing_China%20-%20Peoples%20Republic%20of_7-29-2019.pdf. Accessed November 5, 2020.
63. *China Daily*, 'China's Meat Import Rises Fast in 2019', 14 January 2020. https://www.chinadaily.com.cn/a/202001/14/WS5e1d3308a310128217270c72.html. Accessed 29 September 2020.
64. Reuters Staff, 'China Opens Its Market to Russian Beef Producers', 17 January 2020. https://www.reuters.com/article/russia-china-beef/update-1-china-opens-its-market-to-russian-beef-producers-idUSL8N29M3T1. Accessed 2 August 2020.
65. Keith Bradsher and Ailin Tang, 'China Responds Slowly, and a Pig Disease Becomes a Lethal Epidemic', *New York Times*, 17 December 2019. https://www.nytimes.com/2019/12/17/business/china-pigs-african-swine-fever.html?searchResultPosition=1. Accessed 4 November 2020.
66. *China Daily*, 'China's Meat Import Rises Fast in 2019'.
67. Dominique Patton, 'China's Pork Demand Hits a Peak, Shocking Producers, as Diets Get Healthier', 20 June 2017. https://www.reuters.com/article/us-china-meat-demand-insight/chinas-pork-demand-hits-

a-peak-shocking-producers-as-diets-get-healthier-idUSKBN19A31C. Accessed 4 August 2020.
68. Karlova and Serova, 'Prospects of the Chinese Market'.
69. PRC Ministry of Agriculture, 'Zhongguo nongye'.
70. Brad Gehrke and Lesley Ahmed, 'Agricultural Trade with China: Dairy Import Giant', U.S. International Trade Commission, 2019. https://www.usitc.gov/publications/332/executive_briefings/ebot_brad_gehrke_lesley_ahmed_china_dairy_pdf.pdf. Accessed 29 September 2020.
71. Ganenko, 'Terra inkognita'.
72. Ibid.
73. Wang Ke, 'Guojian duoyuan hua jinkou dadou gongying tixi', 11 August 2018. http://xz.people.com.cn/n2/2018/0811/c138901-31921770.html. Accessed 29 September 2020; Liu Hui, 'Woguo dadou jinkou duoyuan hua geju yijing xingcheng', 10 August 2018. http://www.chinanews.com/gn/2018/08-10/8595520.shtml. Accessed 29 September 2020.
74. Xiao Zhongren and Zhao Yebing, 'Zhongguo qiye zizhu kuoda duoyuan hua jinkou qudao youxiao fensan meiguo dadou jinkou jianshao de fengxian', 14 August 2018. https://www.sohu.com/a/247099209_115239. Accessed 29 September 2020.
75. PRC Ministry of Commerce, 'Zhong e liang guochan yejie gong tan takuan dadou hezuo jujing', 22 November 2019. http://www.mofcom.gov.cn/article/difang/201911/20191102915727.shtml. Accessed 2 August 2020.
76. Kvedomosti.ru, 'Kitai i Rossiia podpishut document o merakh po uvelicheniiu tovarooborota do $200 mlrd', 10 September 2019. https://kvedomosti.ru/news/kitaj-i-rossiya-podpishut-dokument-o-merax-po-uvelicheniyu-tovarooborota-do-200-mlrd.html. Accessed 10 September 2019.
77. Ibid.
78. Alena Uzbekova, 'Boby nastupaiut', 24 November 2019. https://rg.ru/2019/11/24/reg-dfo/soia-vyshla-na-vtoroe-mesto-v-eksporte-produkcii-apk-s-dalnego-vostoka.html. Accessed 20 September 2020.
79. Ivan Zuenko, 'Can Russia's Far East Feed China with Soy?', Carnegie Moscow Center, 9 October 2018. https://carnegie.ru/commentary/77443. Accessed 31 July 2020.
80. IKAR, 'Glava IKAR rasskazal, kak Rossiia mozhet uvelichit' proizvodstvo soi', 24 December 2018. http://ikar.ru/old/press/4679.html. Accessed 29 September 2020.
81. An Yushu, 'Shenru fenxi dangqian zhong e dadou zhongzhi maoyi hezuo: fazhan chengxiao cunzai wenti ji duice jianyi', 3 March 2020. http://www.chinaru.info/zhongejmyw/jingmaotegao/59787.shtml. Accessed 3 August 2020.

82. Zuenko, 'Can Russia's Far East Feed China'.
83. China-Russia Information Network, 'Xuqiu juda eluosi ji zhua yao kou kai zhongguo shichang damen', 24 June 2019. http://chinaru.info/zhongejmyw/zhongemaoyi/57563.shtml. Accessed 29 September 2020.
84. Ganenko, 'Terra inkognita'.
85. PRC Ministry of Commerce, 'Zhonghua remin gongheguo'.
86. Russian Government, 'Ustanovlen zapret na vyrashchivanie i razvedenie genno-inzhenerno-modifitsirovannykh organizmov na territorii Rossii', 29 July 2016. http://council.gov.ru/events/news/69701/. Accessed 3 August 2020.
87. COFCO, 'Zhongguo e nongye hezuo luodi shu qian dun eluosi dadou di su', 2 August 2019. http://www.cofco.com/cn/News/Allnews/Press/2019/0802/47920.html. Accessed 2 August 2020.
88. Karlova and Serova, 'Prospects of the Chinese Market'.
89. Russian Ministry of Agriculture, 'Shokolad i Shokoladhye konditerskie isdeliia na rynke KNR', n.d. https://mcx.gov.ru/upload/iblock/4d6/4d6373a83dd841dcf16891d99b077c01.pdf. Accessed 29 September 2020.
90. Karlova and Serova, 'Prospects of the Chinese Market'.
91. Russian Government, 'Brifing Aleksandra Tkachova po zavershenii zasedaniia', 25 April 2018. http://government.ru/dep_news/32455/. Accessed 29 September 2020.
92. Konstantin Shtepin, 'Nakormit' Kitai po-moskovski', 4 November 2019. https://rg.ru/2019/11/04/rossijskie-selhozproizvoditeli-vyhodiat-na-rynok-podnebesnoj.html. Accessed 29 September 2020.
93. PRC State Council, 'Jinkou rou, woguo 2019 nian you duole 16 ge laiyuan guo', 2019. http://www.scio.gov.cn/m/xwfbh/xwbfbh/wqfbh/42311/42414/xgbd42421/Document/1671755/1671755.htm. Accessed 29 September 2020.
94. Vasily Erokhin, 'Peremirie' v torgovom protivostoianii SShA i Kitaia: vozmozhne posledstviia dlia restrukturizatsii mirovoi torgovli prodovol'stviem', *Marketing i Logistika*, 27, no. 1 (2020): 12–35.
95. RIA Novosti, 'Dmitrii Patrushev: sel'skoe khoziaistvo'.
96. Osinina et al., 'Rossiisko-Kitaiskoe sotrudnichestvo'.
97. Ibid.
98. Ekaterina Burlakova and Tatiana Romanova, 'Magaziny i restorany ishchut zamenu Kitaiskim produktam', 3 February 2020. https://www.vedomosti.ru/business/articles/2020/02/03/822131-zamenu-kitaiskim-produktam. Accessed 3 August 2020.
99. Karlova and Serova, 'Prospects of the Chinese Market'.
100. RIA Novosti, 'Dmitrii Patrushev: sel'skoe khoziaistvo'.
101. Karlova and Serova, 'Prospects of the Chinese Market'; and Sukhorukova, 'Rossiiskoe miaso'.

102. Nielsen Insights, 'New Eating Trends in China: The Healthier the Better', 22 September 2016. https://www.nielsen.com/cn/en/press-releases/2016/New-Eating-Trends-in-China-the-Healthier-the-Better/. Accessed 4 August 2020.
103. Osinina et al., 'Rossiisko-Kitaiskoe sotrudnichestvo'.
104. PRC Government, 'Xi Jinping dui zhizhi canyin langfei xingwei zuochu chong yao zhishi', 11 August 2020. http://www.gov.cn/xinwen/2020-08/11/content_5534026.htm. Accessed 30 September 2020.
105. 'Elousi niurou lai liao: bu ju shichang jingzheng 2020 nian jihua chukou 1 wan dun', 12 May 2020. https://finance.sina.cn/2020-05-12/detail-iirczymk1217263.d.html?cre=tianyi&mod=wpage&loc=6&r=32&rfunc=16&tj=none&tr=32. Accessed 2 August 2020.
106. An, 'Shenru fenxi'.
107. Osinina et al., 'Rossiisko-Kitaiskoe sotrudnichestvo'.
108. Bondarenko, 'Za schet ryby i soi'.
109. Ivan Zuenko, 'Pandemic Changes Face of Farming in Russian Far East', 18 December 2020. https://carnegie.ru/commentary/83484?utm_source=rssemail&utm_medium=email&mkt_tok=eyJpIjoiTUdNMk9UZGhZVGt5TXpCaSIsInQiOiJhTlF5MVZ0OWFCQkxIN0tBOFNpRnhlWnptUlpxOUhcL3JudXJBS2hLRTNcL2tVVXRaYWJHZjJmRjdGcEhtMnY3Mm1WOFVqclFlNCtKTDdTYW5LSVhcL3hLYUtwTm15dEtIUDBWaUNsb3pxekN3YjJKMzlGanhUTnlHUGFLa0ZROGtObiJ9. Accessed 24 December 2020.
110. Interfax, 'V Primor'ye privlekut k posevnoi uchashchikhsia i zaklyuchennykh iz-za nekhvatki migrantov', 28 April 2020. https://www.interfax.ru/russia/706365. Accessed 29 September 2020.
111. Polina Nikolskaya, 'Labour Shortage Crippling Chinese Investments in Russian Soy', 17 August 2020. https://www.nasdaq.com/articles/labour-shortage-crippling-chinese-investments-in-russian-soy-2020-08-17. Accessed 11 October 2020.
112. Kremlin, 'Zasedanie prezidiuma'.

Selected Bibliography

Bolt, Paul and Sharyl Cross. *China, Russia, and Twenty-First Century Global Geopolitics*. Oxford: Oxford University Press, 2018.

Bradsher, Keith and Ailin Tang. 'China Responds Slowly, and a Pig Disease Becomes a Lethal Epidemic'. *New York Times*, 17 December 2019. https://www.nytimes.com/2019/12/17/business/china-pigs-african-swine-fever.html?searchResultPosition=1. Accessed 4 November 2020.

Clover, Charles. 'Russia Resumes Advanced Weapons Sales to China'. *Financial Times*, 3 November 2016.

Food and Agriculture Organization. *Food Outlook: Biannual Report on Global Food Markets*. Rome: FAO, 2019.

Gabuev, Alexander. 'A Pivot to Nowhere: The Realities of Russia's Asia Policy'. Carnegie Moscow Center, 22 April 2016. https://carnegie.ru/commentary/63408.

Gabuev, Alexander. 'China and Russia: Friends with Strategic Benefits'. *The Lowy Interpreter*, 7 April 2017. https://www.lowyinstitute.org/the-interpreter/china-and-russia-friends-strategic-benefits.

Hillman, Jonathan E. 'China and Russia: Economic Unequals'. Center for Strategic and International Studies, July 2020. https://www.csis.org/analysis/china-and-russia-economic-unequals.

Karlova, Natalia and Eugenia Serova. 'Prospects of the Chinese Market for Russian Agri-Food Exports'. *Russian Journal of Economics* 6 (2020): 71–90.

Lo, Bobo. *Axis of Convenience: Moscow: Beijing, and the New Geopolitics*. London: Chatham House, 2008.

Lukin, Alexander. 'Russia's Pivot to Asia: Myth or Reality?'. *Strategic Analysis* 40, no. 6 (2016): 573–89

Lukin, Artyom. 'The Russia-China Entente and Its Future'. *International Politics* (2020). https://doi.org/10.1057/s41311-020-00251-7.

MacFarquhar, Neil. 'As Chinese Flock to Siberia's Lake Baikal, Local Russians Growl'. *New York Times*, 2 May 2019. https://www.nytimes.com/2019/05/02/world/europe/chinese-lake-baikal-tourism-russia.html?searchResultPosition=1.

Nikolskaya, Polina. 'Labour Shortage Crippling Chinese Investments in Russian Soy'. 17 August 2020. https://www.nasdaq.com/articles/labour-shortage-crippling-chinese-investments-in-russian-soy-2020-08-17.

Wegren, Stephen K. 'Can Russia's Food Exports Reach $45 Billion in 2024?' *Post-Communist Economies* 32, no. 2 (2020): 147–75.

Wegren, Stephen K., Alexander Nikulin and Irina Trotsuk. *Food Policy and Food Security: Putting Food on the Russian Table*. Lanham, MD and London, UK: Lexington Books, 2018.

Wegren, Stephen K., Alexander M. Nikulin and Irina Trotsuk. 'Russia's Tilt to Asia and Implications for Agriculture'. *Eurasian Geography and Economics* 56, no. 2 (2015): 127–49.

Zhou, Jiayi. 'Chinese Agrarian Capitalism in the Russian Far East'. *Third World Thematics: A TWQ Journal* 1, no. 5 (2016): 612–32.

Zuenko, Ivan. 'A Milestone, Not a Turning Point: How China Will Develop the Russian Far East'. Carnegie Moscow Center, 8 November 2018. https://carnegie.ru/commentary/77671.

Open Access This chapter is licensed under the terms of the Creative Commons Attribution 4.0 International License (http://creativecommons.org/licenses/by/4.0/), which permits use, sharing, adaptation, distribution and reproduction in any medium or format, as long as you give appropriate credit to the original author(s) and the source, provide a link to the Creative Commons license and indicate if changes were made.

The images or other third party material in this chapter are included in the chapter's Creative Commons license, unless indicated otherwise in a credit line to the material. If material is not included in the chapter's Creative Commons license and your intended use is not permitted by statutory regulation or exceeds the permitted use, you will need to obtain permission directly from the copyright holder.

Chapter 8: Russia's Agri-Food Trade Within the Eurasian Economic Union

Rilka Dragneva

1 Introduction

The pursuit of economic integration has been a key dimension of Russia's policies in the post-Soviet region. After several failed initiatives, the first real achievement was the creation of a Customs Union (CU) with Belarus and Kazakhstan in 2010. It was followed by the launch of a Single Economic Space (SES) in 2012, ultimately culminating in the formation of the Eurasian Economic Union (EAEU) in 2015, to which Armenia and Kyrgyzstan also acceded.[1] As its predecessor, the EAEU aims at 'deep' economic integration: one where not only mutual trade in goods is liberalised, but the formation of a common market is pursued through the harmonisation of domestic regulatory requirements and other non-tariff barriers. In the external plane, the objective has been to exercise a common policy through the adoption of a Union external tariff, a common trade protection regime and the engagement in trade agreements with the rest of the world as a unified trading bloc. To achieve these goals, the EAEU member states have endowed the organisation

R. Dragneva (✉)
University of Birmingham, Birmingham, UK
e-mail: R.DragnevaLewers@bham.ac.uk

© The Author(s) 2022

S. K. Wegren and F. Nilssen (eds.), *Russia's Role in the Contemporary International Agri-Food Trade System*, Palgrave Advances in Bioeconomy: Economics and Policies,
https://doi.org/10.1007/978-3-030-77451-6_9

with a system of bodies with delegated powers and an international legal personality.

Such an ambitious project is bound to affect the economies of its member states, including the production and trade of food, in tangible and fundamental ways. Therefore, the understanding of Russia's role in the international food trade system will be incomplete without taking into account the agency of the EAEU and the opportunities created by it. Yet, while undoubtedly significant, this relationship is not straightforward. Firstly, despite some notable achievements, developments on the ground have been modest or outright disappointing. In mutual trade, in particular, the results have been described as erratic, with significant variations across sectors and member states.[2] Notably, relations have been interlaced with high-profile trade conflicts and back-tracking from previous achievements. Secondly, while some of these dynamics can be explained by external conditions or natural 'growth pains', it is largely symptomatic of the structural problems of the EAEU as an integration project: its highly politicised and decentralised nature, the limitations of its legal regime and the weakness of its common bodies.[3] This has allowed Russia to use its power preponderance in the region to assert its policy priorities and especially its geopolitical considerations *through* the EAEU, where possible, but also *despite* the EAEU, where necessary.

This chapter will unpack this dynamic by analysing the role of the CU and EAEU in Russia's agricultural food trade. In particular, the aim will be to discuss: (1) To what extent has the formation of the EAEU impacted on Russia's food trade with its neighbours, both in terms of the institutional regime set up and the resulting ability of the organisation to affect its members' trade practices? (2) In what ways has the EAEU affected Russia's options as a player in the international food system? Given that the birth of the EAEU coincided with a major reversal in Russia's trading behaviour as a result of the sanctions' war with the West,[4] what role has the bloc performed in this process?

The chapter will begin by providing a background of the key relevant institutional features of the EAEU. It will then focus on some of the most important yet also problematic ways in which the EAEU affects agri-food trade and production, namely the EAEU's food safety regime, the effects of Russia's food import ban, the agenda for agricultural cooperation, including the coordination of food security policy, and the opportunities provided by concluding EAEU free trade agreements with third parties. In conclusion, the chapter will examine some of the changes in agri-food trade flows since the launch of the EAEU, before offering some thoughts on the outlook for the future.

2 The EAEU and Its Institutions

To understand the role of the EAEU in affecting Russia's role in regional and international agri-food trade, it is necessary to point out some of its general characteristics as an institutional regime. The EAEU was set up as an independent interstate actor operating through its bodies on the basis of the powers delegated by its member states. Of particular significance is the Eurasian Economic Commission (EEC), the Union's regulator tasked with the development of integration. The Commission is a two-tiered body consisting of a Council that is composed of the deputy heads of national governments, and a Collegium that is composed of Ministers nominated by the member states who head specialized departments.[5] Despite the intention to model it on the European Union Commission, however, the EEC's autonomy and authority are highly limited.

The EEC has been endowed with significant powers in the area of tariff and customs regulation, technical regulation and the imposition of trade defence measures. Many other areas, such as transport or agricultural policy, are reserved for the member states. In relation to those, the Commission's role is to facilitate cooperation between the member states. Even within the area of delegated powers, however, there is complex mix between Union and national legislation and between Commission and national competences to navigate, as the area of food safety illustrates.

Furthermore, the decision-making process that the EEC follows even in such areas is deeply intergovernmental, putting member states firmly in control. The most important powers of the EEC are exercised by its Council by consensus. The Collegium is the permanent and most professional and independent body of the Union, consisting of departments dealing with day-to-day matters. Its decisions, however, can always be challenged by member states and escalated to the Council of the Commission or the higher bodies of the EAEU, the Inter-Governmental Council (heads of government), and the Supreme Eurasian Economic Council (heads of state), and revoked or reversed by them.

Notably, the powers of the Commission are particularly curtailed by its weak enforcement functions. It can, subject to capacity, monitor member states' practices and notify them of a lack of implementation or breach of Union requirements. Yet, in a reversal from the CU regime, it cannot bring them before the Court of the EAEU. It is notable that the EAEU Treaty asserted the primacy of the member states in several key ways, including by restricting the Court's powers and ensuring that its rulings do not become part of EAEU law.[6]

In this context, the Commission has acted cautiously and conservatively. Even when it demonstrates activism, the fate of its initiatives rests at the highest level of domestic power. Thus, politicised interstate bargaining is the main path to secure progress or resolve disagreements. This characteristic matters for a number of reasons.

Firstly, there is a mismatch between the institutional regime in place and the stated ambition of integration. There is an 'attainment gap' built into the system which is particularly critical in relation to the removal of non-tariff barriers and regulatory alignment. In part, this is connected to the preference for harmonisation similar to the European Union (EU), which is an inherently complex process.[7]

Secondly, it can be argued that the institutional set-up behind the mismatch was the result of the member states' deliberate preference. As the drafting of the EAEU Treaty coincided with the eruption of the Ukraine crisis in early 2014, Russia's partners were keen to limit the scope of integration and, particularly restrict the power of common bodies. With sovereignty sensitivities ignited, Belarus and Kazakhstan were concerned about Russia's ability to dominate the Union and develop a political dimension to economic integration.[8]

Finally, the functioning of the EAEU as well as any improvements of the regime depend on the engagement and continued commitment to the integration of its member states. This is particularly crucial given the large number of areas of cooperation, including the completion of the common market, which are 'in progress' and depend on future actions being taken. Indeed, despite the fact that it inherits developments set in motion with the 2010 Customs Union and 2012 Single Economic Space, the EAEU is best understood as a 'road map' for cooperation.

This links to another important point. In law, the EAEU operates on the basis of formal parity between its members reflected in their voting power and composition of common bodies. Nonetheless, Russia's leadership in the operation of the Union is hard to dispute. It is evident in the staffing of the Collegium of the EEC and Russia's superior ability to lead and participate in various working groups and joint missions, particularly in the area of food safety.[9] It is also a result of its massive structural preponderance within the economy of the EAEU, which translates into a high degree of identification of the EAEU interest with Russia's interest.[10] Ultimately, it represents the political reality behind the EAEU, which is largely based on bilateral, Russia-centred hub-and-spoke patterns of interactions, where the loyalty of members is procured by the provision of collateral benefits, including political support, cheap energy, or enhanced security.[11]

In this sense, it is of particular importance that Russia's key interest in the Eurasian project is primarily (geo-) political. The economic benefits of EAEU integration for Russia, even with the removal of non-tariff barriers, have been estimated as trivial.[12] Russia certainly derives little economic advantage from the bloc above and beyond what it can achieve through bilateral dealings. It is not surprising that Russia has been prepared to let geopolitics trump the constraints of integration at the expense of the Union, but also that its interest in the technical minutiae of integration has not paralleled its enthusiasm for more symbolic wins, such as the launch and expansion of the bloc. It has certainly been selective in driving integration, investing primarily in areas where geopolitical considerations or other domestic priorities have been most prominent.

All this is aptly demonstrated by the case of agri-food trade. In terms of mutual trade in goods, the EAEU inherited the tariff-free trade arrangements already put in place between its members in a web of bilateral free trade agreements and related agreements facilitating trade cooperation. These arrangements were critical in eliminating the various annual exemptions to free trade, which created high uncertainty in bilateral dealings. They did not, however, tackle non-tariff barriers and particularly, the possibility to apply Sanitary and Phyto-Sanitary Measures (SPS) as barriers to trade. Despite Belarus's close alliance with Russia, for example, it periodically experienced food bans and customs restrictions, largely perceived as discriminatory and politically motivated.[13] The launch of the Customs Union in 2010 consolidated the free trade arrangements already in place, brought about a common Customs Code and the highly symbolic removal of internal customs controls in 2011. It also created a new momentum for deeper integration, including the adoption of common technical requirements and other coordination measures. The EAEU inherited these developments with the idea to embed them in a more coherent legal and institutional framework and map out an ambitious agenda for achieving a genuine common market. Nonetheless, agri-food trade under the EAEU regime remains inhibited by several important obstacles linked to the nature of its institutional regime and its limited ability to constrain the diverging preferences of its members, Russia, in particular.

3 Food Safety Requirements

While food safety is fundamental to the functioning of the common market, it is one of the areas where the obstacles to internal trade are most pronounced with disputes between the EAEU members continuing to proliferate. This is largely attributed to the fact that, as aptly described, the EAEU regime does not amount to a workable single food safety system but rather a conglomeration of the national systems of its member states.[14]

To start with, it should be pointed out that at the level of the WTO and the practice of various countries, the regulation of technical barriers to trade and the use of SPS measures are clearly distinguished and defined. Russia, however, has followed an approach where in regulating food safety, the boundaries between the two have been blurred.[15] This approach influenced the practice of the Customs Union,[16] and was then inherited by the EAEU. Thus, food safety in the EAEU straddles issues related to the adoption of Union 'technical regulations', which have included sanitary requirements and procedures with regard to an agreed list of commodities as well as the framework for SPS control.

In this sense, the area of food safety presents some complications in the applicable regimes, particularly in relation to products of animal origin.[17] With regard to technical requirements, the EAEU pursues maximum harmonisation. In law, regulations need to be applied directly in the member states, without the need of implementing legislation, thus aiming to reduce the possibility for divergence. In the area of SPS, however, member states are allowed to impose additional requirements and put in place additional processes for assessing conformity.[18] Indeed, in terms of SPS controls, the EAEU operates an agreed (*soglasovannuiu*) policy,[19] a term which was deliberately used in drafting the Treaty to designate the lowest level of interstate cooperation.

In principle, the EAEU Treaty lays down the fundamentals of food safety policies in line with WTO requirements, dealing with the purposes of food safety measures, scientific risk assessment, regionalisation of food safety risk, transparency and the importance of international standards.[20] The EAEU system is based on the provision of common mandatory requirements and general procedures applying to an agreed list of goods placed under regulatory control. General sanitary requirements and procedures for sanitary control were agreed upon by the CU Commission in 2010.[21] They were developed in a number of horizontal technical regulations, such as the 2011 Technical Regulations 'On Food Safety', 'On the safety of packaging', and 'On food products in relation to labelling'. More detailed mandatory requirements to the products subject to sanitary controls were envisaged in specific technical regulations dealing with certain types of food products, such as meat, milk, grains, fat and oil products, and fruits.[22] These were accompanied by the provision of common rules on conformity assessment, standard forms of documents of compliance, and a register of certification bodies. Similarly, in the area of veterinary controls, there were adopted common requirements applicable to the commodities subject to veterinary control and agreed veterinary control procedure to be applied at the EAEU customs border and throughout its customs territory.[23] This also involved the adoption of uniform veterinary certificates, as well as general rules applying to different aspects of the veterinary control process, such as laboratory controls and joint inspections.

These mandatory requirements and procedures have been developed and continue to be updated at the EAEU level by the EEC, as they were by its predecessor, the Commission of the CU. Nonetheless, the progress in adopting and upgrading technical regulations has been slow and complicated: in the Commission's own assessment, this is an area plagued by the delays and perfunctory attitudes of EAEU member states.[24]

Related to this is the problem of the control over the compliance with technical regulations. This is an area where discrepancies and inconsistencies are common. In a recent example, Russia adopted requirements regarding the marking and marketing of wine, in addition to the EAEU technical regulation 'On the safety of alcohol production', due to enter into force in 2021.[25] However, the EEC has no powers in this regard: control is a prerogative of national authorities in accordance with national systems of food control.[26] Inspection, enforcement, or indeed the pursuit of liability in the case of breaches takes place subject to domestic legislation and procedures, and is open to significant divergence. The EAEU Treaty provides that a future international agreement may harmonise domestic legislations dealing with control over compliance.[27] This, however, has not materialised, nor is there an indication that such a harmonisation will result in more powers of the Commission. Instead, the Commission has sought to respond to problems in this field by issuing recommendations for improved cooperation between member states.[28]

Similarly, the exercise of sanitary and veterinary control is carried out by domestic authorities applying Union as well as national rules. The Commission does not participate in joint inspections nor has the authority to audit the national systems of control.[29] Even more importantly, in contrast to the EU regime,[30] the Commission does not have the right to adopt temporary SPS measures under any circumstances.

The imposition of temporary SPS measures is the exclusive right of the member states. It can be triggered by notification by another member state of problems or measures adopted on its territory, but also by the imposing state's own finding of a violation of technical regulations or a 'deterioration of the sanitary-epidemiological situation on the territory of member state'.[31] This allows for a wide discretion in the imposition of temporary SPS measures, subject only to the requirement to follow a process for mutual notification and consultation, introduced in May 2016.[32] This is especially problematic given the important gaps in the common SPS regime in key areas, such as the definition of deterioration or threat, or how a risk analysis should be conducted.[33] Indeed, in the Commission's own assessment, 'Union law does not define the key terms related to temporary SPS measures, the justification for their introduction and contents, which can give rise to inappropriate use of such measures'.[34]

All this gives rise to two important problems. Firstly, food safety ultimately depends on the capacity and effectiveness of the domestic systems for inspection and enforcement. This underscores the importance of the quality of domestic institutions and the need for their modernisation. However, this conclusion jars against the fact that the EAEU project explicitly lacks a 'governance' dimension. Accession to the EAEU, for example, does not depend on preparedness to implement the various EAEU requirements, nor is support for developing domestic capacity a part of any EAEU equivalent of the EU structural and regional funds. The rudimentary state of SPS control facilities of Kyrgyzstan, for example, was well known to members of the EEC,[35] yet Russia's geopolitical priorities prevailed in pressing for its fast accession. It is telling that Kazakhstan refused to remove its phytosanitary posts from the border with Kyrgyzstan until October 2016, following pressure at the EAEU level.

A closely related problem is that of the corrupt practices of the various national agencies for inspection and certification. Indeed, there have been abundant demonstrations that a domestic 'market for documents' has developed in several countries,[36] undermining the integrity of the system. This is particularly problematic in areas, such as the issuance of veterinary certificates, which are subject to mutual recognition across the Union.[37]

Secondly, this decentralised nature of the SPS regime opens the possibility for arbitrary or opportunistic use of restrictions. The EAEU Treaty provides that SPS measures and import bans should not represent unjustifiable discrimination of a disguised restriction on trade and should only serve a list of agreed purposes.[38] Yet, Russian SPS measures continue to be perceived by Belarus as driven by protectionist or political motivations. Russia's 2018 ban on dried milk, for example, was interpreted as an attempt to curtail the entry of the cheaper, subsidised Belarussian products.[39]

Both these problems culminated in the context of Russia's food embargo, as will be examined next.

4 Russia's Food Import Ban and Its Effects on EAEU Relations

It is not an exaggeration to say that at the same time as the EAEU was being launched as an integration-enhancing project, it was crippled by the consequences of Russia's decision to ban food imports from the EU, the U.S. and a range of other countries, initially imposed in August 2014 and extended to the end of 2022.[40] Given the refusal of Belarus and Kazakhstan to agree on a Union-wide ban, this unilateral action meant that the very logic of functioning as a customs union based on a common external trade policy was undermined.[41] Similarly, complications arose following an import ban on Ukrainian agri-food products in 2016 and also extended to the end of 2022. There were also transit restrictions through Ukraine so that Kazakh and Kyrgyz importers faced higher transaction costs, leading to the actual economic detriment.

In the absence of an EAEU-wide framework, Russia's options to enforce its import ban have been limited. To start with, Belarussian President Lukashenko pledged to cooperate in securing the control of the EAEU external borders.[42] This was also an opportunity to increase Belarus's food exports to Russia as well as help alleviate Russian consumer losses from the collapse in imports. Yet, as widely discussed, the reality was a boom in 'contraband' trade in dairy, fruit, fish products, and others, using a variety of schemes, such as relabelling, falsifying certificates of origin, and violating transit rules. While the case of Belarus has been publicised most, the other partners did not shy from seeking to profit from the sanctions regime either.

With its initial offers to set up joint missions at the Union customs borders and engage in other forms of customs cooperation rejected, Russia resorted to introducing customs and food safety checks in areas bordering on Belarus and Kazakhstan. In effect, this not only caused traffic delays but rolled back the integration achievements already made, resulting in the emergence of a de facto two-tier customs regime.[43] Furthermore, Moscow sought to defend its market as well as place pressure on Belarus to abandon its policy of profiting from the sanctions through the extensive use of temporary SPS measures. For example, while pointing out the presence of antibiotics in violation of EAEU food safety requirements, *Rosselkhoznadzor* also referred to a systemic, organised falsification of milk products and the certificates accompanying them.[44] This pushed the agency to move from enterprise bans to a sectoral ban on the import of some milk products in the spring of 2018, which was eventually retracted.

Given the decentralised nature of the SPS system, throughout this period, the main form of seeking progress in resolving the recurrent disputes was through bilateral dealings, with joint working groups being set up and annual road maps adopted. At the same time, both sides also sought to use the EAEU platform, which exposed the deficiency of the common institutions even further. Belarus was successful in mobilising its Commissioners to lobby for its case, arguing that 'violations unconnected to veterinary risks should not be the basis for the imposition of restrictive veterinary measures'.[45] Following the 2018 'milk war', the EEC Collegium sided with Belarus adopting several decisions calling on Russia to remove various measures representing obstacles to the functioning of the internal market contrary to the requirements of the EAEU Treaty.[46] In particular, the Commission took the view that there is no EAEU legal mechanism for a country to refuse to recognise a veterinary certificate adopted by other country's authorities.[47] Given the limited powers of the Commission, however, the effect of its notifications to Russia remained largely symbolic, with disputes entering the province of highest level of political bargaining.

At the same time, Russia sought to address the problem of contraband goods or 'grey' trade (*seryi oborot*) at the EAEU level by leading on key developments. For example, in February 2018, an agreement on product marking was successfully signed by the EAEU member states. It aims at unifying the different countries' approaches to the product marking and, thus, improving the traceability of certain products. In May 2019, an Agreement on the traceability of products imported into the EAEU customs territory was also signed. It is expected to help reduce the circulation of illegal goods and increase business transparency. It is also unsurprising that Russia has seen the development of the digital agenda in the EAEU as one of its top priorities over other areas in need of attention. Yet, as Kofner points out, there remain a range of technical difficulties in harmonising domestic digital tracing systems, not least because of the prominence of private business interests involved in their operations.[48]

5 Cooperation in the Food Security Agenda

As extensively discussed elsewhere, over the last decade, Russia's food policy has been defined by its food security agenda.[49] Russia's Food Security Doctrine, adopted in 2010, pursued self-sufficiency through assistance for domestic agricultural production in addition to restrictions on specific imports. This was given a new impetus by the food embargo of August 2014, which was followed by Moscow's launch of an extensive import substitution policy in October 2014. Against this background, food security acquired a distinct political and security importance, affecting Russia's preferences vis-à-vis developments in the EAEU.

This is an area where Russia's leadership has been in full display. This was possible also because food security was already an important issue in the region. For example, Armenia adopted a food security law in 2002; Belarus adopted its own Food Security Concept in 2004; Kazakhstan included food independence in its 2005 Law on state regulation of the development of the agricultural complex and rural territories; and Kyrgyzstan passed a law on food security in 2008. These acts were followed by various programmes, concepts, and strategies detailing and updating the food security agenda. While the definitions of food security, the targets set for self-sufficiency of the domestic production of different commodities and the domestic support measures to achieve them varied widely,[50] the general concern was shared as was its association with the wider issue of national security. Furthermore, Food

Security Concepts were adopted at the regional level of some of the preceding integration projects, namely the Eurasian Economic Community in 2009 and the Commonwealth of Independent States in 2010, which to a large extent reflected the Russian concept and food security targets. Recently, a EAEU-wide Concept was drafted and distributed for consultation. As a result, the EEC has monitored the levels of domestic self-sufficiency, producing 'league tables' of the progress of the different countries towards this goal.

Against this background, the EAEU Treaty provided somewhat broadly for the achievement of a coordinated agricultural policy 'to optimise the volumes of production', 'satisfy the needs of the common agricultural market', and 'increase the export of agricultural products and food'.[51] This was a distinctly decentralised policy, carried out by 'regular consultations of the representatives of the member states, organised by the Commission' and followed by the adoption of recommendations.[52] The centrepiece of this coordination was the mutual sharing of the programmes to support the production of an agreed list of sensitive agri-foods. This list adopted in 2016 included milk and milk products, meat and meat products, vegetables, fruits, rice, seeds, sugar, cotton, and tobacco.[53] Furthermore, the Treaty in its Annex 29 attempted to formulate some common principles for the adoption of state support depending on their effect on mutual trade, requiring member states to abstain from the adoption of certain measures. Nonetheless, as in other cases, any disputes with regard to this area of cooperation are to be resolved by interstate consultations, with the Commission performing a purely facilitating function.

The Commission has argued that national import substitution programmes should be developed with a consideration of EAEU imports so as to help the specialisation and competitive advantage of the different member states.[54] In this area, Russia has shown some interest in expanding the import substitution agenda to the level of the EAEU. In July 2020, a EAEU Road-Map on the development of agricultural industry was adopted, which moves forward cooperation in this field.[55] However, Russia was reluctant to open its public procurement market to EAEU companies, which attracted many complaints, especially by Belarus, alleging distortion of the common market. In 2018 Russia finally admitted EAEU companies to its import substitution programme. Nevertheless, as commentators point out, there remain numerous substantial obstacles to EAEU companies taking part in Russian tenders.[56]

6 EAEU's External Agreements

One area where the EAEU boasts a potential to make a difference to its members' external trade is in fostering relations with third parties. Indeed, the EAEU has been active in signing various cooperation memoranda and negotiating trade deals across the globe. To date, the EAEU has successfully signed free trade agreements with Vietnam (2015), Iran (2018), Singapore (2019), and Serbia (2019). Certainly, one might expect that such agreements might contribute to Russia's geographical reorientation of post-sanction imports as well as crate new export opportunities. Yet, the benefits of these agreements so far can be described as marginal.

The agreement with Vietnam is a case in point (see also Chapter 7). It provides for the liberalisation of 88 percent of trade in goods, with 59 percent of tariff eliminated upon entry into force and 29 percent removed over a five to ten-year period.[57] In terms of export opportunities, the agreement hailed the possibility of reaching a market of 90 million people. It secures the immediate removal of tariffs on key commodities, such as wheat and linseed. It also creates opportunities for growing markets in products, such as milk, poultry, and confectionaries, subject to transition periods. In terms of imports, the agreement liberalises the access of goods, such as fish, rice, and fruit. Yet, it excludes competing 'sensitive' commodities, such as meat, milk, tea, coffee, and sugar, thus protecting domestic producers. Furthermore, the EAEU reserves the asymmetric right to apply trigger safeguard measures to control the volume of some imports, such as rice. It similarly relies on quotas and the application of non-tariff barriers, including SPS measures.[58] Protectionist measures were particularly relevant to the case of Belarus, which stood to lose most from free trade with Vietnam.[59]

Five years on, not all EAEU members have benefitted from the agreement.[60] Trade data shows that Russia's total imports from Vietnam have grown, while its exports have been more erratic.[61] Yet, ultimately, the economic significance of this agreement is limited given Vietnam's share in the EAEU members' external trade. Even for Russia, which accounts for the highest volume of EAEU trade with Vietnam, this share is less than 1 percent.[62]

The picture is similar in terms of the temporary FTA with Iran, accounting for 0.28 percent of Russia's external trade in 2018. During the first eight months of 2020, total trade between the EAEU and Iran totalled about $2 billion USD, of which, food and agricultural goods amounted to $939 million USD.[63] Furthermore, the temporary agreement with Iran is limited in its scope and commitments on both sides.[64] It applies to a short list of commodities, representing about 50 percent of existing trade. The EAEU liberalises tariffs on mostly non-sensitive goods, whereas trade in some competing goods, such as vegetables, is restricted to seasonal preferences. In November 2020, however, it was reported that the EAEU and Iran would sign a permanent free trade agreement, which presumably would increase trade and remove current restrictions.[65]

This trend is even more pronounced with regard to the recently signed FTAs with Singapore and Serbia. As Singapore already operates a duty-free access, in the words of the Commission, an FTA 'is not of interest to the CU members by virtue of its foreign trade effects'.[66] Similarly, the agreement with Serbia consolidates existing agreements and offers few new advantages to bilateral trade with Moscow.

The EAEU has also been negotiating agreements with Israel since 2015 and with Egypt and India since 2016. In terms of the attraction of Israel, like with Singapore, its key benefits lie outside trade in goods. While Russia is likely to benefit from grain exports and fruit and vegetable imports from an agreement with Egypt, negotiations have been slow. Reaching an agreement with India is even more problematic. EAEU assessments show significant negative effects of deepened engagement with India particularly for Belarus, short of exemptions relating to dairy and meat products.[67] At the same time, given India's protectionist record, the extent of market access concessions to obtain should not be overestimated.

While some opportunities are created by these agreements, they are not concluded with major trade partners and the primary reason for pursuing them has not been economic. Above all, they align with Russia's particular geopolitical objectives in the respective regions, while promoting an agenda to establish the EAEU as an internationally recognised player.[68] They are more about Russia's regional clout and the economic alignment with important geopolitical shifts rather than about trade liberalisation. Improved market access has been more part of their justification rather than their impetus. Ironically, the very fact that they cover small volumes of trade has helped make them possible in achieving the consensus for signing them in the face of domestic protectionist pressures.[69]

In this sense, it is notable that the bulk of the growth in Russia's external markets since 2014 has been outside the framework of EAEU's free trade agreements. At the same time, while the prominence of trade with China has grown and cooperation opportunities at the level of the EAEU have been explored, the possibility for a free trade agreement is not on the table. Instead, in 2018 the EAEU signed a non-preferential agreement designed to serve as the basis for future economic relations. Yet, in terms of its contents, this is primarily a politically symbolic agreement, with little added value to cooperation other than restating existing WTO commitments.

7 How Trade Flows Have Changed

Against this background, it is not surprising that the picture of agri-food trade in the EAEU presents mixed results. To start with, the EAEU inherited a rising trend in mutual agri-food trade between Russia, Belarus, and Kazakhstan despite declines in total trade in 2012.[70] The launch of the EAEU was marked by a sharp currency depreciation against the U.S. dollar, and the entry into force of Russia's import food ban, which led to a reduction in Russia's total agri-food imports in 2014 and 2015.[71] This trend was also reflected in trade with Russia's EAEU partners (see Fig. 1), even though as the EEC notes, the fall in agri-food trade was not as pronounced as the fall in other commodity groups.[72]

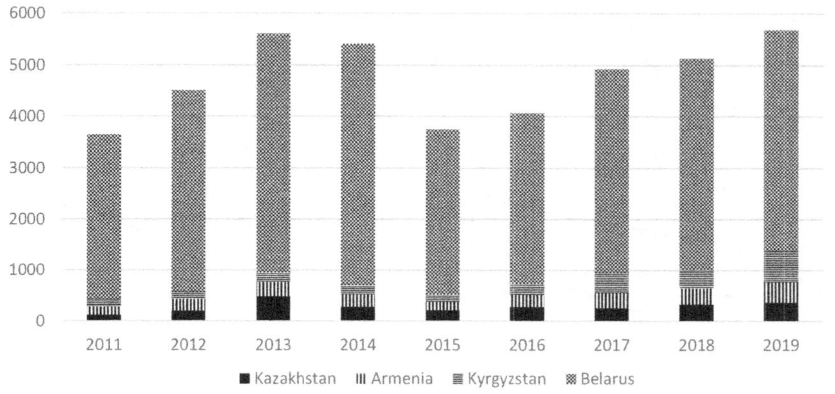

Fig. 1 Value of Russia's agri-food imports from the EAEU (million USD) (*Source* Author's calculations based on EEC's Statistics on trade in agri-food products)

Since 2015, there has been a gradual yet important increase in Russia's agri-food imports from the EAEU, indicating that geographical reorientation as a result of the sanctions war has taken place. This increase has been fairly unequal across EAEU partners: imports from Armenia and Kyrgyzstan have grown at a higher rate than imports from Kazakhstan and Belarus. Nonetheless, imports from Belarus continue to account for the largest share of Russia's food supplies, particularly in commodities such as milk and meat. Indeed, Belarus has been seen as one of the distinct 'winners' in increasing its share of food imports to Russia, even though there has been some scepticism as to how much of this trade has represented re-export of EU foods.[73] A closer look at the dynamics of imports from Belarus (see Fig. 2) suggests that the effect of trade disputes has been significant and USD dollar volumes of trade have still not matched the peak years of 2013–2014.

It should be noted that the value of agri-food imports from the EAEU has grown at a faster rate than imports from the rest of the world (see Fig. 3). Yet, as with external trade, this rate has slowed down significantly after 2017, which may also be attributed to the effects of Russia's import substitution policy. Furthermore, the share of internal trade remains

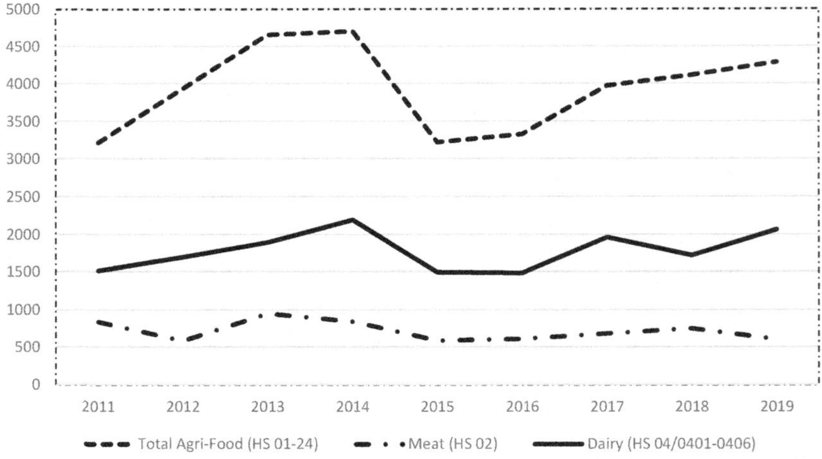

Fig. 2 Dynamics of Russia's agri-food imports from Belarus (million USD) (*Source* Author's calculations based on EEC's Statistics on trade in agri-food products)

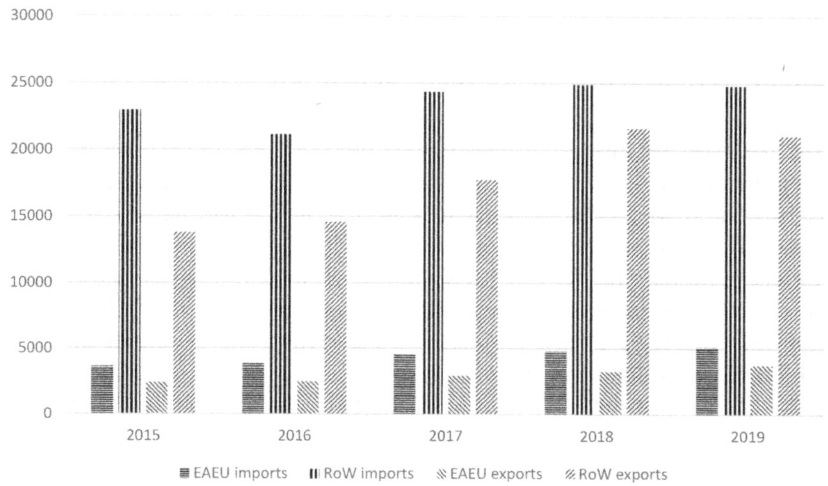

Fig. 3 Russia's agri-food imports and exports from the EAEU and rest of the world (RoW) (million USD) (*Source* Author's calculations based on EEC's Statistics on trade in agri-food products)

significantly lower than external agri-food trade, pointing to the prominence of other geographical regions in replacing the countries subject to the import ban.

Russia remains a net food importer from the EAEU. It has increased its exports to the EAEU albeit at a rate slower than its exports to the rest of the world.[74]

8 Outlook

Over the last decade, Russia sought to increase its influence in the global food trade while promoting its geopolitical priorities. At the same time, it committed to deep economic integration within the 2010 Customs Union and the EAEU, including the creation of a common internal market and the pursuit of a common external trade policy. In this sense, the EAEU has the potential to enhance Russia's policy options in the international arena while growing regional trade.

As the discussion in this chapter shows, however, the EAEU has had a trivial role in affecting Russia's policy choices. Given the bloc's institutional characteristics and structure, Russia's has proved able to deviate from the constraining obligations under the EAEU regime. It has been able to assert its interests regardless of the costs to its partners and the integration project as a whole. At the same time, it has allowed Moscow to use the EAEU platform to further its own priorities with limited commitment to its partners, as the example of the import substitution agenda demonstrates. Given Russia's leadership within the organisation, the EAEU has provided it with the regional clout to enter FTA with politically strategic partners. Yet, in trade terms, the potential of these agreements has been limited.

At the same time, for Russia, dealing in the context of the EAEU framework has not been problem-free. Ironically, the decentralised nature of the EAEU agri-food regime combined with the weakness of domestic institutions in the EAEU member states has meant that Moscow has struggled to enforce its import food ban. Furthermore, the weakness of the common regime has also meant that the EAEU continues to perform below its potential, particularly in growing mutual trade through the elimination of non-tariff barriers.

The problems of the EAEU have often been attributed to 'under-integration', or the insufficient extent to which member states have committed to creating a robust institutional regime for eliminating internal obstacles to trade.[75] The latest 'Strategy for the Development of Eurasian Integration Until 2025' has reflected on this issue, declaring the importance of the completion of the common market and the improvement of the EAEU regulatory regime.[76] Nonetheless, it is questionable if these issues can be sorted out without a radical change in the institutional setting of the Union, even if plans and programmes continue to proliferate. Indeed, as wisely observed, drawing up a roadmap to address sticking points, is 'the EAEU's favourite method for kicking things into the long grass'.[77]

Against this background, it can be expected that some improvements of the Union regime will take place: particularly in areas aligning with Russia's interest, such as digital tracing of origin. However, the deeper structural problems behind it, both at Union and domestic governance levels, are likely to persist without a change in the fundamental preferences and modes of operation of the EAEU member states. In this sense, while the EAEU will continue to add to Russia's image as a bloc leader, it is unlikely to make a major difference to the essence of its policies.

Notes

1. The founding Treaty of the EAEU was signed by Russia, Kazakhstan and Belarus on 29 May 2014. It entered into force on 1 January 2015, the formal birth of the EAEU. Armenia joined the organisation on 2 January 2015 and Kyrgyzstan on 12 August 2015.
2. Irina Gurova, Irina Platonova and Marija Maksakova, 'The Level of Trade Integration in the Eurasian Economic Union', *Studies on Russian Economic Development* 29, no. 4 (2018): 447–53.
3. Rilka Dragneva and Kataryna Wolczuk, 'The Eurasian Economic Union: Deals, Rules and the Exercise of Power', Chatham House Research Paper, May 2017, https://www.chathamhouse.org/sites/default/files/publications/research/2017-05-02-eurasian-economic-union-dragneva-wolczuk.pdf. Accessed 14 October 2020; Rilka Dragneva and Christopher A. Hartwell, 'The Eurasian Economic Union: Integration without Liberalisation?' *Post-Communist Economies* 32, no. 7 (2020). https://doi.org/10.1080/14631377.2020.1793586.
4. See Stephen K Wegren, 'Russia's Foreign Food Trade: An Historical Survey', Chapter 1, in this volume.
5. Maksim Karliuk, 'The Eurasian Economic Union: An EU-like Legal Order in the Post-Soviet Space?', HSE Working Paper BPR/LAW/2015. https://papers.ssrn.com/sol3/papers.cfm?abstract_id=2664519 2015. Accessed 20 September 2020; Rilka Dragneva, 'The Eurasian Economic Union: Balancing Sovereignty and Integration', in *Post-Soviet Constitutions and Challenges of Regional Integration*, eds. Roman Petrov and Peter van Elsewuge (London: Routledge, 2018), 48–70.
6. Karliuk, The Eurasian Economic Union: An EU-like Legal Order in the Post-Soviet Space?'.
7. Alexander Knobel, Andrey Lipin, Andrey Malokostov, David Tarr, and Natalia Turdyeva, 'Deeper Integration in the Eurasian Economic Union: What Are the Benefits of Successful Implementation or Wider Liberalisation?' *Eurasian Geography and Economics* 60, no. 2 (2019): 177–210.
8. Dragneva, 'The Eurasian Economic Union: Balancing Sovereignty and Integration'.
9. David Sedik, Carl Ulbricht, and Nuritdin Dzhamankulov, *The Architecture of Food Safety Control Across Eurasia* (Balti, Moldova: Lambert Academic Publishing, 2017), 46.
10. Ricardo Giucci, 'The Eurasian Economic Union—An Analysis from a Trade Policy Perspective', Presentation at the German Embassy, Moscow,

29 May 2018. https://berlin-economics.com/wp-content/uploads/2018-05-29_Presentation-EAEU_Moscow.pdf. Accessed 23 September 2020.

11. Dragneva and Wolczuk, 'The Eurasian Economic Union: Deals, Rules and the Exercise of Power'.
12. Evgeny Vinokurov, 'Eurasian Economic Union: Current State and Preliminary Results', *Russian Journal of Economics*, no. 3 (2017): 54–70; Knobel et al., 'Deeper Integration in the Eurasian Economic Union'.
13. Alexander Melikishvilli, 'Russia's Economic Pressure on Belarus Escalates to Trade War', Jamestown Foundation Commentaries, 10 June. https://jamestown.org/russias-economic-pressure-on-belarus-escalates-to-trade-war. Accessed 15 September 2020.
14. Sedik, Ulbricht, and Dzhamankulov, *The Architecture of Food Safety Control*, 32.
15. Irina Kireeva and Robert Black, 'Sanitary and Phytosanitary Legislation in the Russian Federation: A General Overview in Light of the WTO SPS Agreement and EU Principles of Food Safety', *Review of Central and East European Law* 35 (2010): 225–55.
16. Robert Black and Irina Kireeva, 'Sanitary and Phytosanitary Issues for the Customs Union of Russian Federation, Belarus and Kazakhstan in Relation to Trade with Other CIS Countries and the EU', *Journal of World Trade* 49, no. 5 (2015): 805–36.
17. Nuritdin Dzhamankulov, 'The Harmonization of Eurasian Economic Union Sanitary and Phytosanitary Measures and Technical Regulation for Agricultural Goods with the Provisions of the WTO for the International Trade Development', FAO Regional Office for Europe and Central Asia Policy Studies on Rural Transition No. 2015-5. http://www.fao.org/3/a-bs205e.pdf. Accessed 14 September 2020.
18. Article 53.2 paragraph 3 of the EAEU Treaty. Available at https://docs.eaeunion.org/docs/ru-ru/0023611/itia_05062014. Accessed 14 October 2020.
19. Article 56. 2 of the EAEU Treaty. Available at https://docs.eaeunion.org/docs/ru-ru/0023611/itia_05062014. Accessed 14 October 2020.
20. Articles 51–52 provide the general framework for technical standards, whereas Articles 56–59 and Annex 12 are specifically dedicated to SPS measures.
21. CU Commission Decision No 299 of 28 May 2010. Available at http://www.tsouz.ru/kts/kts17/pages/r_299.aspx. Accessed 14 October 2020. As technical regulations get adopted, the respective products are deleted from the general list under Decision No. 299.
22. For an up-to-date list, see http://www.eurasiancommission.org/ru/act/texnreg/deptexreg/tr/Pages/TRVsily.aspx. Accessed 17 September 2020.

23. CU Commission Decision No. 317 of 18 June 2010. Available at http://www.tsouz.ru/KTS/KTS17/Pages/R_317.aspx. Accessed 14 October 2020.
24. Evraziiskaia ekonomicheskaia komissiia (hereafter EEK), 'EEK predlagaet izmenit' poryadok razrabotki soyuznykh tehreglamentov i uzhestochit' kontrol' za soblyudeniem ustanovlennykh srokov', 11 October 2019. http://www.eurasiancommission.org/ru/nae/news/Pages/11-10-2019-1.aspx. Accessed 19 September 2020.
25. Il'a Zakharkin, 'Chto ozhidaet rynok vina v EAES?' *Ritm Evrazii*, 30 July 2020. http://www.ritmeurasia.org/news--2020-07-30--chto-ozhidaet-rynok-vina-v-eaes-50195. Accessed 17 September 2020.
26. Article 57.4 of the EAEU Treaty.
27. Such an agreement has been in the making since 2015, with a draft approved by the EEC Council in February 2018 and disseminated to member states for discussion, yet progress has been slow.
28. The Collegium of the EEC adopted two non-binding acts to promote coordination in this field: on how member states' bodies should cooperate with each other when exercising domestic control for compliance with technical regulations (Recommendation No 9 of 19 June 2018) and how they should cooperate with the Commission to prevent the circulation of non-compliant goods (Recommendation no. 22 from 23 July 2019).
29. EEK, 'V EAES dolzhna provodit'sia edinaia politika po primeneniiu sanitarnykh i fitosanitarnykh mer', 25 October 2018. http://www.eurasiancommission.org/ru/nae/news/Pages/25-10-2018-1v.aspx. Accessed 19 September 2020.
30. For a comprehensive comparison between the EAEU and the EU in the area of food safety, see discussion of this aspect see, Sedik, Ulbricht, and Dzhamankulov, *The Architecture of Food Safety Control*.
31. Paragraph 6 of Annex 12 of the EAEU Treaty. Available at https://docs.eaeunion.org/docs/ru-ru/0023611/itia_05062014. Accessed 14 October 2020.
32. Council of the Eurasian Economic Commission. Decision no. 149 from 16 May 2016. Available at http://www.tsouz.ru/KTS/KTS17/Pages/R_317.aspx. Accessed 14 October 2020.
33. For a detailed discussion of this point, see Sedik, Ulbricht, and Dzhamankulov, *The Architecture of Food Safety Control*.
34. EEK, 'Doklad o realizatzii osnovnykh napravlenii integratzii v ramkakh Evraziiskogo ekonomicheskogo soiuza v 2018', n.d. http://www.eurasiancommission.org/ru/act/integr_i_makroec/dep_razv_integr/Documents/%d0%94%d0%be%d0%ba%d0%bb%d0%b0%d0%b4%20%d0%b8%d0%bd%d1%82%d0%b5%d0%b3%d1%80%d0%b0%d1%86%d0%b8%d1%8f.pdf. Accessed 17 September 2020.

35. Author's interview with the EEC's Minister of Integration, Tatyana Valovaya, July 2014.
36. EEK, 'Viktor Nazarenko: Sistema ozenki sootvetstviia i gosudarstvennogo nadzora dolzhny byt' vystroeny takim obrazom, chto na obshcgii rynok postupala tol'ko kachestvennaia i bezopasnaia produkziia', 27 February 2020. http://www.eurasiancommission.org/ru/nae/news/Pages/27-02-2020-1.aspx. Accessed 19 September 2020.
37. Under Article 58.6 of the EAEU Treaty.
38. Article 29.3 of the EAEU Treaty.
39. For example, see Kirill Sokov, 'Molochno-tzenovoi disbalans mezhdu Moskvoi i Minskom', 18 March 2018. https://www.ritmeurasia.org/news--2018-03-08--molochno-cenovoj-disbalans-mezhdu-moskvoj-i-minskom-35313. Accessed 22 September 2020.
40. Government Resolution no. 778 of 7 August 2014 banned imports of certain agricultural products from Australia, Canada, the EU, Norway and the USA. http://government.ru/docs/14195. Accessed 14 October 2020; Government Resolution no. 842 of 13 August 2015 extended the ban to Albania, Iceland, Lichtenstein and Montenegro. From 1 January 2016, the ban was extended to Ukraine. http://government.ru/docs/19265. Accessed 14 October 2020.
41. Alexander Knobel', 'Nevozmozhnaia troitsa; kak rossiiskie sanktsii razrushaiut Tamozhennyi soiuz', 2 December 2014. http://www.forbes.ru/mneniyacolumn/gosplan/274627-nevozmozhnaya-troitsa-kak-rossiiskie-sanktsii-razrushayuttamozhennyi. Accessed 26 September 2020.
42. Volha Charnysh, 'Belarus Hopes to Cash in on Russian Sanctions', 19 August 2014. https://belarusdigest.com/story/belarus-hopes-to-cash-in-on-russian-sanctions/. Accessed 22 September 2020.
43. For a discussion of this issue, see Jurii Kofner, 'Did the EaEU Create a Common Market for Goods, Services, Capital and Labour Within the Union?', 30 October 2019. https://l2v.blogactiv.eu/2019/10/30/did-the-eurasian-economic-union-create-a-common-domestic-market-for-goods-services-capital-and-labor/. Accessed September 9, 2020.
44. Viktor Rogozhin, 'Moloko i myaso is Belarussii ne na stole potrebitelei, v leksikone politikov', 1 April 2018. https://www.ritmeurasia.org/news--2018-04-01--moloko-i-mjaso-iz-belorussii-ne-na-stole-potrebitelej-a-v-leksikone-politikov-35701. Accessed 2 September 2020. See also Rosselkhoznadzor's report from the inspections carried out on Belarus's enterprises in June 2018. https://fsvps.gov.ru/fsvps-docs/ru/importExport/belarus/files/inspection_2018061215_pre.pdf. Accessed 20 September 2020.
45. EEK, 'Sergey Sidorskii: "Produktsiia zhivotnogo proizhozhdeniia Belarusi otvechaet vsem trebovaniiam veterinarno-sanitarnogo kontrolia EAES"',

11 January 2017. http://www.eurasiancommission.org/ru/nae/news/Pages/11-01-2017.aspx. Accessed 22 September 2020.
46. EEC Collegium Decision no. 181 of 12 November 2018, https://docs.eaeunion.org/docs/ru-ru/01424926/clcd_16112018, and Decision no. 11 of 22 January 2019. https://docs.eaeunion.org/docs/ru-ru/01423704/clcd_25012019_11, both accessed 14 October 2020, in relation to restrictions on milk.
47. Il 'ya Zakharkin, 'Kak prekratit' belorussko-rossiiskie 'igry' v ogranicheniia?', 13 May 2019. https://www.ritmeurasia.org/news--2019-05-13--kak-prekratit-belorussko-rossijskie-igry-v-ogranichenija-42604. Accessed 22 September 2020.
48. Kofner, 'Did the EaEU Create a Common Market?'
49. For an analysis of food security and different dimensions that relate to it in Russia see Stephen K. Wegren, Alexander Nikulin, and Irina Trotsuk, *Food Policy and Food Security: Putting Food on the Russian Table* (Lanham, MD and London, UK: Lexington Books, 2018).
50. EEK, 'Monitoring prodovolstvennoi bezopasnosti EAES: 2014', Moscow, 2015. http://www.eurasiancommission.org/ru/act/prom_i_agroprom/dep_agroprom/monitoring/Documents/%D0%9C%D0%BE%D0%BD%D0%B8%D1%82%D0%BE%D1%80%D0%B8%D0%BD%D0%B3%20%D0%BF%D1%80%D0%BE%D0%B4%D0%BE%D0%B2%D0%BE%D0%BB%D1%8C%D1%81%D1%82%D0%B2%D0%B5%D0%BD%D0%BD%D0%BE%D0%B9%20%D0%B1%D0%B5%D0%B7%D0%BE%D0%BF%D0%B0%D1%81%D0%BD%D0%BE%D1%81%D1%82%D0%B8%20%D0%A1%D0%BE%D1%8E%D0%B7%D0%B0%202014.pdf. Accessed 14 October 2020.
51. Article 94.2 of the EAEU Treaty.
52. Article 95.2 of the EAEU Treaty.
53. Decision of the Council of the EEC no. 66 of 12 February 2016. https://docs.eaeunion.org/docs/ru-ru/01414425/cncd_10102016_66. Accessed 14 October 2020.
54. EEK, 'Monitoring prodovolstvennoi bezopasnosti'.
55. EEK, 'V EAES sistemno podoidut k razvitiiu APK', 17 July 2020. http://www.eurasiancommission.org/ru/nae/news/Pages/17.07.2020-5.aspx. Accessed 24 September 2020.
56. Jurii Kofner, 'Did the Other EAEU Member States Profit from Eurasian Integration and Russia's Countersanction Policy?', 3 July 2020. http://greater-europe.org/archives/8091. Accessed 23 September 2020.
57. EEK, 'Obzor kliuchevykh polozhenii soglasheniia o svobodnoi torgovle mezhdu Evraziiskim ekonomicheskim soiuzom i sotzialisticheskoi Respubliki Vietnam', Moscow, 2015. http://eec.eaeunion.org/ru/act/trade/dotp/sogl_torg/Documents/%d0%9e%d0%b1%d0%b7%d0%be%d1%80%20%d0%a1%d0%be%d0%b3%d0%bb%d0%b0%d1%88%d0%b5%d0%bd%d0%b8%d1%8f%20%d0%be%20%d1%81%d0%b2%d0%be%d0%b1%d0%be%d0%

b4%d0%bd%d0%be%d0%b9%20%d1%82%d0%be%d1%80%d0%b3%d0%be%d0%b2%d0%bb%d0%b5%20%d0%bc%d0%b5%d0%b6%d0%b4%d1%83%20%d1%81%d1%82%d1%80%d0%b0%d0%bd%d0%b0%d0%bc%d0%b8%20%d0%95%d0%90%d0%ad%d0%a1%20%d0%b8%20%d0%92%d1%8c%d0%b5%d1%82%d0%bd%d0%b0%d0%bc%d0%be%d0%bc.pdf. Accessed 14 October 2020.

58. For example, rice is subject to 10 thousand tonn quota, which is less than 5 percent of total imports from third countries, and applies to long-grain rice, which is not grown in the EAEU.
59. EEK, 'Annotatzia k rezultatam nauchno-issledovatel'skoi raboty na temu "Opredelenie perspektivnykh partnerov gosudarstv-chlenov Tamozhennogo Soiuza po zakliucheniiu soglashenii o svobodnoi torgovle"', 2013. http://www.eurasiancommission.org/ru/NIR/Lists/List/Attachments/35/18_12_2013_annot.pdf. Accessed 21 September 2020.
60. Sam Bhutia, 'As the Eurasian Union Looks East, Its Deals Do Not Benefit All Members Equally', 19 November 2019. https://eurasianet.org/as-the-eurasian-union-looks-east-its-deals-do-not-benefit-all-members-equally. Accessed 20 September 2020.
61. Author's calculation from data in the EEC's Statistics. http://www.eurasiancommission.org/ru/act/integr_i_makroec/dep_stat/tradestat/tables/Pages/default.aspx. Accessed 28 September 2020.
62. This section uses 2018 data on third countries' share in EAEU and its members' trade, presented in Dragneva and Hartwell, 'The Eurasian Economic Union: Integration Without Liberalisation', 15–16.
63. TASS, 'Iran i EAES mogut sozdat' postoiannuiu zonu svododnoi torgovli do kontsa goda', 2 November 2020. https://www.dairynews.ru/news/iran-i-eaes-mogut-sozdat-postoyannuyu-zonu-svobodn.html. Accessed 2 November 2020.
64. Rilka Dragneva, 'The Eurasian Economic Union: Putin's Geopolitical Project', FPRI Research Paper, 15 October 2018. https://www.fpri.org/wp-content/uploads/2018/10/rpe-6-dragneva-final2.pdf. Accessed 20 September 2020.
65. TASS, 'Iran i EAES mogut sozdat' postoiannuiu zonu svododnoi torgovli do kontsa goda'.
66. EEK, 'Annotatzia k rezultatam nauchno-issledovatel'skoi raboty na temu'.
67. Ibid.
68. Dragneva, 'The Eurasian Economic Union: Putin's Geopolitical Project'.
69. Dragneva and Hartwell, 'The Eurasian Economic Union: Integration Without Liberalisation'.
70. EEK, Doklad 'O rezul'tatakh analiza dinamiki vzaimnoi torgovli gosudarst-chlenovTamozhennogo soiuza i Edinogo ekonomicheskogo prostranstvo v 2010–2014 godakh', 2015. http://www.eurasiancommiss

ion.org/ru/act/integr_i_makroec/dep_stat/tradestat/analytics/Documents/report/Report_2010-2014.PDF. Accessed 24 September 2020.

71. FAO, 'Agricultural Trade Policies in the Post-Soviet countries 2014/2015: A Summary', 2016. http://www.fao.org/3/a-i6160e.pdf. Accessed 24 September 2020.
72. EEK, Doklad 'O rezul'tatakh analiza dinamiki vzaimnoi torgovli'.
73. Kofner, 'Did the Other EAEU Member States Profit from Eurasian Integration and Russia's Countersanction Policy?'
74. FAO, 'Review of Agricultural Trade Policies in the Post-Soviet Countries 2017–2018', 2020. http://www.fao.org/3/CA0879EN/ca0879en.pdf. Accessed 22 September 2020.
75. E.g. see the statements of the then President of the EEC Collegium: "Tigran Sarkisian na PMEF-2019," 7 June 2019, https://xn----8sbeibfw3aojl2n.xn--p1ai/eaes/tigran-sarkisyan-v-vosplamenyayushchemsya-mire-%D0%B5ek-ne-hvataet-polnomochij. Accessed 22 September 2020.
76. EEK, 'Sovet EEK soglasoval eshche 28 punktov proekta Strategii-25', 1 October 2020. http://www.eurasiancommission.org/ru/nae/news/Pages/01-10-2020-3.aspx. Accessed 1 October 2020.
77. Eurasianet, 'Here's Looking at EAEU 4: Belarus Backs Itself into Trade Corner', 3 September 2020. https://eurasianet.org/heres-looking-at-eaeu-4-belarus-backs-itself-into-trade-corner. Accessed 24 September 2020.

Selected Bibliography

Bhutia, Sam. 'As the Eurasian Union Looks East, Its Deals Do Not Benefit All Members Equally'. Eurasianet.org, 19 November 2019. Available at https://eurasianet.org/as-the-eurasian-union-looks-east-its-deals-do-not-benefit-all-members-equally.

Black, Robert and Irina Kireeva. 'Sanitary and Phytosanitary Issues for the Customs Union of Russian Federation, Belarus and Kazakhstan in Relation to Trade with Other CIS Countries and the EU'. *Journal of World Trade* 49, no. 5 (2015): 805–36.

Dragneva, Rilka and Christopher A. Hartwell. 'The Eurasian Economic Union: Integration without Liberalisation?' *Post-Communist Economies* 32, no. 7 (2020). Available at https://doi.org/10.1080/14631377.2020.1793586.

Dragneva, Rilka and Kataryna Wolczuk. 'The Eurasian Economic Union: Deals, Rules and the Exercise of Power'. Chatham House Research Paper, May 2017. Available at https://www.chathamhouse.org/sites/default/files/publications/research/2017-05-02-eurasian-economic-union-dragneva-wolczuk.pdf.

Dragneva, Rilka. 'The Eurasian Economic Union: Balancing Sovereignty and Integration', in *Post-Soviet Constitutions and Challenges of Regional Integration,* eds. Roman Petrov and Peter van Elsewuge. London: Routledge, 2018, 48–70.

Dragneva, Rilka. 'The Eurasian Economic Union: Putin's Geopolitical Project'. FPRI Research Paper, 15 October 2018. Available at https://www.fpri.org/wp-content/uploads/2018/10/rpe-6-dragneva-final2.pdf.

Dzhamankulov, Nuritdin. 'The Harmonization of Eurasian Economic Union Sanitary and Phytosanitary Measures and Technical Regulation for Agricultural Goods with the Provisions of the WTO for the International Trade Development'. FAO Regional Office for Europe and Central Asia Policy Studies on Rural Transition No. 2015-5. Available at http://www.fao.org/3/a-bs205e.pdf.

FAO. 'Agricultural Trade policies in the Post-Soviet countries 2014/2015: A Summary', 2016. Available at http://www.fao.org/3/a-i6160e.pdf.

FAO. 'Review of Agricultural Trade Policies in the Post-Soviet Countries 2017–2018: A Summary', 2020. Available at http://www.fao.org/3/CA0879EN/ca0879en.pdf.

Giucci, Ricardo and Anne Mdinaradze. 'The Eurasian Economic Union—An Analysis from a Trade Policy Perspective', Berlin Economics, 11 April 2017. Available at https://wiiw.ac.at/files/events/giucci-eaeu-11-april-2017-en-n-341.pdf.

Gurova, Irina, Platonova, Irina and Marija Maksakova. 'The Level of Trade Integration in the Eurasian Economic Union'. *Studies on Russian Economic Development* 29, no. 4 (2018): 447–53.

Karliuk, Maksim. 'The Eurasian Economic Union: An EU-like Legal Order in the Post-Soviet Space?', HSE Working Paper BPR/LAW/2015. Available at https://papers.ssrn.com/sol3/papers.cfm?abstract_id=2664519 2015.

Kireeva, Irina and Robert Black. 'Sanitary and Phytosanitary Legislation in the Russian Federation: A General Overview in Light of the WTO SPS Agreement and EU Principles of Food Safety'. *Review of Central and East European Law* 35 (2010): 225–55.

Knobel, Alexander, Lipin, Andrey, Malokostov, Andrey, Tarr, David and Natalia Turdyeva. 'Deeper Integration in the Eurasian Economic Union: What Are the Benefits of Successful Implementation or Wider Liberalisation?' *Eurasian Geography and Economics* 60, no. 2 (2019): 177–210.

Kofner, Jurii. 'Did the EaEU Create a Common Market for Goods, Services, Capital and Labour Within the Union?', 30 October 2019. Available at https://l2v.blogactiv.eu/2019/10/30/did-the-eurasian-economic-union-create-a-common-domestic-market-for-goods-services-capital-and-labor/.

Kofner, Jurii. 'Did the Other EAEU Member States Profit from Eurasian Integration and Russia's Countersanction Policy?', Analytical Media Eurasian Studies, 3 July 2020. Available at http://greater-europe.org/archives/8091.

Sedik, David, Ulbricht, Carl and Nuritdin Dzhamankulov. *The Architecture of Food Safety Control Across Eurasia*. Balti, Moldova: Lambert Academic Publishing, 2017.

Vinokurov, Evgeny. 'Eurasian Economic Union: Current State and Preliminary Results'. *Russian Journal of Economics*, no. 3 (2017): 54–70.

Wegren, Stephen K., Nikulin, Alexander and Irina Trotsuk. *Food Policy and Food Security: Putting Food on the Russian Table*. Lanham, MD and London, UK: Lexington Books, 2018.

Open Access This chapter is licensed under the terms of the Creative Commons Attribution 4.0 International License (http://creativecommons.org/licenses/by/4.0/), which permits use, sharing, adaptation, distribution and reproduction in any medium or format, as long as you give appropriate credit to the original author(s) and the source, provide a link to the Creative Commons license and indicate if changes were made.

The images or other third party material in this chapter are included in the chapter's Creative Commons license, unless indicated otherwise in a credit line to the material. If material is not included in the chapter's Creative Commons license and your intended use is not permitted by statutory regulation or exceeds the permitted use, you will need to obtain permission directly from the copyright holder.

Chapter 9: Russia's Agri-Food Trade with the Middle East and North Africa

Maximilian Heigermoser, Tinoush Jamali Jaghdani, and Linde Götz

1 Introduction

As Russia's food exports started to increase substantially with the turn of the millennium,[1] the Middle East and North Africa (MENA) region became the most important destination region, particularly for grain exports.[2] Due to unfavourable climatic and soil conditions, most MENA countries are dependent on grain imports, as domestic production does not meet consumption. While around one-third of Russia's food exports were destined for MENA countries in 2019, the region's share exhibited a slight downward trend over the past decade, while agricultural exports to Asian markets gradually increased. From 2011 to 2019, Russia's total

M. Heigermoser (✉) · T. J. Jaghdani · L. Götz
Leibniz Institute of Agricultural Development in Transition Economies (IAMO), Halle, Germany
e-mail: heigermoser@iamo.de

T. J. Jaghdani
e-mail: jaghdani@iamo.de

L. Götz
e-mail: Goetz@iamo.de

© The Author(s) 2022

S. K. Wegren and F. Nilssen (eds.), *Russia's Role in the Contemporary International Agri-Food Trade System*, Palgrave Advances in Bioeconomy: Economics and Policies,
https://doi.org/10.1007/978-3-030-77451-6_10

food exports more than doubled from $12 billion USD to over $25 billion USD, and in 2018 the government's declared its objective to increase the volume of food exports to $45 billion USD by the year 2024.[3] The government subsequently had to back off the target date of 2024, but food exports by that date were still expected to be significantly higher than the base year of 2017. Simultaneously, food imports decreased during the immediate period following Russia's decision to implement a complete ban on agricultural imports from Western countries in August 2014. In 2015 Russia's imports fell by almost a third compared to 2014, from 39 billion USD to $27 billion USD, although after 2016 the dollar value of imports began to rise again.[4]

Russia's primary agricultural export item is grain, which accounted for 37 percent of the country's food exports between 2011 and 2019. Wheat is Russia's most important grain export product, accounting for more than 75 percent, followed by barley (11 percent) and maize (11 percent). In the 2015/2016 season, Russia became the world's largest wheat exporter for the first time, a position it has mostly maintained since then.[5] While fish and crustaceans are important food export products, primarily for East Asian markets such as China (frozen fish) and South Korea (crustaceans), the MENA market region is Russia's key market for grain exports. Only 70 percent of grain consumed in this region is produced domestically,[6] while the rest, 90 million tonnes annually, is imported, with Russia and further Black Sea exporters playing an increasingly important role. Against this background, this chapter primarily focuses on Russian wheat exports to the MENA region, while barley, maize, and sunflower oil exports are considered when relevant. We also consider Russia's food imports from the MENA region, which are small compared to exports and mostly consist of fruit, nuts, and vegetables.

We focus on Russia's top four destination markets within the MENA region, namely Egypt, Turkey, Iran, and Saudi Arabia. Jointly, these four countries accounted for close to two-thirds of Russia's food exports to the whole region from 2011 to 2019, while 55 percent of Russia's food imports from MENA originate from these four countries. Grain is the main commodity of this food trade relationship; Egypt and Turkey are the two top wheat export markets for Russia, while Saudi Arabia is the primary destination market for Russian barley. Food trade is largely unidirectional considering Egypt, Iran and especially Saudi Arabia, while Turkey is also a significant supplier of fruits and vegetables to Russia. Considering Russia's total food exports, Turkey is the most important destination market followed by China and Egypt, while Iran and Saudi Arabia fall into the top ten. Regarding Russia's most important suppliers of food, Turkey is fifth, trailing Belarus, Brazil, China, and Germany.

In most MENA countries, including the four considered, State Trading Enterprises (STEs) that manage food imports play a major role in food trade and food security.[7] In most instances, these agencies have a dominant, if not monopolistic position, as primary or exclusive importers of grain in the respective countries. The Egyptian General Authority for Supply of Commodities (GASC), the Turkish Grain Board (TMO), the Saudi Grains Organisation (SAGO), and the Iranian State Livestock Affairs Logistics (SLAL) purchase agricultural commodities on international markets by employing tender systems in order to foster competition among suppliers. These tender markets constitute a central characteristic of the considered regional food trade. Another key feature of Russian food trade with MENA countries is the recurrent disruption caused by political disputes or rapprochement between the respective countries.[8] Further, food trade is frequently impacted by conflicts about the quality and compliance with phytosanitary standards for the supplied products.

In the following, we first briefly outline central characteristics of Russian grain exports, before presenting four individual descriptive analyses of Russia's food trade relationships with Egypt, Turkey, Saudi Arabia, and Iran. We finally project future trends and scenarios in the outlook.

2 General Characteristics of Russian Grain Exports

Russian customs data shows that close to 90 percent of Russia's grain exports flow through ports located at the Black Sea, while smaller quantities are exported by train or via ports at the Caspian Sea, the Baltic Sea, or Far Eastern ports.[9] The deep-water port of Novorossiysk is central to Russia's grain exports via the Black Sea.[10] Together with Tuapse and Taman, Russia's three deep-water ports handle 60 percent of grain exports shipped via the Black Sea. The remaining 40 percent are managed by smaller ports located at the Azov Sea and up the Don River, such as Azov, Rostov-at-Don, Taganrog, and Yeysk. These shallow water ports handle smaller vessels with capacities reaching up to 25,000 tonnes. Turkey—the geographically closest among the four considered trading partners—is usually supplied by these smaller vessels, while barley gets shipped to Saudi Arabia by larger panamax vessels exclusively. In the case of Iran, grain trade partly flows via Black Sea ports and partly via smaller ports located at the Caspian Sea, most notably Astrakhan.

Russian grain exports generally show a strong seasonal pattern. Export volumes are high in the summer months of July through September, when wheat is exported right after the harvest. Elevated exports can be observed until the end of the year before they decrease during the winter and spring months. This pattern partly results from a lack of adequate, modern storage infrastructure, as Russian farmers have no alternative to exporting the new crop right after the harvest, having to accept low prices at the start of a marketing year. However, in recent years, additional storage facilities were set up in Russia. While the United States Department of Agriculture (USDA) estimated Russia's grain storage capacities at 119 million tonnes in 2017,[11] this capacity was estimated at 157 million tonnes in 2019. It can thus be expected that the strong seasonality pattern of Russian grain exports will be dampened in the future.[12]

The climatic and soil conditions in Russia's main agricultural producing regions are generally favourable to grain production. However, Russia's recent ascent as a top wheat exporter also results from a strong devaluation of the Russian ruble since 2014, which supported the competitiveness of Russian exports on the international market.[13] Furthermore, due to close geographical proximity to important destination markets such as Egypt, Russia and further Black Sea exporters, like Ukraine and Romania, benefit from freight cost advantages when competing with other major exporting countries such as France, the United States, or Australia.[14] As agricultural commodities—and grains in particular—have a low value-to-weight ratio, differences in freight costs can become a decisive factor in determining the overall competitiveness of specific exporters in contested destination markets.

3 Focus on Specific MENA Countries

3.1 Egypt

Egypt is the world's largest wheat importer, buying around 12 million tonnes per season, as its domestic production only covers 42 percent of its total consumption.[15] Around half of Egypt's wheat imports are handled by the General Authority for Supply of Commodities (GASC), a STE responsible for the procurement of foodstuffs. In fulfilling its mandate, the GASC alone imports as much wheat as the whole of Japan, making the agency a dominant single player on the international market. To purchase wheat, as well as other food commodities such as rice, soy oil, or sunflower oil, the agency employs a tender system. The GASC usually issues wheat tenders every two weeks, buying three to four cargoes of 60,000 tonnes originating from the destinations that are currently most competitive. GASC tenders are closely watched by the global grain trade, as Egypt is geographically located at a vital chokepoint of international trade, namely the Suez Canal. Therefore, being competitive in GASC tenders typically also implies competitiveness in destination markets beyond the canal, which grants high informational value to the outcome of Egypt's wheat tenders.[16]

The wheat that GASC purchases is processed domestically to produce *baladi* flat bread. This staple food is sold at subsidised prices to Egyptians with lower incomes. Egypt's bread subsidy programme is a politically sensitive issue and efforts to abolish or reform the subsidy system repeatedly caused uprisings and riots.[17] Over the past two decades, Russia and further Black Sea exporters such as Ukraine and Romania have steadily increased their share in the GASC tender market, mostly at the expense of the United States, which had been the top wheat supplier to Egypt for decades. From the 2015/2016 agricultural year onwards, at least 80 percent of wheat imported by the GASC originated from the Black Sea region, with Russia alone accounting for between 40 and 80 percent. This compares to an average share of 33 percent between the 2005/2006 and 2008/2009 agricultural years. As a result of the increasing share of Black Sea wheat in the Egyptian market, the United States Wheat Associates, the U.S. wheat industry's export market development agency, closed their Cairo office in December 2017.[18]

Russia exports significant amounts of wheat and sunflower oil to Egypt, while importing fruits and vegetables from the North African country (see Fig. 1). The food trade between the two countries has repeatedly been affected by conflicts over product quality and compliance with phytosanitary standards regarding the shipped commodities. A major Russo-Egyptian food trade dispute arose after Egypt imposed a zero-tolerance policy regime regarding ergot contamination[19] in wheat cargos shipped to the GASC on 28 August 2016. After requiring that wheat shipped to the GASC must contain zero ergot, which is practically impossible for traders to ensure when wheat is delivered in bulk, Egypt rejected cargos from Romania and Russia in early September 2016, as

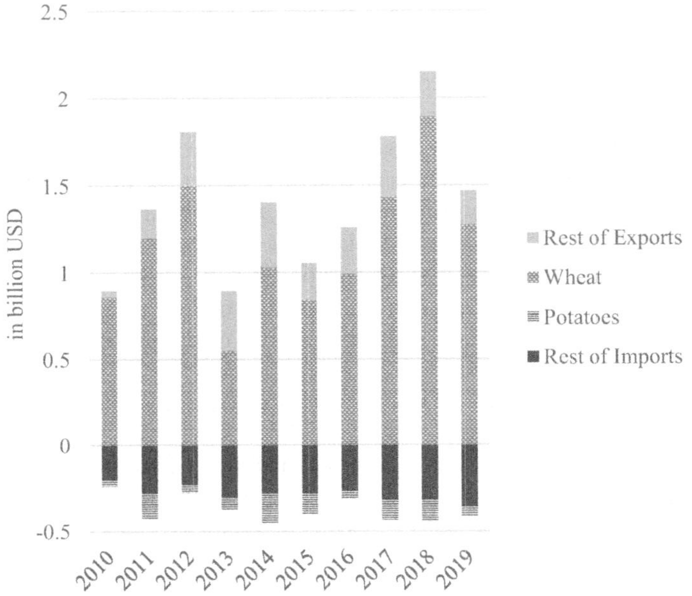

Fig. 1 Russia's Agri-Food trade with Egypt, 2010–2019 (*Source* UN Comtrade. *International Trade Statistics Database*. https://comtrade.un.org/, Accessed 18 August 2020)

they failed to meet the newly established quality standards.[20] In response, wheat traders boycotted several GASC wheat tenders that the agency had to cancel due to a lack of offers. On 16 September, the Russian government announced that fruit and vegetable imports from Egypt would be temporarily halted starting 22 September, due to concerns over food safety. Shortly after, on 21 September, the Egyptian government decided to cancel the zero-tolerance ergot policy.[21] This was followed by the resumption of fruit and vegetable imports from Egypt to Russia on 26 September. Importantly, however, the resumption of food imports did not include Egyptian potatoes, its second most important export to the Russian market after citrus fruits, which remained banned from entry to the Russian market until 14 December (see Fig. 1). Russia itself is a large producer of potatoes and could become a net exporter of potatoes in the future after becoming virtually self-sufficient in potato production recently.[22]

In a similar trade dispute, several shipments of Egyptian potatoes were initially rejected at Russian ports in March and May 2018 due to the cargos reportedly being infested with brown rot disease.[23] On 31 May, Egyptian officials rejected a cargo of Russian wheat because it exhibited ergot contamination levels of 0.06 percent, exceeding the acceptable level of 0.05 percent.[24] Two days after the rejection of the cargo, the Russian government announced that potato imports from specific Egyptian regions that had previously been banned would resume on 6 June 2018. Conducting a second test on ergot levels of the respective Russian wheat cargo, Egyptian officials concluded that the wheat contained 0.01 percent ergot and was therefore allowed to enter the country. However, even as potato exports to Russia resumed, the potato trade volume still declined from $120 million USD annually in 2014 through 2018 to $60 million USD in 2019 (see Fig. 1). While adjustments in trade policy and phytosanitary standards by the Egyptian and Russian governments are usually not explicitly implemented as a response or in retaliation to steps taken by the other side, the sequence of policy changes displayed above suggests that the food trade between the two countries is strongly affected by political considerations.

In 2017, several reports published by Reuters portrayed widespread corruption in the Egyptian food procurement system, with government officials allegedly taking bribes in order to guarantee seamless passage of wheat into Egypt.[25] While the effort to curb corruption resulted in arrests of several government officials responsible for Egypt's food supply, disputes over ergot levels in wheat cargos and adjustments to the quality inspection procedures employed by the GASC continue to cause friction within Egypt's food trade. However, it can be expected that Russia will remain the uncontested top supplier of wheat to Egypt and the GASC due to its competitively priced wheat and the freight cost advantages it enjoys in comparison to competing origins such as the United States or France.

3.2 Turkey

Turkey is Russia's most important trading partner in the MENA region with an average annual food trade volume of $3.15 billion USD from 2017 to 2019 (see Fig. 1). Food trade, however, constituted only 13 percent of total trade between the two countries over the past decade, as Turkey—a country dependent on energy imports—predominantly buys natural gas and crude oil from Russia, making energy trade the prior component in the economic relationship between the two countries located at the Black Sea. Turkey is mostly self-sufficient in wheat and barley production, while total corn consumption exceeds domestic production by around 40 percent. However, grains and wheat in particular still account for more than 55 percent of Turkey's food imports from Russia (see Fig. 2), with excess wheat quantities being processed into wheat flour, which Turkey exports to destination markets in the MENA region, foremost Iraq, as well as Syria and Yemen. With a market share of 20 percent and exports worth $1 billion USD per year, Turkey is the world's largest wheat flour exporter, followed by Kazakhstan (10.5 percent) and Germany (6.5 percent).[26]

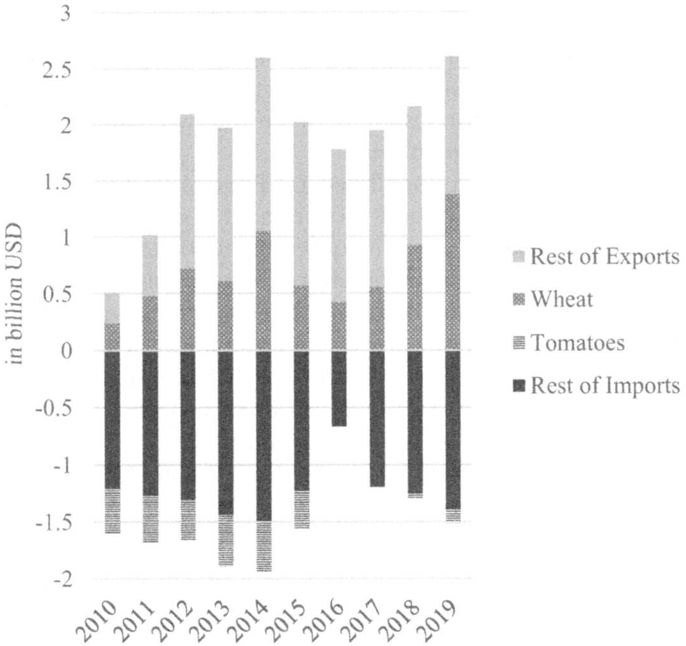

Fig. 2 Russia's Agri-Food trade with Turkey (*Source* UN Comtrade. *International Trade Statistics Database*. https://comtrade.un.org/, Accessed 18 August 2020)

Similar to Egypt, Turkey's grain imports are managed by a state procurement agency, the Turkish Grain Board (TMO). The TMO covers Turkey's wheat and feed corn imports and also purchases feed barley if domestic production does not meet consumption. While the TMO, like its Egyptian counterpart, predominantly purchases Russian wheat, it contrasts the GASC by sourcing grain from smaller Russian shallow water ports located at the Azov Sea and up the Don River, most notably the ports Azov and Rostov-on-Don. Shipping grain using large panamax vessels enables economies of scale if geographically distant destination markets are supplied. Turkey, however, is located in close geographical proximity to the Russian grain export facilities and the TMO thus purchases numerous smaller parcels of between 10,000 and 30,000 tonnes in its grain tenders. Grain exports from Russia's shallow water ports show particularly strong seasonality patterns as some port facilities become inoperable in the winter months due to cold temperatures.[27]

In spite of the generally strong economic entanglement between Russia and Turkey, bilateral food trade was highly affected by political tensions between the two countries in recent years.[28] On 24 November 2015, a Russian fighter jet operating in Syria was downed by the Turkish military close to the country's border. In response, Russia introduced an extensive package of sanctions against Turkey, including a ban on imports of Turkish food products such as tomatoes, onions, cucumbers, grapes, apricots, apples, chicken products, and salt, while imports of lemons and nuts remained unrestricted just like the energy trade that is central to the bilateral trade relationship.[29] After these trade restrictions took effect on 1 January 2016, the Kremlin announced in late June 2016 that Ankara had apologised for downing the military jet. Subsequently, after a meeting between the two countries' presidents in St. Petersburg in early August 2016, the intent to 'normalise' the bilateral relationship and a gradual lifting of the Russian import restrictions were announced.[30]

As a consequence of the implemented trade restrictions, Russia's food imports from Turkey decreased by more than 50 percent, from \$1.5 billion USD per year between 2011 and 2015 to \$663 million USD in 2016 (Fig. 2). Conversely, Russian food exports to Turkey only showed a modest decrease of around 15 percent in 2016. After the agreement to gradually resume food trade in late 2016, Russia's food imports from Turkey rebounded to around \$1.25 billion USD per year in 2017 through 2019, still standing below the levels recorded prior to 2016. This gap in trade volume is almost entirely resulting from diminished imports of Turkish tomatoes, which remained restricted after 2016. Exempting tomatoes from the resumption of food trade corresponds to an effort by the Russian government to support domestic tomato production to ultimately reach self-sufficiency. Indeed, Russian vegetable greenhouse production grew by around 12 percent annually over the past five years.[31]

As Russia's ban on Turkish tomato imports remained in place, Turkey removed Russian food products, most notably wheat, corn, and sunflower oil, from its tax-free import licence list on 15 March 2017, which effectively barred all Russian food exports to Turkey.[32] Following another meeting between the state leaders in Sochi, Russian food exports to Turkey resumed in May 2017, while the ban on Turkish tomato imports was, however, only partially relaxed and converted to an import quota that came into effect on 1 November 2017.[33] This new policy regime allowed only a small number of Turkish companies to sell tomatoes to Russia, which prompted Ankara to threaten a similar limitation on the number of Russian companies accepted to ship food products to Turkey on 19 March 2018.[34] In late April 2018, the limitation on the number of trading companies allowed to sell tomatoes to Russia was finally removed, while the import quota remained unchanged until 28 March 2019, when a tripling of the quota to 150,000 tonnes was announced. This policy adjustment followed an announcement by the Turkish government to implement a 5,000-tonne tax-free import quota per year for beef imports from Russia.[35] A further increase of the Russian import quota to 200,000 tonnes was announced on 26 February 2020. However, as Turkish tomato exports to Russia amounted to around 340,000 tonnes per year before 2016 and in light of Russia's expansion of greenhouse vegetable production over the past five years, a further increase or abolishment of the import quota is likely to have little effect on Turkey's total tomato exports to Russia.

3.3 Saudi Arabia

Until 2016, food trade between Russia and Saudi Arabia was practically limited to Russian barley exports (Fig. 3). For several decades, Saudi Arabia has been the world's largest barley importer with annual imports of around 7.5 million tonnes and a market share of around 30 percent.[36] Today, Saudi Arabia is entirely dependent on the import of barley, which is used as animal feed in the country. Since the early 2000s, Saudi Arabia sources around 40 percent of its barley from the Black Sea

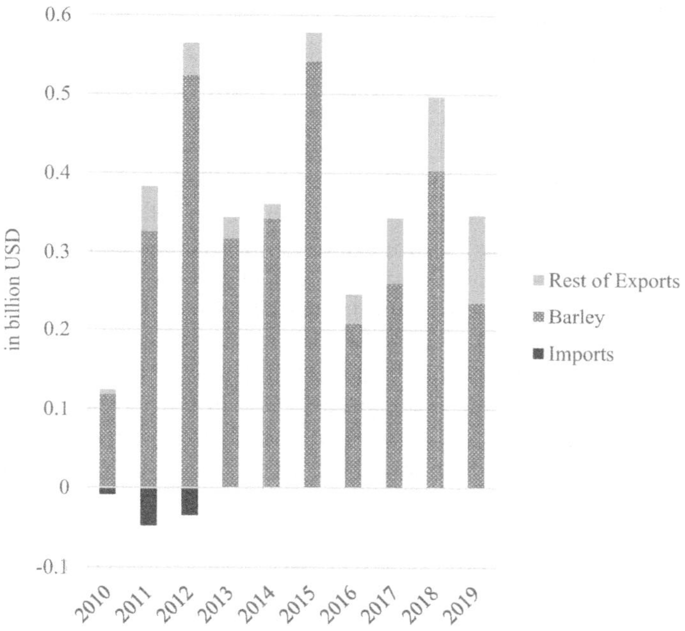

Fig. 3 Russia's Agri-Food trade with Saudi Arabia (*Source* UN Comtrade. *International Trade Statistics Database*. https://comtrade.un.org/, Accessed 18 August 2020)

region, primarily from Ukraine, followed by Russia. In particular years, the Black Sea market share has even exceeded 60 percent. While Saudi Arabia is still the top destination for Russian barley exports, its share has decreased from 60 percent between 2011 and 2015 to 40 percent since 2016, while exports to other MENA countries, particularly Iran and Jordan, increased substantially.

Currently, Saudi Arabia is also among the top 20 wheat importers in the world. However, the country only started importing grain on a large scale in 2008. In the early 1980s, Saudi Arabia had formulated an extensive self-sufficiency policy encouraging and supporting domestic wheat production projects, which were entirely based on irrigation.[37] This policy enabled the country to indeed become a sizeable wheat exporter between 1985 and 1994,[38] before domestic wheat production was scaled back to only supply the domestic market. Due to serious concerns about depleting water reserves, the irrigation-intensive wheat production was gradually phased out between 2007 and 2016. During this time period, Saudi Arabia's wheat imports increased steadily to ultimately reach 3.4 million tonnes annually. In November 2015, the Saudi Grains Organization (SAGO) was established to manage the country's grain imports.[39] The SAGO has a monopoly on the import of milling wheat and is responsible for the vast barley imports, as well. Feed corn, of which Saudi Arabia is also a major importer, is imported by private companies. Similar to the countries discussed previously, the SAGO employs a tender system to purchase grains on the international market. Compared to its counterparts in Egypt and Turkey, the SAGO issues tenders rather infrequently (i.e. roughly every two months) and then buys large quantities at once.

After years of bilateral negotiations, Russian wheat was approved to be offered in SAGO tenders on 8 August 2019.[40] Precisely, tolerated bug damage levels for Russian wheat were adjusted from a practically prohibitive 0 percent level to a manageable level of 0.5 percent. The decision was announced after samples of Russian wheat were sent to Saudi Arabia in late 2018 and multiple meetings between government officials had taken place to discuss amending the quality specification. After Saudi Arabia became a wheat importer, Russian wheat was initially allowed to enter the country. However, a Russian wheat cargo exhibiting strong contamination with the sunn pest on arrival prompted the government to effectively ban Russian wheat in 2012.[41] Following re-approval, the first two cargos of Russian wheat purchased in SAGO tenders were sent to Saudi Arabia in April and May 2020.[42]

The opening of the Saudi Arabian market for Russian wheat must be seen in the context of a steadily improving relationship between the two countries in recent years. After bilateral relations reached a low point due to opposing involvements in the Syrian civil war, Saudi Arabia and Russia, the two largest crude oil exporters worldwide, initially started to cooperate in oil markets in 2016 in view of crude oil prices falling to historic low levels.[43] An agreement to cut oil production between the Organization of Petroleum Exporting Countries (OPEC)—which is virtually led by Saudi Arabia—and Russia was signed on 10 December 2016, resulting in rising oil prices in the following years. Similarly, food exports from Russia to Saudi Arabia, which had halved from around $500 million USD annually in 2012 through 2015 to $250 million USD in 2016, returned to previous levels (see Fig. 3). Additionally, since 2016, Russia's food exports to Saudi Arabia show a gradual diversification, as cocoa products, as well as poultry, started to be exported to Saudi Arabia in 2017 and 2018, respectively. This resulted in a decreasing share of barley in Russia's food exports to Saudi Arabia, from 95 percent in 2014 to 68 percent in 2019.

On 14 October 2019, during the first state visit by the Russian president Vladimir Putin to Riyadh since 2007, the heads of state signed a comprehensive Memorandum of Understanding (MoU) aiming to further improve the bilateral relationship. Alongside various agreements on joint investments and expanded cooperation, both governments reaffirmed their intent to increase the mutual food trade. Particularly, the Russian side expressed interest in the export of animal and dairy products, among others, while Saudi Arabia proclaimed the intent to export fish and shrimp products, as well as fruit and dates to Russia.[44] During a preceding bilateral meeting in early September 2019, the Russian Minister for Agriculture had underlined the goal of quadrupling Russian food exports to Saudi Arabia to reach USD 2 billion in 2024.[45] The MoU should be seen in the context of his ambitious goal regarding the food trade volume between the two countries.

3.4 Iran

After the collapse of the Soviet Union, there was bilateral political will to expand trade relations between the Russian Federation and the Islamic Republic of Iran (Iran, hereafter). The 'Look to the East' policy defined by Tehran in 2006,[46] promoted the improvement of Iran's economic and political relations with Russia and China after many years of a no-alliance policy.[47] However, while the bilateral economic relationship remains insignificant if total trade is considered, agricultural and food trade has increased substantially since 2017 (see Fig. 4). In 2018, Iran had imported food products worth $856 million USD from Russia, while food exports to Russia showed a volume of $450 million USD.[48] As such, the Russo-Iranian food trade accounted for around two-thirds of the total trade between 2017 and 2019. Russia and Iran both have large oil and natural gas reservoirs, and both depend on fossil fuel exports. However, Iran has an arid to semi-arid climate and is confronted with severe water scarcity issues. Despite this fact, Iran has implemented self-sufficiency policies, particularly for its domestic grain production, which is affected by varying levels of precipitation. As Russia turned into a major grain exporter, Iran has started to diversify its cereal import portfolio by relying more on Russia, while imports from other countries remain

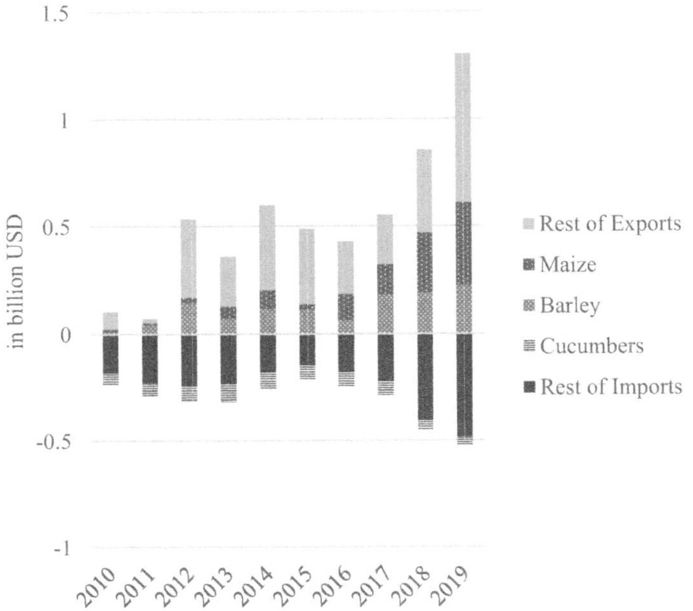

Fig. 4 Russia's Agri-Food trade with Iran (*Source* UN Comtrade. *International Trade Statistics Database*. https://comtrade.un.org/, Accessed 18 August 2020)

substantial, as well.[49] In 2018, maize was Iran's primary food import from Russia followed by sunflower oil and barley. The top food exports from Iran to Russia are fruits, nuts, and vegetables. It must be added that there is a volatile pattern of Iranian wheat imports from Russia, which mainly depends on the domestic wheat production in Iran and thus on annual precipitation levels (see Fig. 4).[50]

While Russia and Iran do not have a land border, they are connected by the Caspian Sea and its sea transport facilities. The food trade over the Caspian Sea is mainly conducted via the Russian port of Astrakhan and the ports of Amirabad and Anzali in Iran. However, bilateral seaborne trade is impeded by a lack of adequate infrastructure, as well as bureaucratic hurdles. For instance, the available port facilities are not well prepared for handling container trade, as well as the storage of fresh agricultural products.[51] Furthermore, non-Russian ships are only allowed to use inland waterways in Russia after paying a fee of $30,000 USD. As this fee is essentially prohibitive, non-Russian vessels need to either unload cargos at the ports of Astrakhan or Makhachkala or switch to Russian vessels.[52] Facing these impediments, a mutual protocol aimed at the improvement of trade infrastructure and the reduction of bureaucratic hurdles was signed in 2020.[53] Furthermore, the first permanent container shipping line between Iran and Russia was planned to be established in September 2020, which could increase the trade of fresh food products.[54] Further reports have announced the construction of additional Russian port infrastructure in Lagan at the Caspian Sea, which could also facilitate food trade with Iran.[55] Railway and road infrastructure between Russia and Iran is not well developed and the contribution of non-marine transport of agricultural commodities is currently low. On the Iranian side, the constant intervention of the government in the domestic agricultural market is another issue that impedes the long-term provision of fruit and vegetable exports to the Russian market, as a state organisation called the Market Control Centre frequently implements restrictions on the export of agricultural and food commodities once food shortages appear in Iran.[56]

Despite the deficiencies in transport infrastructure, bilateral food trade has increased in recent years and can be expected to further develop in the future. After years of negotiations, on 27 October 2019, a free trade agreement between the Eurasian Economic Union and Iran took effect.[57] This was an important decision for expanding Iran's trade relationships with former members of the Soviet Union, and Russia in particular. The main objective of the agreement is the liberalisation and facilitation of the trade between the parties through, inter alia, reduction, or elimination of tariff and non-tariff barriers.[58] This interim preferential trade agreement should lead to a free trade agreement within three years (Article 1.3, §3). At its primary stage, the EAEU-Iran interim preferential trade agreement (PTA) covers approximately 55 percent of the total trade between the partners and focuses on selected agricultural and industrial products. Iran grants preferential treatment for meat and other food commodities, as well as metals, electronics, and other items. The average import tariff applied by Iran to imports from the EAEU is reduced from 22.4 percent to 15.4 percent for manufactured commodities and from 32.2 percent to 13.2 percent for agricultural commodities. A total of 360 commodity categories are covered in the agreement. Furthermore, Iran receives preferential treatment for exports of fruits and vegetables and other selected products. The average import tariff applied by the EAEU on Iran is reduced for agricultural commodities from 9.6 percent to 4.6 percent and for industrial commodities from 8 percent to 4.7 percent, with 502 commodity categories being covered.[59] The available data on tariff changes show, however, that barley and corn are not included in the list of goods with reduced tariffs by Iran at this stage. Conversely, there are complaints that the agreement disregards goods that are important to Iranian producers and exporters. While tariff reductions on additional goods could be considered in the next round of negotiations,[60] the trade between Iran and EAEU has already increased compared to the same period before the agreement, despite the presence of U.S. sanctions against Iran since 2018.[61] A first study investigating the effects of this EAEU-Iran free trade agreement employing a gravity model framework projected a higher increase of exports by EAEU members to Iran than by Iran to the other EAEU members.[62]

4 Outlook

This chapter examined Russia's food trade with its top four destination markets in the MENA region. Food trade is the most important component of the bilateral economic relationships with Saudi Arabia, Iran, and Egypt, which are energy net-exporters like Russia. Regarding Turkey, the sole energy net importer among the considered cases, food trade only accounts for 13 percent of total trade with Russia, which is dominated by energy trade. In all four cases, Russian food exports to the MENA clearly outweigh its food imports. Due to unfavourable climatic conditions, the majority of MENA countries are unable to produce enough grain to meet the consumption of growing populations and Russia thus emerged as a main supplier of wheat, as well as barley and maize for the neighbouring region. After Saudi Arabia approved the import of Russian wheat in August 2019, only few MENA countries continue to disallow the import of Russian wheat, most notably Algeria, the world's third-largest wheat importer, as well as Iraq.[63] However, regardless of Algeria approving wheat imports from Russia, its overall grain exports to the MENA region are unlikely to increase much further in the future, as the region already sources most of its grain from Russia or competing Black Sea exporters, such as Ukraine, Kazakhstan, or Romania.

As a consequence, a goal outlined by Russian trade officials is the diversification of Russia's food exports, and thus the development of new destination markets for food export products other than grains and vegetable oils. In this respect, Russia recently started to export notable amounts of chocolate products and poultry meat to Saudi Arabia, which had previously almost exclusively imported barley from Russia. This diversification in Russia's exports to the high-income gulf country follows an improvement in the bilateral relations due to a fruitful cooperation in the energy market since 2016 and corresponds to Russia's proclaimed effort to quadruple food exports to Saudi Arabia by 2024. Since 2018, growing volumes of chocolate products and lamb meat have also been exported to Iran. Russo-Iranian food trade shows a clear upward trend after Iran's free trade agreement. Regarding Egypt and Turkey, total food trade does not exhibit a clear upwards or downwards trend over the past decade.

The considered food trade relationships are strongly shaped by political disputes and/or the improvement of diplomatic ties. Russia appears to use import restrictions on specific food products as an instrument of support for domestic production to substitute its imports, reach self-sufficiency and even gain the capacity to export, an approach that several studies focusing on Russia's import restrictions versus Western countries in 2014 have previously analysed.[64] The trade dispute surrounding the imports of Turkish tomatoes especially illustrates how Russian import quotas are maintained to (successfully) encourage domestic greenhouse tomato production. Regarding food trade between Russia and the MENA countries, food exports are often restricted using non-tariff measures, as products are rejected over concerns about food safety, product quality or the alleged non-compliance with prevailing phytosanitary standards. While it must be expected that non-compliant food cargos be rejected from government agencies that control the quality of food imports, the sequence of cargo rejections in the considered cases suggests that the product quality tests are partly influenced by bilateral political relations or previous adjustments in trade policies or quality standards introduced by the other side.

By exporting wheat and other grains to the import-dependent MENA region, Russia has achieved building meaningful economic trade relationships with countries that are also primarily energy-exporters and thus competitors. After reaching low points in 2016 due to inter alia Russia's involvement in the Syrian civil war, a stand-off in international energy markets and various disputes over product quality, the food trade relationships with the selected MENA countries have largely improved recently. While the food trade was repeatedly disrupted by political interventions in recent years, its central component, grain trade, can be expected to remain stable in the long run due to its unequivocal mutual benefit. Because of climatic and geographic advantages, Russia can competitively produce and ship grains to the MENA countries that lack sufficient production of grains to meet domestic consumption.

Notes

1. In the following, we define all products falling under the two-digit HS-2 codes 01 through 23 as food products. The trade statistics are presented as provided by the Russian Federation to the UN Comtrade database.
2. The MENA region includes Algeria, Bahrain, Djibouti, Egypt, Iran, Iraq, Israel, Jordan, Kuwait, Lebanon, Libya, Morocco, Oman, Qatar, Saudi Arabia, Syria, Tunisia, Turkey, United Arab Emirates and Yemen.
3. Stephen K. Wegren, 'Can Russia's Food Exports Reach $45 Billion in 2024?' *Post-Communist Economies* 32, no. 2 (2020): 147–175.
4. William M. Liefert and Olga Liefert, 'Russia's Economic Crisis and Its Agricultural and Food Economy', *Choices* 30, no. 1, 2015, 1–6; Stephen K. Wegren, 'The Russian Food Embargo and Food Security: Can Household Production Fill the Void?' *Eurasian Geography and Economics* 55, no. 5 (2014): 491–513; and Martin Banse, Ivan Duric, Linde Götz and Verena Laquai, 'From the Russian Food Import Ban to Free Trade from Lisbon to Vladivostok—Will Farmers Benefit?' *Journal of International Studies* 12, no. 4 (2019): 20–31.
5. William M. Liefert and Olga Liefert, 'Russian Agricultural Trade and World Markets', *Russian Journal of Economics* 6 (2020): 56–70; Maximilian Heigermoser and Linde Götz, 'Russia's Rise to Become the World's Largest Wheat Exporter: Implications for the Global Grain Trade', *Russian Analytical Digest* no. 244 (17 December 2019): 7–11.
6. United States Department of Agriculture, Foreign Agriculture Service, 'Production, Supply and Demand Online Database', n.d. https://apps.fas.usda.gov/psdonline/app/index.html#/app/advQuery. Accessed 18 August 2020.
7. Ghada Ahmed, Danny Hamrick and Gary Gereffi, 'Shifting Governance Structures in the Wheat Value Chain: Implications for Food Securityin the Middle East and North Afric', Presentation held at the Global Value Chains and Trade Policies for Food and Nutrition Security Workshop in Rome, 26 September 2014. https://gvcc.duke.edu/wp-content/uploads/2014-09-26_Shifting-Governance-Structures-in-the-Wheat-GVC.pdf. Accessed 13 October 2020; and Ahmed F. Ghonein, 'The Political Economy of Food Price Policy in Egypt', in *Food Price Policy in an*

Era of Market Instability, ed. Per Pinstrup-Andersen (Oxford: Oxford University Press, 2015), 253–274.

8. Stephen K. Wegren, Frode Nilssen and Christel Elvestad, 'The Impact of Russian Food Security Policy on the Performance of the Food System', *Eurasian Geography and Economics* 57, no. 6 (2016): 671–699; and Stephen K. Wegren, Alexander M. Nikulin and Irina Trotsuk, 'The Russian Variant of Food Security', *Problems of Post-Communism* 64, no. 1 (2016): 47–62.
9. Zerno on-lain, 'Zerno Traffic Database', n.d. http://www.zolbase.ru/. Accessed 18 August 2020.
10. Deep-water ports are equipped to handle large supramax and panamax vessels that can load up to 65,000 tonnes of grain.
11. United States Department of Agriculture, Foreign Agriculture Service, 'Russian Federation. Grain and Feed Annual', 14 April 2017. GAIN Report RS1726. www.fas.usda.gov/data. Accessed 18 August 2020.
12. Maximilian Heigermoser and Linde Götz, 'Russia's Rise to Become the World's Largest Wheat Exporter'.
13. Thomas Glauben, Linde Götz and Ulrich Koester, 'The Rouble Crisis and the Russian Grain Export Controls', IAMO Policy Brief No. 22, 2015. https://www.iamo.de/fileadmin/documents/IAMOPolicyBrief22_en.pdf. Accessed 13 October 2020.
14. French grain exports mostly flow through the port of Rouen, located in the English Channel.
15. International Grains Council, Supply & Demand Database, 2020. https://www.igc.int/en/markets/marketinfo-sd.aspx. Accessed 11 August 2020.
16. Maximilian Heigermoser, Linde Götz and Miranda Svanidze, 'Egypt's Wheat Tenders—A Public Noticeboard for Black Sea Grain Notations?' Proceedings of the Gewisola Annual Meeting in Kiel, Germany, September 2018. https://ageconsearch.umn.edu/record/275853. Accessed 13 October 2020.
17. Ahmed F. Ghonein, 'The Political Economy of Food Price Policy in Egypt'.
18. Arvin Donley, 'U.S. Wheat Associates to Close Cairo Office', 18 October 2017. https://www.world-grain.com/articles/8814-u-s-wheat-associates-to-close-cairo-office. Accessed 5 August 2020.
19. The common ergot fungus often infests wheat crops and causes harm to humans if it is consumed in large quantities. However, small amounts of ergot are harmless, and the international trade considers ergot levels in wheat of less than 0.05 percent acceptable.
20. Emiko Terazono and Heba Saleh, 'Wheat Trade Hit Hard by Egypt Quarantine Crackdown', 19 September 2016. https://www.ft.com/content/e92d0caa-7b2e-11e6-ae24-f193b105145e. Accessed 6 August 2020.

21. Eric Knecht, 'Egypt Cancels Zero Ergot Wheat Policy Amid Mounting Pressure'. 21 September 2016. https://www.reuters.com/article/us-egypt-wheat-ergot-idUSKCN11R1WX. Accessed 6 August 2020.
22. United States Department of Agriculture, Foreign Agriculture Service, 'Russian Federation: Strategy for Development of Agriculture and Fisheries Through 2030', Report RS2020-026. 14 May 2020. www.fas.usda.gov/data. Accessed 18 August 2020.
23. Enterprise Press, 'Russia Bans 140-Tonne Shipment of Egyptian Potatoes Over Pest Infection', 6 May 2018. https://enterprise.press/stories/2018/05/06/russia-bans-140-tonne-shipment-of-egyptian-potatoes-over-pest-infection/. Accessed 18 August 2020.
24. Reuters Staff, 'Egypt's Rejection of Russian Wheat Over Ergot Creates Latest Supply Snag', 31 May 2018. https://www.reuters.com/article/egypt-wheat/update-3-egypts-rejection-of-russian-wheat-over-ergot-creates-latest-supply-snag-idUSL5N1T22DW. Accessed 6 August 2020.
25. Eric Knecht and Maha El Dahan, 'Inspection Battle Threatens Egypt's Wheat Supply', 17 October 2017. https://www.reuters.com/article/us-egypt-wheat-inspections-insight/inspection-battle-threatens-egypts-wheat-supply-idUSKBN1CM10N?utm_content=buffer2f4c4&utm_medium=social&utm_source=twitter.com&utm_campaign=buffer. Accessed 6 August 2020.
26. United Nations, 'UN Comtrade Database', n.d. https://comtrade.un.org/. Accessed 18 August 2020.
27. Heigermoser and Götz, 'Russia's Rise to Become the World's Largest Wheat Exporter'.
28. Ziya Önis and Suhnaz Yilmaz, 'Turkey and Russia in a Shifting Global Order: Cooperation, Conflict and Asymmetric Interdependence in a Turbulent Region', *Third World Quarterly* 37, no. 1 (2016): 71–95.
29. Reuters Staff, 'Russia Approves Detailed Sanctions Against Turkey Over Downed Plane', 1 December 2015. https://www.reuters.com/article/us-mideast-crisis-russia-turkey-sanction/russia-approves-detailed-sanctions-against-turkey-over-downed-plane-idUSKBN0TK4SD20151201. Accessed 18 August 2020.
30. Reuters Staff, 'Turkey, Russia Agree on Need to Normalize Ties: Turkish Official', 9 August 2016. https://www.reuters.com/article/us-russia-turkey-erdogan-official/turkey-russia-agree-on-need-to-normalize-ties-turkish-official-idUSKCN10K1EQ. Accessed 18 August 2020.
31. Institut Kon'iunktury Agrarnogo Rynka, 'IKAR: Itogi Goda—2019. Rynok Kartofelia', 8 January 2020. http://ikar.ru/1/lenta/709/. Accessed 18 August 2020.
32. Gus Trompiz and Michael Hogan, 'Turkish Mills Buy EU, Black Sea Wheat to Replace Russian Imports', 5 April 2017. https://www.reuters.

com/article/turkey-wheat-europe/turkish-mills-buy-eu-black-sea-wheat-to-replace-russian-imports-idUSL5N1HD3X9. Accessed 18 August 2020.
33. Kamila Aliyeva, 'First Truck with Turkish Tomatoes Arrives in Russia', 16 November 2017. https://www.azernews.az/region/122341.html. Accessed 18 August 2020.
34. Hurriyet Daily News, 'Turkey Objects to Russia's Import Quota on Tomatoes', 19 March 2018. https://www.hurriyetdailynews.com/turkey-objects-to-russias-import-quota-on-tomatoes-128981. Accessed 18 August 2020.
35. Russia remains a net importer of beef and exports only very small quantities of beef so far.
36. United Nations, 'UN Comtrade Database'. Most recently, China's barley imports have increased substantially and have exceeded Saudi Arabian barley imports, particularly in 2015.
37. Arani K. Grindle, Afreen Siddiqi and Laura Diaz Anadon, 'Food Security Amidst Water Scarcity: Insights on Sustainable Food Production from Saudi Arabia', *Sustainable Production and Consumption* 2 (2015): 67–78; and Thomas W. Lippmann, 'Saudi Arabia's Quest for Food Security', *Middle East Policy* 17, no. 1 (2010): 90–98.
38. 'United States Department of Agriculture, Foreign Agriculture Service, Production, Supply and Demand Online Database'. n.d. https://apps.fas.usda.gov/psdonline/app/index.html#/app/advQuery. Accessed 18 August 2020.
39. United States Department of Agriculture, Foreign Agriculture Service, 'Saudi Arabia: Grain and Feed Annual', 2 April 2017. www.fas.usda.gov/data. Accessed 18 August 2020.
40. Maha El Dahan and Polina Devitt, 'Exclusive: Saudi Boosts Russia Ties with Welcome for Black Sea Wheat', 8 August 2019. https://www.reuters.com/article/us-saudi-wheat-exclusive/exclusive-saudi-boosts-russia-ties-with-welcome-for-black-sea-wheat-idUSKCN1UY0ZW. Accessed 18 August 2020.
41. Anatoly Medetsky and Javier Blas, 'Russia Eyes Up Saudi Wheat Market Dominated by EU Supplies', 21 December 2017. https://www.bloomberg.com/news/articles/2017-12-21/russia-is-eyeing-up-saudi-wheat-market-dominated-by-eu-supplies. Accessed 18 August 2020.
42. An increasing share of Russian wheat in the Saudi Arabian market could negatively affect exporters from Germany and the Baltic states, which were previously the top suppliers of wheat to Saudi Arabia.
43. Ruby Lian, Josephine Mason and El Gamal, 'Saudi Arabia, Russia Sign Oil Pact, May Limit Output in Future', 5 September 2016. https://www.reuters.com/article/us-g20-china-saudi-russia-oil-idUSKCN11B0UF. Accessed 17 August 2020.

44. Interfax, 'Russia, Saudi Arabia Sign Memorandum to Boost Agricultural Exports', 14 October 2019. https://interfax.com/. Accessed 17 August 2020.
45. Reuters Staff, 'Russian Agri Minister, Saudi's Falih to Discuss Russia-Saudi Trade', 4 September 2019. https://www.reuters.com/article/us-saudi-wheat-russia/russian-agri-minister-saudis-falih-to-discuss-russia-saudi-trade-idUSKCN1VP0Y7. Accessed 17 August 2020.
46. Ali Adami, 'Look to the East Strategy in the Foreign Affairs of Islamic Republic of Iran; Perspectives, Basics and Opportunities', *Quarterly Journal in Political Studies* 7 (2010): 97–127 (Originally in Persian).
47. Adam Tarock, 'Russo-Iranian Relations in the Post-Soviet Era', *Diplomacy and Statecraft* 28, no. 3 (2017): 518–537.
48. AWNRC, 'Summary of Iran Food and Agricultural Trade in 2018', 2019. https://bit.ly/2EvvmwY. Accessed 30 August 2020 (Original in Persian). The data available in Iranian sources present different trade volumes compared to data provided by the UN Comtrade Database. Following these sources, Iran has imported USD 661 million agricultural and food products from Russia and exported USD 218 million of the same commodity groups to Russia.
49. ITC, 'Trade Map—Trade Statistics Between Iran and Russia', https://www.trademap.org/Index.aspx. Accessed 24 August 2020; and Kevin Lim, *Bumped Crops: Iran's Grain Imports and Geopolitical Shocks* (Washington, DC: The Washington Institute, 2020).
50. Recently, plans to import Russian wheat to Iran to process it into flour for re-exporting to Iraq have been formulated. However, such activity, which would put Iranian flour producers in competition with Turkish producers on the Iraqi market, has not yet materialised.
51. Wali Kuzehgarkaleji, 'Five Important Essentialities on Iran-Russia Trade', 16 August 2020. http://fdn.ir/44562. Accessed 24 August 2020 (Original in Persian).
52. Wali Kuzehgarkaleji, 'Sanctions and Marine Transport in Caspian Sea', 22 August 2020. http://fdn.ir/44850. Accessed 24 August 2020 (Original in Persian).
53. Mehr News Agency, 'The Mutual Protocol Signed Between Iran and Russia on Increasing Sea Trade', 5 December 2019. mehrnews.com/xQJLX. Accessed 24 August 2020 (Original in Persian).
54. Tejaratgardan, 'Establishing the First Permanent Container Ship Between Iran and Russia in September 2020', 11 August 2020. https://tejaratgardan.ir/?p=64503. Accessed 17 August 2020 (Original in Persian).
55. Global Construction Review Staff, 'Russia Approves $1.6bn Caspian Seaport to Increase Trade with Iran, India and China', 3 August 2020. https://www.globalconstructionreview.com/news/russia-approves-16bn-caspian-seaport-increase-trad/. Accessed 24 August 2020; and RT, 'Russia

Building New Seaport to Boost Trade with Iran, India & Kazakhstan', 1 August 2020. https://www.rt.com/business/496775-russia-new-seaport-construction/. Accessed 17 August 2020 (Original in Persian).
56. Kuzehgarkaleji, 'Five Important Essentialities on Iran-Russia Trade'.
57. Eurasian Economic Commission, 'EAEU and Iran Pass on to Preferential Trade Conditions', 29 August 2019. http://www.eurasiancommission.org/en/nae/news/Pages/28-08-2019-3.aspx. Accessed 17 August 2020.
58. 'Interim Agreement Leading to Formation of a Free Trade Area Between the Eurasian Economic Union (EAEU) and Its Member States, of the One Part, and the Islamic Republic of Iran, of the Other Part', 27 October 2019. http://www.eurasiancommission.org/ru/act/trade/dotp/sogl_torg/Documents/Interim_Agreement_EAEU-Iran_final.pdf. Accessed 13 October 2020.
59. Amat Adarov and Mahdi Ghodsi, 'The Impact of the EAEU-Iran Preferential Trade Agreement', WIIW Working Paper No. 179, May 2020. https://wiiw.ac.at/the-impact-of-the-eaeu-iran-preferential-trade-agreement-p-5335.html. Accessed 13 October 2020.
60. Amir Nikkhah, 'Corona Crisis and Expansion Trade Relation Between Iran and Russia', 15 May 2020. https://www.eghtesadonline.com/n/2EZ5. Accessed 24 August 2020 (Original in Persian).
61. It is not evident whether there are complications on money transfers between financial institutions of Iran and EAEU countries at this point.
62. Adarov and Ghodsi, 'The Impact of the EAEU-Iran Preferential Trade Agreement'.
63. Iraq, however, imports large quantities of wheat flour from Turkey, which imports more wheat than it needs from Russia. Thus, Iraq virtually already imports Russian wheat via Turkey in an indirect way.
64. Liefert and Liefert, 'Russia's Economic Crisis and Its Agricultural and Food Economy', 1–6; Wegren, 'The Russian Food Embargo and food Security: Can Household Production Fill the Void?', 491–513; and Banse et al., 'From the Russian Food Import Ban to Free Trade from Lisbon to Vladivostok—Will Farmers Benefit?', 20–31.

Selected Bibliography

Adami, Ali. 'Look to the East Strategy in the Foreign Affairs of Islamic Republic of Iran; Perspectives, Basics and Opportunities'. *Quarterly Journal in Political Studies* 7 (2010): 97–127.

Adarov, Amat, and Mahdi Ghodsi. *The Impact of the EAEU-Iran Preferential Trade Agreement*. Vienna: WIIW Working Paper No. 179, 2020, 1–20.

Ahmed, Ghada, Danny Hamrick and Gary Gereffi. 'Shifting Governance Structures in the Wheat Value Chain: Implications for Food Securityin the Middle East and North Africa'. *Presentation held at the Global Value Chains and Trade Policies for Food and Nutrition Security Workshop in Rome*, 26 September 2014. https://gvcc.duke.edu/wp-content/uploads/2014-09-26_Shifting-Governance-Structures-in-the-Wheat-GVC.pdf.

Banse, Martin, Ivan Duric, Götz Linde and Verena Laquai. 'From the Russian Food Import Ban to Free Trade from Lisbon to Vladivostok—Will Farmers Benefit?' *Journal of International Studies* 12, no. 4 (2019): 20–31.

Ghonein, Ahmed F. 'The Political Economy of Food Price Policy in Egypt'. In *Food Price Policy in an Era of Market Instability*, ed. Per Pinstrup-Andersen. Oxford: Oxford University Press, 2015, 253–274.

Glauben, Thomas, Linde Götz, and Ulrich Koester. *The Rouble Crisis and the Russian Grain Export Controls*. IAMO Policy Brief No. 22. Halle, Germany, 2015.

Grindle, Arani K., Afreen Siddiqi, and Laura Diaz Anadon. 'Food Security Amidst Water Scarcity: Insights on Sustainable Food Production from Saudi Arabia'. *Sustainable Production and Consumption* 2 (2015): 67–78.

Heigermoser, Maximilian and Linde Götz. 'Russia's Rise to Become the World's Largest Wheat Exporter: Implications for the Global Grain Trade'. *Russian Analytical Digest*, no. 244 (17 December 2019): 7–11.

Heigermoser, Maximilian, Linde Götz and Miranda Svanidze. *Wheat Price Formation in the Black Sea Region: The Role of Egypt's GASC*. Washington, DC: Proceedings of the IATRC Annual Meeting, 2017.

Liefert, William M. and Olga Liefert. 'Russia's Economic Crisis and Its Agricultural and Food Economy.' *Choices* 30, no. 1 (2015): 1–6.

Liefert, William M. and Olga Liefert. 'Russian Agricultural Trade and World Markets'. *Russian Journal of Economics* 6 (2020): 56–70.

Lim, Kevin. *Bumped Crops: Iran's Grain Imports and Geopolitical Shocks*. Washington, DC: The Washington Institute, 2020.

Lippmann, Thomas W. 'Saudi Arabia's Quest for Food Security'. *Middle East Policy* 17, no. 1 (2010): 90–98.

Önis, Ziya and Suhnaz Yilmaz. 'Turkey and Russia in a Shifting Global Order: Cooperation, Conflict and Asymmetric Interdependence in a Turbulent Region'. *Third World Quarterly* 37, no. 1 (2016): 71–95.

Tarock, Adam. 'Russo-Iranian Relations in the Post-Soviet Era'. *Diplomacy and Statecraft* 28, no. 3 (2017): 518–537.

Wegren, Stephen K. 'The Russian Food Embargo and Food Security: Can Household Production Fill the Void?' *Eurasian Geography and Economics* 55, no. 5 (2014): 491–513.

Wegren, Stephen K. 'Can Russia's Food Exports Reach $45 Billion in 2024?'. *Post-Communist Economies* 32, no. 2 (2020): 147–175.

Wegren, Stephen K., Alexander M. Nikulin and Irina Trotsuk. 'The Russian Variant of Food Security'. *Problems of Post-Communism* 64, no. 1 (2016): 47–62.

Wegren, Stephen K., Frode Nilssen and Christel Elvestad. 'The Impact of Russian Food Security Policy on the Performance of the Food System'. *Eurasian Geography and Economics* 57, no. 6 (2016): 671–699.

Open Access This chapter is licensed under the terms of the Creative Commons Attribution 4.0 International License (http://creativecommons.org/licenses/by/4.0/), which permits use, sharing, adaptation, distribution and reproduction in any medium or format, as long as you give appropriate credit to the original author(s) and the source, provide a link to the Creative Commons license and indicate if changes were made.

The images or other third party material in this chapter are included in the chapter's Creative Commons license, unless indicated otherwise in a credit line to the material. If material is not included in the chapter's Creative Commons license and your intended use is not permitted by statutory regulation or exceeds the permitted use, you will need to obtain permission directly from the copyright holder.

Chapter 10: Agri-Food Trade Between the United States and Russia: From Divergence to Irrelevance

Stephen K. Wegren

1 Introduction

Historically, the U.S.-Russia agricultural trade relationship has been one-sided with the United States as the exporting country. Starting in the 1970s, the former USSR became a prominent importer of grain from the United States. For the remainder of the Cold War, even though the bilateral political relationship was tense, the United States supplied and even increased grain shipments to its adversary. Since August 2014, however, the U.S. has been almost entirely shut out of the Russian food market and its 146 million consumers due to Russia's embargo, called countersanctions. Although Russia's food embargo against the West has been widely discussed in the media and among scholars, the fact is that even prior to 2014, American agricultural exports to Russia already were already declining in dollar amount and quantity. Russia's 2014 food embargo

S. K. Wegren (✉)
Department of Political Science, Southern Methodist University, Dallas, TX, USA
e-mail: swegren@smu.edu

© The Author(s) 2022

S. K. Wegren and F. Nilssen (eds.), *Russia's Role in the Contemporary International Agri-Food Trade System*, Palgrave Advances in Bioeconomy: Economics and Policies,
https://doi.org/10.1007/978-3-030-77451-6_11

merely took the agricultural trade relationship with the U.S. one step further, to irrelevance.

This chapter examines whether political relations affect agricultural trade. It surveys bilateral agricultural trade between the United States and Russia, starting in the 1970s and continuing to the present.[1] The Cold War period suggests that political relations do not need to affect food trade. The period since 2014 raises the question of whether it may be possible to re-start agricultural exports to Russia based on the Cold War precedent, or whether the post-Cold War pattern of convergence will continue.

This historical survey leads to several conclusions. First, during the Cold War, the link between the political relationship and food trade often was weak. In other words, political relations between the United States and Russia and agricultural trade were divergent, which means that agricultural exports were maintained or increased even as the political relationship deteriorated. Second, the divergence between worsening political relations and increasing agricultural exports ended in the post-Soviet period. Instead, the relationship between politics and agricultural exports became convergent. With Putin in office, U.S. agricultural exports have fallen into irrelevance, a trend that predates 2014 but has become pronounced since 2014. To the extent that the U.S. ever had a 'food weapon' in its arsenal, this lever to influence Russian behaviour going forward would appear to be lost. The next section presents the analytical framework and subsequent sections examine the interplay between political relations and agricultural trade during the Cold War 1970s and 1980s, the 1990s, and since 2000.

2 Analytical Framework

The analytical framework draws ideas from two literatures. The first, Realism, holds that leaders act to ensure national security; national security is in turn is a function of power and power is a function of military strength. In short, national leaders are interested in maximising their own national security and minimising the strength of an adversary. The second literature argues that food may be weaponised to advance foreign policy interests and national security. States frequently use food to enhance power and when they do, government's food exports are utilised to gain economic, diplomatic, or security advantages.[2] Paarlberg observes that with regard to diplomatic or security advantages, exporters may use food power to reward allies or punish adversaries with embargoes. Importers may adopt a defensive form of food power by reducing food imports or diversifying their imports away from an adversary.[3]

Intuitively, one would think that trade follows political relations. Indeed, Gowa argues that trade creates security externalities and for that reason, trade is more likely to occur within alliances than across alliances, especially in a bipolar world.[4] That said, the fact is that the United States exported strategically important food to its rival the USSR during the Cold War. Broadly speaking, adversaries have different motivations for trading with one another. One side tries to initiate trade to lower tensions or to improve relations. The exporting side may want to create dependence by the importer and thus gain potential leverage. The importing side may want access to goods that it cannot produce itself or are cost-prohibitive to produce. That said, the core motivation of state security and preservation can also be threatened by international trade with adversaries. In agricultural trade, for example, exporting food allows that adversary to allocate resources to its military to make itself stronger instead of growing food. A state that imports food from an adversary helps its rival earn income that allows it to use that higher income for its military. A rise in disposable income in an adversary state thereby lessens the security of the first state.

Concerning bilateral relations between the United States and the USSR, American presidents from the beginning considered the Soviet regime to be illegitimate, but that does not mean that they were prepared to dedicate resources to force its overthrow or replacement. Gaddis argues that however distasteful the Soviet regime was, no U.S. president ever tried for regime change in the USSR, even going so far as to help Soviet leaders twice in their darkest hour.[5] During 1921–1922, the United States offered food aid to the nascent Soviet government instead of working for the overthrow of Bolshevism; and in 1941, following Hitler's attack on the USSR, the United States sided with Stalin against Germany rather than try to bring Stalinism to an end. The question, therefore, is not merely why the United States did not press its advantage against its main adversary in the post-World War II period, but also why it did not take advantage of Soviet systemic weaknesses in later decades. In particular, it is curious why did the U.S. not utilise its 'food weapon' against a rival that suffered from chronic food shortages.

U.S. policymakers have been aware of their food power. The politicalisation of food trade dates has existed for decades. In the years following

World War II, both food aid and commercial food sales were used repeatedly by the United States to support its foreign policy goals in different regions of the world.[6] The politicalisation of food aid dates to the 1950s. The Eisenhower administration used food to exacerbate tensions between the communist regime in East Germany and its population following the death of Stalin in March 1953.[7] In the early 1960s, the Kennedy administration advocated making 'full use of our agricultural abundance in furtherance of U.S. foreign policy'.[8]

Commercial food sales were also politicised. In 1974, Secretary of Agriculture Earl Butz referred to food as a 'weapon' that the U.S. should utilise. In the early 1980s, conservative analysts in the U.S. recognised the disadvantaged position the Soviets were in and called for using American grain as leverage by threatening or actually withholding grain to change Soviet international behaviour and to make the USSR pay an economic price for violating international norms.[9] Specifically, conservatives argued that the grain weapon could be used to force a reduction in Soviet livestock herds that ultimately would affect meat consumption levels, with the intent to foment consumers' dissatisfaction with the Soviet regime. Some evidence suggests that the food weapon was at least partially effective. Following the U.S. ban on grain sales to the USSR in 1980, the CIA noted 'a rising incidence of strikes related to food shortages in the 1980–1982 period', although the dysfunctional retail price and distribution system also contributed to spotty food supplies.[10] Thus, it is reasonable to conclude that food exports are another weapon in states' arsenals to protect and project their interests.

3 Cold War Foreign Policy Context: 1970–1985

Dating from 1946, the USSR and the United States were adversaries who during the next forty-five years would engage in espionage, assassinations, coups, and support puppet governments in an effort to gain a geopolitical advantage against the other. The Cold War represented economic, psychological, ideological, and geopolitical warfare, stopping just short of direct military conflict between the two countries. During the second half of the 1970s and into the 1980s the Soviet Union reached the apex of its global political influence and its military might. During this period there was a significant increase in Soviet military forces. The build-up included a dramatic increase in ICBMs; modernisation of the navy, including the deployment of submarines with nuclear warheads, nuclear-powered attack submarines, and an expansion in the number of guided missile cruisers, frigates, destroyers, and aircraft carriers; the development of intermediate nuclear weapons; the modernisation of ground forces and ground attack capability; the deployment of advanced strategic bombers and attack aircraft; and the development of air defences. The Soviet intent was to challenge U.S. hegemony on the land, sea, air, and in nuclear force. Improvements in Soviet military capability were also accompanied by the spread of political influence into Central America, North Africa, and the Middle East, an improvement in relations with India and China, and forging alliances with Vietnam and North Korea.[11] By the late 1970s-early 1980s the USSR reached nuclear parity or even surpassed the United States based on sheer numbers of nuclear weapons and warheads. In short, the national security of the United States was threatened by Soviet advances militarily and politically.

Although the 1970s is sometimes called the 'decade of détente', in fact, it was at its height only during 1972-1974. By mid-decade, the détente relationship already showed signs of unraveling. Soviet support for rebels in regional conflicts such as Angola, Ethiopia, and Mozambique strained the relationship and in the opinion of U.S. leaders violated the 1972 political 'code of conduct'. Soviet pressure on Poland in the wake of widespread protests in 1976 led President Gerald Ford to stop referring to détente during his reelection campaign, reflecting the fact that conservatives were souring on détente and its supposed benefits. In 1979, the U.S. raised alarms that the Soviets were stationing combat troops in Cuba. Although in many ways that crisis was manufactured and did not constitute a new phase of Soviet adventurism in the Caribbean, it did cause enough of a ruckus as to prevent the SALT II Treaty from being approved in 1979,[12] and following the Soviet's December 1979 invasion of Afghanistan, the treaty was removed from consideration in the Senate. The U.S. also raised objections over Soviet support for Sandinistas in Nicaragua that threatened American interests in Central America. The decade ended with the Soviet Union invading Afghanistan which at the time was feared by U.S. conservatives to be a drive to cut off the U.S. from Saudi oil. By the end of the 1970s, U.S. political willingness to cooperate with the USSR had waned.

The first half of the 1980s witnessed the Cold War at its coldest. There was a general war scare among the general population in both the U.S. and USSR. In the West, the peace movement ramped up as the superpowers seemed headed for conflict. President Ronald Reagan distrusted the Soviet leaders and accused them of being 'the focus of evil in the modern world' and being behind all of the global political instability that was occurring in different regions.[13] Numerous crises exacerbated tensions: the imposition of martial law in Poland and a threatened Soviet invasion over the challenge represented by Solidarity to communist rule in 1980; the standoff over the deployment of U.S. medium-range missiles in Europe in 1982–1983; and the shooting down of a Korean passenger plane in August 1983. After August 1983 then-General Secretary Yurii Andropov indicated that he was done talking to the Americans. The Soviets stationed submarines armed with SLBMs off the East coast that could reach Washington, DC in less than ten minutes. Muscle-flexing in Berlin in 1984 led to the shooting death of an American soldier near the Berlin Wall.

The existential threat posed by Soviet nuclear forces in the early 1980s is easily forgotten today but was very real then. Coit Blacker noted that in the early 1980s the Soviets could devote 3,000–4,000 warheads from their SS17, SS18, and SS19 ICBMs that could destroy 90 percent of the U.S. ICBM force. He argued that 'the development of this Soviet option [to strike first] deeply disturbs some Western military and political leaders because….it enhances the Kremlin's ability to "intimidate" or to "coerce" the United States and its allies during times of severe tension or crisis'.[14] Such a strike would not only destroy U.S. retaliatory capacity but render its economy and society unable to function. Together with Secretary of State Alexander Haig, Reagan's intent was 'the management of global Soviet power', a strategy, which relied more on the stick than the carrot.[15] In reaction to these trends, during Reagan's first term, the U.S. engaged in a significant military modernisation and introduced new nuclear land-based, sea-based, and air-based weapons to counter the Soviet military build-up. The Strategic Defence Initiative, or 'Star Wars' as it came to be called, was directed at the Soviet Union and threatened to neutralise its nuclear deterrent.

Despite a rising political and security threat, the United States sold wheat and feed grain to the adversary who threatened its survival. To be sure, rivals trade with each other during periods when they are not at war.[16] That said, there had never been a global rivalry on the scale of the Cold War. Thus, Soviet-American bilateral food trade was paradoxical because the two nations were competing globally while simultaneously engaging in trade which helped the other country.

The seeming paradox of American food exports to the country that most threatened it is compounded by two other factors. First, in the 1970s and 1980s, the U.S. was the global food hegemon, accounting for 55 percent of international wheat and coarse grain exports in 1980.[17] France and Canada were second and third, respectively, accounting for 10 percent of global wheat and coarse grain exports in that same year.[18] In other words, the U.S. had the food resources that could not be matched by any other country. It had the leverage, at least in theory, to disrupt Soviet society and foster political instability. In the current vernacular, the U.S. could have worked for regime change. Second, the U.S. had options about to whom to sell its surplus grain. The U.S. was not forced to sell grain to the Soviet Union. There were other potential and real customers besides the Soviet Union: Eastern bloc satellites were eager customers; surplus grain could be offered as concessionary food aid; or surplus grain could be commercially sold to developing nations. Members of OPEC in particular were interested in the purchase of American wheat.[19] Thus, while the U.S. was interested in the economic advantages of exporting its surplus grain, there was nothing that dictated that the purchaser had to be the Soviet Union.

4 U.S. Agricultural Exports to USSR, 1972–1984

When political relations and agricultural trade move in the same direction I refer to it as convergence; divergence occurs when political relations and agricultural trade move in opposite directions. The 1972–1985 period is an example of convergence (1972–1974) and then divergence (1975–1985), during which the political relationship deteriorated but U.S. agricultural exports to the USSR reached unprecedented levels in value and quantity.

4.1 1972–1974

In 1972, at the beginning of détente, former Secretary of State Henry Kissinger had wanted to cultivate Soviet dependence on U.S. grain and link trade to Soviet behaviour in Jewish emigration and other foreign policy.[20] In the second half of the decade, that dependence certainly existed, but the U.S. did not deploy its food weapon to its political or security advantage.

As political relations warmed in the early détente period, the United States extended a $750 million USD Commodity Credit Corporation loan in 1972 to the Soviet Union to purchase U.S. grain. The agreement included an understanding that U.S. cargo ships would be used.[21] The grain agreement required the Soviets to purchase a *minimum* of $200 million USD in each year of the three-year deal. In reality, the Soviets utilised the entire $750 million USD credit in year one by misrepresenting their true needs. Ultimately, in 1972 the Soviets purchased 25 percent of the American wheat harvest at subsidised prices, the largest grain purchase in history, as well as large quantities of corn and soybeans.[22] The total purchase value exceeded $1 billion USD. When the full extent of Soviet purchases became known, the Nixon administration was embarrassed and American consumers were faced with higher retail prices for bread. The deal became known as the 'great grain robbery'.[23]

In 1974, after another large Soviet purchase, and remembering the bad experience of 1972, President Gerald Ford canceled $500 million USD in export contracts with the USSR in order to ensure sufficient domestic supply and to prevent further food inflation.[24] As a result, the value of agricultural exports to the USSR dropped nearly 70 percent compared to 1973. Again in 1975, the U.S. government suspended export contracts with the Soviets during a record American wheat harvest. American farmers claimed that the export ban cost them $200 million USD from lower domestic prices and lost business abroad.[25] The 1975 suspension was short-lived, however, as farm states organised to oppose the move. Thus, the embargo lasted only two months and for all of 1975 the value of U.S. agricultural exports to the USSR jumped to over $1.1 billion USD, beginning a string of years when agricultural sales surpassed $1 billion USD.

4.2 1975–1984

Another poor Soviet harvest led to a new five-year deal in October 1975 to buy American grain (1976–1981). The agreement almost fell apart over the U.S. insistence on a long-term commitment which the Soviets initially rejected.[26] The final agreement required that the Soviet Union purchase a minimum of six million metric tonnes (mmt) of grain each year, evenly divided between corn and wheat. If U.S. production surpassed 225 mmt, the Soviets could buy up to 8 mmt without consultation; above 8 mmt required prior notification and permission from the

Table 1 U.S. Agricultural Exports to USSR, 1975–1979 (dollar values are USD)

	Total value of U.S. agricultural exports to USSR	*Value of US grain exports to USSR*	*U.S. grain sales to USSR (million metric tonnes)*
1975	$1.17 billion	$1.13 billion	7.61
1976	$1.60 billion	$1.46 billion	11.60
1977	$1.05 billion	$852.5 million	6.86
1978	$1.76 billion	$1.47 billion	13.44
1979	$3.00 billion	$2.39 billion	18.87

Source Kathryn A. Zeimetz, *USSR Agricultural Trade*, Statistical Bulletin 808 (Washington, DC: United States Department of Agriculture, Economic Research Service, 1991), 36, 38

U.S. government.[27] In reality, the Soviets purchased much more than the minimum stipulated in the agreement. In 1976 they were allowed to purchase 11.6 mmt of grain, 13.4 mmt in 1978, and 18.8 mmt in 1979 without objection from the U.S. government. The dollar value of U.S. agricultural exports to the USSR during 1975–1979 is shown in Table 1.

The fact that agricultural trade did not suffer even as the détente relationship deteriorated after 1974 reflects divergence between politics and economics. Despite a rise in bilateral political tensions, U.S. agricultural exports to the USSR remained strong, surpassing $1 billion USD each year during 1975–1979 and reaching $3 billion USD in 1979. Ironically, both rivals helped each other. Soviet imports of American grain contributed to the rise of American food power. The U.S. share of world agricultural trade increased from 13.5 percent in 1970 to 17 percent in 1978. Moreover, during the 1970s the U.S. accounted for more than 80 percent of the increase in global grain exports.[28] Conversely, American grain exports allowed the USSR to continue to allocate large amount of money and other resources to its military and towards expanding its influence around the world.

Thus, the second half of the 1970s witnessed divergence between political relations and agricultural exports, which meant that America's use of food as a weapon of foreign policy was weak and the deterioration in the political relationship became secondary to economic considerations. If U.S. security considerations had dominated, there certainly were available levers given the fact that U.S. grain accounted for over 60 percent of Soviet grain imports from 1972 through 1979.[29] In the 1978/1979 agricultural year, U.S. grain exports accounted for 67 percent of Soviet grain imports.[30]

The 1980s began with a U.S. grain embargo in retaliation for the Soviet invasion of Afghanistan. President Jimmy Carter suspended delivery of grain sales in December 1979 for purchases in excess of the 8 mmt permitted in the 1975 grain agreement. Paarlberg notes that 'never before had U.S. food exports to the USSR been suspended in pursuit of a noncommercial, foreign policy objective'.[31] It appeared that the 'food weapon' had been taken from the shelf.

The U.S. grain embargo was an important symbolic act, along with the U.S. boycott of the 1980 Olympics in Moscow. But the embargo was not successful. This occurrence in and of itself is not surprising since the literature on sanctions is generally negative about the effectiveness of sanctions.[32] Lindsay places sanctions into five categories: (1) compliance—to alter another state's behaviour; (2) subversion—to remove the target's leaders; (3) deterrence—to dissuade the target from repeating disputed behaviour in the future; (4) international symbolism—to send a message to other members of the world community; and (5) domestic symbolism—to increase domestic support and thwart domestic criticism of its policies.[33] Carter's grain embargo was most concerned with domestic symbolism and according to Paarlberg was not intended to force the Soviets out of Afghanistan but simply to punish them for their behaviour.[34]

The U.S. grain embargo was not successful for a variety of reasons. First, the U.S. was unable to enforce an embargo coalition and thus there was considerable 'leakage', meaning other states filled the U.S. void. Canada, Australia, Argentina, and the European Community all expanded their grain sales to the Soviet Union following the announcement of the U.S. embargo. Even India sold grain to the USSR for the first time, a modest 2 mmt. In short, the Soviet Union was able to substitute U.S. grain and thus paid a very small price for its 'adventurism' in Afghanistan. Second, the embargo motivated Soviet leaders to lessen their dependence on U.S. grain, although doing so proved more difficult. During the first half of the 1980s, the U.S. share of Soviet grain imports did not exceed 40 percent, compared to more than 60 percent in the 1970s. Third, the U.S. grain embargo was not expanded to Warsaw Pact countries to prevent 'leakage' to the USSR. Instead, the U.S. expanded grain sales to Eastern Europe from an original 16 mmt to 18 mmt despite favourable harvests in the communist bloc.[35]

Perhaps most important, the embargo did not even meet its limited goal of punishing the Soviets for their behaviour in Afghanistan. A long-term 'leak proof' embargo combined with a reduction in agricultural exports *may* have forced the Soviet leaders to reallocate resources away from the military, but that was not done for domestic political reasons in the U.S. Carter's embargo was designed to trigger a distress slaughter of livestock due to feed shortages, thereby affecting Soviet meat supply and consumption. Instead, in 1980 the Soviet Union fed 126 mmt of grain to livestock, 1 mmt *more* than the year before.[36] In reality, there was no distress slaughter. In the Russian Republic during 1979–1984 the number of long-horned cattle rose from 58.6 million to 60 million head; the number of dairy cows remained constant at 22.2 million; and the number of pigs increased from 36.4 million to 38.7 million.[37] Finally, in April 1981, four months into the new administration of Ronald Reagan, the arch-anti-communist, the U.S. embargo ended.[38]

The five-year period 1980–1984 period overall witnessed significant divergence between political relations, which fell to their nadir, and agricultural trade which increased. Instead of the U.S. maximising its leverage at a time when the enemy was vulnerable, the value of U.S. agricultural exports increased from $1.1 billion USD in 1980 to $2.8 billion USD in 1984. Even as the two sides threatened each other militarily, the volume of U.S. grain sales increased from 6.6 mmt in 1980 to over 18 mmt in 1984. Moreover, U.S. grain sales averaged 10.7 mmt during 1980–1984, more than double the level of the détente years 1970–1974 when the political relationship warmed. During 1980–1984, the average annual value of America's agricultural exports to the Soviet Union was $1.80 billion USD, higher than the $1.69 billion USD average during 1975–1979, as shown in Table 2.

As the 1980s came to a close, U.S. agricultural exports to the USSR were at their peak. During 1988–1991 U.S. agricultural exports totaled more than $10.55 billion USD, more than in any other four-year period. This high point in U.S. agricultural exports to the Soviet Union reflected the partial opening of the Soviet economy and improving bilateral political relations. During the 1988–1991 period, political relations and agricultural trade were convergent.

Rising American agricultural exports also reflected political support by the Reagan and Bush administrations for President Mikhail Gorbachev and his perestroika efforts, particularly in foreign policy where he was making unilateral concessions in Eastern Europe and supporting the U.S.

Table 2 U.S. Agricultural Exports to USSR, 1980–1984 (dollar values are USD)

	Total value of U.S. agricultural exports to USSR	*Value of U.S. grain exports to USSR*	*U.S. grain sales to USSR (million metric tonnes)*
1980	$1.13 billion	$1.02 billion	6.66
1981	$1.68 billion	$1.57 billion	9.65
1982	$1.87 billion	$1.63 billion	11.42
1983	$1.47 billion	$1.20 billion	7.86
1984	$2.87 billion	$2.62 billion	18.26

Source Kathryn A. Zeimetz, *USSR Agricultural Trade*, Statistical Bulletin 808 (Washington, DC: United States Department of Agriculture, Economic Research Service, 1991), 37, 39

in its first Gulf War against Iraq.[39] Unfortunately for Gorbachev, the broad-based economic assistance that he had counted on was not forthcoming from the United States, a fact that was deeply disappointing to Soviet leaders.[40] But the Americans were willing to sell food, and thus agricultural trade reached a single year high point in 1989 at $3.59 billion USD. In that year, the USSR purchased over 21 mmt of American wheat and corn.

5 1990s Foreign Policy Context

Following the breakup of the Soviet Union in December 1991, the remainder of decade ushered in significant changes in world politics and the U.S.-Russia bilateral relationship. The end of the Soviet Union lowered bilateral political tensions and witnessed multilateral economic cooperation as post-Soviet Russia joined international and regional organisations. It also meant that the U.S.-USSR ideological competition that had dominated world politics during the Cold War faded away. The zero-sum game that had defined bilateral relations was replaced by a search for mutual security, although this desire was often frustrated by mistrust and misunderstanding especially with regard to political arrangements in Europe.

Further, the collapse of the Soviet Union diminished military-strategic competition. With the subsequent collapse of the Russian economy and deep cuts in its military spending, Russia was no longer a global threat, at least in conventional weaponry. Competition between the two nations was characterised by asymmetrical power in favour of the United States.[41] One constant in the bilateral relationship was the U.S. as a provider of economic assistance and as the dominant player in the global financial system. In the late Gorbachev period and early post-Soviet period, political leaders in Moscow were hoping for assistance from the U.S. along the lines of the Marshall Plan, but by about 1994 it became clear that that level of assistance would not be forthcoming.[42]

Even without a massive aid package that the Russians had hoped for, the 1990s represented a honeymoon decade in U.S.-Russian relations during which the relationship was warmer and more cooperative than at any other time in the twentieth century. Russian President Boris Yeltsin and U.S. President Bill Clinton were on a first name basis and met no less than eight times during 1993–1999. The core reasons for this new phase in the bilateral relationship were the demise of Marxist-Leninist ideology that viewed international relations as inherently conflictual between capitalist and socialist states, and the rise of a pro-Western vision of national identity and foreign policy.[43] Russia's post-Soviet leaders saw their country as part of Western civilisation whose identity had been 'hijacked' by the Bolsheviks and the Soviet system.[44] Tsygankov argues that the new concept of the post-Soviet identity emphasised partnership with the West and was predicated on rapid membership in Western international organisations; radical economic reforms that would usher in a market economy; and isolationism from the former Soviet region. This new foreign policy concept was signed into law in 1993.[45]

During the decade, the two sides signed the START 2 arms control treaty in 1993 and an agreement to ban chemical weapons in 1996; adhered to the Nunn-Lugar programme to help Russia destroy its nuclear weapons; and conducted on-site inspections to enforce the Intermediate-range Nuclear Force treaty. The two sides also cooperated on the construction of democracy, civil society, and human rights in Russia. There were regular meetings between the Russian Foreign Minister and the U.S. Secretary of State; and in 1995 regular meetings convened between Russian Prime Minister Viktor Chernomyrdin and U.S. Vice President Albert Gore. There were also economic achievements: a $24 billion USD aid package from the U.S. in 1992; an American-led G-7 commitment for an aid package of more than $43 billion USD; the rescheduling of $70 million USD of Soviet debt with the Paris Club; and a U.S.-backed $10 billion USD aid package from the IMF in 1998.

In short, the relationship moved from being defined by conflicting and diverging interests to parallel and common interests.[46]

The improvement in bilateral relations did not imply an absence of problems. The December 1993 Duma election witnessed the emergence of powerful nationalist politicians that led to 'a series of tactical concessions that reflected the changing balance of domestic power' away from Westernism.[47] In an embarrassing moment, Foreign Minister Andrei Kozyrev had asked for a special session of NATO foreign ministers at which he would presumably announce Russia's membership in the Partnership for Peace. Instead, at the December 1994 meeting, Kozyrev indicated that Russia was not yet ready to join. Then-Secretary of State Warren Christopher recalls being 'flabbergasted and embarrassed….Russia was putting a thumb in our eye'.[48] After the meeting, Kozyrev explained to Christopher that hardliners had convinced Yeltsin not to join the Partnership for Peace. Russia finally joined the Partnership for Peace in May 1995. Russian leaders also complained about patronising and condescending treatment by the United States, claims that would seem to be justified given that the Clinton administration expected Russia to adopt Western views of security for Europe. By 1995, pro-Western Foreign Minister Kozyrev was openly asking the West whether it wanted 'Partnership or Cold Peace' between the two countries by way of complaining about U.S. unilateralism in the Balkans.[49] There were other tensions—U.S. support for an independent Kosovo in 1997, economic aid that Russia felt was insufficient before and after the 1998 financial crisis in Russia, and the U.S. bombing of Serbia in 1999, which was an ally of Russia.

The decision to expand NATO to include former communist satellite nations in Eastern Europe in 1999 was especially contentious. Christopher notes that Russia's opposition to NATO enlargement seemed to centre around a lack of respect from the United States. From Christopher's own descriptions, the U.S. essentially dictated to Russia that NATO would enlarge and bring in former communist nations in Europe.[50] Christopher's successor, Secretary Madeline Albright, also noted that 'part of our strategy, of course, was to convince the Russians that enlargement would go forward with or without their agreement'.[51] Robert Gates, who served as Secretary of Defence from 2006 to 2011, observed that during the 1990s, 'we did not take Russian interests seriously. We did a poor job of seeing the world from their point of view, and of managing the relationship for the long term'.[52]

Eventually, Albright admits that 'we wore the Russians down'.[53] Not only did NATO expand, but the NATO-Russia Charter shut Russia out of a formal role in NATO's decision-making process. Yeltsin had little choice but to accept what the Americans decided.[54] But Russian unhappiness with the way they were treated was reflected in their negotiation strategy which was characterised as similar to a 'dental root canal'. Albright writes that 'Moscow wanted the ordeal [NATO enlargement] to be so painful that we would forget about further rounds'.[55]

Despite tensions in the relationship, the U.S. remained fully invested in Boris Yeltsin and supported him through his extra-constitutional actions in September–October 1993 when he disbanded Parliament; the brutal conduct Chechen war of 1994–1996 during which rape, genocide, and murder were common; flagrant violations of a free and fair presidential election in 1996; and Russia's 1998 financial meltdown that effectively ended Russia's experiment with de-statisation. The broader point is that the bilateral relationship was generally positive during the 1990s and cooperation, even if strained at times, replaced military confrontation.

6 U.S. Agricultural Exports in the 1990s

Building on a record value of U.S. grain exports to the USSR in 1989 ($3.59 billion USD), in 1990 the United States and the Soviet Union signed a new grain agreement. This agreement raised the Soviet Union's minimum annual purchase to 10 mmt and included barley and sorghum for the first time. The Soviets were given the right to buy up to 14 mmt without advance notification, up from 12 mmt. The Soviets also agreed to buy a minimum of 4 mmt of wheat and feed grain.[56] As a result, 1990–1991 witnessed continued high levels of U.S. agricultural exports, with more than $4.5 billion USD in agricultural exports to the USSR despite its limited hard currency reserves.

With the fall of communism and the emergence of a democratic and market-oriented government in Moscow, it could be expected that the improving bilateral political relationship would build upon the trade momentum of 1988–1991, especially considering the economic difficulties that Russia's transition to a market economy were experiencing. It would be reasonable to expect that warmer political relations would be accompanied by much higher agricultural trade. In fact, however, higher valuations of agricultural exports did not occur, instead of dropping from $2.45 billion USD in 1991 to $1.12 billion USD in 1992 and never exceeding $1.5 billion USD for the rest of the decade. The volume of the main U.S. export in the past, grain, began to decline precipitously. The improving political relationship after 1992 contrasts with trends in agricultural trade which were lower than 1990–1991 and lower than the 1980–1984 period. Thus, the relationship between politics and agricultural trade was divergent, but not as much as during the 1980–1984 period. Annual U.S. agricultural exports during the 1990s are shown in Table 3.

The table demonstrates three occurrences about U.S. food exports to Russia: (1) the value of U.S. agricultural exports declined after 1992; (2) the value of grain exports comprised a smaller percentage of total agricultural exports as the decade progressed; and (3) the quantity of grain exports declined after 1992.

Mild divergence is further witnessed by lower annual valuations of U.S. agricultural exports than in the last decade of the Soviet period. During 1992–1999, the value of U.S. agricultural exports totaled $9.01 billion USD, or an annual average of $1.1 billion USD for the eight-year period. In comparison, during the 1980–1984 period, U.S. agricultural exports

Table 3 U.S. Agricultural Exports to USSR/Russia in 1990s (dollar values are USD)

	Total value of U.S. agricultural exports to USSR/Russia	*Value of grain exports to USSR/Russia*	*Quantity of grain export to USSR/Russia*
1990	$2.26 billion	$1.68 billion	13.2 mmt
1991	$2.45 billion	$1.78 billion	16.5 mmt
1992	$1.12 billion	$738 million	5.9 mmt
1993	$1.22 billion	$682 million	6.0 mmt
1994	$1.00 billion	$45 million	303.9 tt
1995	$1.45 billion	$80 million	444.0 tt
1996	$1.32 billion	$56 million	223.2 tt
1997	$1.20 billion	$27 million	114.3 tt
1998	$988.5 million	$9 million	40.6 tt
1999	$728.0 million	$257 million	1.90 mmt

Notes (a) Data for agricultural exports in 1990–1991 are for USSR, thereafter they are for Russia (b) mmt = million metric tonnes (c) tt = thousand metric tonnes. *Sources* Kathryn A. Zeimetz, *USSR Agricultural Trade*, Statistical Bulletin 808 (Washington, DC: United States Department of Agriculture, Economic Research Service, 1991), 37, 39; and Foreign Agricultural Service database at https://apps.fas.usda.gov/GATS/default.aspx

totaled $9.02 billion USD, or an annual average of $1.8 billion USD during the five-year period. Further, U.S. grain exports declined from 16.5 mmt in 1991 to about 6 mmt in 1992 and 1993, and thereafter did not come close to 500 thousand tonnes for the rest of the decade. Another perspective on the decline is to note that during 1982–1989, a period generally considered to be one of poor agricultural performance and high grain imports, the average annual domestic grain production was 98.8 mmt per year. During 1992–1999, Russia's annual average domestic grain harvests declined to 76.3 mmt a year.[57] And yet, Russian grain imports declined after 1992.

The decline in U.S. grain exports to Russia was due to economic changes in demand within Russia. Due to high food inflation and contraction in real per capita income, Russian consumer demand for meat plummeted after 1992 as consumers turned to cheaper starches, carbohydrates, and grains which domestic production could fulfill.[58] Consumers responded to price changes for food, especially for high-cost livestock products. Farms in turn responded to falling consumer demand and rising prices for fuel, feed, and other inputs by slashing livestock herds. The result was a decline in animal husbandry that rivaled the mass slaughter of the early 1930s when peasants resisted collectivisation. In 1996, for example, the number of cattle was 70 percent and the number of pigs was 59 percent of the 1990 level. The number of cattle and pigs continued to decline, falling to 49 percent and 48 percent of the 1990 level by 2000, respectively.[59] As demand for meat plummeted and the number of farm animals decreased, the need (demand) for imported feed grain evaporated.

As Russian consumers shifted their demand to cheaper proteins, Russia quickly became the largest importer of poultry meat in the world. Russia's poultry imports rose from about 46 thousand tonnes in 1992 to 500 thousand tonnes in 1994, and then to 1.14 million tonnes in 1997. In 1997, 70 percent of Russia's poultry imports came from the United States.[60] U.S. poultry exporters earned in excess of $1 billion USD annually from trade with Russia from about mid-decade onward. Chicken meat replaced grain as the main U.S. agricultural export to Russia.

Russia's dependence on foreign meat and poultry impacted Russia's food import policy.[61] Protectionist policies began to emerge in mid-decade to protect the domestic food market from imports. Advocates of more protectionism cited Russia's comparative disadvantage in land productivity and harsher climatic conditions that made it difficult to compete with lower international prices.[62] To assist domestic producers to retain market share, food import tariffs were increased in mid-1995. The tariff on meat (non-poultry) increased from 8 to 15 percent; on poultry and sugar from 20 to 25 percent; and on butter from 15 to 20 percent.[63] In 1996, the Russian government raised import tariffs on alcohol, chicken, and other food products that resulted in an average weighted tariff of 14 percent.[64] Further, in July 1996 import quotas were introduced for the first time on meat, milk, and poultry products, but withdrawn in December 1996 under U.S. pressure.

In addition, in 1996 the first of several disputes over U.S. chicken exports arose. In February 1996, a controversy arose when the Russian Ministry of Agriculture announced that its veterinary service would deny import certification to many U.S. poultry processing plants, in effect placing a temporary ban of American poultry exports. Critics in the U.S. argued that the sanitary issue was Russia's pretext for what was really a political demonstration of power by Russian conservatives whose influence was rising following the departure of Foreign Minister Andrei Kozyrev and First Vice Premier Yegor Gaidar from Yeltsin's cabinet. The controversy was settled in March 1996 following negotiations that led to Russia accepting the U.S. poultry inspection system. The issuance of import licenses was resumed and chicken imports that had been shipped when the dispute arose were admitted into the country by Russian customs. The 'chicken war' between the U.S. and Russia would extend into the next decade.[65]

America's agricultural exports to Russia encompassed not only commercial sales. U.S. food aid was first extended to the Soviet Union in 1990–1991 when the Bush administration was informed of the possibility of hunger and even starvation. Those forecasts turned out to be exaggerated but nonetheless food aid was continued during the Clinton administration. By 1993–1994 it became clear that U.S. food aid to Russia was suffering from waste, loss, and corruption. The Russian state grain monopoly colluded with a small group of banks and grain auction houses to buy up U.S. supplies of grain at artificially low prices. These supplies undercut existing private farmers and kept domestic grain prices so low that they were a formidable barrier to entry for prospective growers. According to estimates by the United States Department of Agriculture, no more than 5 percent of aid reached intended recipients.[66] In 1994, the U.S. reoriented its distribution away from state-owned grain distributors to private farmers. During fiscal years 1994–1998, the U.S.

government underwrote the delivery of millions of tonnes of wheat, corn, and soybeans, as well as tens of thousands of tonnes of rice, barley, and rye to Russia.[67]

As one aid package came to an end, another began in late 1998. Following a very poor harvest in 1998, in November of that year the United States set up a $1 billion USD food aid package to avoid mass hunger in the Far East and other remote regions of Russia. The aid package consisted of 1.5 mmt of wheat worth $600 million USD as humanitarian assistance, and a $400 million USD line of credit to purchase additional food at 2 percent interest repayable over twenty years after a five-year grace period. The U.S. also agreed to pay shipping costs, which totaled more than $300 million USD. Food aid began to arrive in Russia in March 1999, although the bulk of aid was not shipped until late summer 1999, and even then few small towns in remote areas where aid was needed actually received food. A large share of the aid remained in Moscow and St. Petersburg.[68] In January 1999, the U.S. donated additional seed for Russia's spring sowing.[69]

7 Foreign Policy Context Since 2000

At the turn of the century, both countries were disappointed in the other. The U.S. was losing hope that Russia would democratise; U.S. leaders were frustrated with the level of corruption in the Russian government; and they were concerned about stalled economic reform following Russia's financial collapse of August 1998. The incoming Bush administration downplayed the geostrategic importance of Russia and instead articulated other priorities.[70] President Clinton's engagement with Russia in the 1990s gave way to 'Russia fatigue'. The Kremlin was disillusioned as well. Secretary of Defense Donald Rumsfeld recounts how President Vladimir Putin argued that Russia was being 'pushed out' of collective defense with the West for which Putin blamed the West.[71] Russian political leaders continued to be offended at the lack of respect by the Americans, an issue that Rumsfeld says he explicitly tried to address.[72] Lingering bitterness over NATO expansion led to early tension between the two countries. The tension escalated when FBI agent Philip Hanssen was arrested and charged with spying for Moscow for 15 years. The Bush administration ordered the expulsion of 50 Russian diplomats from the U.S. in March 2001.[73] Russia retaliated and expelled U.S. diplomats, behaviour reminiscent of the Cold War. Unlike the Soviet period, however, the rivalry between the two countries flowed from big power competition and increasing nationalism in Russia rather than incompatible political ideologies.

The bilateral drift came to an abrupt halt with the 9/11 attacks. Not only was Putin among the first world leaders to offer condolences to President George W. Bush, the aftermath brought concrete cooperation in counterterrorism as the U.S. began military action against the Taliban in Afghanistan. There was also cooperation in nuclear proliferation as Russia joined the West in trying to limit Iran's nuclear capabilities. The reemergence of common interests was able to withstand the announcement of another round of NATO expansion in 2002 that brought in the Baltic states and the announcement of a 'big bang' expansion of the European Union that witnessed almost all former Soviet satellite nations in Eastern Europe join the Western sphere of influence in 2004. Further, after notifying the Russians of intent, in June 2002 the United States withdrew from the ABM Treaty that had existed since 1972, a move denounced by Putin. The U.S. also continued with the development of a modest missile defense system in Europe, which, according to Rumsfeld, Putin said he understood did not threaten Russia's security interests.[74]

By 2003, however, disagreements outweighed cooperation. Putin made clear his opposition to the U.S. invasion of Iraq in March 2003. Later in 2003, the Russian government took over oil giant Yukos in 2003 and subsequently imprisoned its CEO, Mikhail Khodorkovsky, in 2004.[75] Stent argues that the Yukos affair had a minimal impact on the political relationship.[76] However, in the financial sphere, foreign direct investment (FDI) into Russia collapsed in the fourth quarter of 2003 and declined from a net of + $1.79 billion USD in 2003 to net -$1.62 billion USD in 2004, which reflected concerns over the sanctity of private property in Putin's Russia.[77]

Even as Western FDI dried up, the bilateral trade relationship between the United States and Russia began to take off. Total U.S. exports in goods to Russia increased from $2.4 billion USD in 2003 and eventually reached a high of $11.1 billion USD in 2013. Even more impressive was the growth in Russia's exports of goods to the U.S., which increased from $8.6 billion USD in 2003 to a high of $34.6 billion USD in 2011. Most of Russia's exports to the U.S. were energy-related and in general, there were several cooperative energy projects up to 2008.[78] The U.S. trade balance in goods since 2000 is presented in Table 4, showing that the

Table 4 U.S. Trade Balance with Russia (dollar values are USD)

	Total value of U.S. exports to Russia	*Total value of U.S. imports from Russia*	*Trade balance*
1992–1999 annual average	\$2.85 billion	\$3.63 billion	\$−780 million
2000	\$2.09 billion	\$7.65 billion	\$−5.56 billion
2001	\$2.71 billion	\$6.26 billion	\$−3.54 billion
2002	\$2.39 billion	\$6.87 billion	\$−4.47 billion
2003	\$2.44 billion	\$8.61 billion	\$−6.17 billion
2004	\$2.96 billion	\$11.89 billion	\$−8.93 billion
2005	\$3.96 billion	\$15.30 billion	\$−11.34 billion
2006	\$4.70 billion	\$19.82 billion	\$−15.12 billion
2007	\$7.28 billion	\$19.31 billion	\$−12.03 billion
2008	\$9.33billion	\$26.78 billion	\$−17.44 billion
2009	\$5.33 billion	\$18.19 billion	\$−12.86 billion
2010	\$5.99 billion	\$25.69 billion	\$−19.69 billion
2011	\$8.31 billion	\$34.61 billion	\$−26.30 billion
2012	\$10.69 billion	\$29.36 billion	\$−18.66 billion
2013	\$11.14 billion	\$27.08 billion	\$−15.94 billion
2014	\$10.75 billion	\$23.65 billion	\$−12.90 billion
2015	\$7.98 billion	\$16.37 billion	\$−9.28 billion
2016	\$5.83 billion	\$14.54 billion	\$−8.71 billion
2017	\$7.00 billion	\$17.05 billion	\$−10.05 billion
2018	\$6.65 billion	\$20.87 billion	\$−14.21 billion
2019	\$5.78 billion	\$22.28 billion	\$−16.49 billion

Sources https://www.census.gov/foreign-trade/balance/c4621.html; and Author's calculations

U.S. began to run a chronic trade deficit with Russia after having trade surpluses through 1994.

Even as bilateral trade ramped up, the political relationship drifted. Following the tragic loss of life in the 2004 Beslan school murders, Putin seemed to implicate the United States for the event in a speech to the Russian people.[79] In the wake of Beslan, Putin imposed stricter control over domestic politics by changing the election system for the State Duma in a way that benefited the pro-Kremlin party United Russia; he ended gubernatorial elections; banned electoral blocs in the Duma; revised the way members of the Federation Council were selected; and replaced elected city mayors with appointed city managers in many regions. The cumulative political effect was a significant backsliding from democracy and the rise of human rights abuses that caused concern in Washington.[80]

The next few years deepened the political mistrust between the two countries. In 2006, Russia felt mislead in its quest to join the World Trade Organisation (WTO), accusing the United States of double standards that held up Russia's membership.[81] In a February 2007 speech at a security conference in Munich, Putin recited a long list of complaints about the American-dominated unipolar world. He excoriated the United States for provoking a new nuclear arms race, undermining international institutions, destabilising the Middle East by invading Iraq, and increasing tensions through the expansion of NATO, which he said, can only be interpreted as directed at Russia.[82] Secretary of Defence Robert Gates, who was in attendance at the Munich security conference, was stunned by Putin's 'harshness' but decided to respond in a humourous manner, observing that 'by the nods and smiles throughout the hall, I knew I had taken the right tack'.[83]

In 2008, during Russia's abbreviated war with Georgia, Foreign Minister Sergei Lavrov tried to enlist the support of the United States to remove Georgian President Saaskashvili whom the Russians considered an annoyance. Washington, of course, refused. In the aftermath of the war, Russia withdrew from the NATO-Russia Council, followed by NATO's declaration of support for Georgia and its territorial integrity and independence. NATO called on Russia to withdraw its troops. Immediately after the war ended, the U.S. signed a missile defence pact with Poland, the timing of which former Secretary of State Condoleeza Rice claims was coincidental but even if that claim is true, the Russians perceived it as ratcheting up tensions in Europe.[84] Robert Gates, who was Secretary of Defence during the Georgian war, gives the impression that the missile defence pact with Poland was a response to Russian aggression in Georgia. Further, he indicated that Russian behaviour 'called into question the entire premise of our dialogue'. He continued that, 'all of the nations of Europe are looking at Russia through a different set of lenses'.[85] In the aftermath of the Georgian war, the U.S. tabled Russia's application to the WTO to show its opposition to Russia's unilateral redefinition of borders of Georgia.[86] Russia's entry into the WTO would not be reconsidered until the Obama administration, which led to eventual membership in 2012.

The 2009 'reset' in bilateral relations and subsequent 2010 START arms control agreement were exceptions to the downward trend in relations. During the 'reset', the two countries experienced some cooperative successes—sanctions against Iran and North Korea, opening a northern supply route to Afghanistan, getting a UN resolution on a no-fly zone in Libya passed, and Russia's membership in the World Trade Organization. Yet, once Putin retook the presidency in 2012, relations cooled. Putin declined President Obama's invitation to the G8 meeting at Camp David in May 2012; Russia adopted an uncooperative stance with regard to Syria by backing the Assad regime; and Putin cracked down on internal dissent and protest (for which he blamed former Secretary of State Hillary Clinton for instigating). Clinton writes that 'for those who expected the reset to open a new era of goodwill between Russia and the United States, it proved to be a bitter disappointment'.[87] Perhaps the failure of the reset was inevitable. Stent argues that 'U.S.-Russian relations were indeed overburdened by a legacy of disagreements and mutual mistrust from both the Cold War and post-Cold-War periods'.[88] From Russia's perspective, contested issues such as U.S. missile defence, U.S. meddling in Russia's domestic affairs, European security, and U.S. behaviour in the Middle East continued to affect relations negatively. In December 2012, the so-called 'Magnitsky Act' passed in the U.S. Senate 92–4, denying visas and freezing the assets of Russian nationals who U.S. officials believed were complicit in the murder of Sergei Magnitsky, the former accountant from Hermitage Capital who died in a Russian prison in 2009 after weeks of torture and abuse.[89] Putin was furious over the Magnitsky Act and tried to prevent its passage, but when he could not, Russia retaliated by adopting the Dima Yakovlev Law two weeks later, which permanently banned the adoption of Russian children by U.S. parents.

Heightened tensions surrounding the Ukraine crisis of late 2013-early 2014 were symptoms rather than causes for a relationship that would fall to new lows after summer 2014 and continued into 2020. The 2014 political crises in Ukraine—the Yanukovych presidency, the annexation of Crimea, and independence movements in Ukraine's eastern provinces—poisoned the relationship and created a trap of acrimony that neither side seems willing or able to end. In March 2014, following Russia's annexation of Crimea, Putin threw down the gauntlet when he accused the West of 'primitive, blunt cynicism'. He alleged that the West has 'lied to us many times, made decisions behind our backs, [and] placed before us an accomplished fact', referring specifically to the expansion of NATO and missile defence. He continued that 'they are constantly trying to sweep us into a corner because we have an independent position, because we maintain it and because we call things like they are and do not engage in hypocrisy. But there is a limit to everything'.[90]

The breadth and depth of animosity led journalists and some academics to speak of a 'New Cold War'.[91] To be sure, there were differences with the original Cold War, for instance the lack of ideological competition, different Russian motivations, and certainly a change in Russia's capabilities.[92] Nonetheless, heightened tensions after 2014 were unparalleled in the post-Soviet period. Intensified rivalry, competition, and 'hybrid warfare' replaced cooperation. A representative but not exhaustive summary includes the following. The United States feared a potential Russian attack on the Baltics or even worse, a 'frozen conflict' in countries with a high percentage of ethnic Russians. Russia opposed a modest increase in NATO troops in Poland and Lithuania while engaging in actions that motivated that increase. The U.S. contested Russia's military support for Syrian President Bashar al-Assad starting in 2015, which came without any advance notification to the U.S., and which former Secretary of State John Kerry characterised as eviscerating U.S. leverage in Syria and setting the stage for even more blood-letting.[93] Despite opposing Russian troops in Syria, the U.S. took no direct action against Russian forces in Syria. The U.S. criticised Russia's closer relations with Iran.[94] Russian energy supplies to Europe became a contentious policy issue and the U.S. pressed its European allies to diversify their sources in order to lower dependence on Russia. In March 2018, the U.S. expelled 60 Russian diplomats over the allegation that the Russian government was behind the nerve agent attack against former military intelligence officer Sergei Skripal and his daughter in England. Putin retaliated by expelling 60 U.S. diplomats and closing the U.S. consulate in St. Petersburg. The U.S. withdrew from the Joint Comprehensive Plan of Action in May 2018. In October 2018, the U.S. informed Russia of its intention to leave the Intermediate Range Nuclear Force Treaty (INF) which had been in effect since 1987. According to former National Security Advisor John Bolton, the Russians used the announcement to play on Europeans' fears that the U.S. was abandoning them, a notion that Bolton dismisses.[95] Following the U.S. withdrawal from the INF Treaty in August 2019, Putin announced a new hypersonic weapon that could defeat missile defence. Allegations of Russian meddling in the U.S. 2016 presidential election coloured the relationship during the entirety of Trump's presidency. Thus, the political relationship since early 2014 was characterised by nearly unending disagreement and mistrust.

8 U.S. Agricultural Exports to Russia Since 2000

In the post-Soviet period, U.S. agricultural exports to Russia shifted away from grain. As previously noted, Russia imported large quantities of poultry meat from the U.S. in the 1990s. After 1999, poultry and other meat imports continued to increase rapidly as the economy began to grow again and consumers began to realise real gains in their standard of living and income. By 2002, Russia imported double the level of meat compared to 2000, and meat imports as a percentage of total supply increased from 12 percent in 2000 to 24 percent in 2002.[96] The dollar value of Russia's food imports would continue to increase for another decade, although not linearly due to the financial crisis of 2008–2009.

Against this context, the story of U.S. agricultural exports to Russia since 2000 is one of decline compared to the 1990s, a brief and modest increase during 2007–2012, and then renewed decline to the point of irrelevance after 2014. U.S. agricultural exports declined for three reasons: (1) the recovery in Russia's agricultural sector, which was able to meet more of domestic demand; (2) an expansion in Russia's other trading partners; and (3) a significant deterioration in the political relationship revolving around the crisis in Ukraine in 2014 that continues to the present. U.S. agricultural exports to Russia during 2000–2019 are presented in Table 5.

For analytical purposes, U.S. agricultural trade with Russia since 2000 may be separated into three periods. In the first period, 2000–2006, the value of U.S. agricultural exports did not exceed $1 billion USD, despite the fact that political tensions were between Washington and Kremlin were generally low.[97] For context, during this period the total value of Russia's agricultural imports increased from $7.3 billion USD in 2000 to $21.5 billion USD in 2006, a rise that reflects higher consumer demand within Russia. The European Union in particular became a major trading partner. Russia was a main export market for agricultural products from the EU. In 2013, the EU exported €10.9 billion of agricultural goods to Russia, equal to more than 10 percent of its total agricultural exports. By 2016, however, EU food exports to Russia declined to €5.4 billion before rebounding to €7 billion in 2019, equal to about 3.9 percent of non-EU food exports.[98]

In contrast, U.S. agricultural exports to Russia became progressively less important and by 2006 accounted for less than 5 percent of the

Table 5 U.S. Agricultural Exports to Russia After 2000 (dollar values are USD)

	Total value of U.S. agricultural exports to Russia	*Value of grain exports to Russia*	*Quantity of grain exports to Russia*	*Percent of U.S. agricultural exports to Russia comprised of foodstuffs (%)*
2000	$580 million	$116 million	779.5 tt	68
2001	$917 million	$65 million	133.9 tt	87
2002	$552 million	$21 million	53.9 tt	88
2003	$579 million	$11 million	13.4 tt	87
2004	$802 million	$84 million	90.1 tt	83
2005	$972 million	$72 million	25.2 tt	87
2006	$820 million	$53 million	43.6 tt	87
2007	$1.32 billion	$86 million	60.2 tt	88
2008	$1.83 billion	$92 million	35.1 tt	90
2009	$1.42 billion	$90 million	116.7 tt	88
2010	$1.13 billion	$67 million	65.6 tt	86
2011	$1.24 billion	$71 million	69.1 tt	79
2012	$1.65 billion	$99 million	102.2 tt	71
2013	$1.20 billion	$230 million	309.0 tt	60
2014	$900 million	$246 million	362.0 tt	56
2015	$426 million	$236 million	524.8 tt	23
2016	$250 million	$95 million	164.7 tt	36
2017	$193 million	$24 million	6.6 tt	47
2018	$233 million	$17 million	5.1 tt	39
2019	$191 million	$17 million	4.7 tt	23

Notes (a) Total value of U.S. agricultural exports includes foodstuffs, intermediate products, and bulk goods. In this table, grain exports are defined as bulk goods. The value of U.S. exports excludes agricultural-related products which are non-food products as defined by the USDA. See Table 6 for full definitions. (b) Numbers have been rounded. (c) Data for agricultural exports in 1990–1991 are for USSR, thereafter they are for Russia. (d) tt = thousand metric tonnes. *Sources* Kathryn A. Zeimetz, *USSR Agricultural Trade*, Statistical Bulletin 808 (Washington, DC: United States Department of Agriculture, Economic Research Service, 1991), 37, 39; Foreign Agricultural Service database at https://apps.fas.usda.gov/GATS/default.aspx; and Author's calculations

value of Russia's food imports. The relatively low level of U.S. agricultural exports to Russia marked a departure from the 1990s when all but two years surpassed $1 billion USD and those two years, 1998–1999, were due to financial crisis and the devaluation of the ruble that made imports more expensive. Thus, the value of U.S. agricultural exports to Russia during 2000–2006 was lower than in the 1980s and 1990s and comprised an insignificant percentage of Russia's total food imports.

Table 6 Distribution of U.S. Agricultural Exports to Russia 2014–2019 (dollar values are USD)

	Total value of U.S. agricultural exports to Russia	*Intermediate products*	*Consumer oriented products*	*Bulk products*
2014	$900 million	$151 million	$502 million	$245 million
2015	$4269 million	$90 million	$99 million	$236 million
2016	$250 million	$64 million	$90 million	$95 million
2017	$193 million	$77 million	$90 million	$24 million
2018	$233 million	$123 million	$91 million	$17 million
2019	$191 million	$90 million	$83 million	$17 million

Notes (a) Numbers have been rounded. (b) Intermediate goods include: soybean oil, soybean meal, vegetable oil, animal fat, live animals, hides and skins, hay, distiller grain, planting seeds, sugars and sweeteners, and other intermediate goods. (c) Consumer oriented goods are essentially foodstuffs and include: beef and beef products, pork and pork products, poultry and poultry products, eggs and egg products, dairy products, fresh fruit, fresh vegetables, processed vegetables, fruit and vegetable juices, tree nuts, chocolate and cocoa products, snack foods, breakfast cereals, condiments and sauces, prepared foods, wine and beer, non-alcoholic beverages, dog and cat food, and other consumer-oriented products. (d) Bulk goods are crop products and include: wheat, corn, coarse grains, rice, soybeans, cotton, pulses, tobacco, and other bulk commodities. (e) Agricultural-related goods are excluded from the total value of agricultural exports. They are defined as: distilled spirits, ethanol, biodiesel, forest products, and fish products. All definitions are taken from United Stated Department of Agriculture. *Source* Foreign Agricultural Service database at https://apps.fas.usda.gov/GATS/default.aspx

During the 2000–2006 period, the value of U.S. grain exports comprised a small percentage of the overall value of bilateral agricultural trade. The volume of U.S. grain exports to Russia did not exceed 100 thousand tonnes during 2002–2006. That said, agricultural exports from the U.S. during the 2000–2006 period were overwhelming 'consumer-oriented products', a term used by the U.S. Department of Agriculture that basically refers to foodstuffs. In 2000, foodstuffs comprised 68 percent of the dollar value of U.S. agricultural exports to Russia; thereafter and through 2006, the percentage did not drop below 83 percent and most years was 87–88 percent. In short, the overwhelming majority of U.S. agricultural exports to Russia consisted of food.

From the Russian side, the 2000–2006 period brought stabilisation and then rebound in agricultural production. The period also served to lay a legislative and policy foundation for future growth, guided by a strategic plan that led to the creation of a state-owned agricultural bank through which credits and subsidies could be channeled; financial debt relief for large farms; the creation of a mechanism for state intervention in the grain market; the introduction of a new credit policy; and in 2005 the development of a 'national project' that channeled unprecedented levels of financial assistance, credit, and subsidies to agriculture during 2006–2007.[99] The strategy of 'bringing the state back in' paid off, as growth in agricultural production on large farms averaged more than 4 percent per annum during 2000–2006.[100]

During the second period, 2007–2013, the political relationship had its ups and downs while U.S. agricultural exports to Russia increased modestly from $832 million USD in 2006 to $1.32 billion USD in 2007. Exports stayed above the $1 billion USD threshold through 2013, though never exceeding $1.65 billion USD. The political relationship was framed by Putin's February 2007 speech in Munich; the 2008 Georgian war; a largely inconsequential 'reset' in 2009; the START arms control agreement in 2010; and U.S. support for Russia's entry into the WTO in 2011 with membership finalised in 2012. Because the political relationship had aspects of cooperation and competition during 2007–2013, I characterise the relationship between politics and agricultural trade as neither convergent nor divergent. During the 2007–2013 period, foodstuffs remained the dominant U.S. agricultural export to Russia, but their percentage declined over time. During 2007–2009, foodstuffs accounted for 88–90 percent of U.S. agricultural exports to Russia, but this percentage declined to 71 percent in 2012 and to 60 percent in 2013 even as the level of agricultural imports from the U.S. remained above $1 billion USD.

The third period, 2014-present, has witnessed a significant decrease in U.S. agricultural exports to Russia brought about by Russia's countersanctions that ban the importation of most agricultural products from the United States and other Western nations. The decline in the value of U.S. agricultural exports is convergent with the deterioration in political relations. Prior to Russia's food embargo in August 2014, U.S. agricultural exports were on track to surpass the $1 billion USD threshold, but the food embargo brought immediate curtailment. After 2014, U.S. agricultural exports continued to decline, eventually falling to just $191 million USD in 2019. Grain had historically accounted for a large percentage of U.S. exports to Russia, although we saw that situation began to change in the 1990s and continued into the 2000s. Starting in 2003, U.S. wheat exports to Russia fell to zero and remained at zero through 2018 but rose to 433 thousand tonnes in 2019, still a small quantity. Soy was the dominant grain export to Russia during 2014–2016, but soy exports to Russia fell to zero in 2017–2019.

Russia's food embargo brought about a significant redistribution in U.S. agricultural exports away from foodstuffs and towards intermediate goods that are used in processing. The transition is shown in Table 6.

The table depicts the effects of Russia's countersanctions which led to an 80 percent decline in the value of agricultural imports from the United States. Within the overall decline in the value of agricultural exports, the table also shows that from 2014 through 2019 exports of foodstuffs fell from 55 percent of U.S. agricultural exports to Russia in 2014 to 43 percent in 2019; bulk goods, or crop products, also declined, from 27 percent in 2014 to 9 percent in 2019; while intermediate goods increased from 17 percent in 2014 to 47 percent in 2019. Assorted agricultural-related goods (products that are not directly consumable) are excluded from the table because this category generally is not very significant in volume or value. For example, agricultural-related goods fell from 6 percent of the dollar value of U.S. exports to Russia in 2014 to 2.5 percent in 2019.

9 Outlook

This chapter documented how U.S. agricultural exports to Russia have changed from being a significant factor in the USSR's food security to being essentially irrelevant to food security in the contemporary period. This contemporary irrelevance is measured by a low dollar valuation of U.S. agricultural exports to Russia and the transition away from foodstuffs as the dominant agricultural export.

The historical trading patterns during the Cold War demonstrate that agricultural trade is not dependent on good political relations. However, the difference between now and then is that now Russia has a strong agricultural sector that provides food self-sufficiency in many basic commodities, including grain. For this reason, the outlook for U.S.-Russian agricultural trade appears reasonably clear. Russia's 2014 food embargo, which continues through the end of 2022, has rendered U.S. agricultural exports insignificant to Russia. Given the commitment by the Putin regime to food security, food self-sufficiency, and the expansion of its own export capacity, it is difficult to foresee how U.S. exporters can re-gain any significant market share in Russia's food market in the near to medium term, and that is significant because Russia is the largest consumer market in Europe. Putin himself noted that once markets are lost, they are hard to recapture. Thus, the contemporary story of U.S.-Russia agricultural trade represents the loss of the 'food weapon' as leverage by the exporter and the rise of the power of the importer.

Notes

1. In this chapter, I use the terms 'agricultural trade' and 'food trade' synonymously although I acknowledge that not all agricultural exports are edible. Moreover, the terms 'agricultural trade' and 'food trade' refer to U.S. exports to the Soviet Union/Russia unless otherwise stipulated; food imports by the U.S. from Russia are minuscule and not discussed.
2. Robert L. Paarlberg, *Food Trade and Foreign Policy: India, the Soviet Union, and the United States* (Ithaca: Cornell University Press, 1985), 15.
3. Ibid.
4. Joanne Gowa, *Allies, Adversaries, and International Trade* (Princeton: Princeton University Press, 1994), 120–121.
5. John Gaddis, 'The Evolution of U.S. Policy Goals Toward the USSR in the Postwar Era', in *Gorbachev's Russia and American Foreign Policy*, eds. Seweryn Bialer and Michael Mandelbaum (Boulder: Westview Press, 1988), 305–313.
6. Paarlberg, *Food Trade and Foreign Policy*, chaps, 4, 5, 6.
7. Barry Riley, *The Political History of American Food Aid: An Uneasy Benevolence* (Oxford: Oxford University Press, 2017), 173–177.
8. Ibid., 220.
9. Paige Bryan, 'The Soviet Grain Embargo', *The Heritage Foundation Backgrounder* no. 130 (12 January 1981), 3.
10. Directorate of Intelligence, CIA, 'USSR: The Food Supply Situation', Report SOV 85–10,042, March 1985. Approved for release on 5 February 2010. https://www.cia.gov/library/readingroom/docs/CIA-RDP86T00591R000100140005-4.pdf. Accessed 1 February 2020.
11. Nicolai N. Petro and Alvin Z. Rubinstein, *Russian Foreign Policy: From Empire to Nation-State* (New York: Longman, 1997), chaps. 7, 9, 10 11.
12. See Raymond L. Garthoff, *Détente and Confrontation: American-Soviet Relations From Nixon to Reagan* (Washington, DC: The Brookings Institution, 1985), 842–848.
13. Ibid., 1010.
14. Coit D. Blacker, 'Military Forces', in *After Brezhnev: Sources of Soviet Conduct in the 1980s*, ed. Robert F. Byrnes (Bloomington: Indiana University Press, 1983), 130.

15. Garthoff, Détente and Confrontation, 1111.
16. Paarlberg, *Food Trade and Foreign Policy*; VanGrasstek, *Trade and American Leadership*, 282–308; and Jeffrey M. Pilcher, *Food in World History*, 2nd edn. (New York and London: Routledge Publishers, 2017), 80–89.
17. Author's calculations based on data in Robert L. Paarlberg, 'Food as an Instrument of Foreign Policy', *Proceedings of the Academy of Political Science*, 34, no. 3 (1982): 27. In 1980 the U.S. accounted for 42 percent of international wheat exports and 65 percent of coarse grain exports.
18. Paarlberg, 'Food as an Instrument of Foreign Policy', 27.
19. Ibid., 29.
20. Henry Kissinger, *White House Years* (Boston: Little, Brown and Co., 1979), 1269–1273.
21. Philip Shabecoff, 'Moscow Agrees to Buy U.S. Grain for $750 Million', *The New York Times*, 9 July 1972. https://www.nytimes.com/1972/07/09/archives/moscow-agrees-to-buy-us-grain-for-750million-credits-planned.html. Accessed 5 March 2020.
22. Mark J. Penn, 'America Gets the Shaft', *The Harvard Crimson*, 16 November 1973. https://www.thecrimson.com/article/1973/11/16/america-gets-the-shaft-pthe-1972/. Accessed 5 March 2020.
23. James Trager, *The Great Grain Robbery* (New York: Ballantine Books, 1975).
24. Garthoff, *Détente and Confrontation*, 456.
25. Robert L. Paarlberg, 'The Soviet burden on the world food system: Challenge and response', *Food Policy* 1, no. 5 (1976): 398.
26. Clyde H. Farnsworth, 'U.S.-Soviet Grain Deal Nearly Failed', *The New York Times*, 25 October 1975. https://www.nytimes.com/1975/10/25/archives/ussoviet-grain-deal-nearly-failed-mood-is-tense-during-27day.html. Accessed 6 April 2020.
27. Josef C. Brada, 'The Soviet-American Grain Agreement and the National Interest', *American Journal of Agricultural Economics* 65, no. 4 (November 1983): 652.
28. Richard K. Abrams and C. Edward Harshbarger, 'U.S. Agricultural Trade in the 1970s: Progress and Problems', *The Economic Review* (May 1979). https://www.kansascityfed.org/~/media/files/publicat/econrev/econrevarchive/1979/2q79abra.pdf. Accessed March 13, 2020.
29. Lester R. Brown, 'The U.S.-Soviet Food Connection', *Challenge* 25, no. 6 (January–February 1983): 47.
30. Joseph Hajda, The Outlook for East–West Agricultural Trade', in *East–West Relations: Prospects for the 1980s*, ed. Giuseppe Schiavone (New York: St. Martin's Press, 1982), 49.
31. Robert L. Paarlberg, 'Lessons of The Grain Embargo', *Foreign Affairs* 59, no. 1 (Fall 1980): 144. That said, American policymakers faced

several constraints when using food as a weapon in the 1980s. First, the federal government did not control the entire supply chain for grain exports. There was no central marketing board in U.S. and grain exporters are private companies. Thus, the federal government did not have complete control over grain exports. Second, the International Longshoreman's Association (ILA) influenced grain export policy. During the 1980 grain embargo against the USSR, for example, the ILA refused to load grain that was bound for the Soviet Union. Third, domestic political forces influenced food export policy. In 1975, for example, representatives from farm states prevented President Ford from maintaining the grain embargo against the USSR.

32. VanGrasstek, *Trade and American Leadership*, 254.
33. See James L. Lindsay, 'Trade Sanctions as Policy Instruments: A Re-examination', *International Studies Quarterly* 30, no. 2 (June 1986): 155–156.
34. Paarlberg, 'Lessons of The Grain Embargo', 155.
35. Ibid., 150.
36. Ibid., 156.
37. Rosstat, *Sel'skoe khoziaistvo, okhota, i okhtnich'e khoziaistvo, lesovodstvo v Rossii 2015* (Moscow: Rosstat, 2015), 92.
38. Steven R. Weisman, 'Reagan Ends Curbs on Export of Grain to Soviet Union', *The New York Times*, 25 April 1981. https://www.nytimes.com/1981/04/25/world/reagan-ends-curbs-on-export-of-grain-to-the-soviet-union-office.html. Accessed 18 March 2020.
39. Michael R. Beschloss and Strobe Talbott, *At the Highest Levels: The Inside Story of the End of the Cold War* (Boston: Little, Brown and Co. 1993), 69–125.
40. Anatoly Dobrynin, *In Confidence* (New York: Times Books, 1995), 632–636.
41. Andrei P. Tsygankov, *Russia and America: The Asymmetric Rivalry* (Cambridge: Polity Press, 2019), 9–10, 284–295.
42. Peter Shearman, 'Russian Foreign Policy Toward the United States', in *Russian Foreign Policy Since 1990*, ed. Peter Shearman (Boulder: Westview Press, 1995), 116.
43. See Andrei P. Tsygankov, *Russia's Foreign Policy: Change and Continuity in National Identity*, 4th edn. (Lanham: Rowman and Littlefield, 2016), 59–96.
44. Ibid., 61.
45. Ibid., 62–64.
46. See Sergey M. Rogov, 'The Changing Perspective of Russian-American Relations', in *From Rivalry to Cooperation: Russian and American Perspectives on the Post-Cold War Era*, eds. Manus I. Midlarsky, John

A. Vasquesz, and Peter V. Gladkov (New York: HarperCollins, 1994), 116–25.

47. Tsygankov, *Russia's Foreign Policy*, 81.
48. Warren Christopher, *Chances of a Lifetime: A Memoir* (New York: Scribner, 2001), 281.
49. Andrei Kozyrev, 'Partnership of Cold Peace?' *Foreign Policy* no. 99 (Summer 1995): 3–14.
50. Christopher, *Chances of a Lifetime*, 281–288.
51. Madeline Albright, *Madam Secretary: A Memoir* (New York: Harper Perennial, 2003), 256.
52. Robert M. Gates, *Duty: Memoirs of a Secretary at War* (New York: Vintage Books, 2014), 158.
53. Albright, *Madam Secretary*, 259.
54. Christopher, *Chances of a Lifetime*, 288.
55. Albright, *Madam Secretary*, 258.
56. Robert D. Hershey, 'U.S.-Soviet Grain Pact is Reached', *The New York Times*, 23 March 1990. https://www.nytimes.com/1990/03/23/business/us-soviet-grain-pact-is-reached.html. Accessed 6 April 2020.
57. Author's calculations from data in Rosstat, *Sel'skoe khoziaistvo, okhota i okhotnich'e khoziaistva, lesovodstvo v Rossii 2015*, 80.
58. William Liefert, 'Food Security in Russia: Economic Growth and Rising Incomes are Reducing Insecurity', in *Food Security Assessment*, GFA-15, Economic Research Service, United States Department of Agriculture (Washington, DC: USDA, 2004), 37.
59. Author's calculations from data in Goskomstat, *Regiony Rossii*, vol. 2 (Moscow: Goskomstat 2001), 508, 510.
60. V. V. Doikov, 'Rynok miasa i miasoproduktov', *Ekonomika sel'skokhozi-aistvennykh i pererabatyvaiushchikh predpriatii* no. 7 (July 1999): 7.
61. See Stephen K. Wegren, 'The Russian Food Problem: Domestic and Foreign Consequences', *Problems of Post-Communism* 47, no. 1 (2000): 44–45.
62. See V. Brichko, 'APK i vneshniaia torgovlia', *Ekonomist* no. 3 (March 1997): 89.
63. Iurii Savin, 'Shag vynuzhdennyi, no neobkhodimyi', *Sel'skaia zhizn'*, 3 June 1995, 2.
64. Stephen K. Wegren with Alexander Nikulin and Irina Trotsuk, *Russia's Food Revolution: The Transformation of the Food System* (London and New York: Routledge Publishers, 2021), 48.
65. Stephen K. Wegren, *Russia's Food Policies and Globalization* (Lanham: Lexington Books, 2005), 141–144.
66. See Mark Kramer, 'Food Aid to Russia: The Fallacies of US Policy', Ponars Policy Memo 86, October 1999, 3. http://www.ponarseurasia.org/sites/default/files/policy-memos-pdf/pm_0086.pdf, accessed 12 April 2020.

67. Ibid.
68. Ibid., 4.
69. Stephen K. Wegren, Alexander Nikulin, and Irina Trotsuk, *Food Policy and Food Security: Putting Food on the Russian Table* (Lanham: Lexington Books, 2018), 144.
70. Condoleeza Rice, *No Higher Honor: A Memoir of My Years in Washington* (New York: Crown Publishers, 2011), 23–37; and see also Condoleezza Rice, 'Campaign 2000: Promoting the National Interest', *Foreign Affairs*, 79, no. 1 (January–February 2000). https://www.foreignaffairs.com/articles/2000-01-01/campaign-2000-promoting-national-interest. Accessed 3 April 2020.
71. Donald Rumsfeld, *Known and Unknown: A Memoir* (New York: Penguin Group, 2011), 309.
72. Ibid., 307.
73. James Risen and Jane Perez, "Russian Diplomats Ordered Expelled in a Countermove," *The New York Times*, 22 March 2001. https://www.nytimes.com/2001/03/22/world/russian-diplomats-ordered-expelled-in-a-countermove.html. Accessed 18 June 2020.
74. Rumsfeld, *Known and Unknown*, 309.
75. For background, see Leon Aron, 'The Yukos Affair', American Enterprise Report, 1 October 2003. https://www.aei.org/research-products/report/the-yukos-affair/. Accessed 15 April 2020.
76. Angela E. Stent, *The Limits of Partnership: U.S.-Russian Relations in the Twenty-first Century* (Princeton: Princeton University Press, 2014), 202.
77. The World Bank, 'Foreign direct investment, net (BoP, current US$)—Russian Federation', n.d. https://data.worldbank.org/indicator/BN.KLT.DINV.CD?locations=RU&view=chart. Accessed 15 April 2020.
78. Stent, *The Limits of Partnership*, 203–210.
79. Task Force for Council on Foreign Relations, *Russia's Wrong Direction: What the United States Can and Should Do*, Report no. 57 (New York: Council on Foreign Relation, 2006), 27.
80. Committee on International Relations, U.S. House of Representatives, and Committee on Foreign Relations, U.S. Senate, *Country Reports on Human Rights Practices for 2005*, vol. 1, 109th Congress, 2nd Session (Washington, DC: Government Printing Office, 2006), 1509–1554.
81. Stephen K. Wegren, 'Russian Agriculture and the WTO', *Problems of Post-Communism* 54, no. 4 (2007): 46–59.
82. See 'Speech and Following Discussion at the Munich Conference on Security Policy', February 10, 2007. http://en.kremlin.ru/events/president/transcripts/24034. Accessed April 18, 2020. The speech is summarized in Thom Shanker and Mark Landler, 'Putin Says U.S. Is Undermining Global Stability', *The New York Times*,

11 February 2007. https://www.nytimes.com/2007/02/11/world/europe/11munich.html. Accessed 15 April 2020.

83. Robert M. Gates, *Duty: Memoirs of a Secretary at War* (New York: Vintage Books, 2015), 156.
84. Rice, *No Higher Honor*, 692.
85. Gates, *Duty*, 170.
86. Charles King, 'The Five-Day War', *Foreign Affairs* 87, no. 6 (2008): 2–11; and Stephen Sestanovich, 'What Has Moscow Done?' *Foreign Affairs* 87, no. 6 (2008): 12–28.
87. Hillary Rodham Clinton, *Hard Choices* (New York: Simon and Schuster, 2014), 236.
88. Stent, *The Limits of Partnership*, 212.
89. See Bill Browder, *Red Notice: A True Story of High Finance, Murder, and One Man's Fight for Justice* (New York: Simon and Schuster, 2015).
90. All quotes from official site of the President of Russia, 'Address by the President of the Russian Federation', 18 March 2014. http://eng.news.kremlin.ru/news/6889/print. Accessed 22 March 2014.
91. Edward Lucas, *The New Cold War: Putin's Russia and the Threat to the West* (New York: Palgrave Mcmillan, 2009); Robert Levgold, *Return to Cold War* (Cambridge: Polity Press, 2016).
92. Tsygankov, *Russia and America*, 5–7.
93. John Kerry, *Every Day is Extra* (New York: Simon and Schuster, 2018), 548–549.
94. One aspect of the closer relationship between Russia and Iran that is almost completely missed by analysts is expanding agricultural ties, witnessed by Iran signing a free trade agreement with the Eurasian Economic Union, bilateral memoranda of intent to increase agricultural trade and cooperation, and a rise in Iran's imports of Russian wheat.
95. John Bolton, *The Room Where It Happened: A White House Memoir* (New York: Simon and Schuster, 2020), 165.
96. Goskomstat, *Rossiia v tsifrakh* (Moscow: Goskomstat, 2003), 214, 378–379.
97. The $1 billion USD threshold is based on the export of consumer-oriented agricultural products, intermediate commodities used for processing, and bulk commodities. It excludes agricultural-related commodities such as distilled spirits, ethanol, biodiesel, forest products, and fish products. See Table 6 for components of consumer-oriented agricultural products, intermediate commodities used for processing, and bulk commodities. These definitions are taken from the United States Department of Agriculture.
98. European Commission, 'Russia', n.d., https://webgate.ec.europa.eu/isdb_results/factsheets/country/overview_russia_en.pdf. Accessed 9 May 2020; and European Commission, 'Agri-Food Trade Statistical

Factsheet: European Union-Russia', 17 March 2020. https://ec.europa.eu/info/sites/info/files/food-farming-fisheries/farming/documents/agrifood-russia_en.pdf. Accessed 9 May 2020.

99. Wegren, Nikulin, and Trotsuk, *Food Policy and Food Security*, 54–61.
100. Author's calculations from data in Rosstat, *Sel'skoe khoziaistvo, okhota i okhotnich'e khoziaistva, lesovodstvo v Rossii 2004* (Moscow: Rosstat, 2004), 37; and Rosstat, *Sel'skoe khoziaistvo, okhota i okhotnich'e khoziaistva, lesovodstvo v Rossii 2009* (Moscow: Rosstat, 2009), 50.

Selected Bibliography

Albright, Madeline. *Madam Secretary: A Memoir*. New York: Harper Perennial, 2003.

Beschloss, Michael R. and Strobe Talbott. *At the Highest Levels: The Inside Story of the End of the Cold War*. Boston: Little, Brown and Co. 1993.

Blacker, Coit D. 'Military Forces'. In *After Brezhnev: Sources of Soviet Conduct in the 1980s*, ed. Robert F. Byrnes. Bloomington: Indiana University Press, 1983, 125–85.

Bolton, John. *The Room Where It Happened: A White House Memoir*. New York: Simon and Schuster, 2020.

Brada, Josef C. 'The Soviet-American Grain Agreement and the National Interest'. *American Journal of Agricultural Economics,* 65, no. 4 (November 1983): 651–56.

Browder, Bill. *Red Notice: A True Story of High Finance, Murder, and One Man's Fight for Justice*. New York: Simon and Schuster, 2015.

Brown, Lester R. 'The U.S.-Soviet Food Connection'. *Challenge*, 25, no. 6 (January-February 1983): 40–49.

Clinton, Hillary Rodham. *Hard Choices*. New York: Simon and Schuster, 2014.

Christopher, Warren. *Chances of a Lifetime: A Memoir*. New York: Scribner, 2001.

Dobrynin, Anatoly. *In Confidence*. New York: Times Books, 1995.

Frost, Ellen L. and Angela E. Stent, 'Troubles with East-West Trade'. *International Security* 8, no. 1 (Summer 1983): 179–200.

Gaddis, John. 'The Evolution of U.S. Policy Goals Toward the USSR in the Postwar Era'. In *Gorbachev's Russia and American Foreign Policy*, eds. Seweryn Bialer and Michael Mandelbaum. Boulder: Westview Press, 1988, 305–313.

Garthoff, Raymond L. *Détente and Confrontation: American-Soviet Relations From Nixon to Reagan*. Washington, DC: The Brookings Institution, 1985.

Gates, Robert M. *Duty: Memoirs of a Secretary at War*. New York: Vintage Books, 2015.

Gowa, Joanne. *Allies, Adversaries, and International Trade*. Princeton: Princeton University Press, 1994.

Hajda, Joseph. 'The Outlook for East-West Agricultural Trade'. In *East-West Relations: Prospects for the 1980s*, ed. Giuseppe Schiavone. New York: St. Martin's Press, 1982, 47–58.

Kerry, John. *Every Day is Extra*. New York: Simon and Schuster, 2018.

King, Charles. 'The Five-Day War'. *Foreign Affairs* 87, no. 6 (2008): 2–11.

Kissinger, Henry. *White House Years*. Boston: Little, Brown and Co., 1979.

Kozyrev, Andrei. 'Partnership of Cold Peace?' *Foreign Policy* no. 99 (Summer 1995): 3–14.

Levgold, Robert. *Return to Cold War*. Cambridge: Polity Press, 2016.

Liefert, William. 'Food Security in Russia: Economic Growth and Rising Incomes are Reducing Insecurity'. In *Food Security Assessment*, GFA-15, Economic Research Service, United States Department of Agriculture. Washington, DC: USDA, 2004, 35–43.

Lindsay, James L. 'Trade Sanctions as Policy Instruments: A Re-examination'. *International Studies Quarterly* 30 no. 2 (June 1986): 153–73.

Lucas, Edward. *The New Cold War: Putin's Russia and the Threat to the West*. New York: Palgrave Mcmillan, 2009.

Paarlberg, Robert L. 'The Soviet burden on the world food system: Challenge and response'. *Food Policy* 1 no. 5 (1976): 392–404.

Paarlberg, Robert L. 'Lessons of The Grain Embargo'. *Foreign Affairs* 59 no. 1 (Fall 1980): 144–62.

Paarlberg, Robert L. *Food Trade and Foreign Policy: India, the Soviet Union, and the United States*. Ithaca: Cornell University Press, 1985.

Petro, Nicolai N. and Alvin Z. Rubinstein. *Russian Foreign Policy: From Empire to Nation-State*. New York: Longman, 1997.

Pilcher, Jeffrey M. *Food in World History*, 2nd edn. New York and London: Routledge Publishers, 2017.

Rice, Condoleeza. *No Higher Honor: A Memoir of My Years in Washington*. New York: Crown Publishers, 2011.

Riley, Barry. *The Political History of American Food Aid: An Uneasy Benevolence*. Oxford: Oxford University Press, 2017.

Rogov, Sergey M. 'The Changing Perspective of Russian-American Relations'. In *From Rivalry to Cooperation: Russian and American Perspectives on the Post-Cold War Era*, eds. Manus I. Midlarsky, John A. Vasquesz, and Peter V. Gladkov. New York: HarperCollins, 1994, 116–25.

Rumsfeld, Donald. *Known and Unknown: A Memoir*. New York: Penguin Group, 2011.

Sestanovich, Stephen. 'What Has Moscow Done?' *Foreign Affairs* 87, no. 6 (2008): 12–28.

Shearman, Peter. 'Russian Foreign Policy Toward the United States'. In *Russian Foreign Policy Since 1990*, ed. Peter Shearman. Boulder: Westview Press, 1995, 111–33.

Stent, Angela E. *The Limits of Partnership: U.S.-Russian Relations in the Twenty-first Century*. Princeton: Princeton University Press, 2014.

Trager, James. *The Great Grain Robbery*. New York: Ballantine Books, 1975.

Tsygankov, Andrei P. *Russia and America: The Asymmetric Rivalry*. Cambridge: Polity Press, 2019.

Tsygankov, Andrei P. *Russia's Foreign Policy: Change and Continuity in National Identity*, 4th ed. Lanham: Rowman and Littlefield, 2016.

VanGrasstek, Craig. *Trade and American Leadership: The Paradoxes of Power and Wealth from Alexander Hamilton to Donald Trump*. Cambridge: Cambridge University Press, 2019.

Wegren, Stephen K. 'Russian Agriculture and the WTO'. *Problems of Post-Communism* 54, no. 4 (2007): 46–59.

Wegren, Stephen K. *Russia's Food Policies and Globalization*. Lanham: Lexington Books, 2005.

Wegren, Stephen K. 'The Russian Food Problem: Domestic and Foreign Consequences'. *Problems of Post-Communism* 47, no. 1 (2000): 38–48.

Wegren, Stephen K. with Alexander Nikulin and Irina Trotsuk. *Russia's Food Revolution: The Transformation of the Food System*. London and New York: Routledge Publishers, 2021.

Wegren, Stephen K., Alexander Nikulin, and Irina Trotsuk. *Food Policy and Food Security: Putting Food on the Russian Table*. Lanham: Lexington Books, 2018.

Open Access This chapter is licensed under the terms of the Creative Commons Attribution 4.0 International License (http://creativecommons.org/licenses/by/4.0/), which permits use, sharing, adaptation, distribution and reproduction in any medium or format, as long as you give appropriate credit to the original author(s) and the source, provide a link to the Creative Commons license and indicate if changes were made.

The images or other third party material in this chapter are included in the chapter's Creative Commons license, unless indicated otherwise in a credit line to the material. If material is not included in the chapter's Creative Commons license and your intended use is not permitted by statutory regulation or exceeds the permitted use, you will need to obtain permission directly from the copyright holder.

Notes on Contributors

Rilka Dragneva is Professor of International Legal Studies at the Birmingham Law School, University of Birmingham. Her latest research focuses on the internal and external dynamics of Eurasian economic integration, including its relation to EU's initiatives in the Post-Soviet region and to cooperation within the wider Eurasian space.

Christel Elvestad is professor in international business and trade at Nord University Business School, Norway. In addition to her academic career, Elvestad has been working with food trade issues, and national and international fisheries and aquaculture management in governmental positions (Nordland County Council, Norwegian Ministry of Trade, Industry and Fisheries). She is also a member in the board of directors at NIBIO - Norwegian Institute of Bioeconomy Research (2019–2023).

Linde Götz is deputy head of the Agricultural Markets Department at the Institute of Agricultural Development in Transition Economies (IAMO) in Halle, Germany, and a lecturer at Martin-Luther University also in Halle. Her research focuses on price formation and competition in the food supply chain and agricultural policy and trade. Specifically, she analyses agricultural market development in the Black Sea region and its role for global food security. She obtained her PhD in agricultural economics from the University of Göttingen and a MSc in Applied Economics from the University of Minnesota (USA).

© The Editor(s) (if applicable) and The Author(s) 2022

S. K. Wegren and F. Nilssen (eds.), *Russia's Role in the Contemporary International Agri-Food Trade System*, Palgrave Advances in Bioeconomy: Economics and Policies,
https://doi.org/10.1007/978-3-030-77451-6

Maximilian Heigermoser is a researcher at the Department of Agricultural Markets at the Institute of Agricultural Development in Transition Economies (IAMO) in Halle. He investigates the processes of price formation in Black Sea grain markets, focusing on trade relations with major grain importers in the Middle East and North Africa region, with a focus on Egypt. His methodological focus is on time series econometric models to analyse price transmission and price volatility.

Tatiana Isachenko is a Doctor of Economics and Professor at the Moscow State Institute of International Relations, Russian Ministry of Foreign Affairs. The area of her scientific and teaching expertise is multilateral trading systems and trade policy, including regional trade agreements and Russia's participation in the WTO. She is an author and co-author of many publications in Russian and English. Her most recent article is 'WTO Dispute Settlement Mechanism: Overcoming the Crisis and the Need for Reform', *Journal of International Trends* (2020).

Tinoush Jamali Jaghdani is research associate at the Institute of Agricultural Development in Transition Economies (IAMO) in Halle, Germany. He received his Ph.D. in agricultural economics with a minor in applied statistics and a Master of Science in rural development from the University of Göttingen (Germany). He also holds a Bachelor of Science in agricultural economics from Tehran University (Iran). His current research interests are agricultural markets and food supply chain, focusing on price volatility, governance and market power. Furthermore, he is pursuing research on water economics issues in the Middle East.

William M. Liefert is a senior agricultural economist with the Economic Research Service of the United States Department of Agriculture. He is a specialist on macroeconomics and trade as related to agriculture, with regional expertise on Russia and the former Soviet Union. He has published extensively in USDA outlets, books, and journals, such as the *American Journal of Agricultural Economics, Review of Income and Wealth*, and *Eurasian Geography and Economics*. William was on the faculty of economics at Kent State University, and has also been a consultant with the World Bank and the Organization for Economic Cooperation and Development in Paris.

Olga Liefert is the international coarse grains analyst with the Economic Research Service of the United States Department of Agriculture. She has a regional specialization on Russia and the other countries of the former Soviet Union. She has also worked as a consultant with the Food and Agriculture Organization, World Bank, and Organization for Economic Cooperation and Development in Paris. Olga has published in USDA outlets, books, and journals.

Frode Nilssen is Professor in International Trade and Marketing at Nord University Business School, Norway. He is also a research professor at Fridtjof Nansens Institute, Oslo Norway. His research has mainly focused on the strategy and conditions for international food trade on state level governance and the effect on companies internationalisation abilities and opportunities.

Nikolai M. Svetlov is a Doctor of Economics and is a researcher at All-Russian Institute of Agrarian Problems and Informatics A. A. Nikonov (Moscow); a part-time researcher at the Central Economics and Mathematics Institute (Moscow); a part-time researcher at the Center of Agricultural and Food Policy of the Russian Presidental Academy of National Economy and Public Administration (Moscow); a part-time professor at Russian State Agricultural University/Timiryazev Agricultural Academy (Moscow); and a corresponding member of Russian Academy of Sciences. He is an expert in the application of simulation modelling of agricultural policy analyses and a leading developer of the production frontier plus partial equilibrium model of Russia's regional wholesale markets of agricultural production.

Stephen K. Wegren is Distinguished University Professor and Professor of Political Science at Southern Methodist University, Dallas, TX, USA. He has published extensively on Russia's political economy in a wide array of journals. Among his 18 books, the three most recent are: *Food Policy and Food Security: Putting Food on the Russian Table* (Lexington Books, 2018); *Putin's Russia* (Rowman and Littlefield, 2019); and *Russia's Food Revolution: The Transformation of the Food System* (Routledge, 2021).

Jiayi Zhou is a Researcher in the Climate Change and Risk Programme of the Stockholm International Peace Research Institute (SIPRI). She works on the geopolitics of sustainable development, with an area focus on Russia and China.

Index

© The Editor(s) (if applicable) and The Author(s) 2022

S. K. Wegren and F. Nilssen (eds.), *Russia's Role in the Contemporary International Agri-Food Trade System*, Palgrave Advances in Bioeconomy: Economics and Policies,
https://doi.org/10.1007/978-3-030-77451-6

The manufacturer's authorised representative in the EU is Springer Nature Customer Service Centre GmbH, Europaplatz 3, 69115 Heidelberg, Germany. If you have any concerns regarding our products, please contact ProductSafety@springernature.com

Printed and bound by CPI Group (UK) Ltd, Croydon, CR0 4YY
30/09/2026
02225455-0016